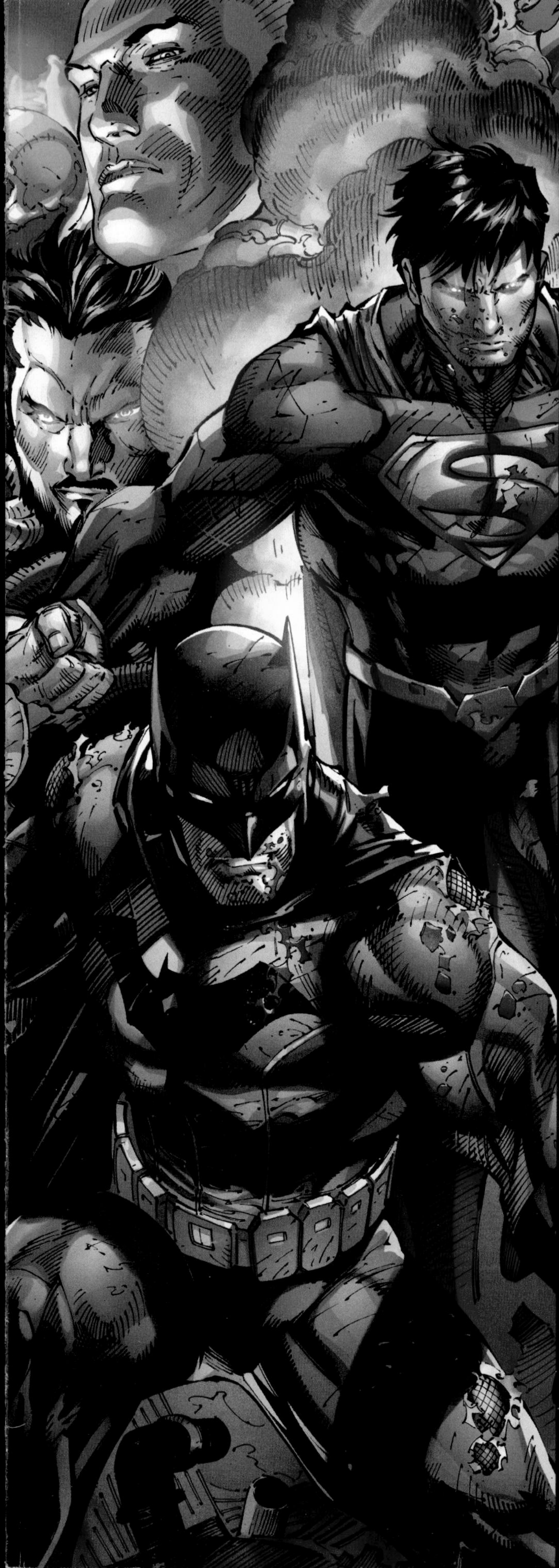

BATMAN/SUPERMAN

VOLUME 4

SIEGE

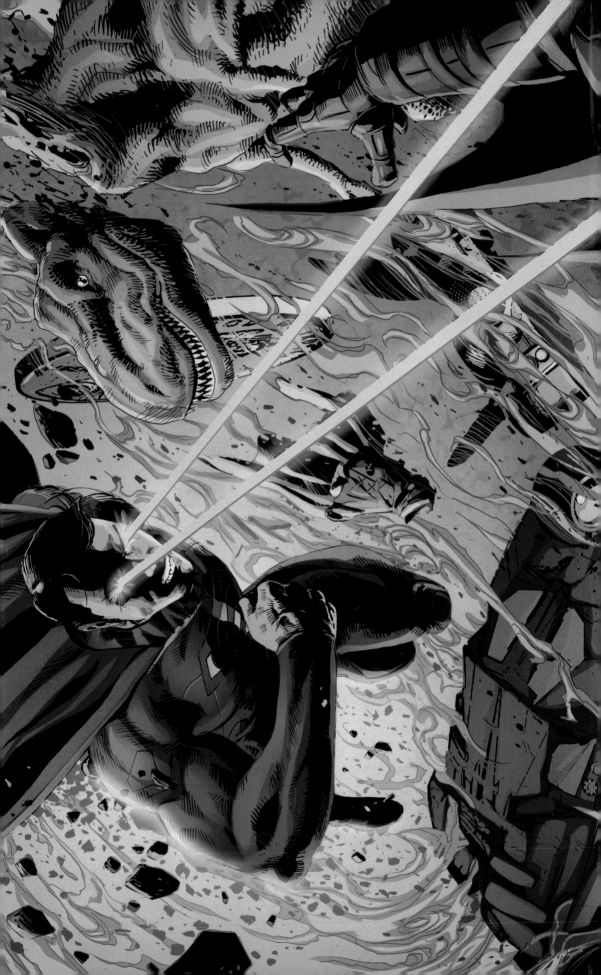

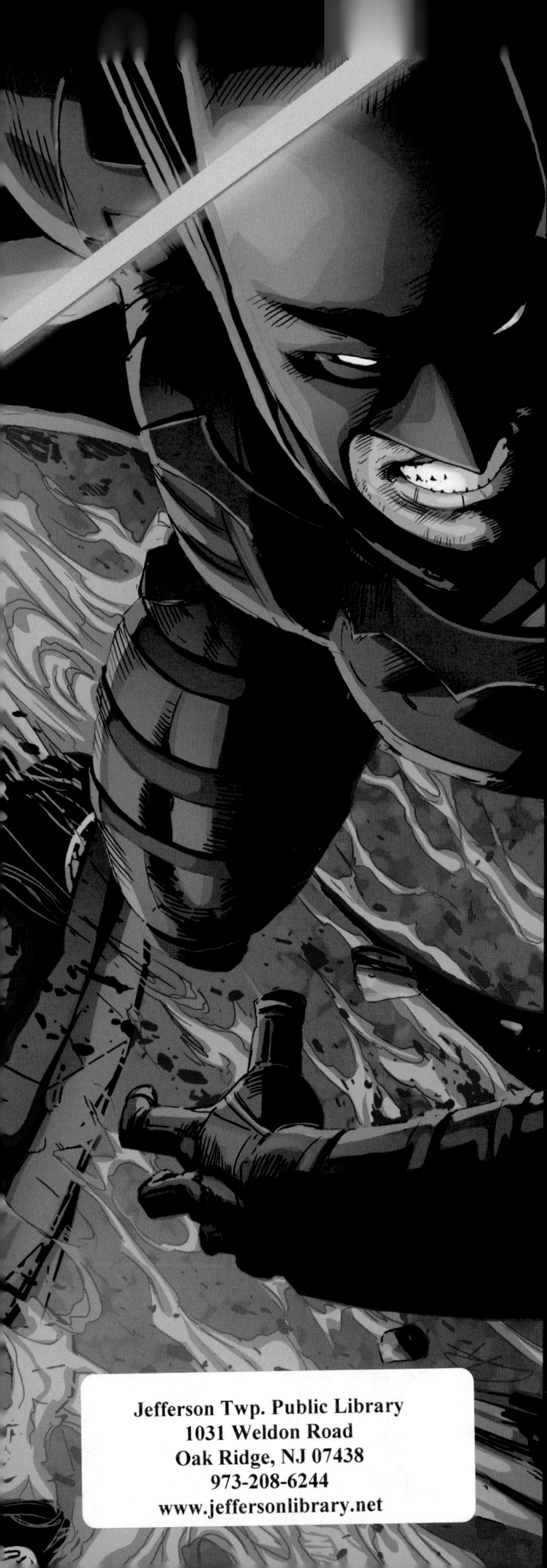

BATMAN/SUPERMAN

VOLUME 4
SIEGE

WRITTEN BY
GREG PAK

PENCILS BY
ARDIAN SYAF
TOM DERENICK
TYLER KIRKHAM
IAN CHURCHILL
EMANUELA LUPACCHINO
CLIFF RICHARDS
JACK HERBERT

INKS BY
SANDRA HOPE ARCHER
JONATHAN GLAPION
JAIME MENDOZA
MARK MORALES
DON HO
VICENTE CIFUENTES
DAVID MEIKIS
RAY MCCARTHY
TYLER KIRKHAM
CLIFF RICHARDS

COLOR BY
ULISES ARREOLA
ARIF PRIANTO
FAHRIZA KAMAPUTRA
JESSICA KHOLINNE
GLORIA CAELI
HI-FI

LETTERS BY
ROB LEIGH

COLLECTION COVER BY
ARDIAN SYAF, DANNY MIKI
AND **WIL QUINTANA**

BATMAN CREATED BY
BOB KANE

SUPERMAN CREATED BY
JERRY SIEGEL & JOE SHUSTER
BY SPECIAL ARRANGEMENT WITH
THE JERRY SIEGEL FAMILY

BATMAN/SUPERMAN VOLUME 4: SIEGE

Published by DC Comics. Compilation and all new material Copyright © 2016 DC Comics. All Rights Reserved.

Originally published in single magazine form in BATMAN/SUPERMAN 16-20; BATMAN/SUPERMAN ANNUAL 2; BATMAN/SUPERMAN: FUTURES END 1 © 2014, 2015 DC Comics. All Rights Reserved. All characters, their distinctive likenesses and related elements featured in this publication are trademarks of DC Comics. The stories, characters and incidents featured in this publication are entirely fictional. DC Comics does not read or accept unsolicited submissions of ideas, stories or artwork.

DC Comics, 2900 West Alameda Avenue, Burbank, CA 91505
Printed by RR Donnelley, Owensville, MO, USA. 7/8/16. First Printing.
ISBN: 978-1-4012-6368-3

Library of Congress Cataloging-in-Publication Data

Pak, Greg.
Batman/Superman. Volume 4 / Greg Pak, writer ; Ardian Syaf, artist.
pages cm.
ISBN 978-1-4012-6368-3
1. Graphic novels. I. Syaf, Ardian, illustrator. II. Title.
PN6728.B36P345 2015
741.5'973--dc23
2015031181

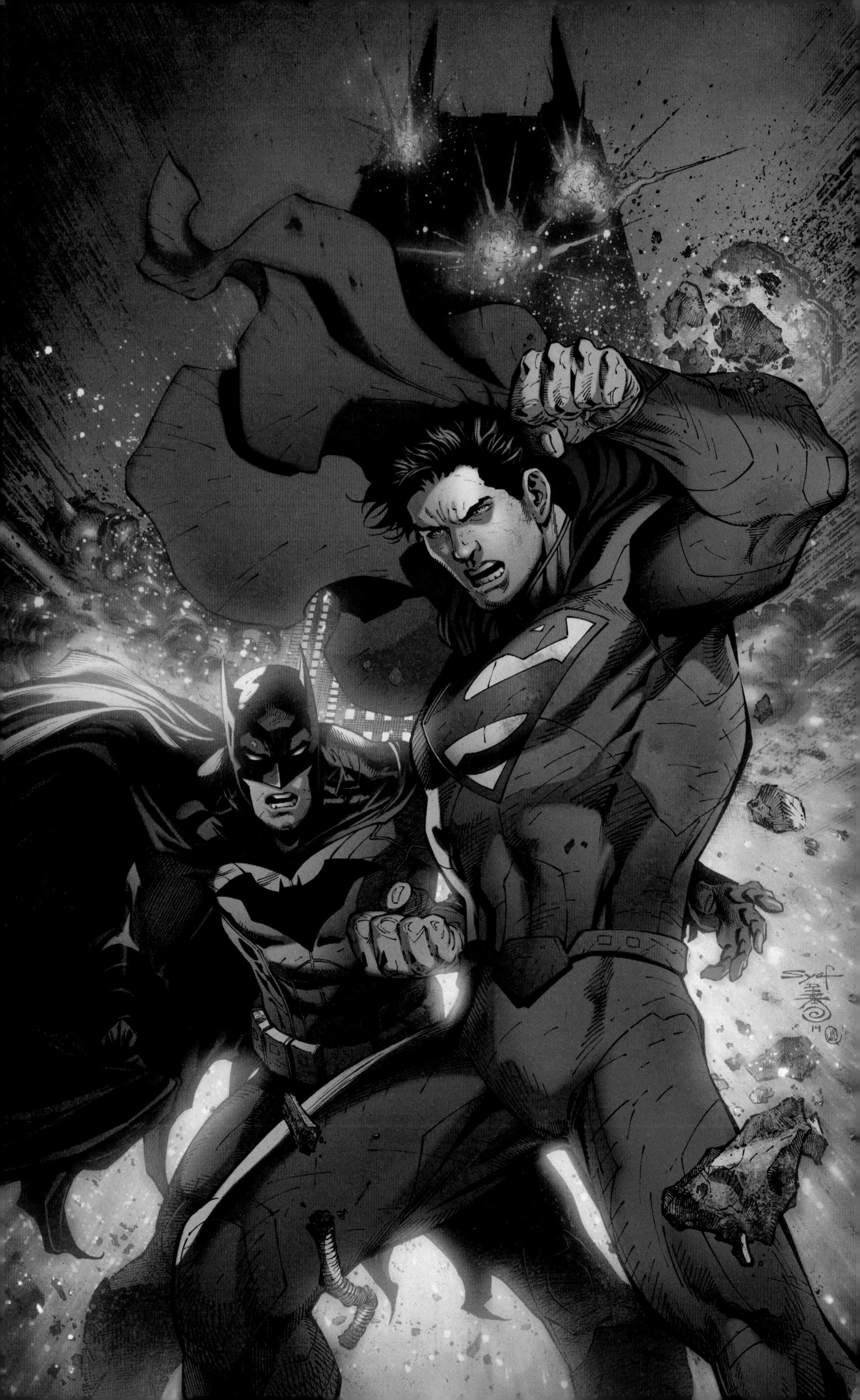

cover by ARDIAN SYAF, DANNY MIKI and WIL QUINTANA

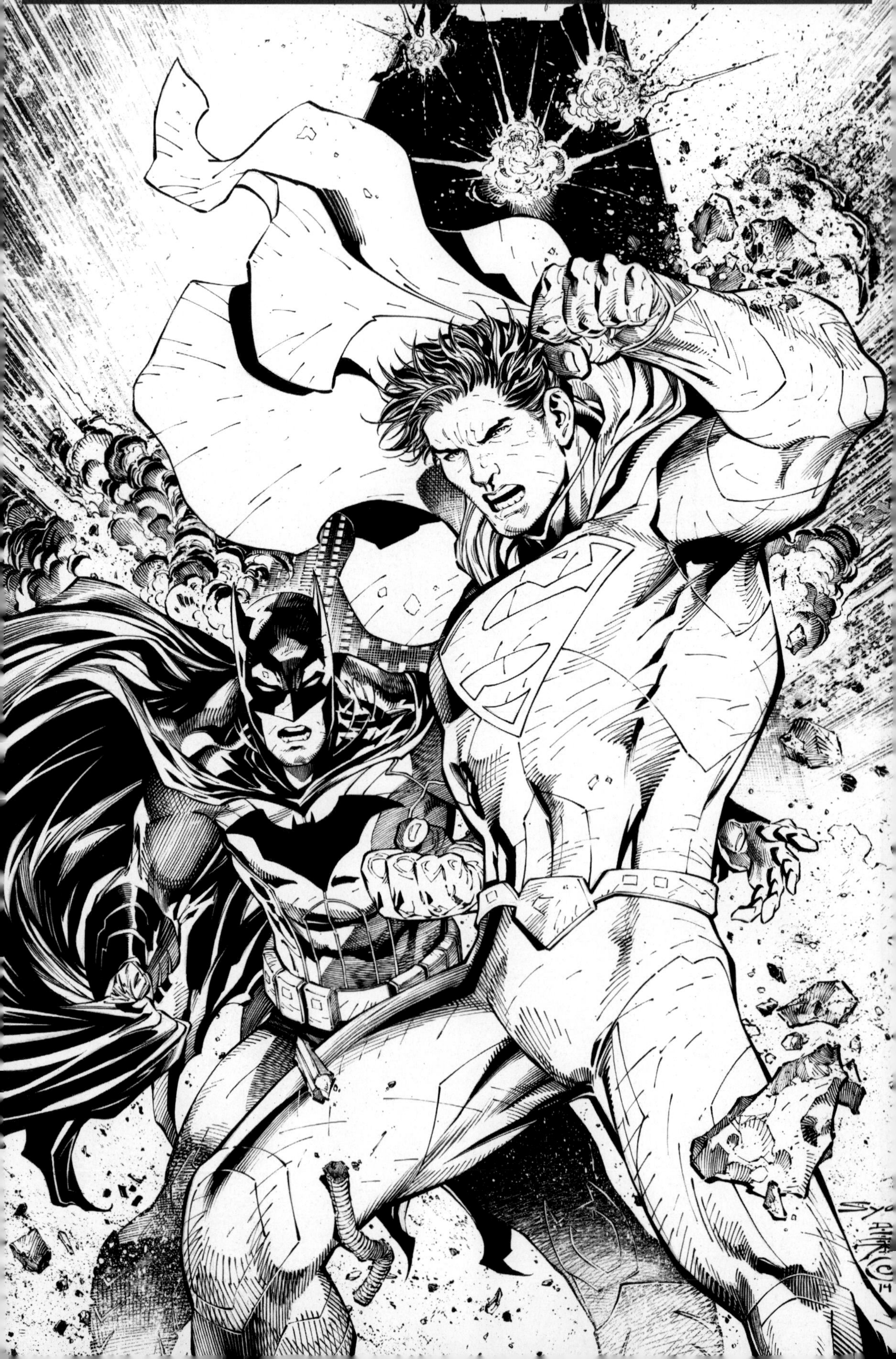

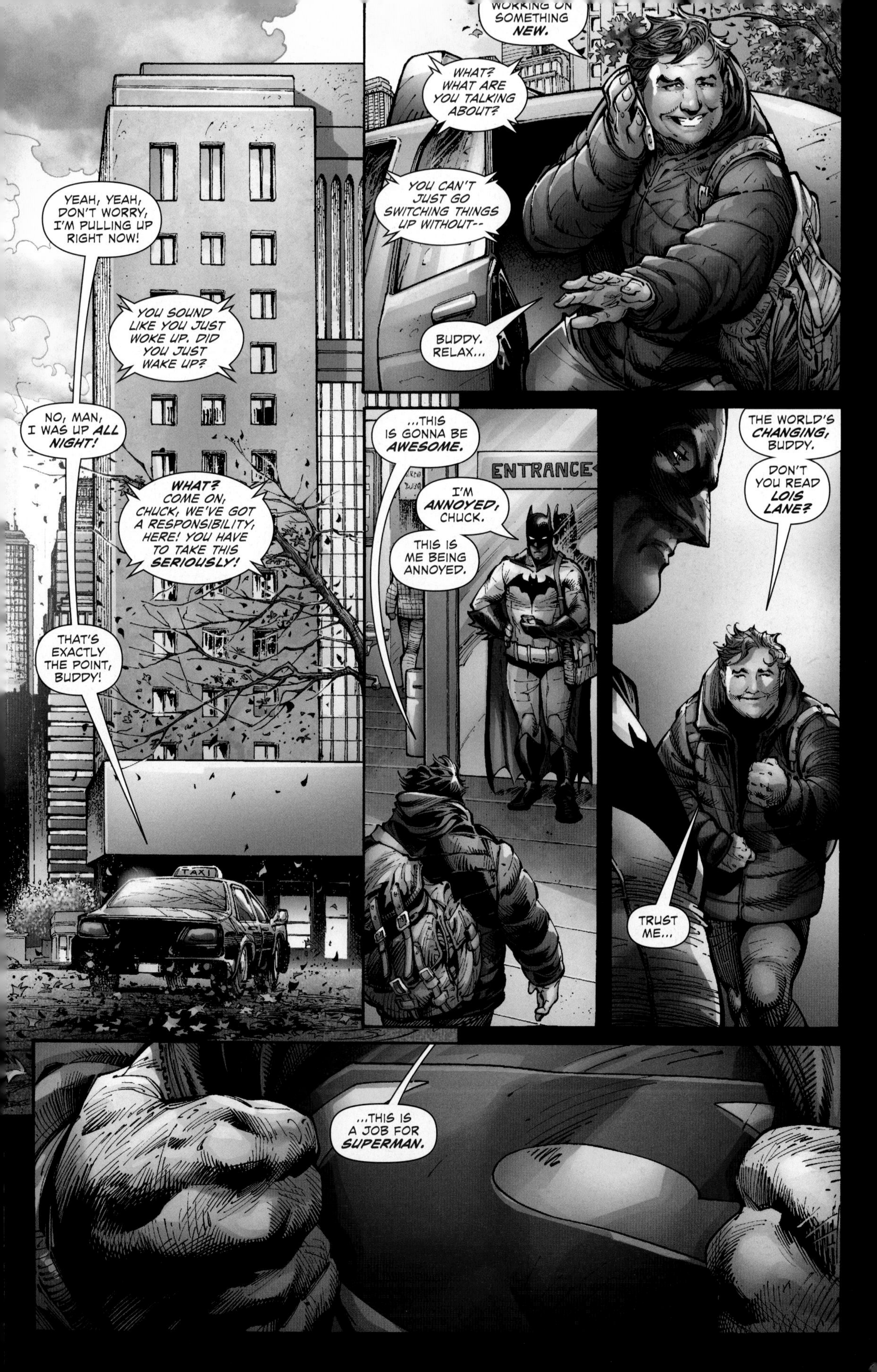
YEAH, YEAH, DON'T WORRY, I'M PULLING UP RIGHT NOW!
YOU SOUND LIKE YOU JUST WOKE UP. DID YOU JUST WAKE UP?
NO, MAN, I WAS UP ALL NIGHT!
WHAT? COME ON, CHUCK, WE'VE GOT A RESPONSIBILITY, HERE! YOU HAVE TO TAKE THIS SERIOUSLY!
THAT'S EXACTLY THE POINT, BUDDY!
TAXI
WORKING ON SOMETHING NEW.
WHAT? WHAT ARE YOU TALKING ABOUT?
YOU CAN'T JUST GO SWITCHING THINGS UP WITHOUT--
BUDDY. RELAX...
...THIS IS GONNA BE AWESOME.
ENTRANCE
I'M ANNOYED, CHUCK.
THIS IS ME BEING ANNOYED.
THE WORLD'S CHANGING, BUDDY.
DON'T YOU READ LOIS LANE?
TRUST ME...
...THIS IS A JOB FOR SUPERMAN.

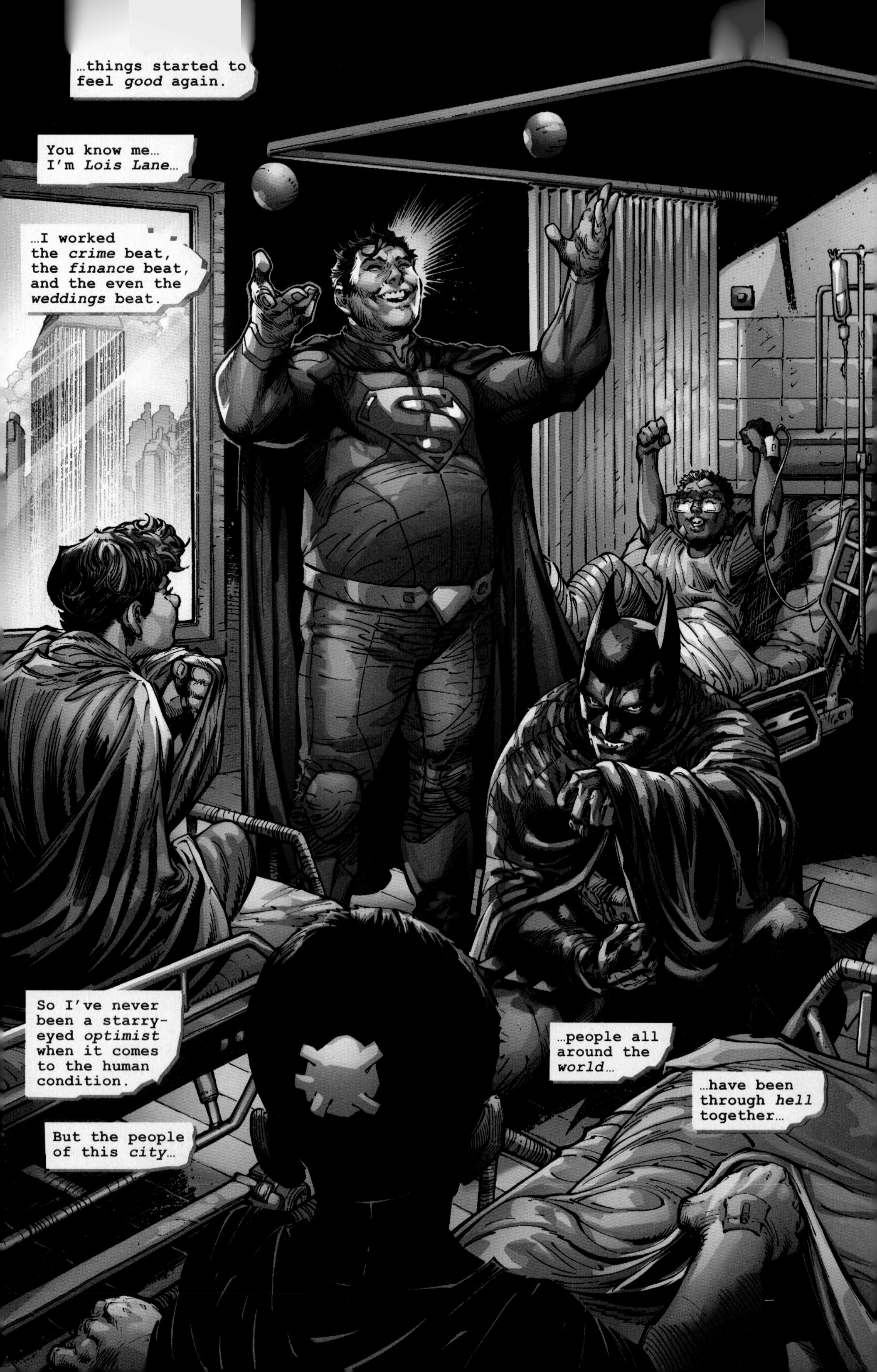

...things started to feel good again.
You know me... I'm Lois Lane...
...I worked the crime beat, the finance beat, and the even the weddings beat.
So I've never been a starry-eyed optimist when it comes to the human condition.
But the people of this city...
...people all around the world...
...have been through hell together...

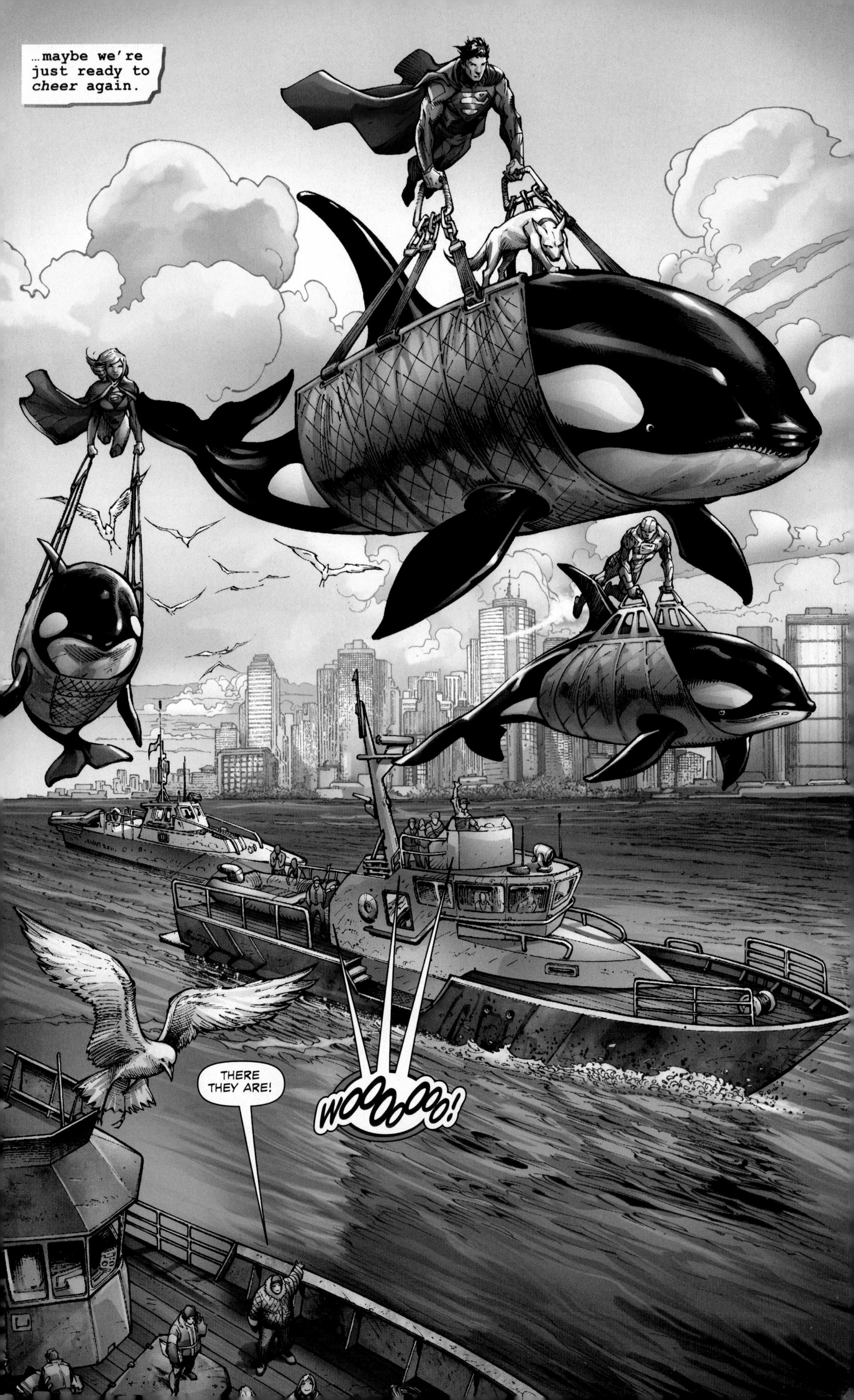
…maybe we're just ready to cheer again.
THERE THEY ARE!
WOOOOOOO!

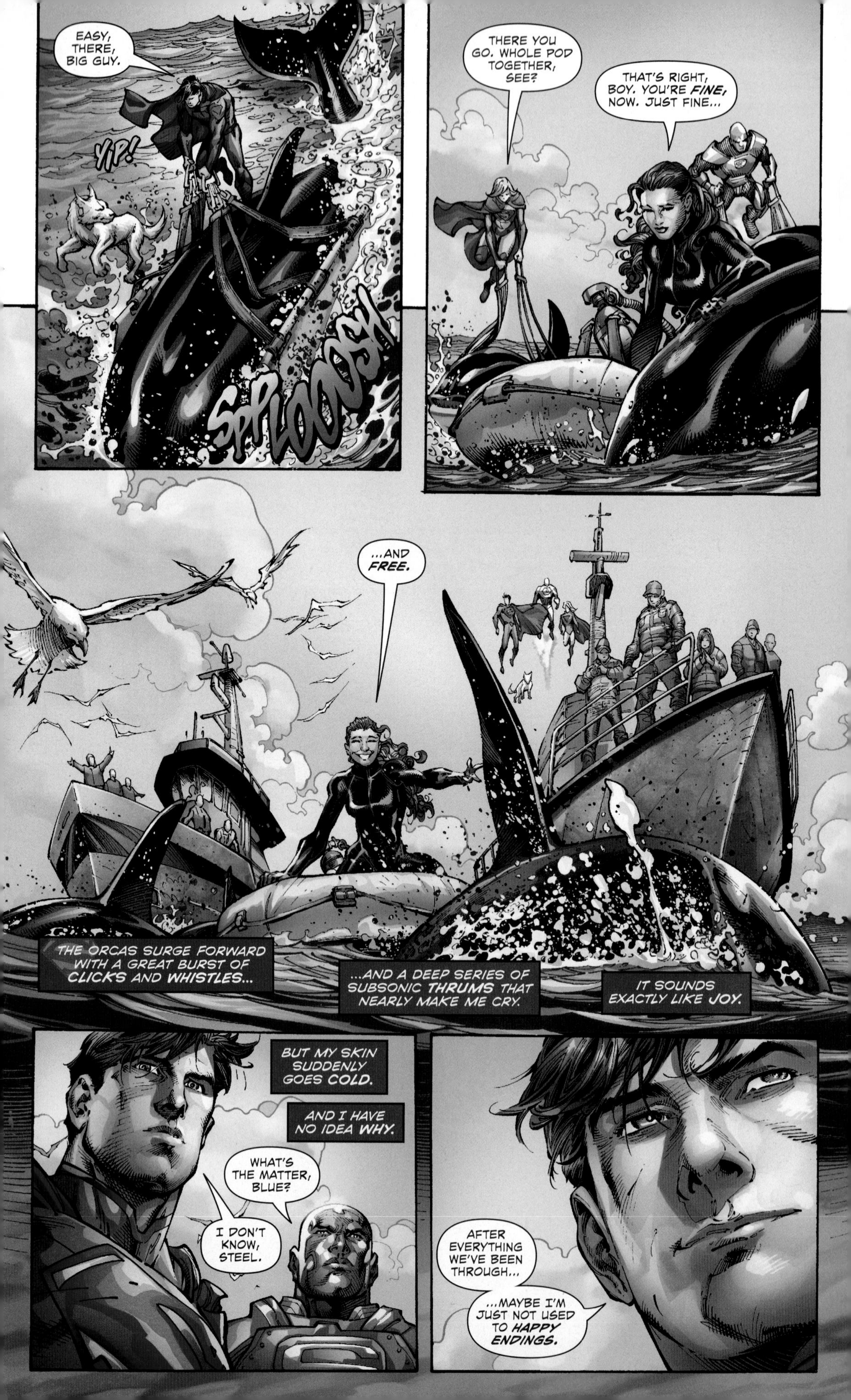
EASY, THERE, BIG GUY.
YIP!
SPLOOOSH
THERE YOU GO. WHOLE POD TOGETHER, SEE?
THAT'S RIGHT, BOY. YOU'RE FINE, NOW. JUST FINE...
...AND FREE.
THE ORCAS SURGE FORWARD WITH A GREAT BURST OF CLICKS AND WHISTLES...
...AND A DEEP SERIES OF SUBSONIC THRUMS THAT NEARLY MAKE ME CRY.
IT SOUNDS EXACTLY LIKE JOY.
BUT MY SKIN SUDDENLY GOES COLD.
AND I HAVE NO IDEA WHY.
WHAT'S THE MATTER, BLUE?
I DON'T KNOW, STEEL.
AFTER EVERYTHING WE'VE BEEN THROUGH...
...MAYBE I'M JUST NOT USED TO HAPPY ENDINGS.

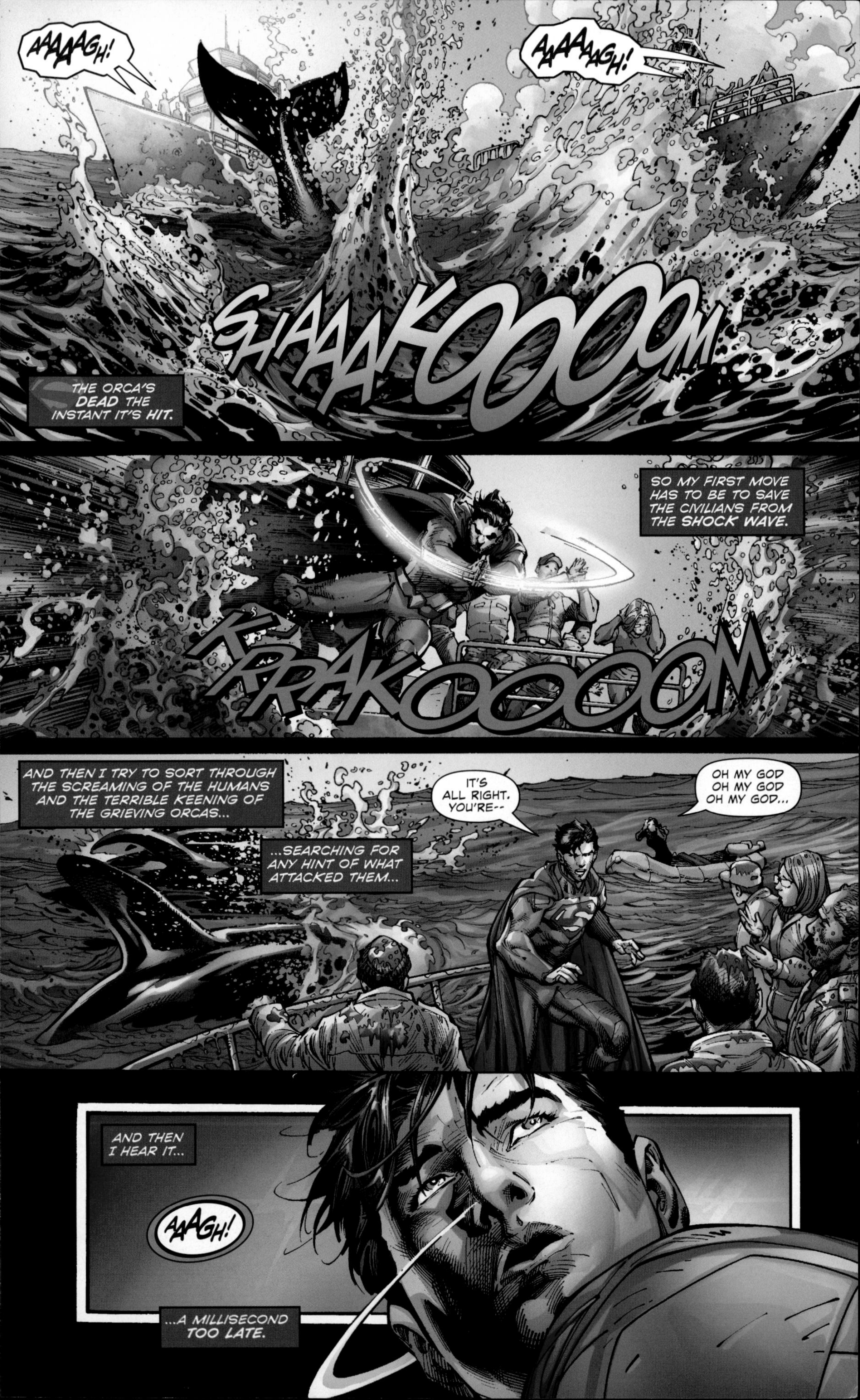
AAAAAGH!
AAAAAAGH!
SHAAAKOOOOOM
THE ORCA'S DEAD THE INSTANT IT'S HIT.
SO MY FIRST MOVE HAS TO BE TO SAVE THE CIVILIANS FROM THE SHOCK WAVE.
KRRAKOOOOOOM
AND THEN I TRY TO SORT THROUGH THE SCREAMING OF THE HUMANS AND THE TERRIBLE KEENING OF THE GRIEVING ORCAS...
IT'S ALL RIGHT. YOU'RE--
OH MY GOD OH MY GOD OH MY GOD...
...SEARCHING FOR ANY HINT OF WHAT ATTACKED THEM...
AND THEN I HEAR IT...
AAAGH!
...A MILLISECOND TOO LATE.

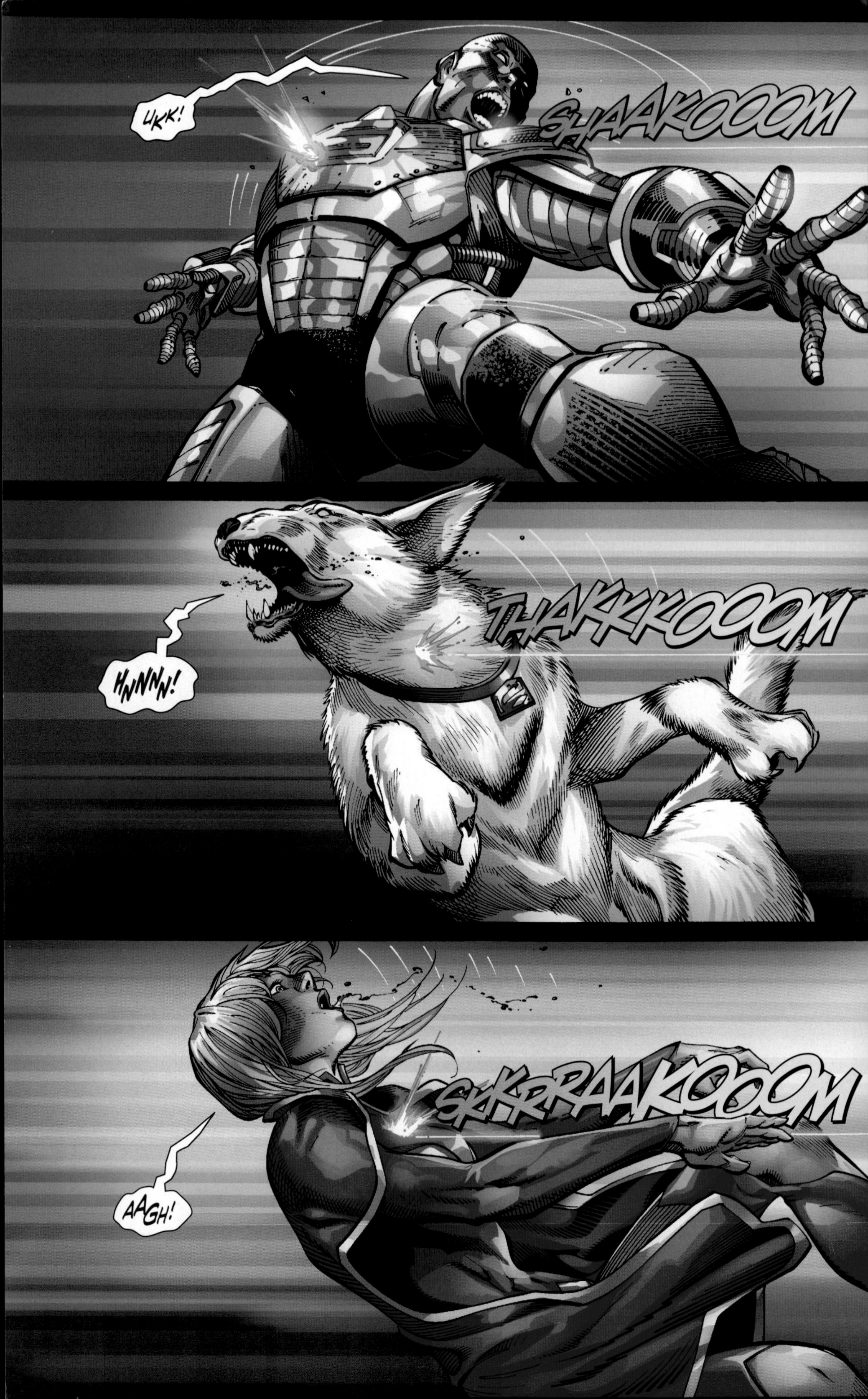
UKK!
SHAAKOOOM
HNNNN!
THAKKOOOM
AAGH!
SKKRRAAKOOOM

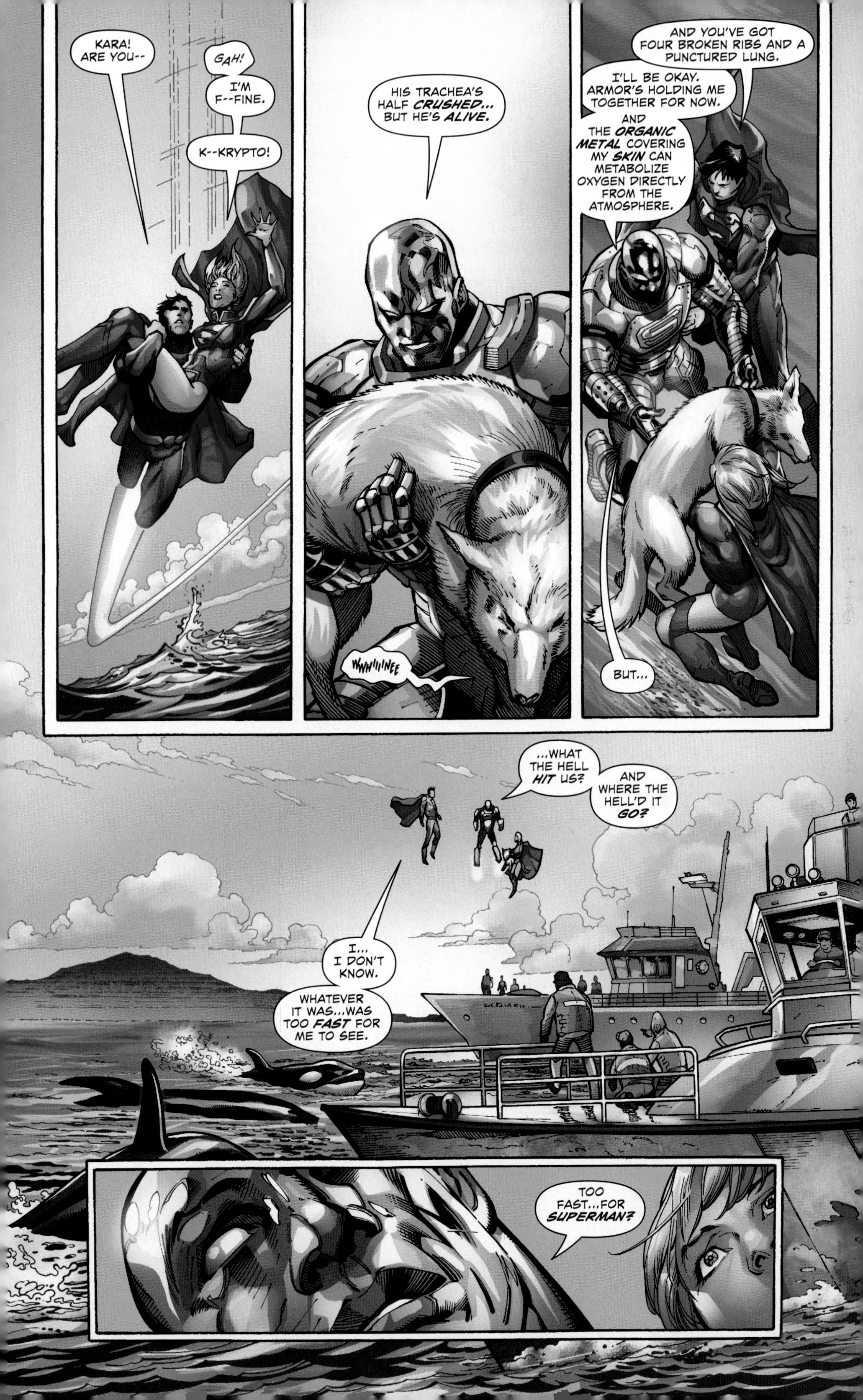
KARA! ARE YOU--
GAH!
I'M F--FINE.
K--KRYPTO!
HIS TRACHEA'S HALF *CRUSHED...* BUT HE'S *ALIVE.*
WWHIIINEE
AND YOU'VE GOT FOUR BROKEN RIBS AND A PUNCTURED LUNG.
I'LL BE OKAY. ARMOR'S HOLDING ME TOGETHER FOR NOW.
AND THE *ORGANIC METAL* COVERING MY *SKIN* CAN METABOLIZE OXYGEN DIRECTLY FROM THE ATMOSPHERE.
BUT...
...WHAT THE HELL *HIT* US?
AND WHERE THE HELL'D IT *GO?*
I... I DON'T KNOW.
WHATEVER IT WAS...WAS TOO *FAST* FOR ME TO SEE.
TOO FAST...FOR *SUPERMAN?*

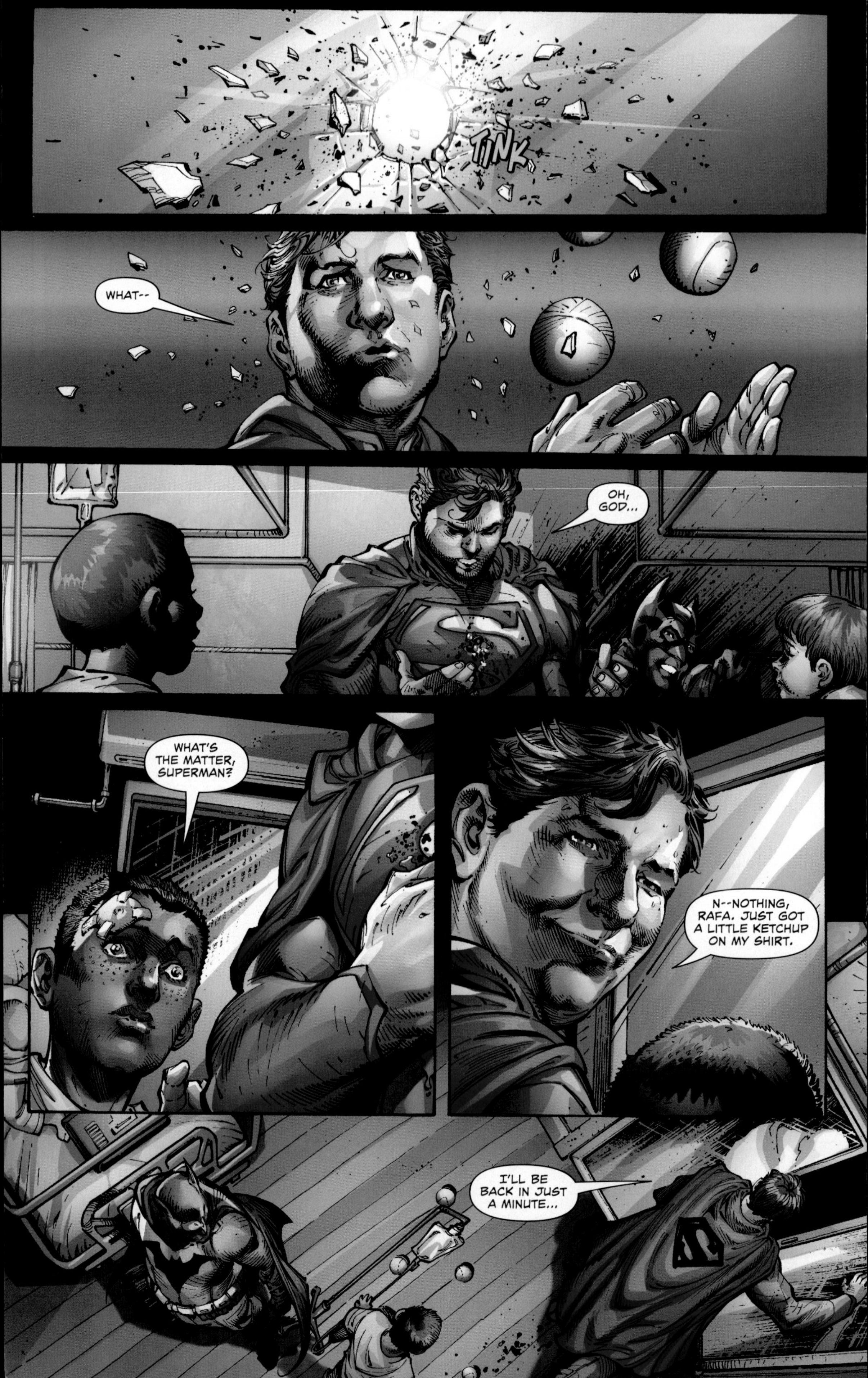
TINK
WHAT--
OH, GOD...
WHAT'S THE MATTER, SUPERMAN?
N--NOTHING, RAFA. JUST GOT A LITTLE KETCHUP ON MY SHIRT.
I'LL BE BACK IN JUST A MINUTE...

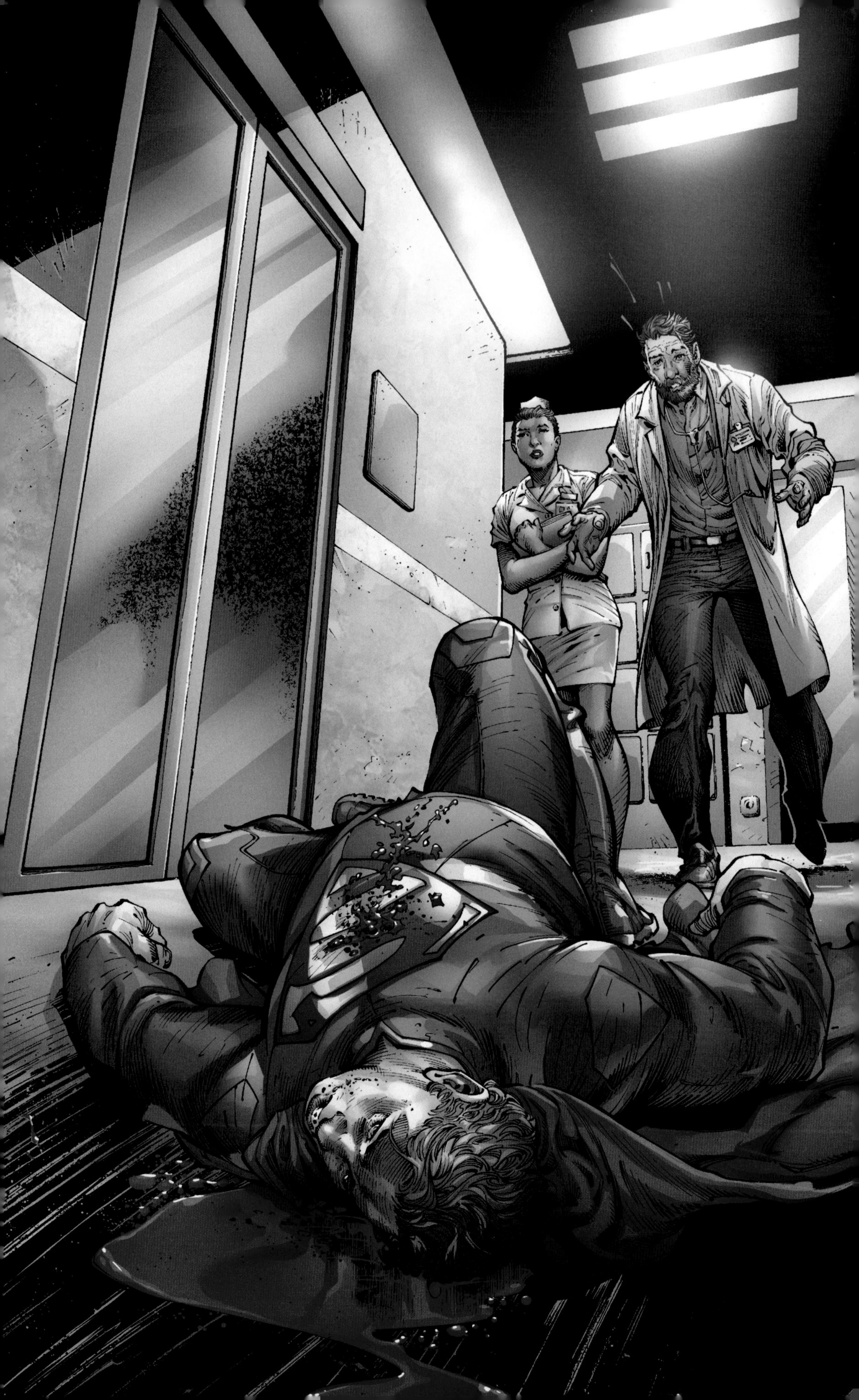

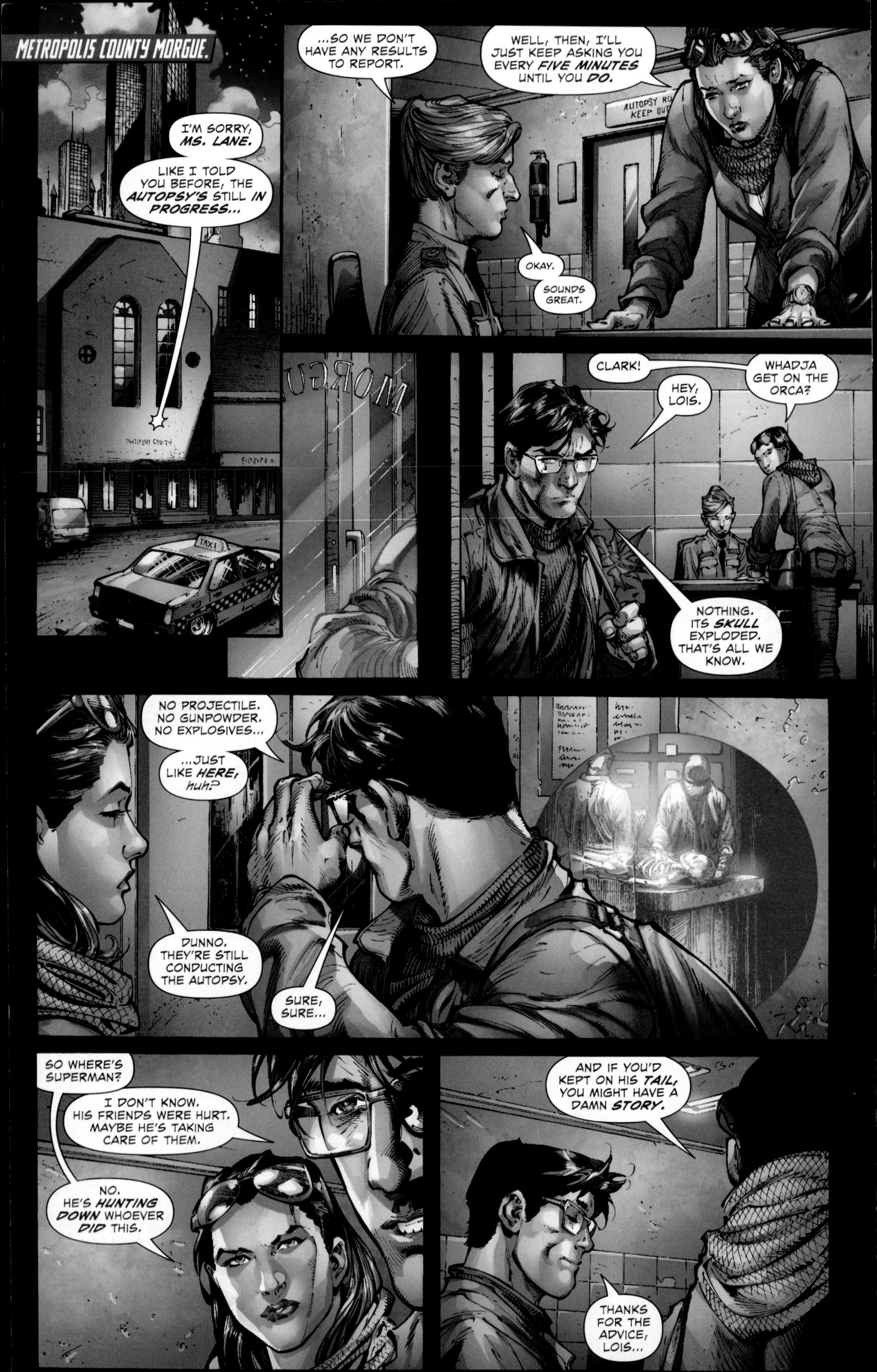
METROPOLIS COUNTY MORGUE.
I'M SORRY, MS. LANE.
LIKE I TOLD YOU BEFORE, THE AUTOPSY'S STILL IN PROGRESS...
...SO WE DON'T HAVE ANY RESULTS TO REPORT.
WELL, THEN, I'LL JUST KEEP ASKING YOU EVERY FIVE MINUTES UNTIL YOU DO.
OKAY.
SOUNDS GREAT.
AUTOPSY RO
KEEP OUT
MORGU
CLARK!
HEY, LOIS.
WHADJA GET ON THE ORCA?
NOTHING. ITS SKULL EXPLODED. THAT'S ALL WE KNOW.
NO PROJECTILE. NO GUNPOWDER. NO EXPLOSIVES...
...JUST LIKE HERE, huh?
DUNNO. THEY'RE STILL CONDUCTING THE AUTOPSY.
SURE, SURE...
SO WHERE'S SUPERMAN?
I DON'T KNOW. HIS FRIENDS WERE HURT. MAYBE HE'S TAKING CARE OF THEM.
NO. HE'S HUNTING DOWN WHOEVER DID THIS.
AND IF YOU'D KEPT ON HIS TAIL, YOU MIGHT HAVE A DAMN STORY.
THANKS FOR THE ADVICE, LOIS...

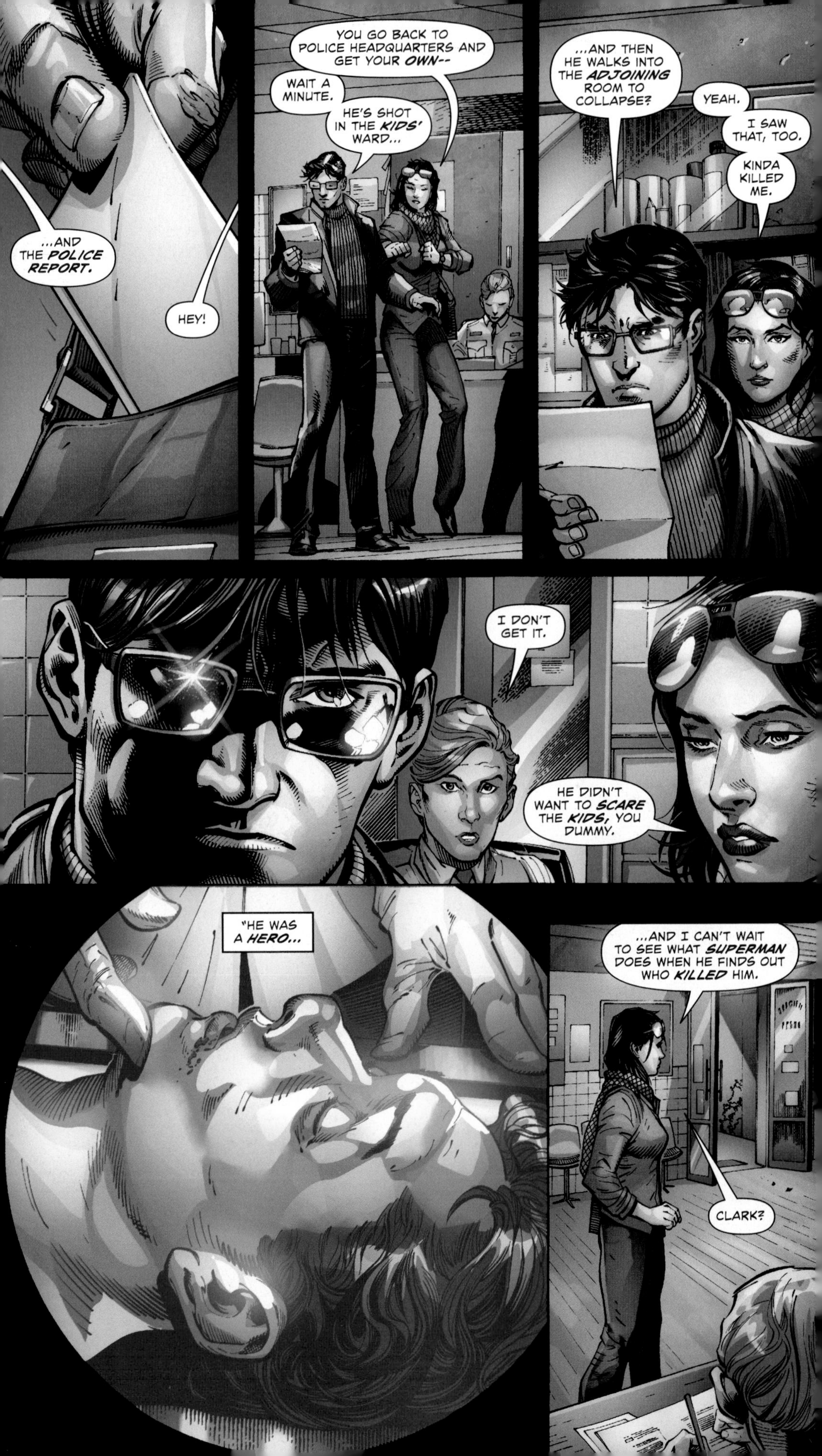
...AND THE POLICE REPORT.
HEY!
YOU GO BACK TO POLICE HEADQUARTERS AND GET YOUR OWN--
WAIT A MINUTE.
HE'S SHOT IN THE KIDS' WARD...
...AND THEN HE WALKS INTO THE ADJOINING ROOM TO COLLAPSE?
YEAH.
I SAW THAT, TOO.
KINDA KILLED ME.
I DON'T GET IT.
HE DIDN'T WANT TO SCARE THE KIDS, YOU DUMMY.
"HE WAS A HERO...
...AND I CAN'T WAIT TO SEE WHAT SUPERMAN DOES WHEN HE FINDS OUT WHO KILLED HIM.
CLARK?

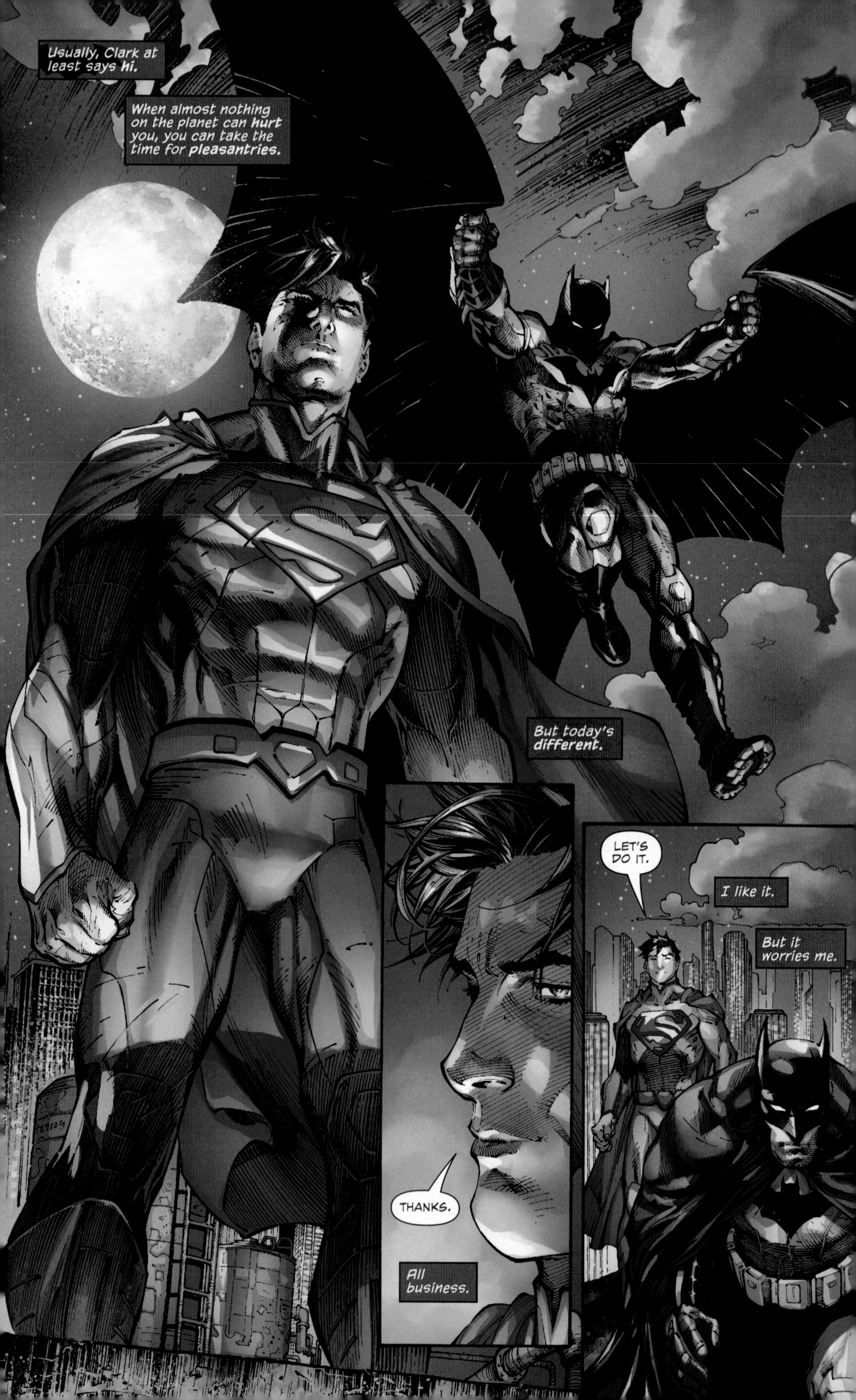
Usually, Clark at least says hi.
When almost nothing on the planet can hurt you, you can take the time for pleasantries.
But today's different.
THANKS.
All business.
LET'S DO IT.
I like it.
But it worries me.

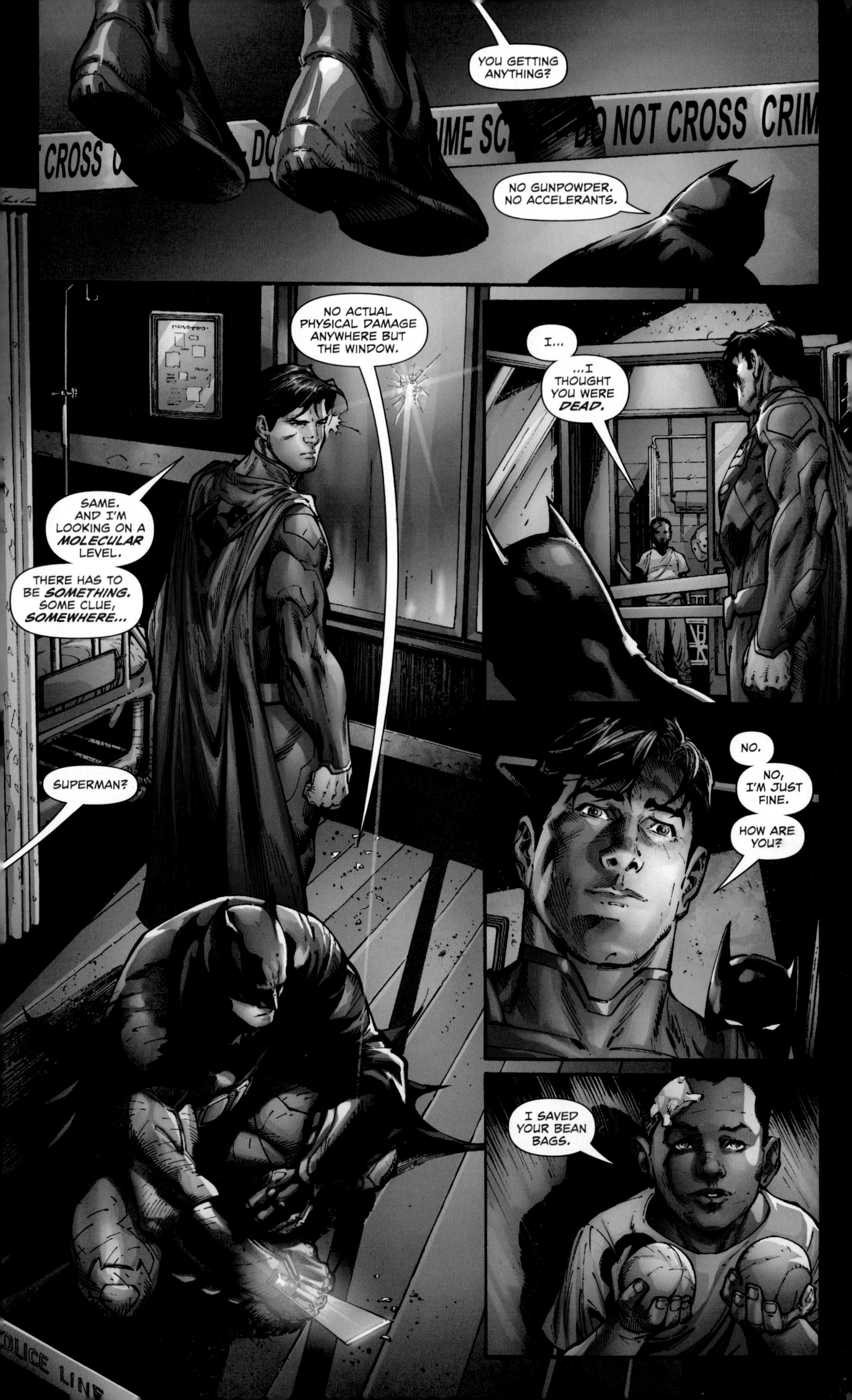
YOU GETTING ANYTHING?
CRIME SCE DO NOT CROSS CRIM
CROSS
NO GUNPOWDER. NO ACCELERANTS.
NO ACTUAL PHYSICAL DAMAGE ANYWHERE BUT THE WINDOW.
SAME. AND I'M LOOKING ON A *MOLECULAR* LEVEL.
THERE HAS TO BE *SOMETHING.* SOME CLUE, *SOMEWHERE...*
SUPERMAN?
I...
...I THOUGHT YOU WERE *DEAD.*
NO.
NO, I'M JUST FINE.
HOW ARE YOU?
I SAVED YOUR BEAN BAGS.
OLICE LINE

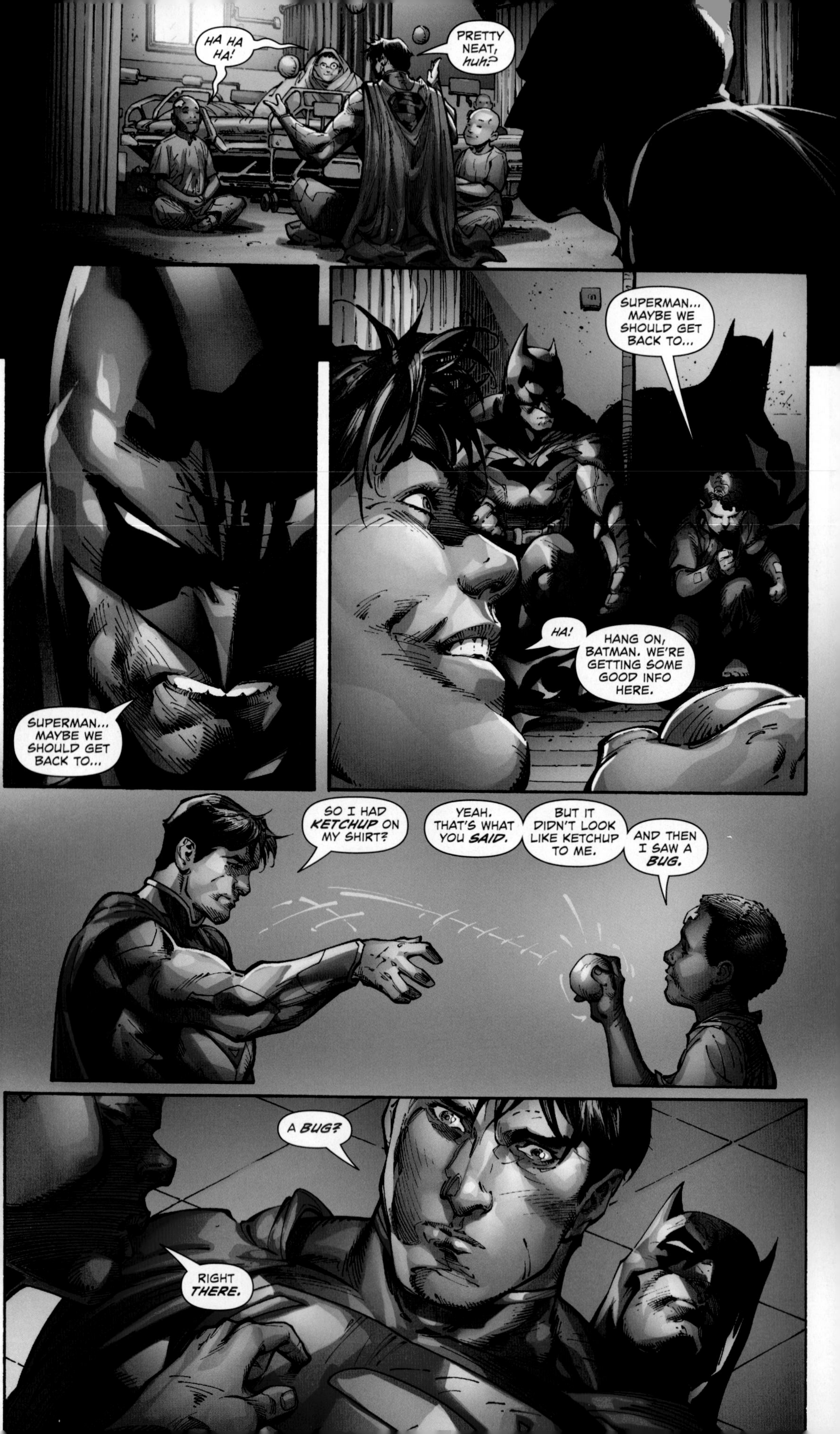
HA HA HA!
PRETTY NEAT, huh?
SUPERMAN... MAYBE WE SHOULD GET BACK TO...
SUPERMAN... MAYBE WE SHOULD GET BACK TO...
HA!
HANG ON, BATMAN. WE'RE GETTING SOME GOOD INFO HERE.
SO I HAD KETCHUP ON MY SHIRT?
YEAH. THAT'S WHAT YOU SAID.
BUT IT DIDN'T LOOK LIKE KETCHUP TO ME.
AND THEN I SAW A BUG.
A BUG?
RIGHT THERE.

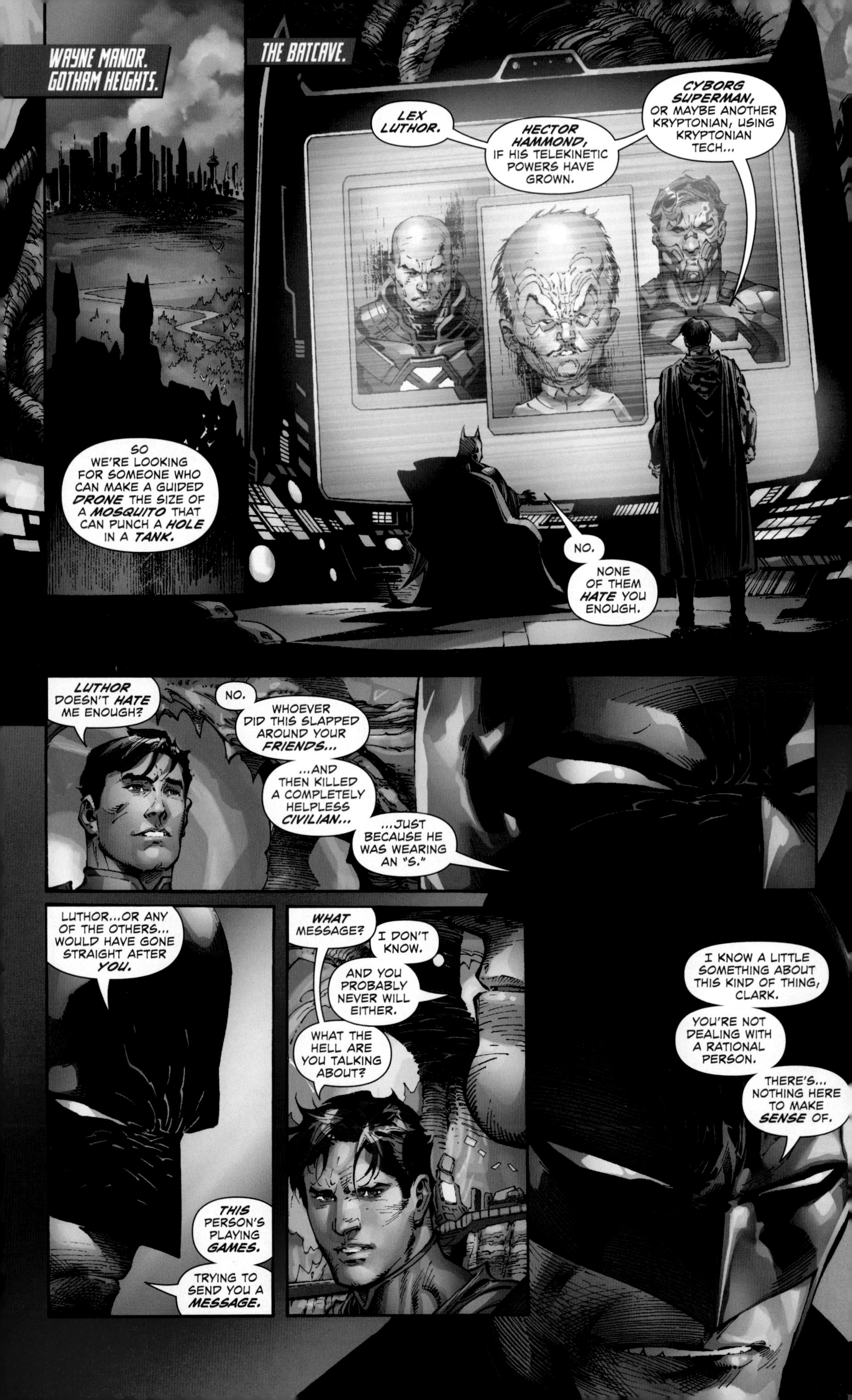
WAYNE MANOR. GOTHAM HEIGHTS.
THE BATCAVE.
LEX LUTHOR.
HECTOR HAMMOND, IF HIS TELEKINETIC POWERS HAVE GROWN.
CYBORG SUPERMAN, OR MAYBE ANOTHER KRYPTONIAN, USING KRYPTONIAN TECH...
SO WE'RE LOOKING FOR SOMEONE WHO CAN MAKE A GUIDED DRONE THE SIZE OF A MOSQUITO THAT CAN PUNCH A HOLE IN A TANK.
NO.
NONE OF THEM HATE YOU ENOUGH.
LUTHOR DOESN'T HATE ME ENOUGH?
NO.
WHOEVER DID THIS SLAPPED AROUND YOUR FRIENDS...
...AND THEN KILLED A COMPLETELY HELPLESS CIVILIAN...
...JUST BECAUSE HE WAS WEARING AN "S."
LUTHOR...OR ANY OF THE OTHERS... WOULD HAVE GONE STRAIGHT AFTER YOU.
THIS PERSON'S PLAYING GAMES.
TRYING TO SEND YOU A MESSAGE.
WHAT MESSAGE?
I DON'T KNOW.
AND YOU PROBABLY NEVER WILL EITHER.
WHAT THE HELL ARE YOU TALKING ABOUT?
I KNOW A LITTLE SOMETHING ABOUT THIS KIND OF THING, CLARK.
YOU'RE NOT DEALING WITH A RATIONAL PERSON.
THERE'S... NOTHING HERE TO MAKE SENSE OF.

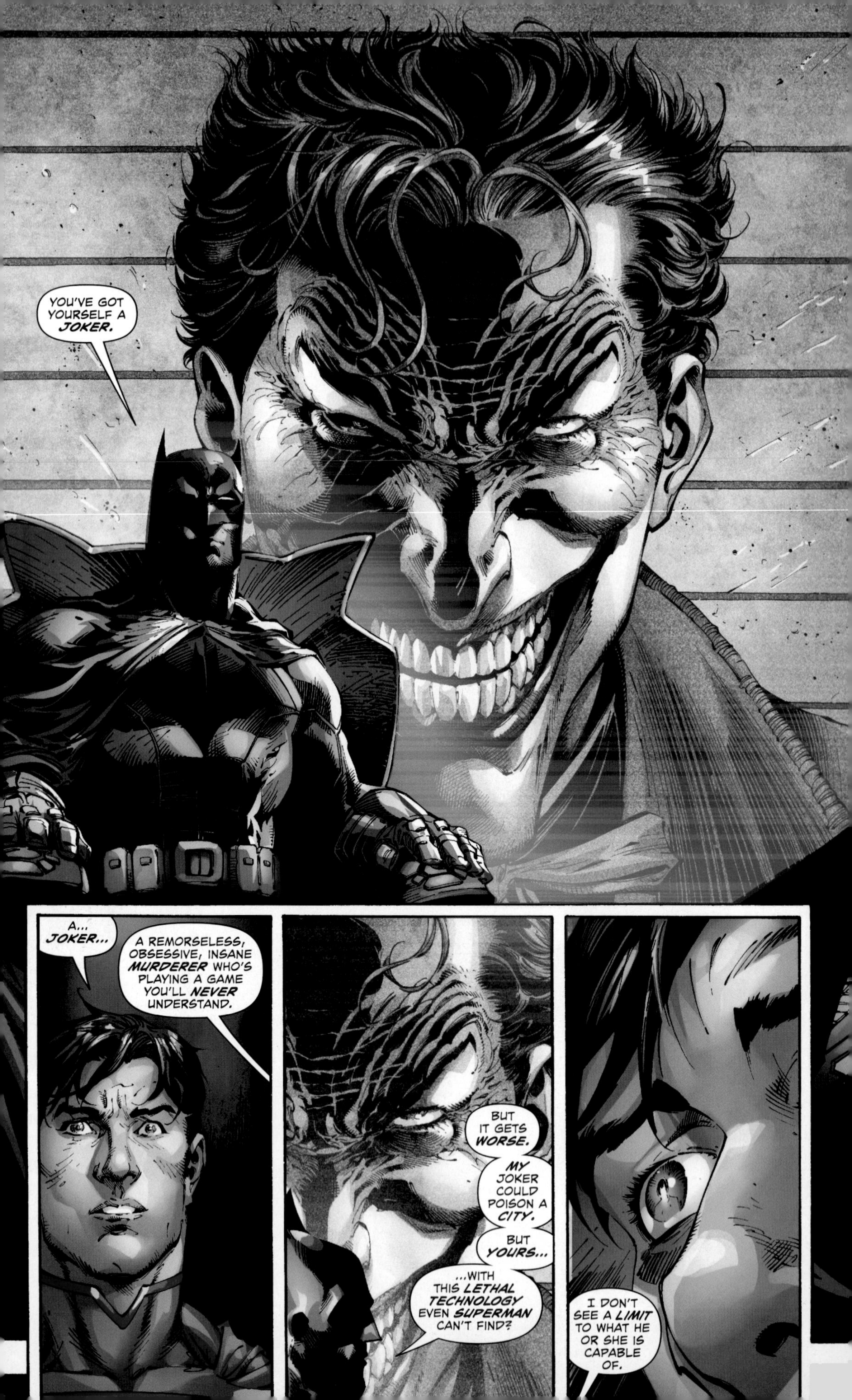
YOU'VE GOT YOURSELF A JOKER.
A... JOKER...
A REMORSELESS, OBSESSIVE, INSANE MURDERER WHO'S PLAYING A GAME YOU'LL NEVER UNDERSTAND.
BUT IT GETS WORSE.
MY JOKER COULD POISON A CITY.
BUT YOURS...
...WITH THIS LETHAL TECHNOLOGY EVEN SUPERMAN CAN'T FIND?
I DON'T SEE A LIMIT TO WHAT HE OR SHE IS CAPABLE OF.

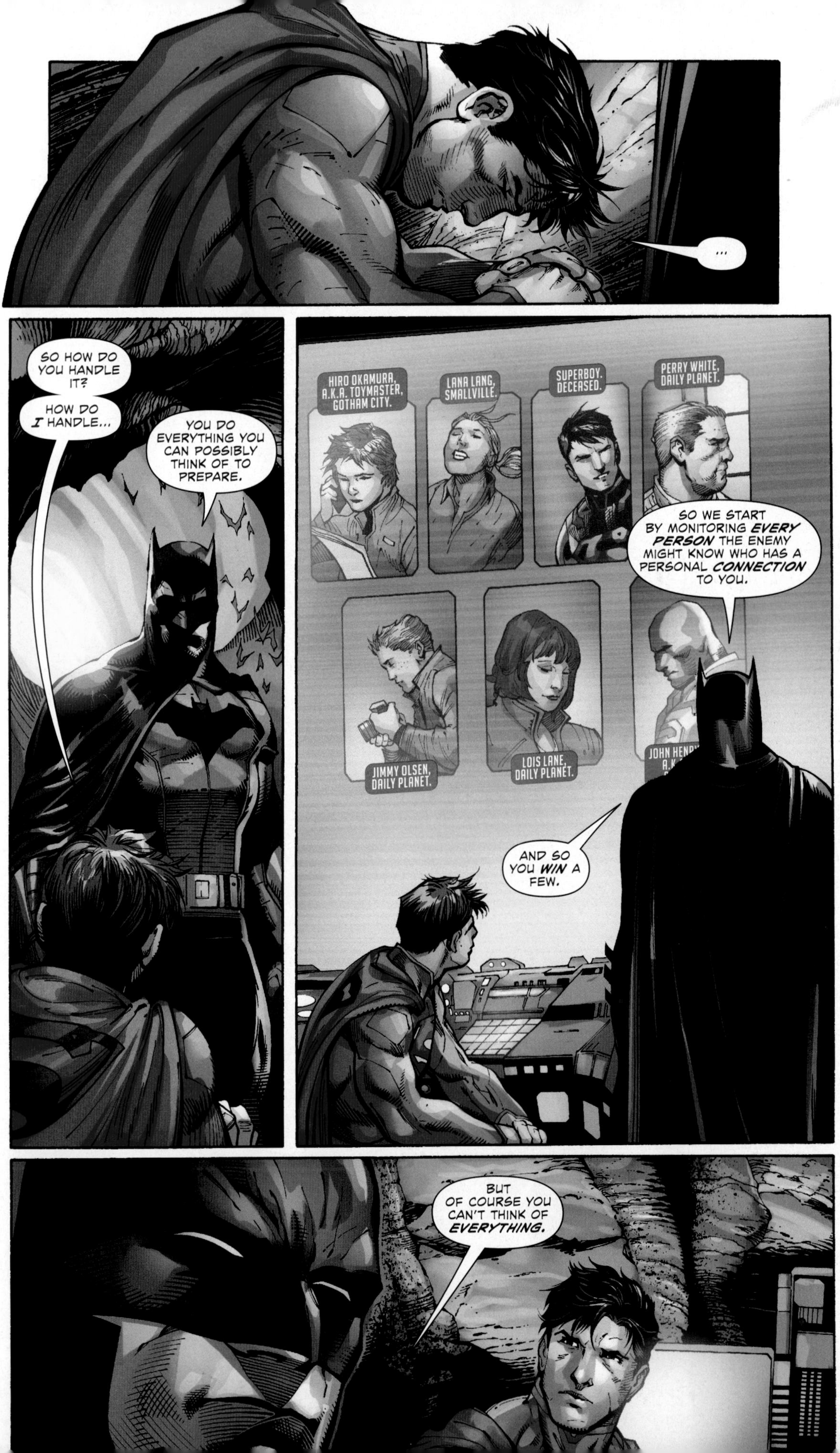
...
SO HOW DO YOU HANDLE IT?
HOW DO I HANDLE...
YOU DO EVERYTHING YOU CAN POSSIBLY THINK OF TO PREPARE.
HIRO OKAMURA, A.K.A. TOYMASTER, GOTHAM CITY.
LANA LANG, SMALLVILLE.
SUPERBOY, DECEASED.
PERRY WHITE, DAILY PLANET.
SO WE START BY MONITORING EVERY PERSON THE ENEMY MIGHT KNOW WHO HAS A PERSONAL CONNECTION TO YOU.
JIMMY OLSEN, DAILY PLANET.
LOIS LANE, DAILY PLANET.
AND SO YOU WIN A FEW.
BUT OF COURSE YOU CAN'T THINK OF EVERYTHING.

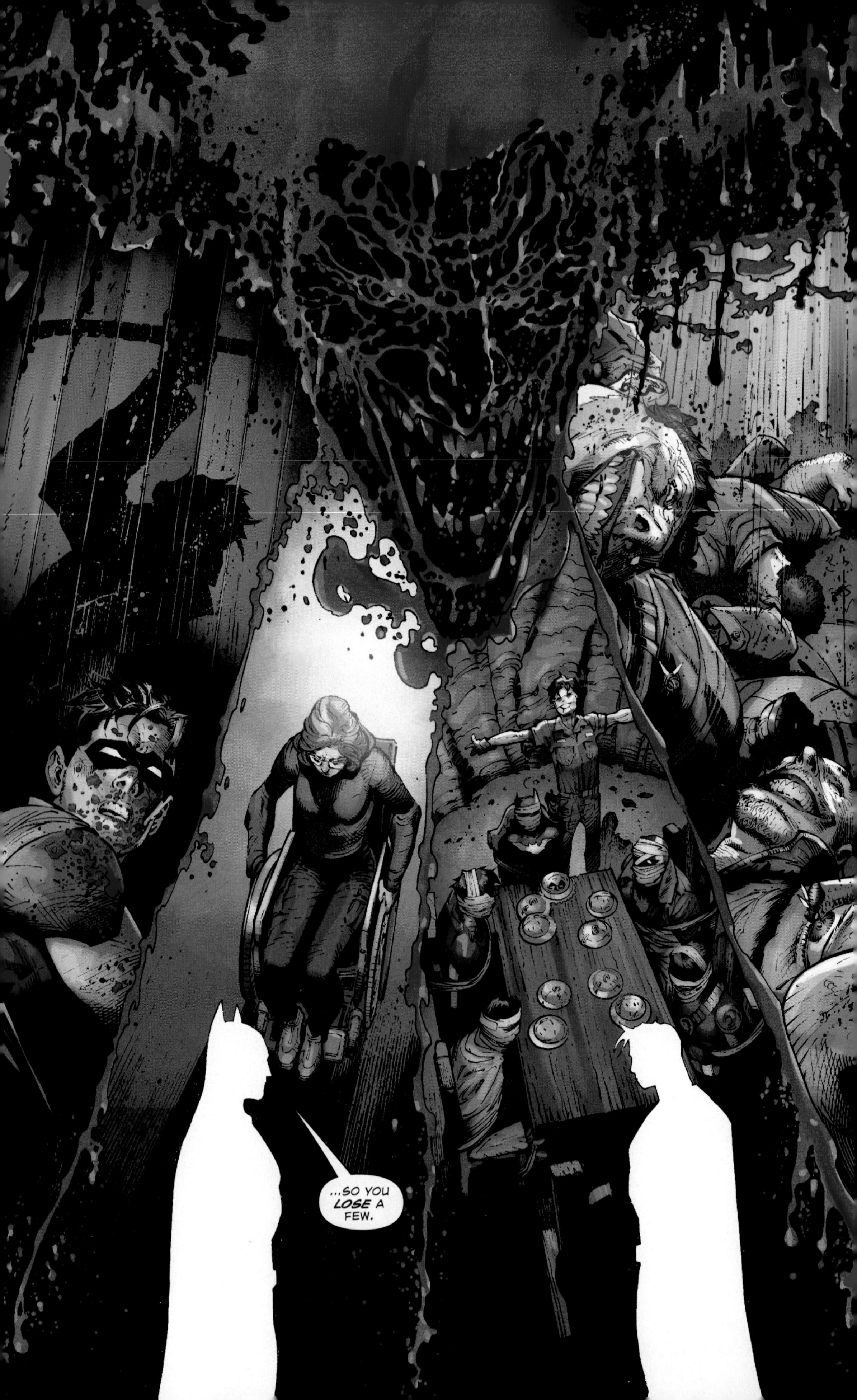
...SO YOU LOSE A FEW.

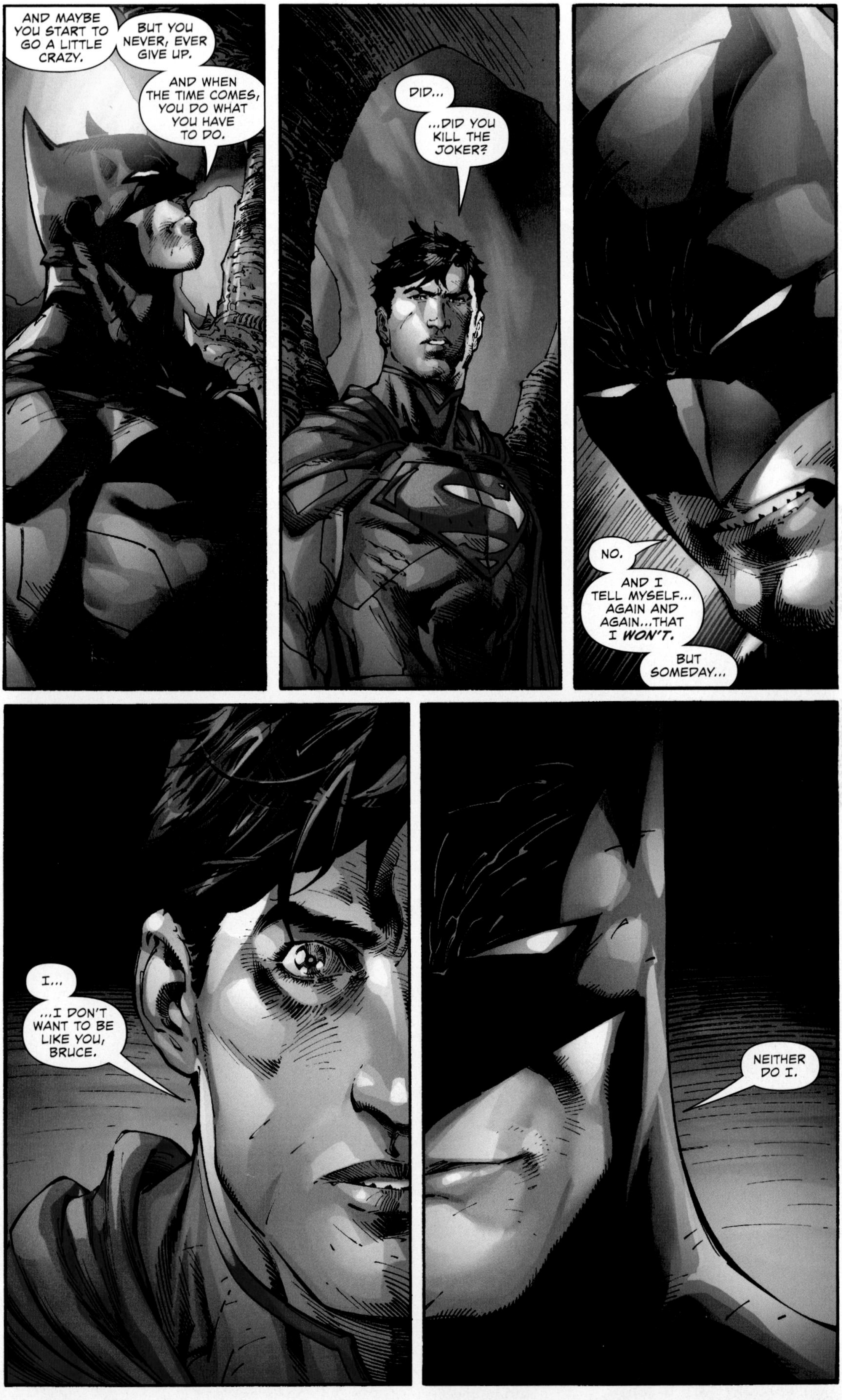
AND MAYBE YOU START TO GO A LITTLE CRAZY.
BUT YOU NEVER, EVER GIVE UP.
AND WHEN THE TIME COMES, YOU DO WHAT YOU HAVE TO DO.
DID...
...DID YOU KILL THE JOKER?
NO.
AND I TELL MYSELF... AGAIN AND AGAIN...THAT I *WON'T.*
BUT SOMEDAY...
I...
...I DON'T WANT TO BE LIKE YOU, BRUCE.
NEITHER DO I.

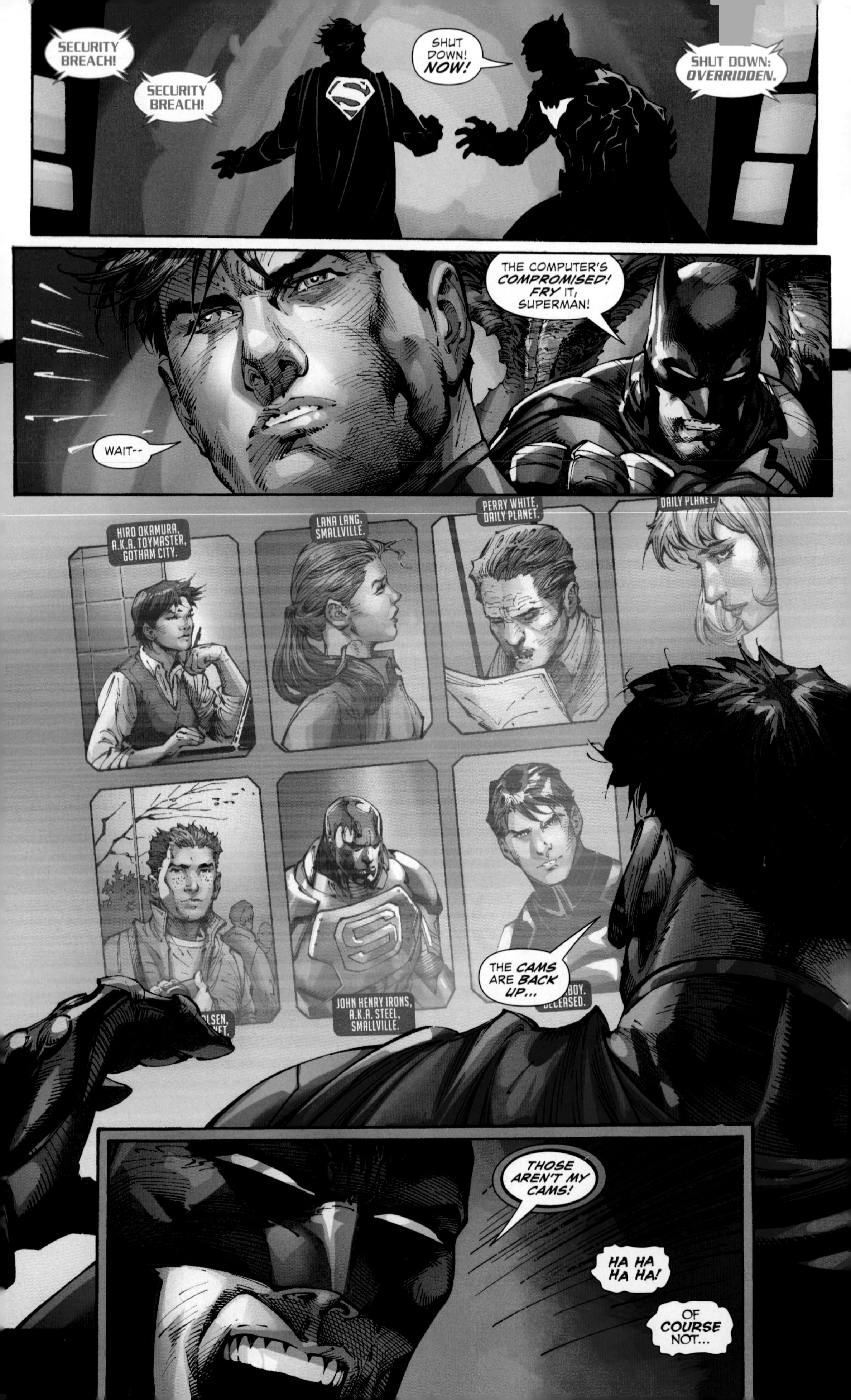
SECURITY BREACH!
SECURITY BREACH!
SHUT DOWN! NOW!
SHUT DOWN: OVERRIDDEN.
THE COMPUTER'S COMPROMISED! FRY IT, SUPERMAN!
WAIT--
HIRO OKAMURA, A.K.A. TOYMASTER, GOTHAM CITY.
LANA LANG, SMALLVILLE.
PERRY WHITE, DAILY PLANET.
DAILY PLANET.
JOHN HENRY IRONS, A.K.A. STEEL, SMALLVILLE.
THE CAMS ARE BACK UP...
THOSE AREN'T MY CAMS!
HA HA HA HA!
OF COURSE NOT...

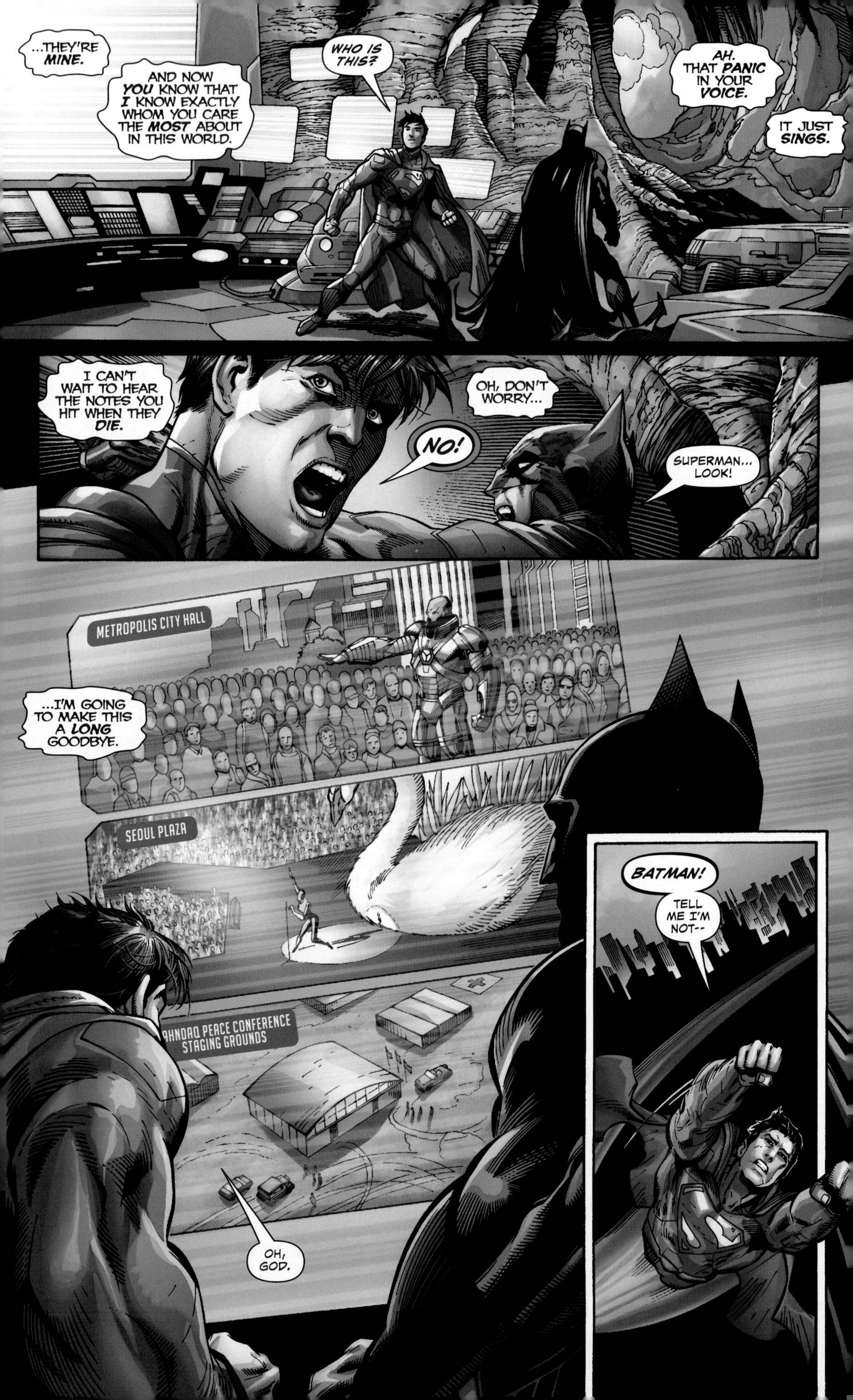
...THEY'RE MINE.
AND NOW YOU KNOW THAT I KNOW EXACTLY WHOM YOU CARE THE MOST ABOUT IN THIS WORLD.
WHO IS THIS?
AH. THAT PANIC IN YOUR VOICE.
IT JUST SINGS.
I CAN'T WAIT TO HEAR THE NOTES YOU HIT WHEN THEY DIE.
OH, DON'T WORRY...
NO!
SUPERMAN... LOOK!
METROPOLIS CITY HALL
...I'M GOING TO MAKE THIS A LONG GOODBYE.
SEOUL PLAZA
KAHNDAQ PEACE CONFERENCE STAGING GROUNDS
OH, GOD.
BATMAN!
TELL ME I'M NOT--

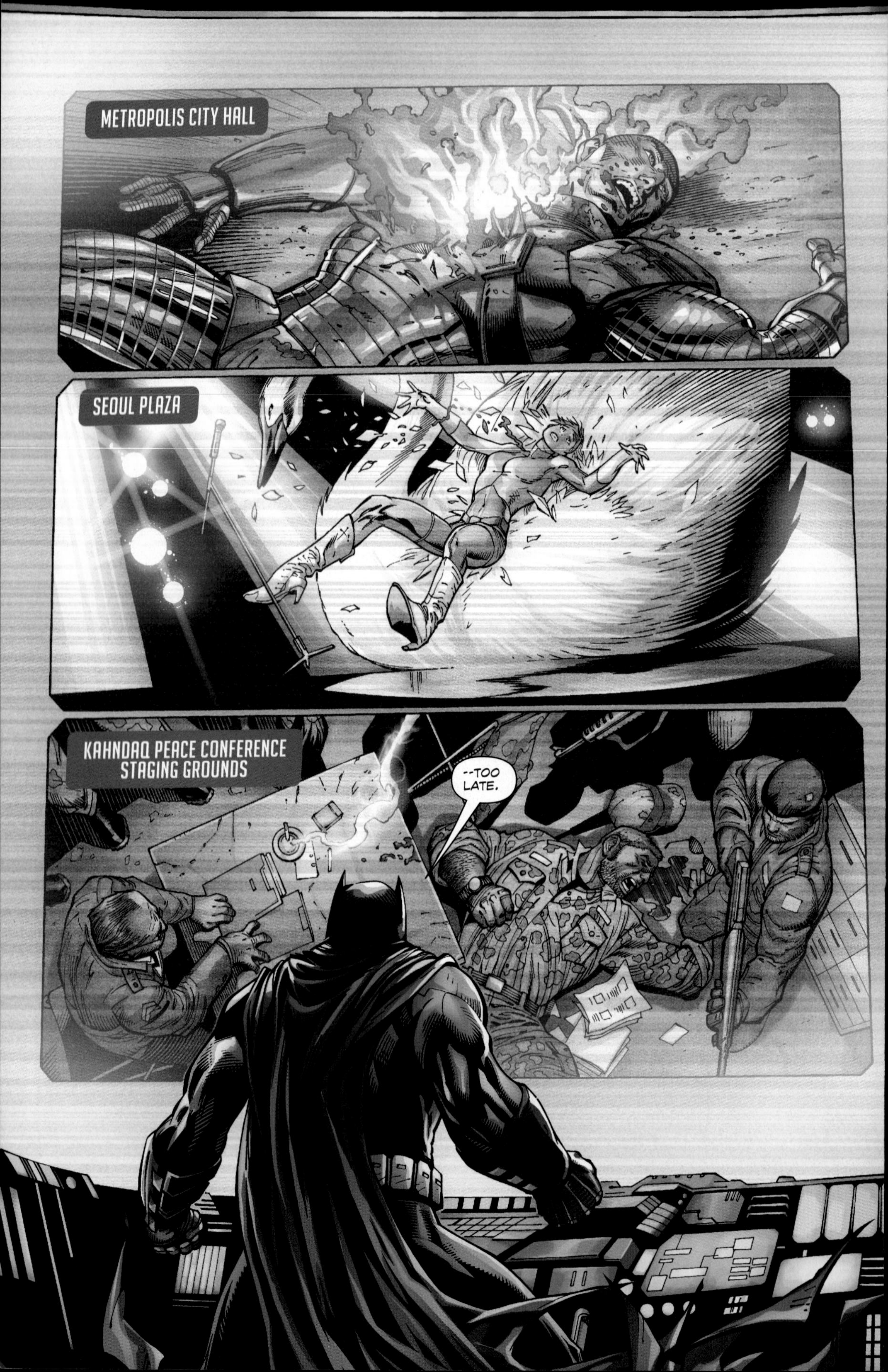
METROPOLIS CITY HALL
SEOUL PLAZA
KAHNDAQ PEACE CONFERENCE STAGING GROUNDS
--TOO LATE.

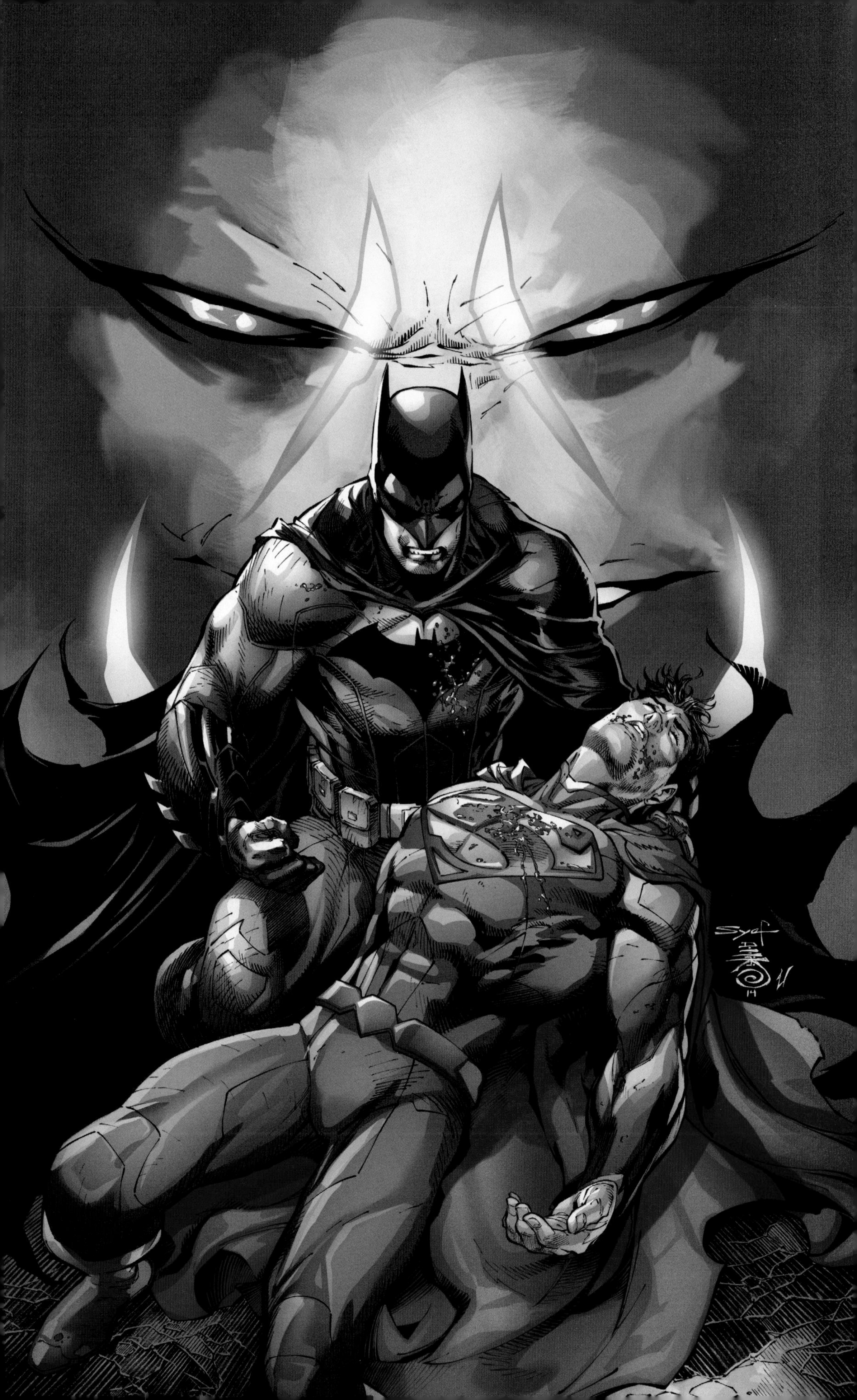

cover by ARDIAN SYAF, DANNY MIKI and ULISES ARREOLA

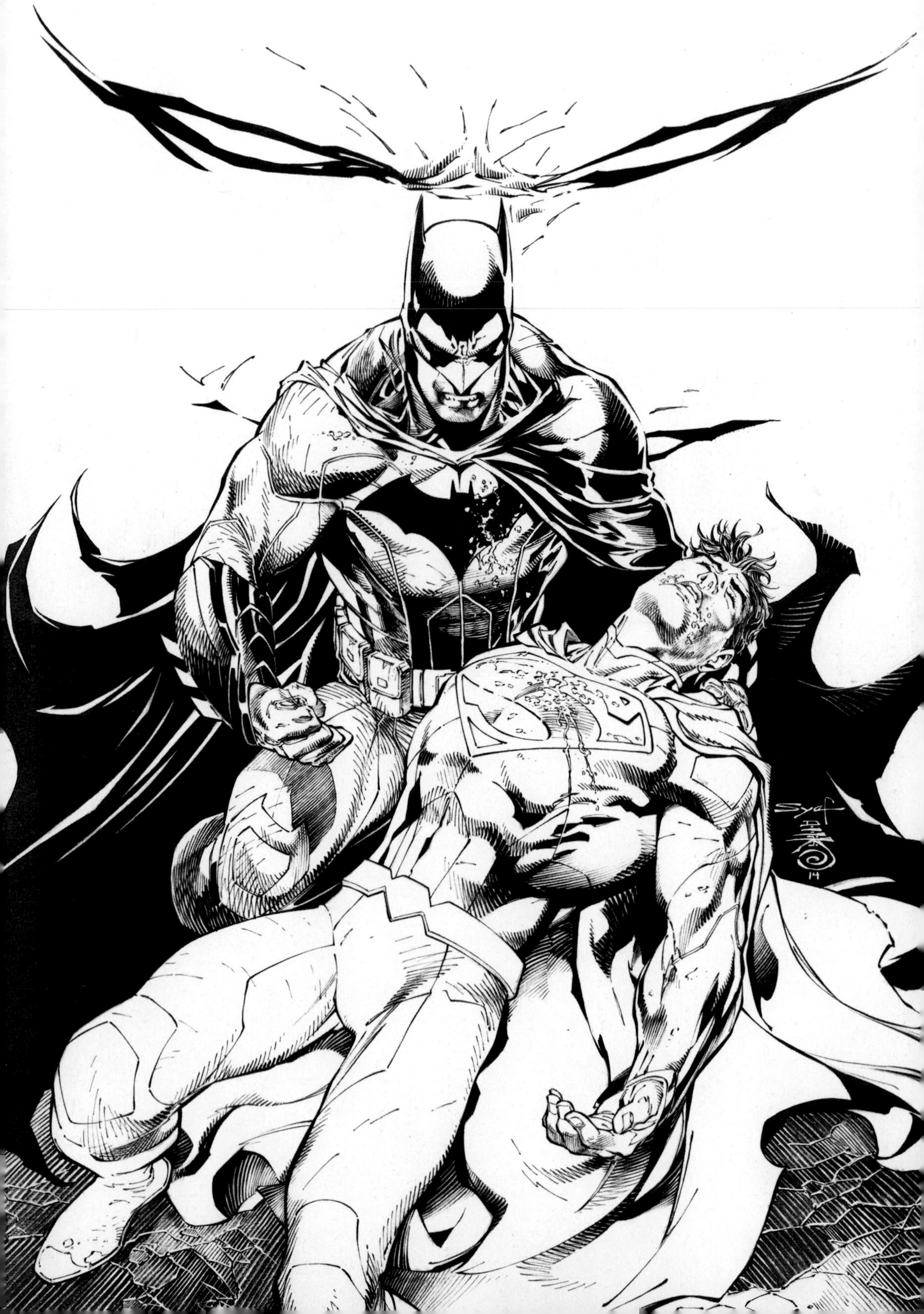

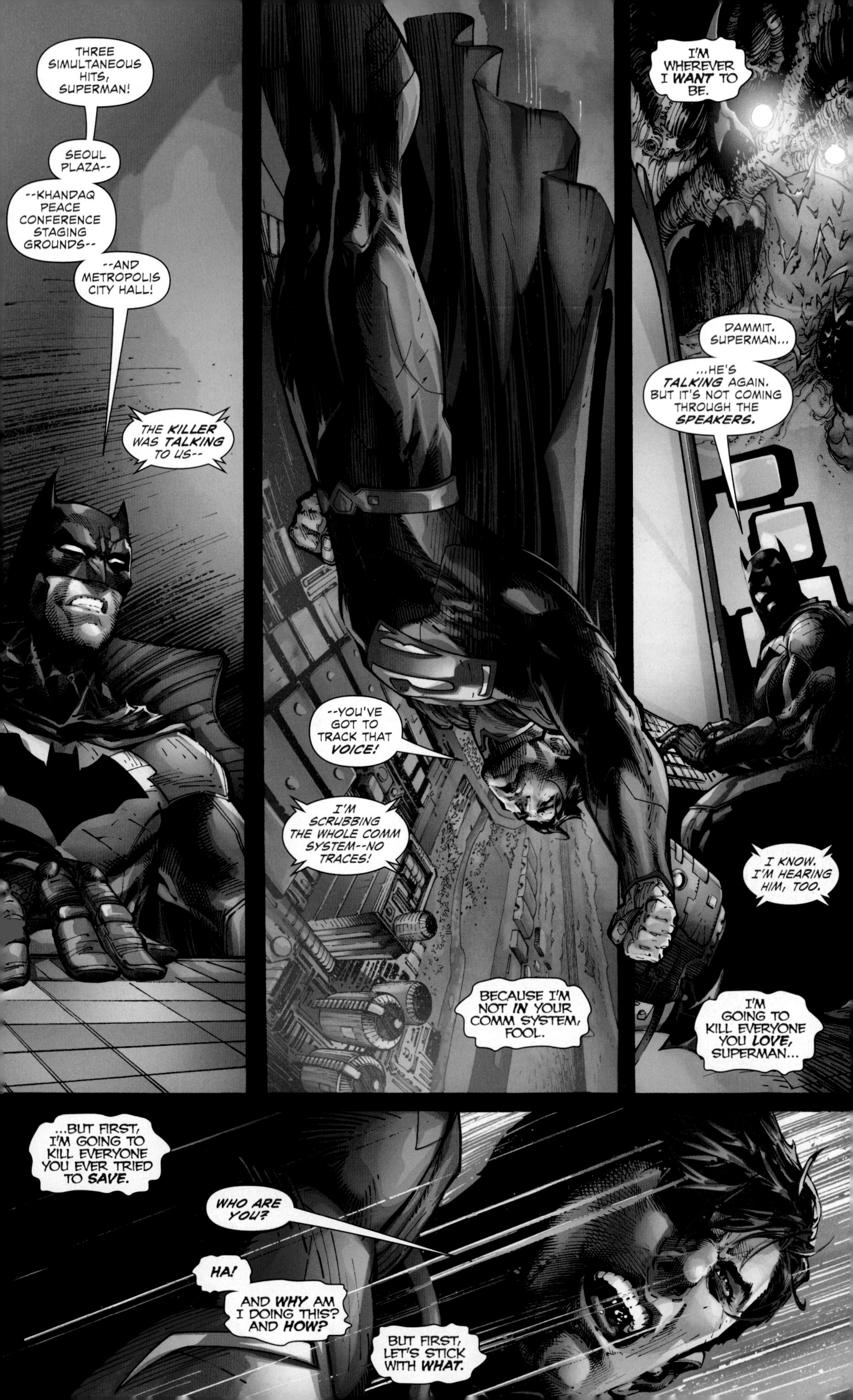
THREE SIMULTANEOUS HITS, SUPERMAN!
SEOUL PLAZA--
--KHANDAQ PEACE CONFERENCE STAGING GROUNDS--
--AND METROPOLIS CITY HALL!
THE KILLER WAS TALKING TO US--
--YOU'VE GOT TO TRACK THAT VOICE!
I'M SCRUBBING THE WHOLE COMM SYSTEM--NO TRACES!
BECAUSE I'M NOT IN YOUR COMM SYSTEM, FOOL.
I'M WHEREVER I WANT TO BE.
DAMMIT. SUPERMAN...
...HE'S TALKING AGAIN. BUT IT'S NOT COMING THROUGH THE SPEAKERS.
I KNOW. I'M HEARING HIM, TOO.
I'M GOING TO KILL EVERYONE YOU LOVE, SUPERMAN...
...BUT FIRST, I'M GOING TO KILL EVERYONE YOU EVER TRIED TO SAVE.
WHO ARE YOU?
HA!
AND WHY AM I DOING THIS? AND HOW?
BUT FIRST, LET'S STICK WITH WHAT.

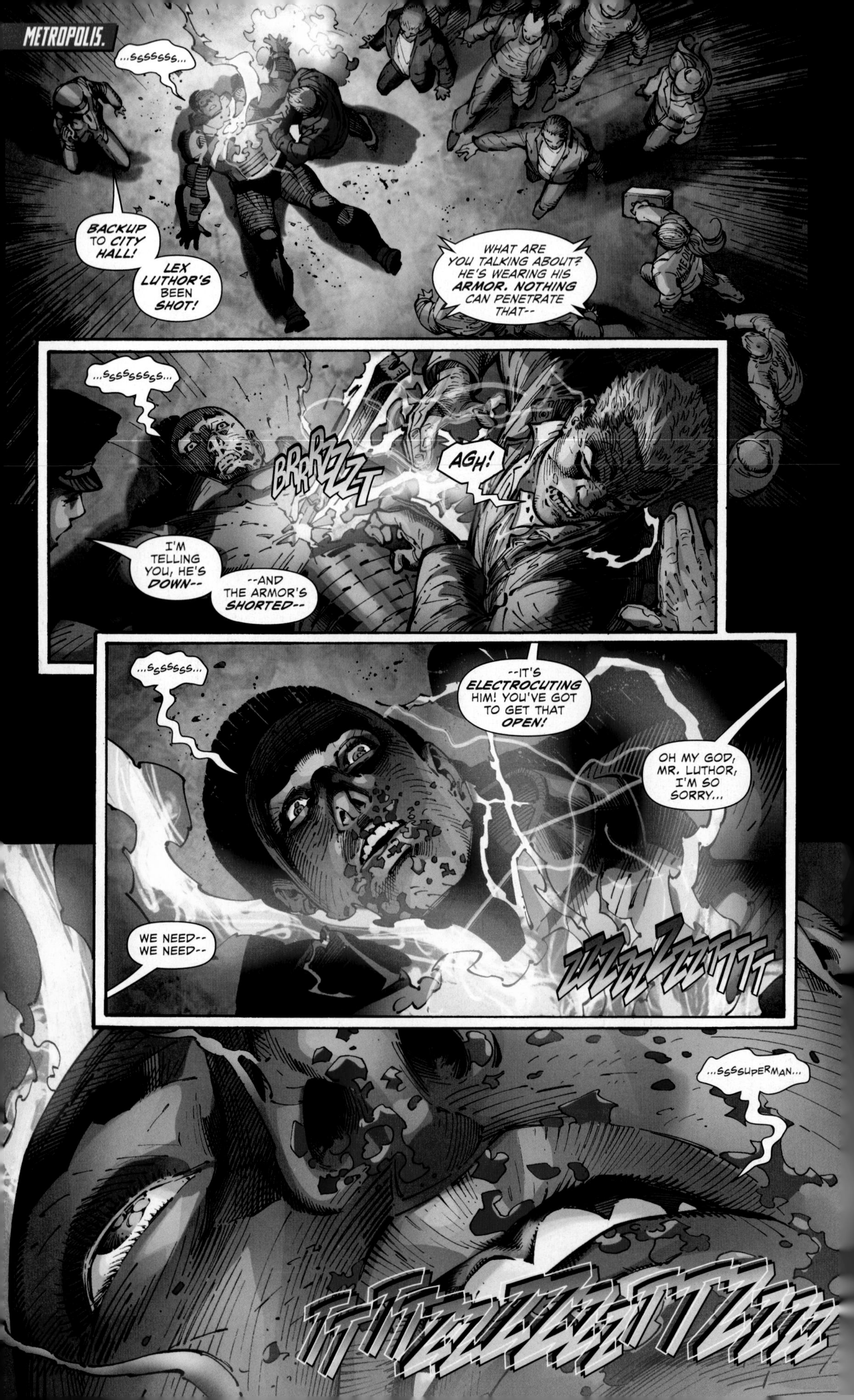
METROPOLIS.
...SSSSSSS...
BACKUP TO CITY HALL!
LEX LUTHOR'S BEEN SHOT!
WHAT ARE YOU TALKING ABOUT? HE'S WEARING HIS ARMOR. NOTHING CAN PENETRATE THAT--
...SSSSSSSS...
BRRRZZZT
AGH!
I'M TELLING YOU, HE'S DOWN--
--AND THE ARMOR'S SHORTED--
...SSSSSS...
--IT'S ELECTROCUTING HIM! YOU'VE GOT TO GET THAT OPEN!
OH MY GOD, MR. LUTHOR, I'M SO SORRY...
WE NEED-- WE NEED--
ZZZZZZZZTTTT
...SSSSUPERMAN...
TTTTZZZZZZTTTZZZ

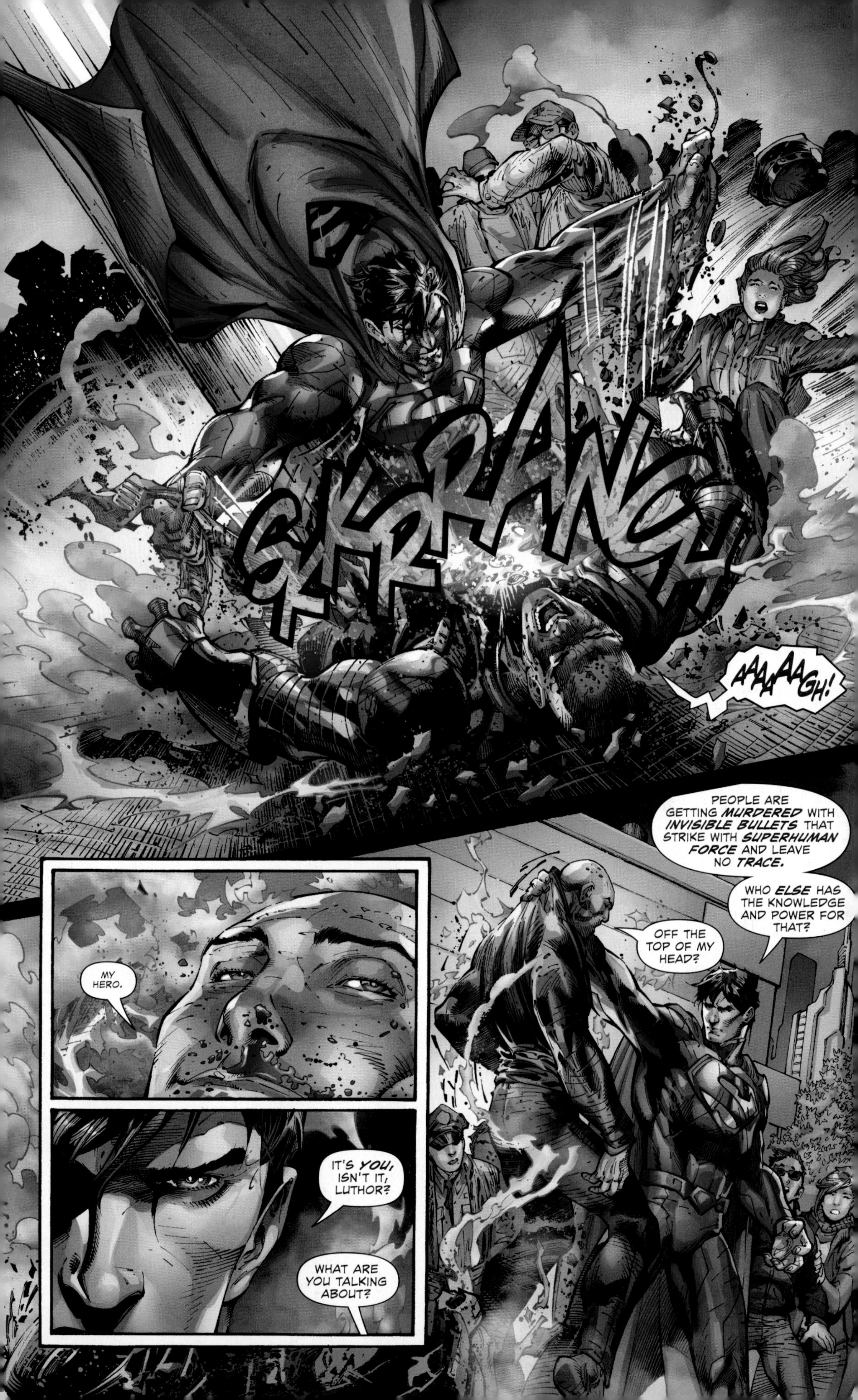
SKRANCH
AAAAAAGH!
PEOPLE ARE GETTING MURDERED WITH INVISIBLE BULLETS THAT STRIKE WITH SUPERHUMAN FORCE AND LEAVE NO TRACE.
WHO ELSE HAS THE KNOWLEDGE AND POWER FOR THAT?
OFF THE TOP OF MY HEAD?
MY HERO.
IT'S YOU, ISN'T IT, LUTHOR?
WHAT ARE YOU TALKING ABOUT?

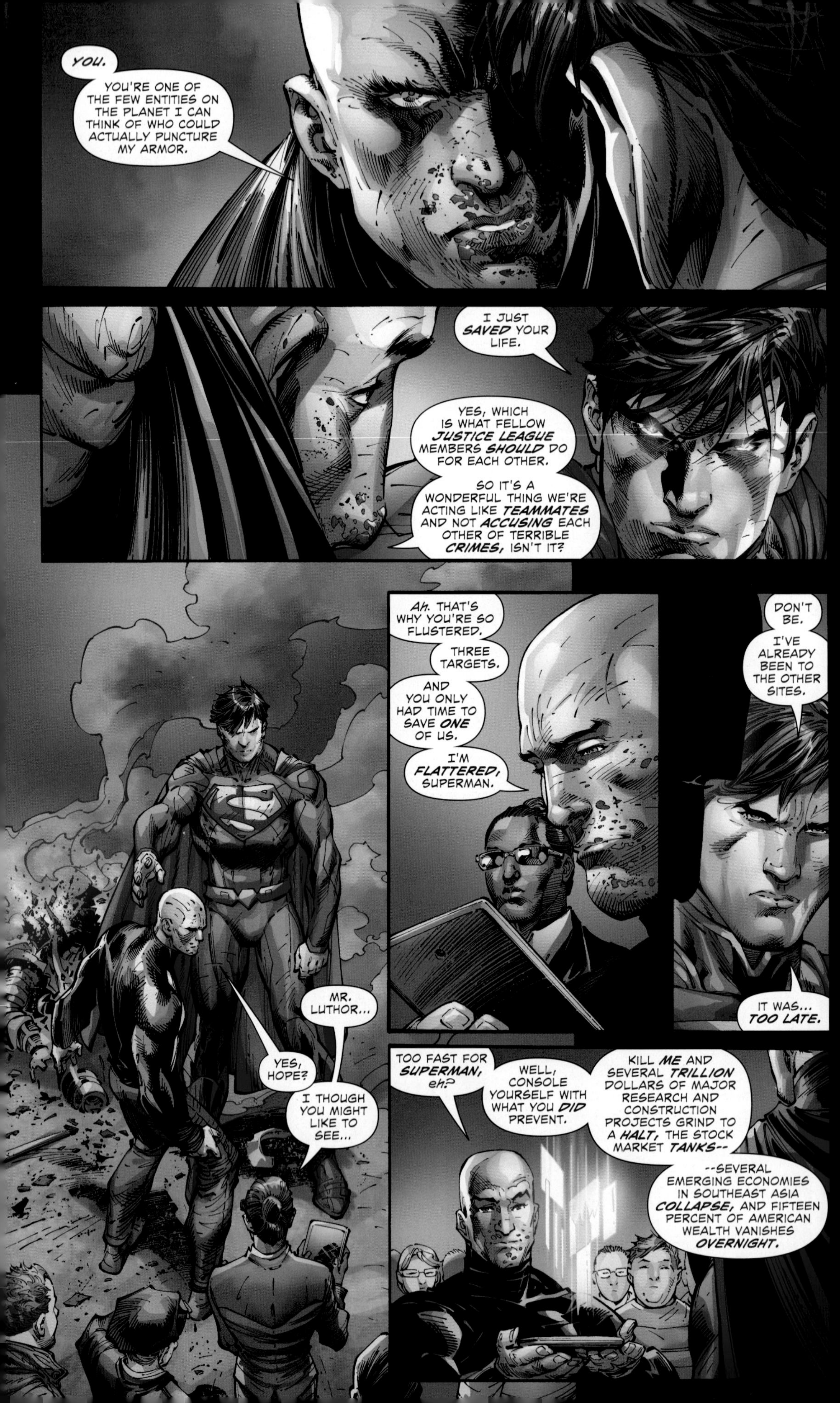
YOU.
YOU'RE ONE OF THE FEW ENTITIES ON THE PLANET I CAN THINK OF WHO COULD ACTUALLY PUNCTURE MY ARMOR.
I JUST SAVED YOUR LIFE.
YES, WHICH IS WHAT FELLOW JUSTICE LEAGUE MEMBERS SHOULD DO FOR EACH OTHER.
SO IT'S A WONDERFUL THING WE'RE ACTING LIKE TEAMMATES AND NOT ACCUSING EACH OTHER OF TERRIBLE CRIMES, ISN'T IT?
MR. LUTHOR...
YES, HOPE?
I THOUGH YOU MIGHT LIKE TO SEE...
Ah. THAT'S WHY YOU'RE SO FLUSTERED.
THREE TARGETS.
AND YOU ONLY HAD TIME TO SAVE ONE OF US.
I'M FLATTERED, SUPERMAN.
DON'T BE.
I'VE ALREADY BEEN TO THE OTHER SITES.
IT WAS... TOO LATE.
TOO FAST FOR SUPERMAN, eh?
WELL, CONSOLE YOURSELF WITH WHAT YOU DID PREVENT.
KILL ME AND SEVERAL TRILLION DOLLARS OF MAJOR RESEARCH AND CONSTRUCTION PROJECTS GRIND TO A HALT, THE STOCK MARKET TANKS--
--SEVERAL EMERGING ECONOMIES IN SOUTHEAST ASIA COLLAPSE, AND FIFTEEN PERCENT OF AMERICAN WEALTH VANISHES OVERNIGHT.

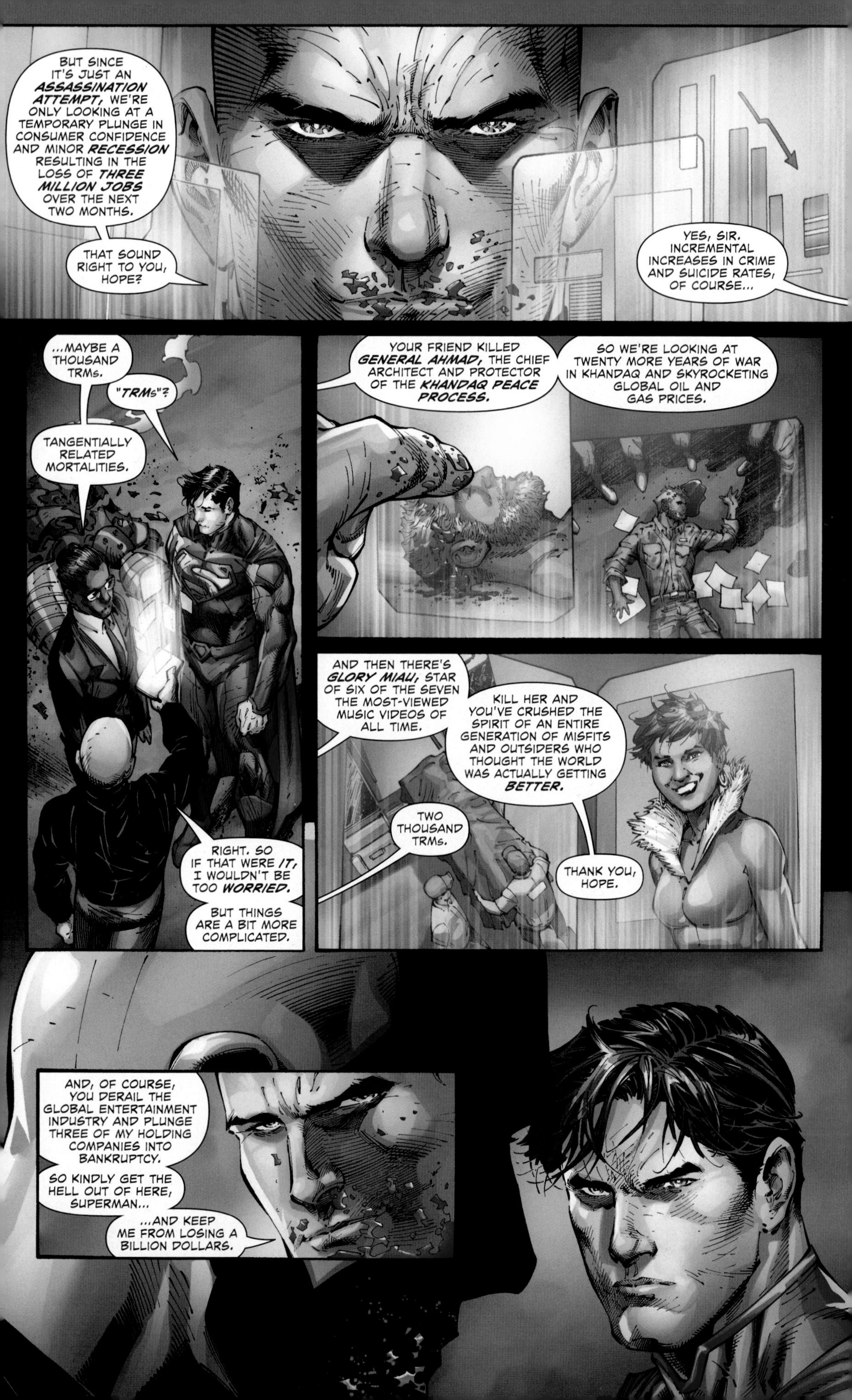
BUT SINCE IT'S JUST AN ASSASSINATION ATTEMPT, WE'RE ONLY LOOKING AT A TEMPORARY PLUNGE IN CONSUMER CONFIDENCE AND MINOR RECESSION RESULTING IN THE LOSS OF THREE MILLION JOBS OVER THE NEXT TWO MONTHS.
THAT SOUND RIGHT TO YOU, HOPE?
YES, SIR. INCREMENTAL INCREASES IN CRIME AND SUICIDE RATES, OF COURSE...
...MAYBE A THOUSAND TRMs.
"TRMs"?
TANGENTIALLY RELATED MORTALITIES.
RIGHT. SO IF THAT WERE IT, I WOULDN'T BE TOO WORRIED.
BUT THINGS ARE A BIT MORE COMPLICATED.
YOUR FRIEND KILLED GENERAL AHMAD, THE CHIEF ARCHITECT AND PROTECTOR OF THE KHANDAQ PEACE PROCESS.
SO WE'RE LOOKING AT TWENTY MORE YEARS OF WAR IN KHANDAQ AND SKYROCKETING GLOBAL OIL AND GAS PRICES.
AND THEN THERE'S GLORY MIAU, STAR OF SIX OF THE SEVEN MOST-VIEWED MUSIC VIDEOS OF ALL TIME.
KILL HER AND YOU'VE CRUSHED THE SPIRIT OF AN ENTIRE GENERATION OF MISFITS AND OUTSIDERS WHO THOUGHT THE WORLD WAS ACTUALLY GETTING BETTER.
TWO THOUSAND TRMs.
THANK YOU, HOPE.
AND, OF COURSE, YOU DERAIL THE GLOBAL ENTERTAINMENT INDUSTRY AND PLUNGE THREE OF MY HOLDING COMPANIES INTO BANKRUPTCY.
SO KINDLY GET THE HELL OUT OF HERE, SUPERMAN...
...AND KEEP ME FROM LOSING A BILLION DOLLARS.

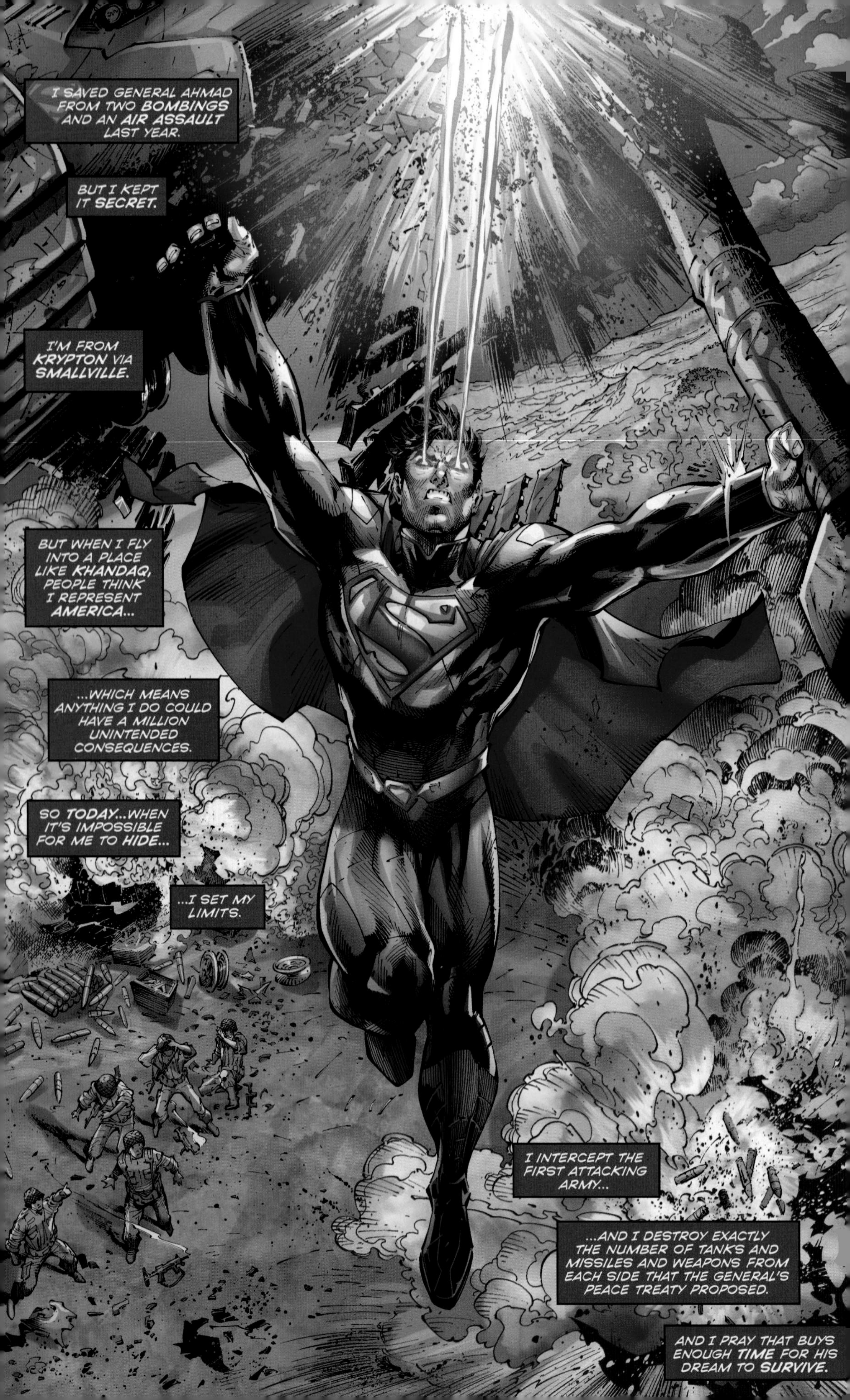
I SAVED GENERAL AHMAD FROM TWO BOMBINGS AND AN AIR ASSAULT LAST YEAR.
BUT I KEPT IT SECRET.
I'M FROM KRYPTON VIA SMALLVILLE.
BUT WHEN I FLY INTO A PLACE LIKE KHANDAQ, PEOPLE THINK I REPRESENT AMERICA...
...WHICH MEANS ANYTHING I DO COULD HAVE A MILLION UNINTENDED CONSEQUENCES.
SO TODAY...WHEN IT'S IMPOSSIBLE FOR ME TO HIDE...
...I SET MY LIMITS.
I INTERCEPT THE FIRST ATTACKING ARMY...
...AND I DESTROY EXACTLY THE NUMBER OF TANKS AND MISSILES AND WEAPONS FROM EACH SIDE THAT THE GENERAL'S PEACE TREATY PROPOSED.
AND I PRAY THAT BUYS ENOUGH TIME FOR HIS DREAM TO SURVIVE.

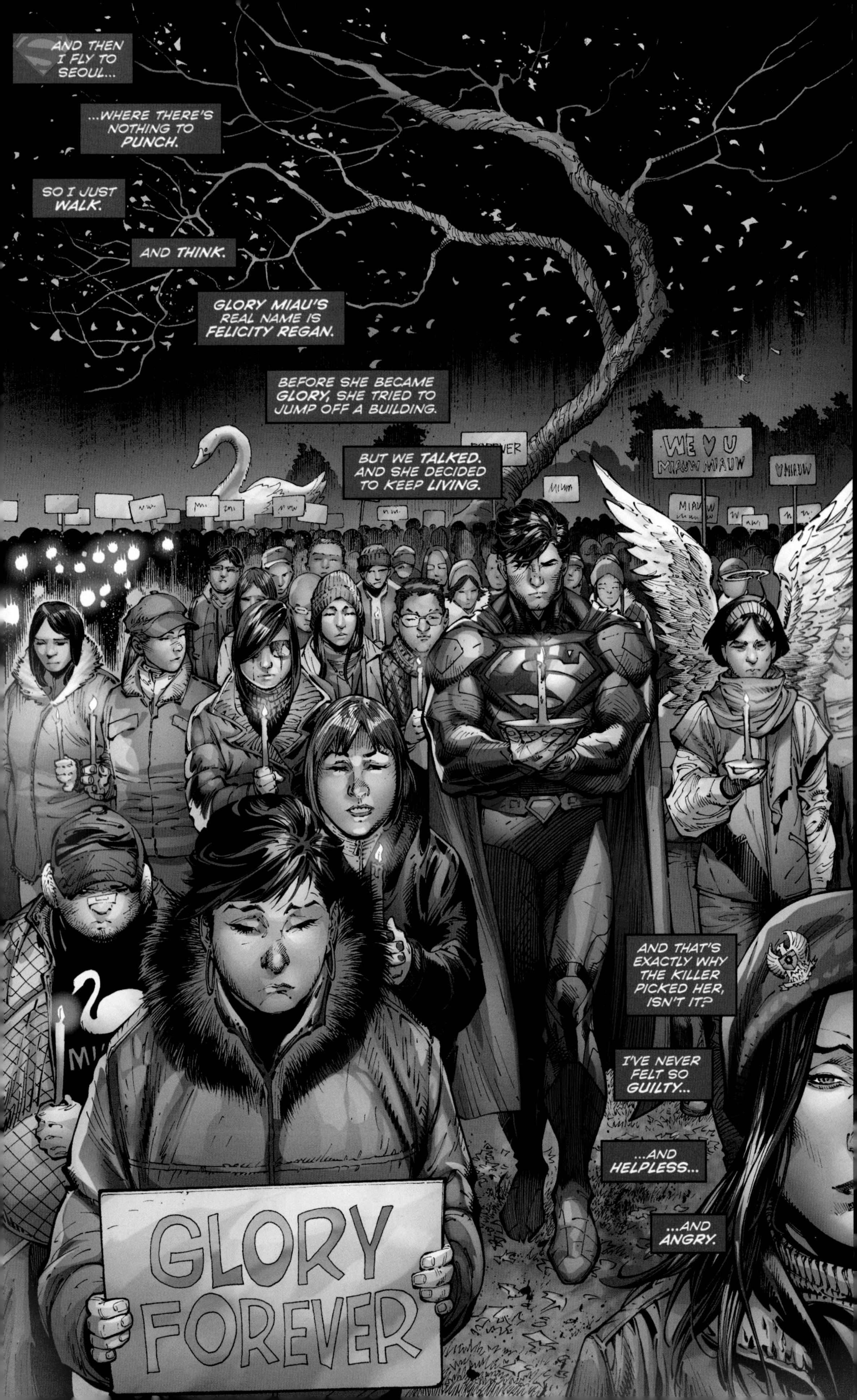
AND THEN I FLY TO SEOUL...
...WHERE THERE'S NOTHING TO PUNCH.
SO I JUST WALK.
AND THINK.
GLORY MIAU'S REAL NAME IS FELICITY REGAN.
BEFORE SHE BECAME GLORY, SHE TRIED TO JUMP OFF A BUILDING.
BUT WE TALKED. AND SHE DECIDED TO KEEP LIVING.
WE ♥ U MIAUW MIAUW
AND THAT'S EXACTLY WHY THE KILLER PICKED HER, ISN'T IT?
I'VE NEVER FELT SO GUILTY...
...AND HELPLESS...
...AND ANGRY.
GLORY FOREVER

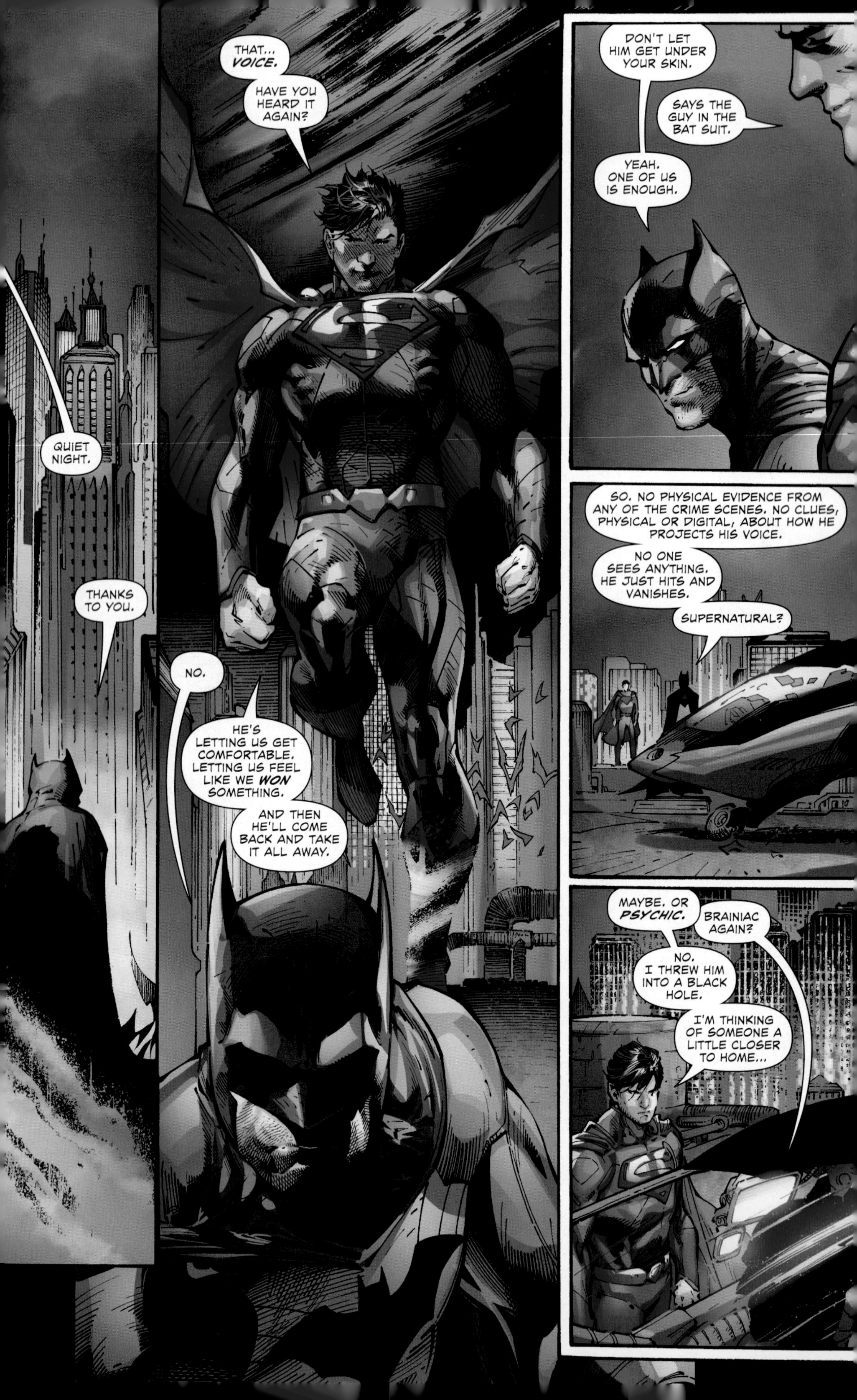
QUIET NIGHT.
THANKS TO YOU.
THAT... VOICE.
HAVE YOU HEARD IT AGAIN?
NO.
HE'S LETTING US GET COMFORTABLE. LETTING US FEEL LIKE WE WON SOMETHING.
AND THEN HE'LL COME BACK AND TAKE IT ALL AWAY.
DON'T LET HIM GET UNDER YOUR SKIN.
SAYS THE GUY IN THE BAT SUIT.
YEAH. ONE OF US IS ENOUGH.
SO. NO PHYSICAL EVIDENCE FROM ANY OF THE CRIME SCENES. NO CLUES, PHYSICAL OR DIGITAL, ABOUT HOW HE PROJECTS HIS VOICE.
NO ONE SEES ANYTHING. HE JUST HITS AND VANISHES.
SUPERNATURAL?
MAYBE. OR PSYCHIC.
BRAINIAC AGAIN?
NO. I THREW HIM INTO A BLACK HOLE.
I'M THINKING OF SOMEONE A LITTLE CLOSER TO HOME...

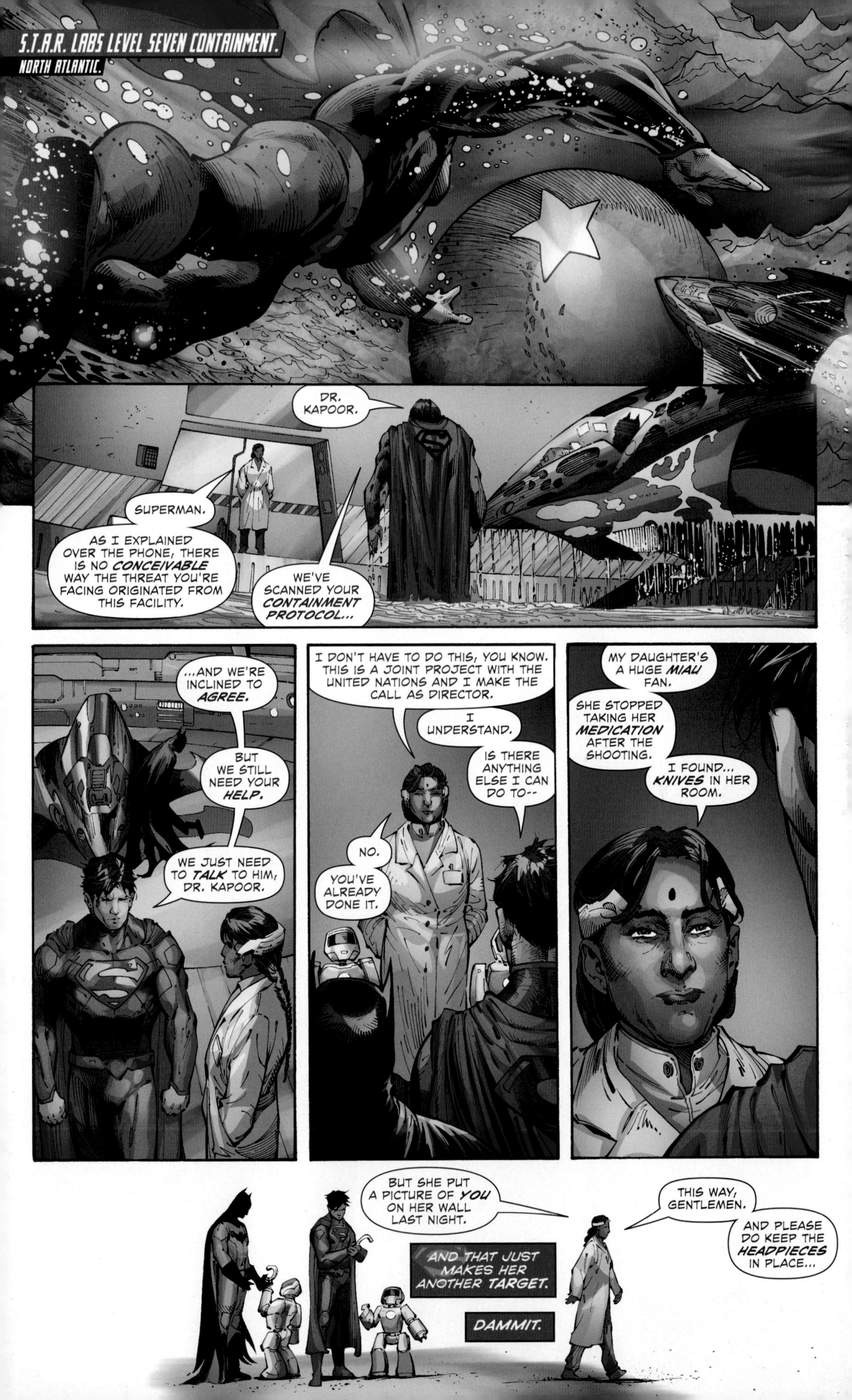

S.T.A.R. LABS LEVEL SEVEN CONTAINMENT.
NORTH ATLANTIC.
DR. KAPOOR.
SUPERMAN.
AS I EXPLAINED OVER THE PHONE, THERE IS NO CONCEIVABLE WAY THE THREAT YOU'RE FACING ORIGINATED FROM THIS FACILITY.
WE'VE SCANNED YOUR CONTAINMENT PROTOCOL...
...AND WE'RE INCLINED TO AGREE.
BUT WE STILL NEED YOUR HELP.
WE JUST NEED TO TALK TO HIM, DR. KAPOOR.
I DON'T HAVE TO DO THIS, YOU KNOW. THIS IS A JOINT PROJECT WITH THE UNITED NATIONS AND I MAKE THE CALL AS DIRECTOR.
I UNDERSTAND.
IS THERE ANYTHING ELSE I CAN DO TO--
NO.
YOU'VE ALREADY DONE IT.
MY DAUGHTER'S A HUGE MIAU FAN.
SHE STOPPED TAKING HER MEDICATION AFTER THE SHOOTING.
I FOUND... KNIVES IN HER ROOM.
BUT SHE PUT A PICTURE OF YOU ON HER WALL LAST NIGHT.
AND THAT JUST MAKES HER ANOTHER TARGET.
DAMMIT.
THIS WAY, GENTLEMEN.
AND PLEASE DO KEEP THE HEADPIECES IN PLACE...

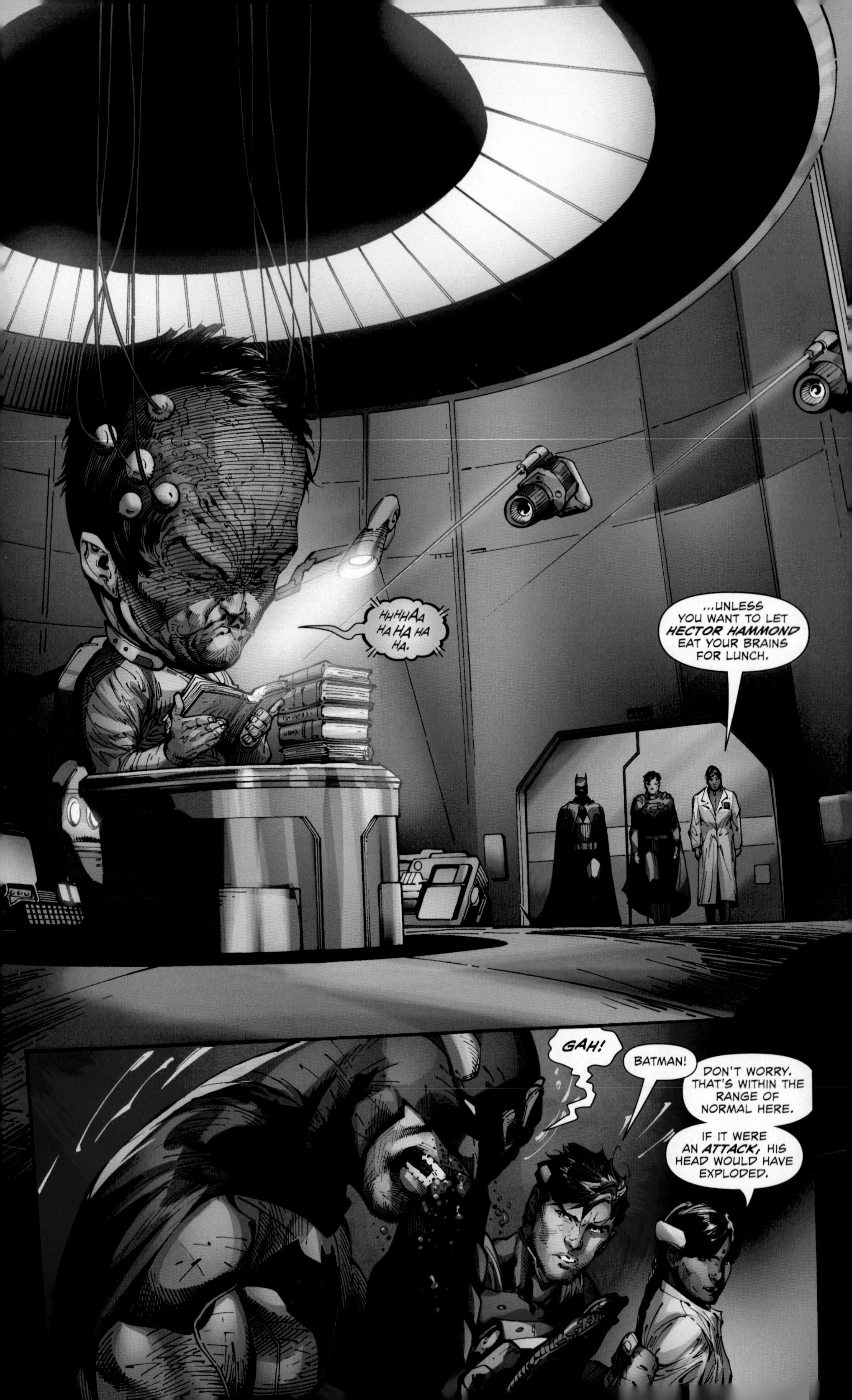
HHHHAA HA HA HA HA HA.
...UNLESS YOU WANT TO LET HECTOR HAMMOND EAT YOUR BRAINS FOR LUNCH.
GAH!
BATMAN!
DON'T WORRY. THAT'S WITHIN THE RANGE OF NORMAL HERE.
IF IT WERE AN ATTACK, HIS HEAD WOULD HAVE EXPLODED.

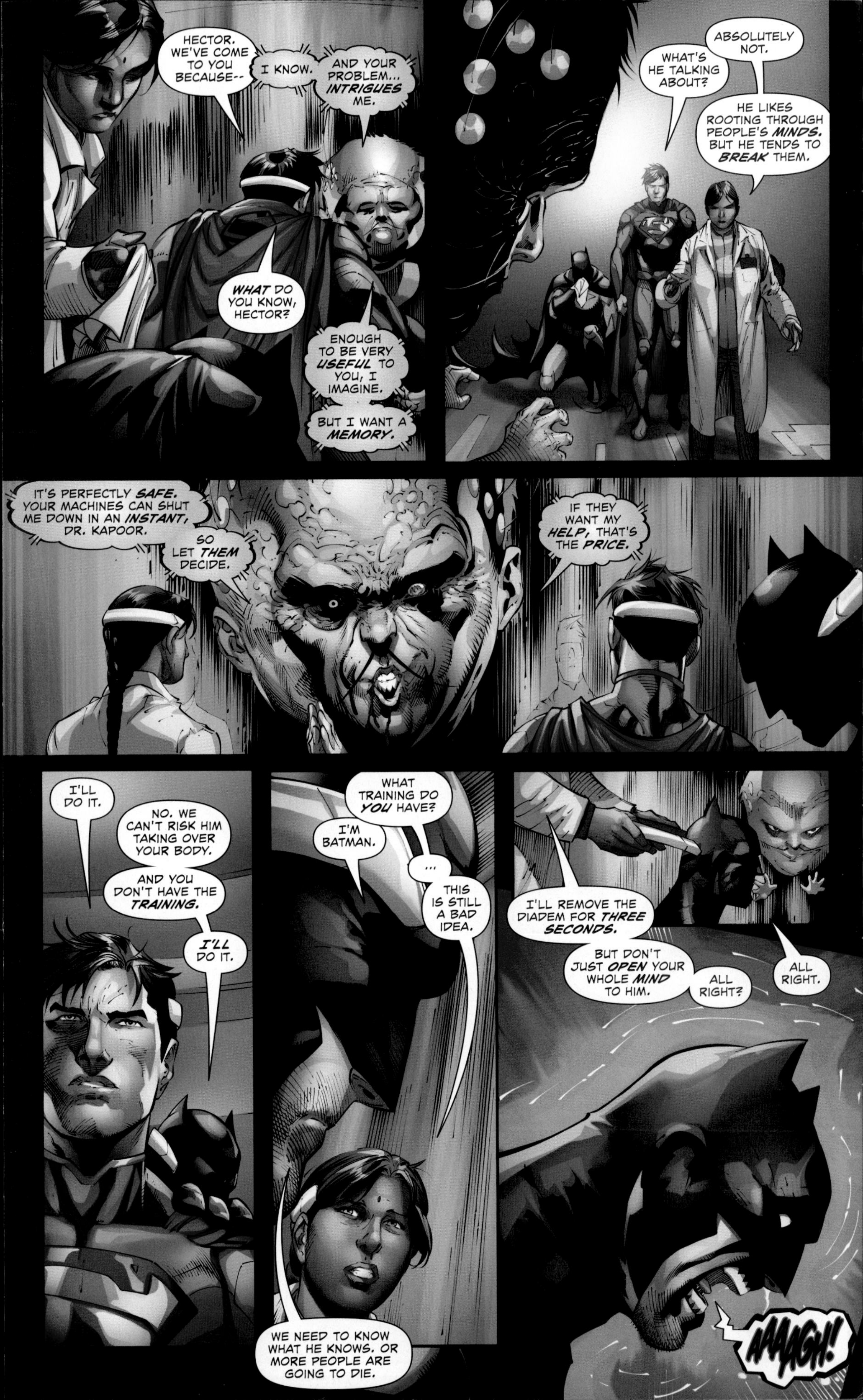
HECTOR. WE'VE COME TO YOU BECAUSE--
I KNOW.
AND YOUR PROBLEM... INTRIGUES ME.
WHAT DO YOU KNOW, HECTOR?
ENOUGH TO BE VERY USEFUL TO YOU, I IMAGINE.
BUT I WANT A MEMORY.
WHAT'S HE TALKING ABOUT?
ABSOLUTELY NOT.
HE LIKES ROOTING THROUGH PEOPLE'S MINDS. BUT HE TENDS TO BREAK THEM.
IT'S PERFECTLY SAFE. YOUR MACHINES CAN SHUT ME DOWN IN AN INSTANT, DR. KAPOOR.
SO LET THEM DECIDE.
IF THEY WANT MY HELP, THAT'S THE PRICE.
I'LL DO IT.
NO. WE CAN'T RISK HIM TAKING OVER YOUR BODY.
AND YOU DON'T HAVE THE TRAINING.
I'LL DO IT.
WHAT TRAINING DO YOU HAVE?
I'M BATMAN.
...
THIS IS STILL A BAD IDEA.
WE NEED TO KNOW WHAT HE KNOWS. OR MORE PEOPLE ARE GOING TO DIE.
I'LL REMOVE THE DIADEM FOR THREE SECONDS.
BUT DON'T JUST OPEN YOUR WHOLE MIND TO HIM.
ALL RIGHT?
ALL RIGHT.
AAAAGH!

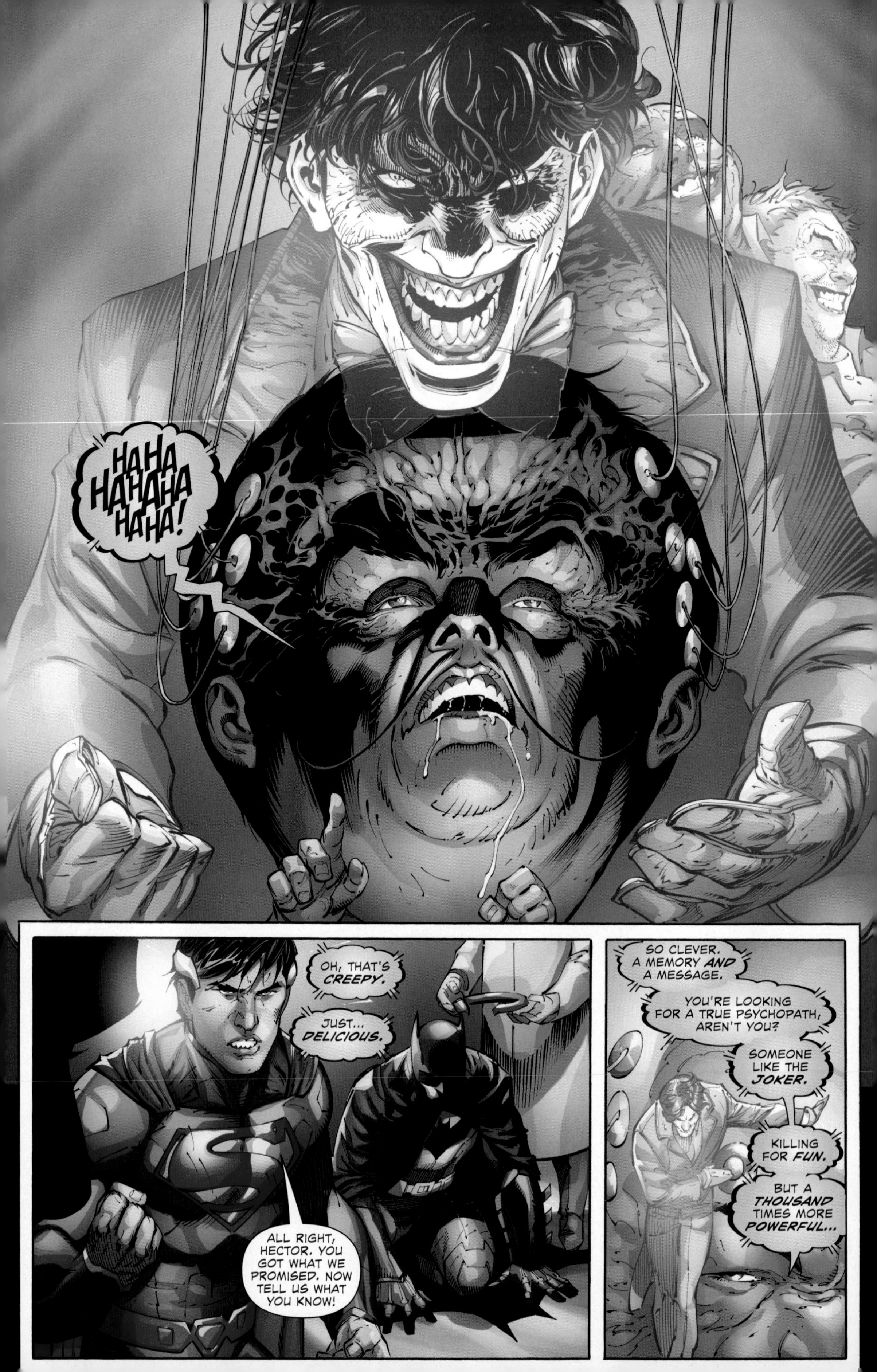
HAHA HAHAHA HAHA!
OH, THAT'S CREEPY.
JUST... DELICIOUS.
ALL RIGHT, HECTOR. YOU GOT WHAT WE PROMISED. NOW TELL US WHAT YOU KNOW!
SO CLEVER. A MEMORY AND A MESSAGE.
YOU'RE LOOKING FOR A TRUE PSYCHOPATH, AREN'T YOU?
SOMEONE LIKE THE JOKER.
KILLING FOR FUN.
BUT A THOUSAND TIMES MORE POWERFUL...

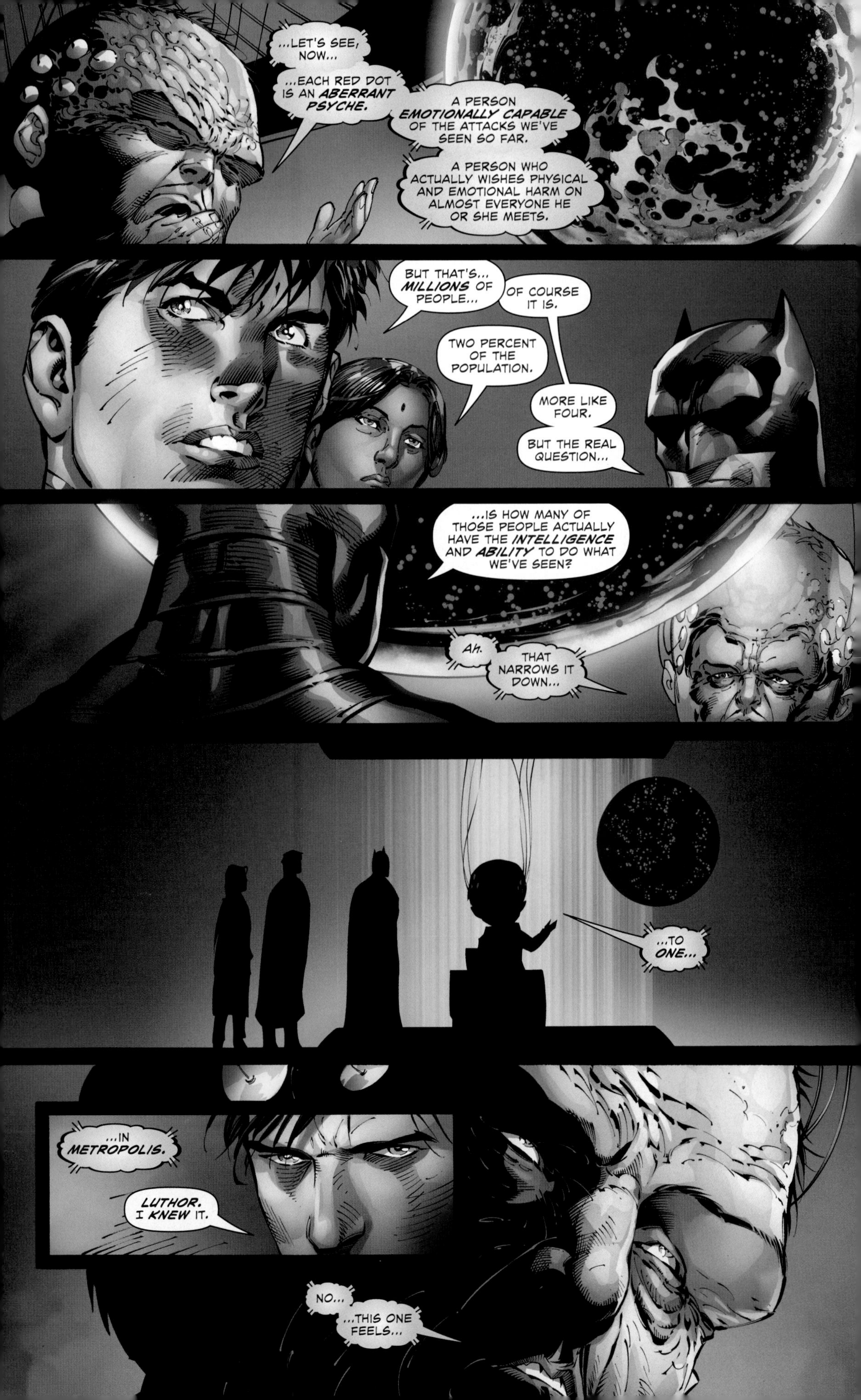
...LET'S SEE, NOW...
...EACH RED DOT IS AN ABERRANT PSYCHE.
A PERSON EMOTIONALLY CAPABLE OF THE ATTACKS WE'VE SEEN SO FAR.
A PERSON WHO ACTUALLY WISHES PHYSICAL AND EMOTIONAL HARM ON ALMOST EVERYONE HE OR SHE MEETS.
BUT THAT'S... MILLIONS OF PEOPLE...
OF COURSE IT IS.
TWO PERCENT OF THE POPULATION.
MORE LIKE FOUR.
BUT THE REAL QUESTION...
...IS HOW MANY OF THOSE PEOPLE ACTUALLY HAVE THE INTELLIGENCE AND ABILITY TO DO WHAT WE'VE SEEN?
Ah.
THAT NARROWS IT DOWN...
...TO ONE...
...IN METROPOLIS.
LUTHOR. I KNEW IT.
NO...
...THIS ONE FEELS...

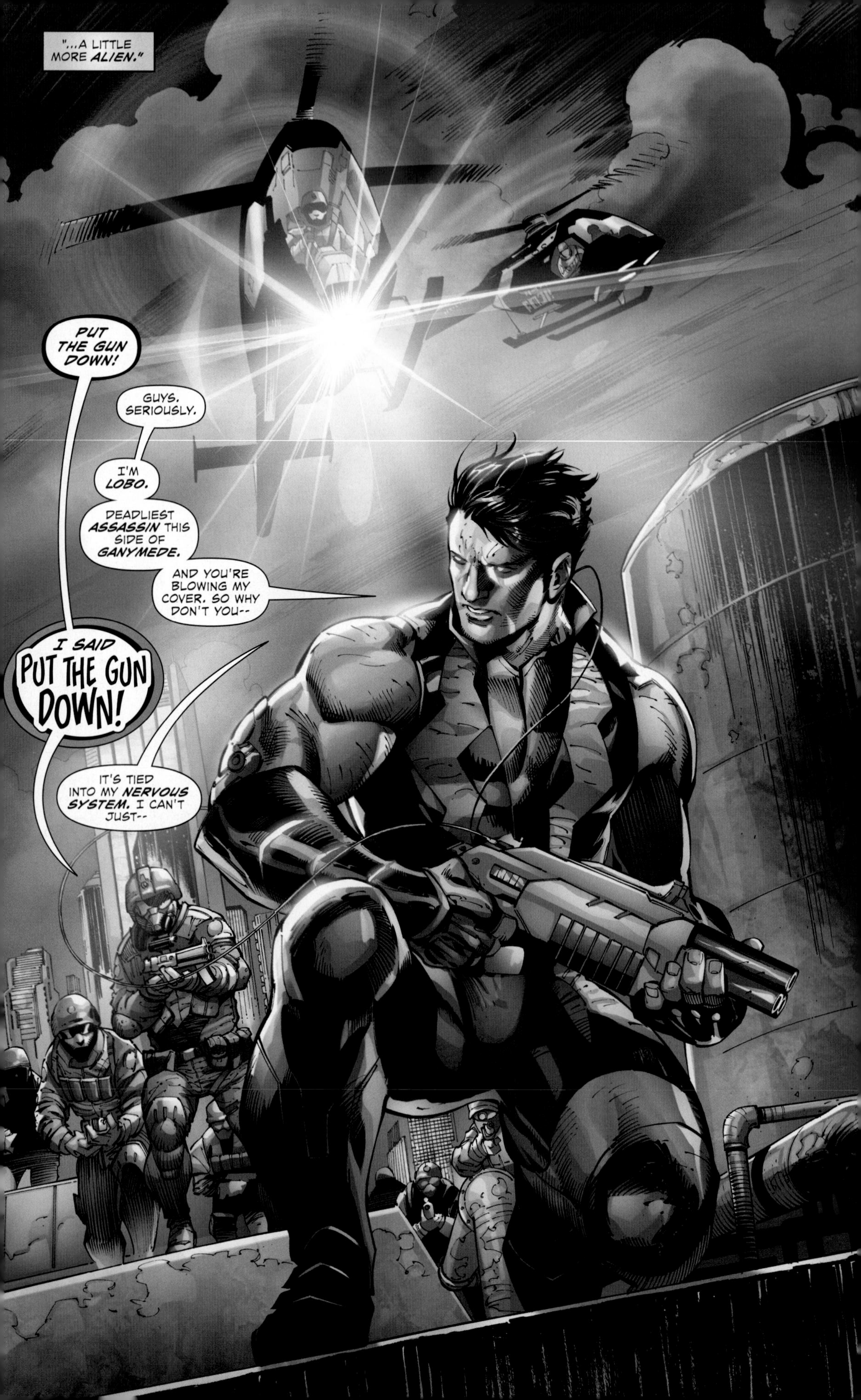
"...A LITTLE MORE ALIEN."
PUT THE GUN DOWN!
GUYS. SERIOUSLY.
I'M LOBO.
DEADLIEST ASSASSIN THIS SIDE OF GANYMEDE.
AND YOU'RE BLOWING MY COVER. SO WHY DON'T YOU--
I SAID PUT THE GUN DOWN!
IT'S TIED INTO MY NERVOUS SYSTEM. I CAN'T JUST--

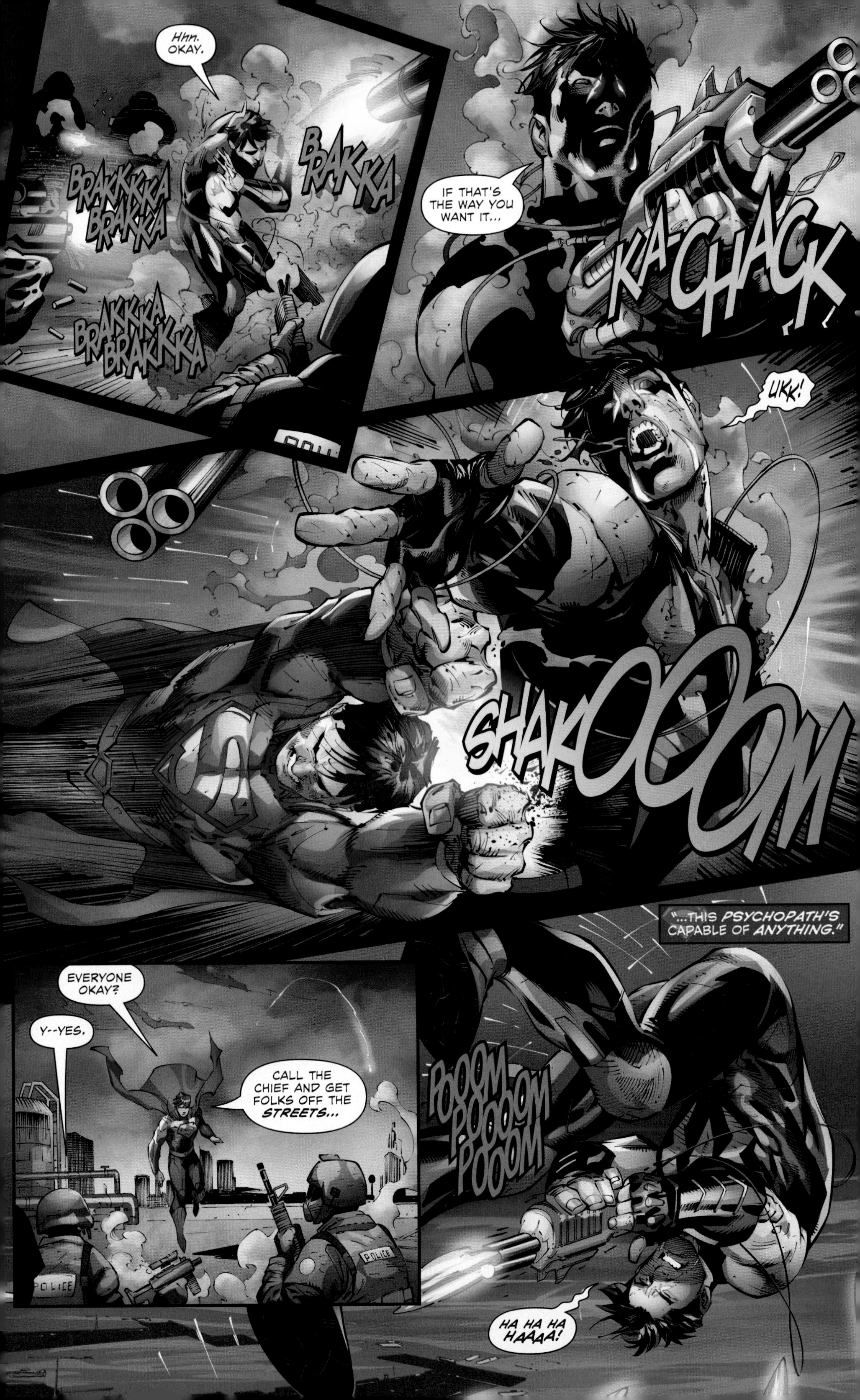

Hhn. OKAY.
BRAKKKKA BRAKKA
BRAKKA
BRAKKKA BRAKKKA
IF THAT'S THE WAY YOU WANT IT...
KA-CHACK
UKK!
SHAKOOOOM
"...THIS PSYCHOPATH'S CAPABLE OF ANYTHING."
EVERYONE OKAY?
Y--YES.
CALL THE CHIEF AND GET FOLKS OFF THE STREETS...
POLICE
POLICE
POOOM POOOOM POOOM
HA HA HA HAAAA!

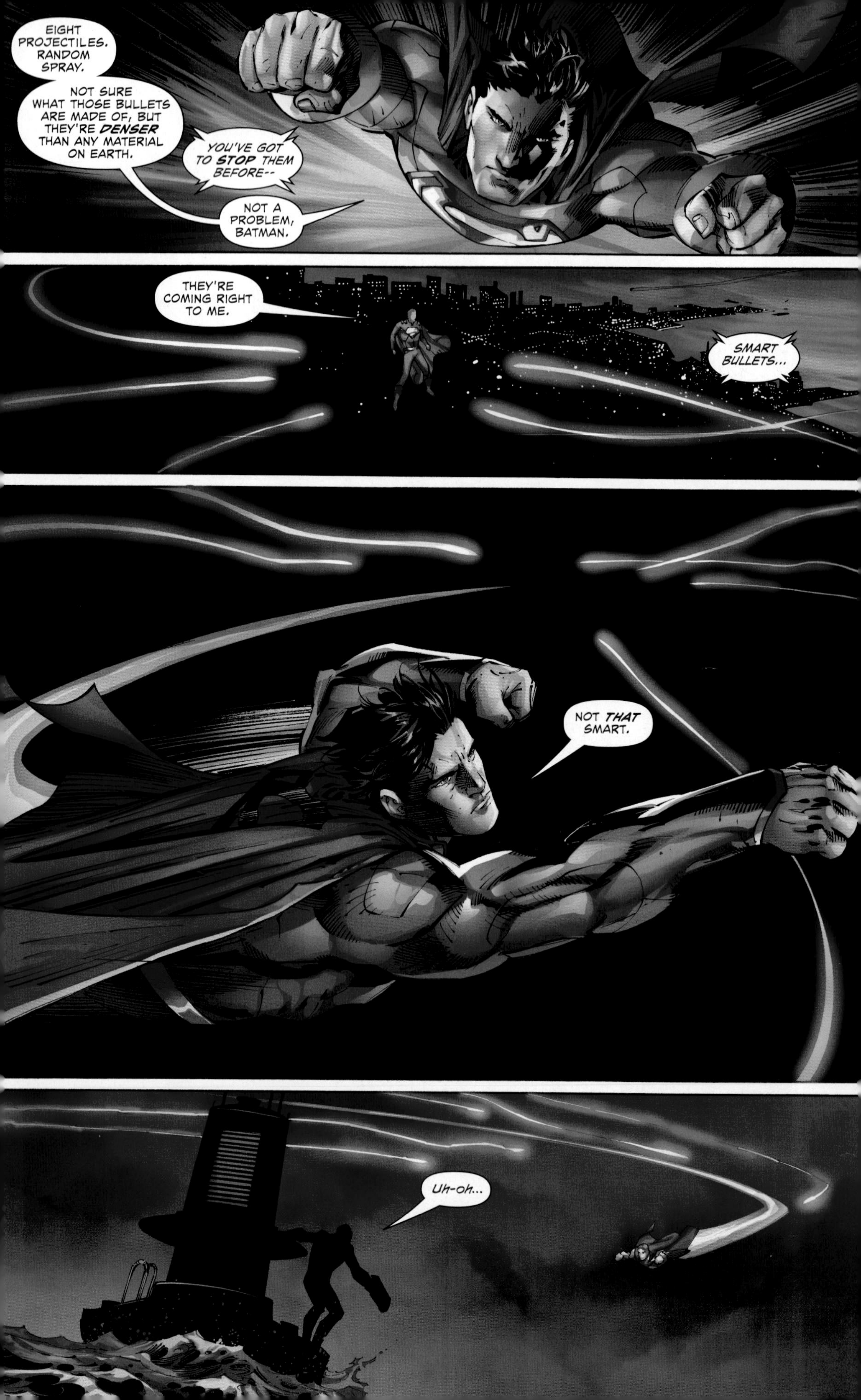
EIGHT PROJECTILES. RANDOM SPRAY.
NOT SURE WHAT THOSE BULLETS ARE MADE OF, BUT THEY'RE DENSER THAN ANY MATERIAL ON EARTH.
YOU'VE GOT TO STOP THEM BEFORE--
NOT A PROBLEM, BATMAN.
THEY'RE COMING RIGHT TO ME.
SMART BULLETS...
NOT THAT SMART.
Uh-oh...

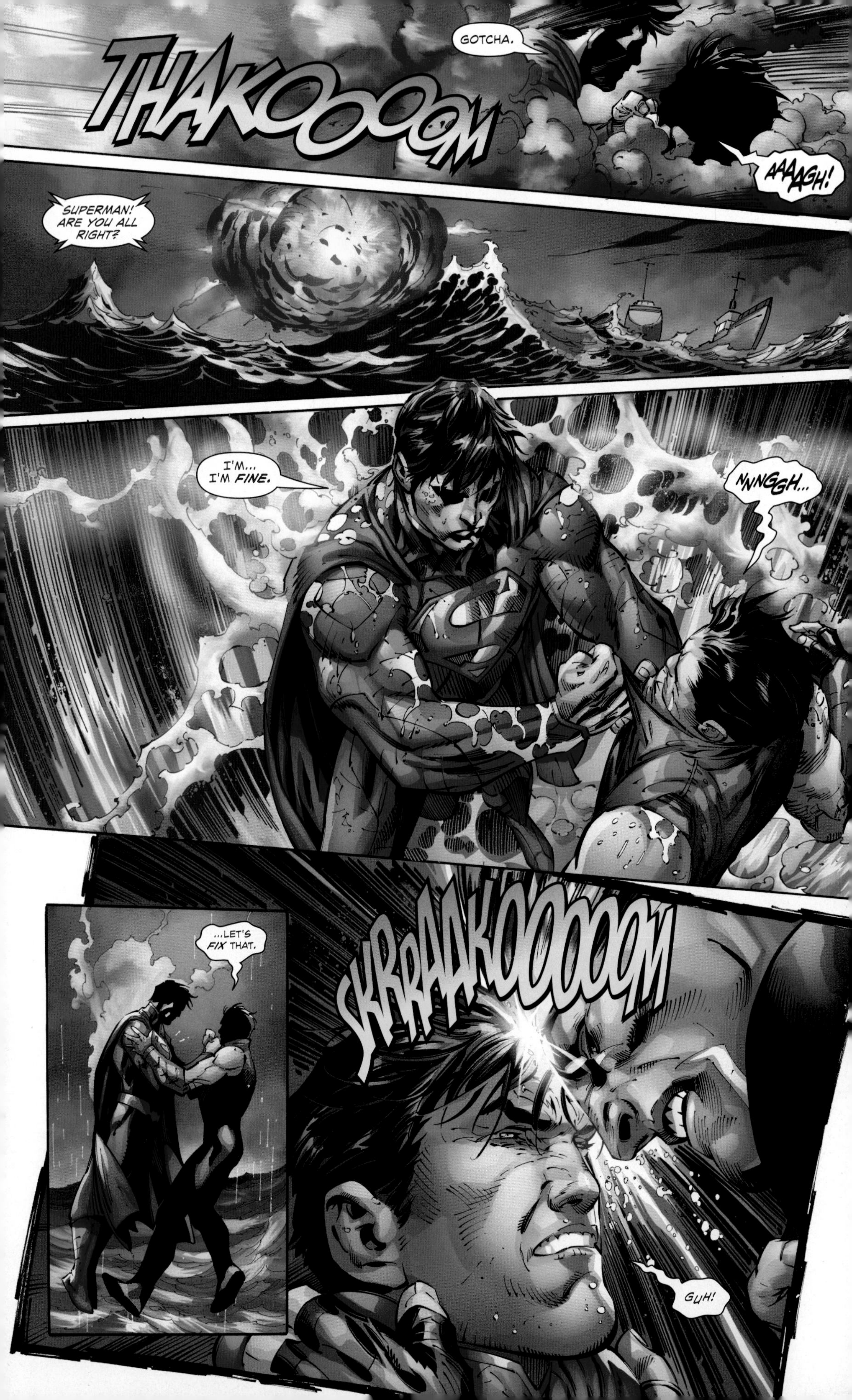
GOTCHA.
THAKOOOOOM
AAAAAGH!
SUPERMAN! ARE YOU ALL RIGHT?
I'M... I'M FINE.
NNNGGH...
...LET'S FIX THAT.
SKRRAAKOOOOOM
GUH!

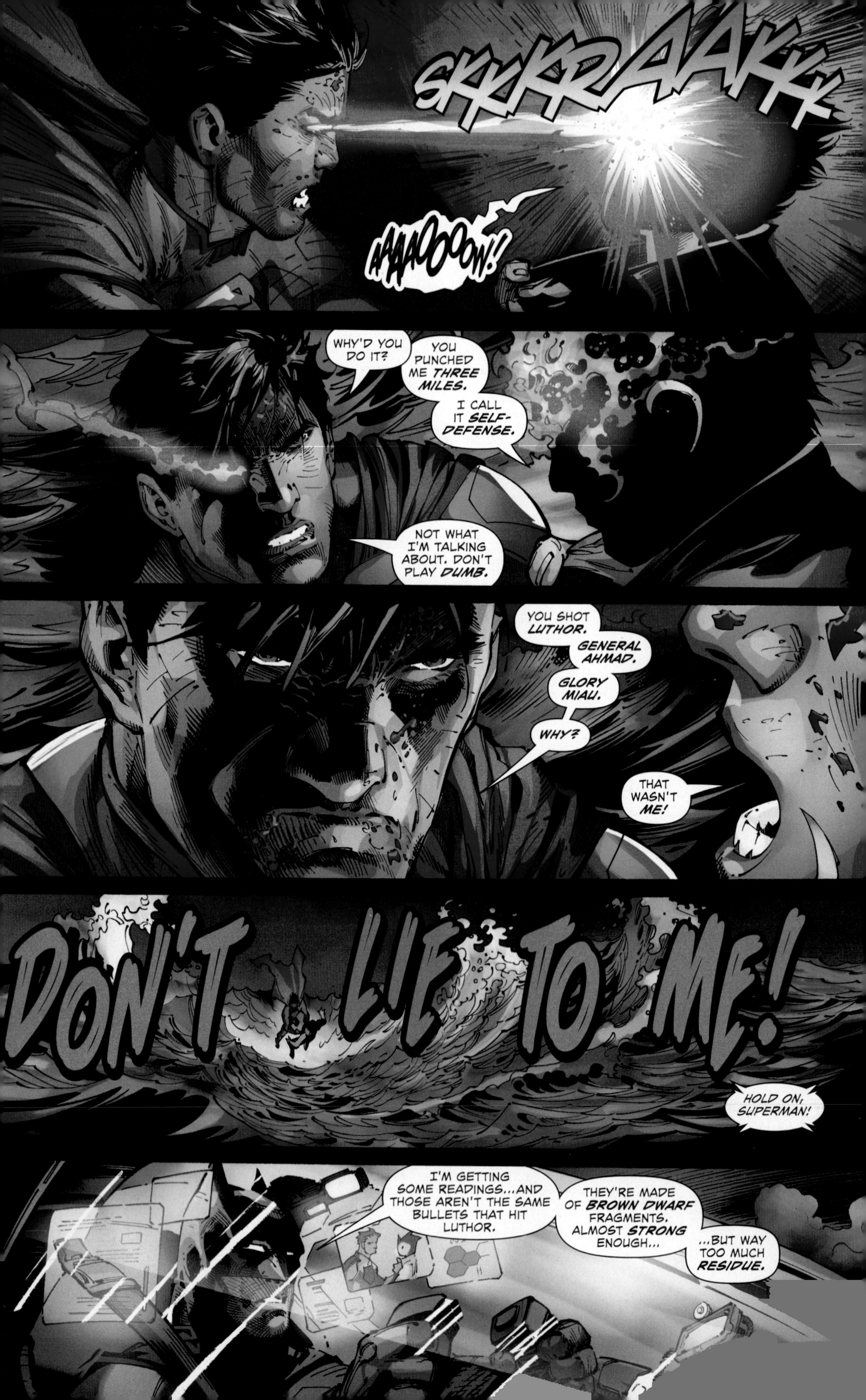
SKKKRAAAKKK
AAAAOOOOW!
WHY'D YOU DO IT?
YOU PUNCHED ME THREE MILES.
I CALL IT SELF-DEFENSE.
NOT WHAT I'M TALKING ABOUT. DON'T PLAY DUMB.
YOU SHOT LUTHOR.
GENERAL AHMAD.
GLORY MIAU.
WHY?
THAT WASN'T ME!
DON'T LIE TO ME!
HOLD ON, SUPERMAN!
I'M GETTING SOME READINGS...AND THOSE AREN'T THE SAME BULLETS THAT HIT LUTHOR.
THEY'RE MADE OF BROWN DWARF FRAGMENTS. ALMOST STRONG ENOUGH...
...BUT WAY TOO MUCH RESIDUE.

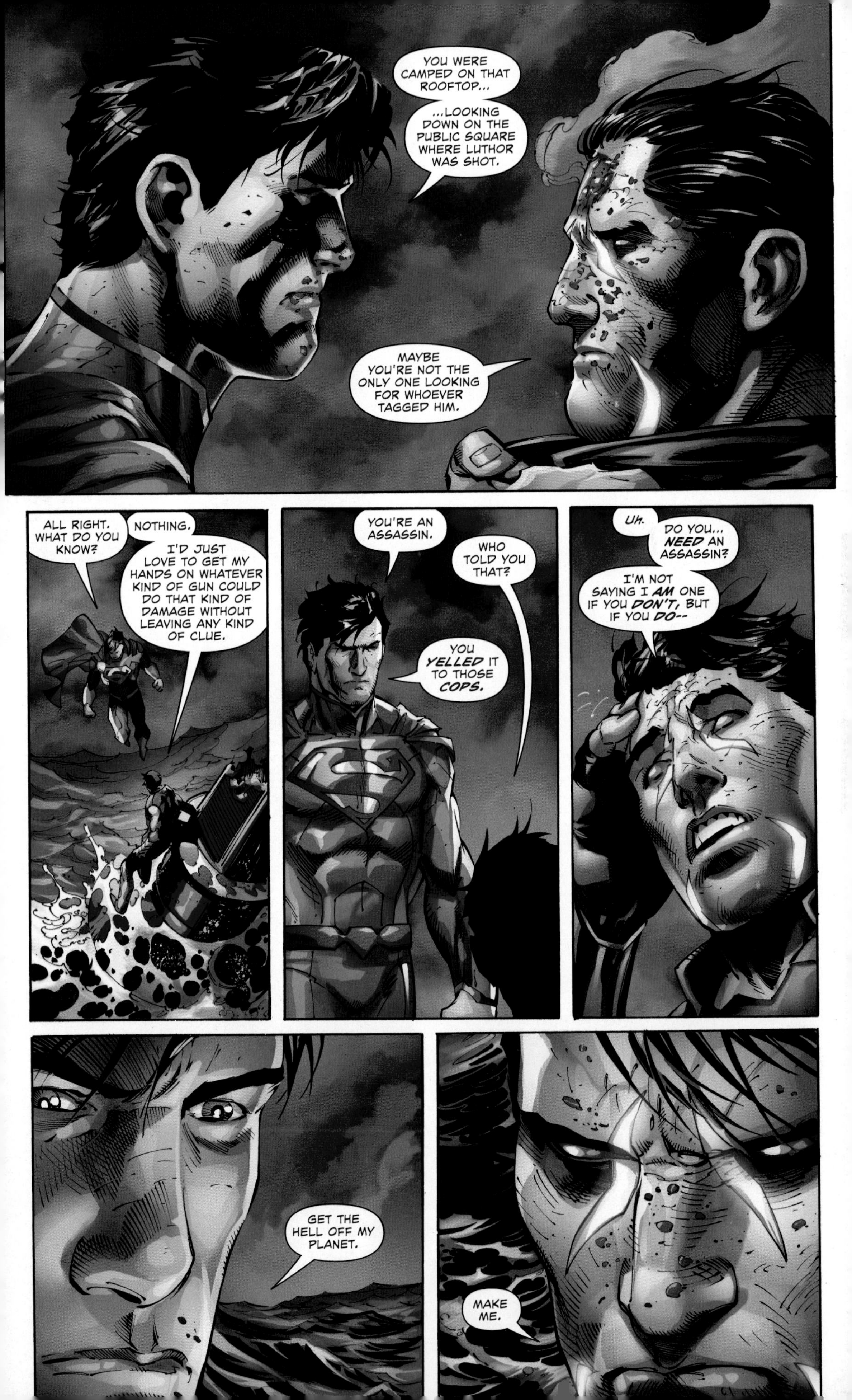
YOU WERE CAMPED ON THAT ROOFTOP...
...LOOKING DOWN ON THE PUBLIC SQUARE WHERE LUTHOR WAS SHOT.
MAYBE YOU'RE NOT THE ONLY ONE LOOKING FOR WHOEVER TAGGED HIM.
ALL RIGHT. WHAT DO YOU KNOW?
NOTHING.
I'D JUST LOVE TO GET MY HANDS ON WHATEVER KIND OF GUN COULD DO THAT KIND OF DAMAGE WITHOUT LEAVING ANY KIND OF CLUE.
YOU'RE AN ASSASSIN.
WHO TOLD YOU THAT?
YOU *YELLED* IT TO THOSE *COPS.*
Uh.
DO YOU... *NEED* AN ASSASSIN?
I'M NOT SAYING I *AM* ONE IF YOU *DON'T,* BUT IF YOU *DO*--
GET THE HELL OFF MY PLANET.
MAKE ME.

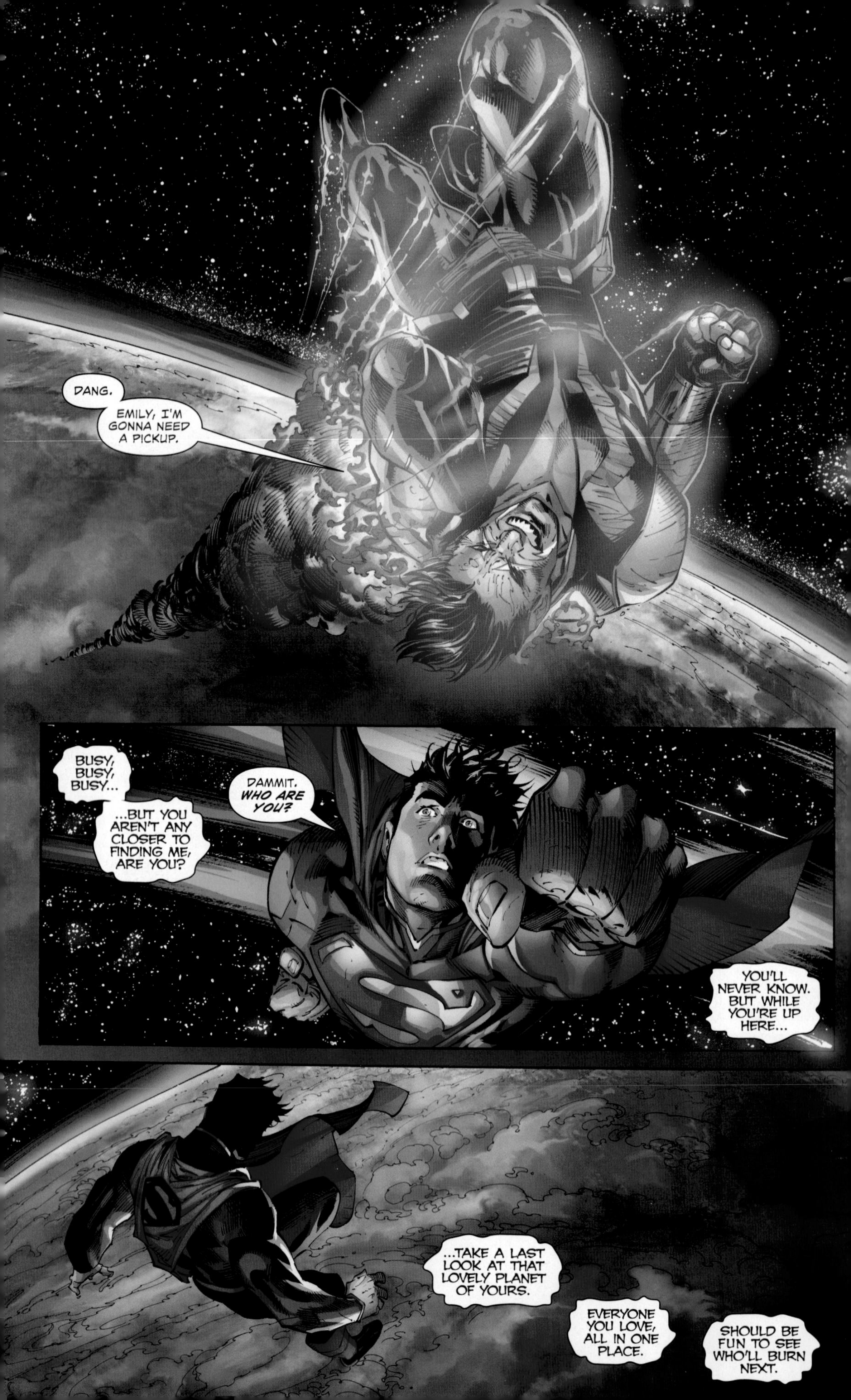
DANG.
EMILY, I'M GONNA NEED A PICKUP.
BUSY, BUSY, BUSY...
...BUT YOU AREN'T ANY CLOSER TO FINDING ME, ARE YOU?
DAMMIT. *WHO ARE YOU?*
YOU'LL NEVER KNOW. BUT WHILE YOU'RE UP HERE...
...TAKE A LAST LOOK AT THAT LOVELY PLANET OF YOURS.
EVERYONE YOU LOVE, ALL IN ONE PLACE.
SHOULD BE FUN TO SEE WHO'LL BURN NEXT.

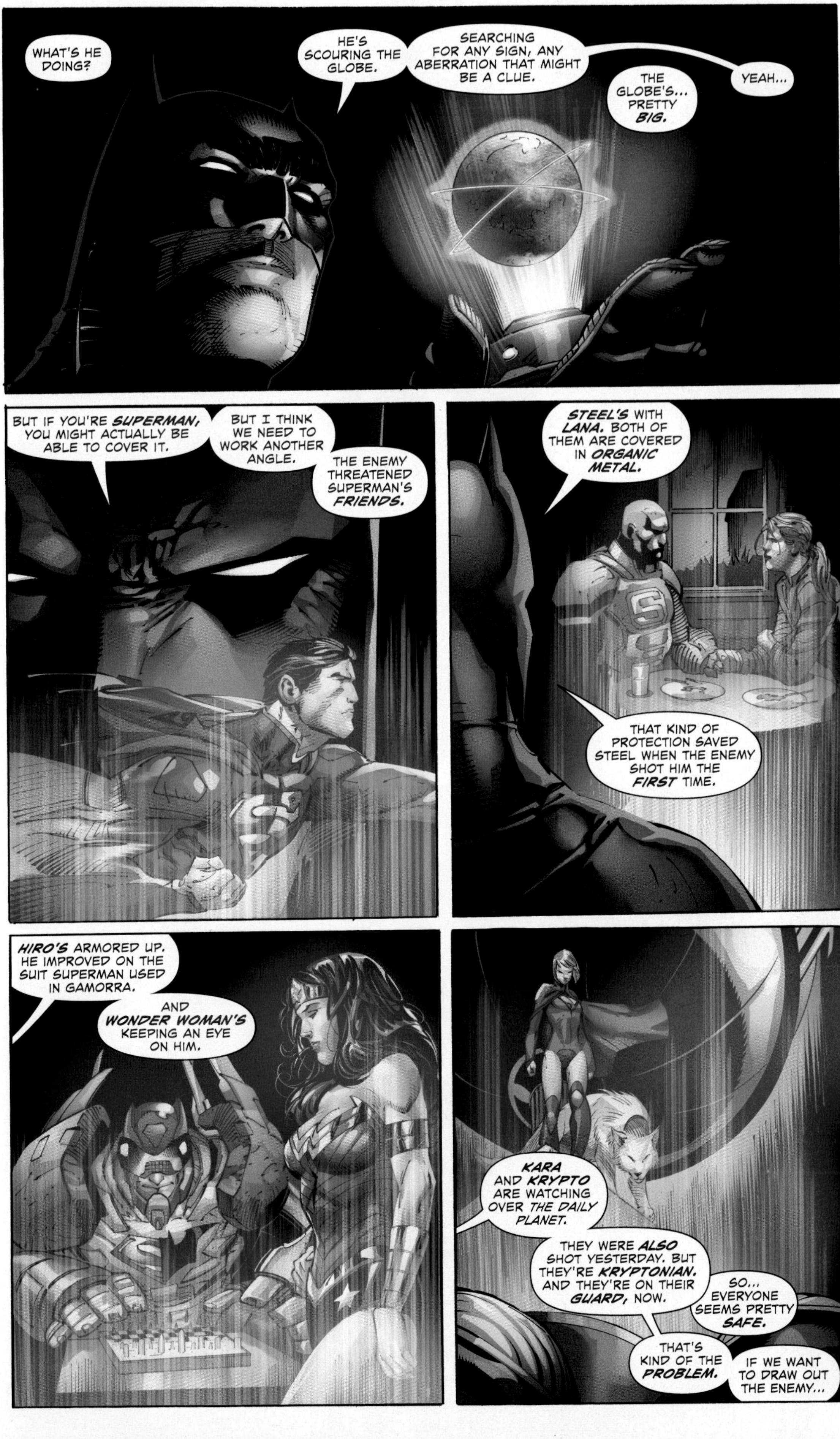
WHAT'S HE DOING?
HE'S SCOURING THE GLOBE.
SEARCHING FOR ANY SIGN, ANY ABERRATION THAT MIGHT BE A CLUE.
YEAH...
THE GLOBE'S... PRETTY BIG.
BUT IF YOU'RE SUPERMAN, YOU MIGHT ACTUALLY BE ABLE TO COVER IT.
BUT I THINK WE NEED TO WORK ANOTHER ANGLE.
THE ENEMY THREATENED SUPERMAN'S FRIENDS.
STEEL'S WITH LANA. BOTH OF THEM ARE COVERED IN ORGANIC METAL.
THAT KIND OF PROTECTION SAVED STEEL WHEN THE ENEMY SHOT HIM THE FIRST TIME.
HIRO'S ARMORED UP. HE IMPROVED ON THE SUIT SUPERMAN USED IN GAMORRA.
AND WONDER WOMAN'S KEEPING AN EYE ON HIM.
KARA AND KRYPTO ARE WATCHING OVER THE DAILY PLANET.
THEY WERE ALSO SHOT YESTERDAY. BUT THEY'RE KRYPTONIAN. AND THEY'RE ON THEIR GUARD, NOW.
SO... EVERYONE SEEMS PRETTY SAFE.
THAT'S KIND OF THE PROBLEM.
IF WE WANT TO DRAW OUT THE ENEMY...

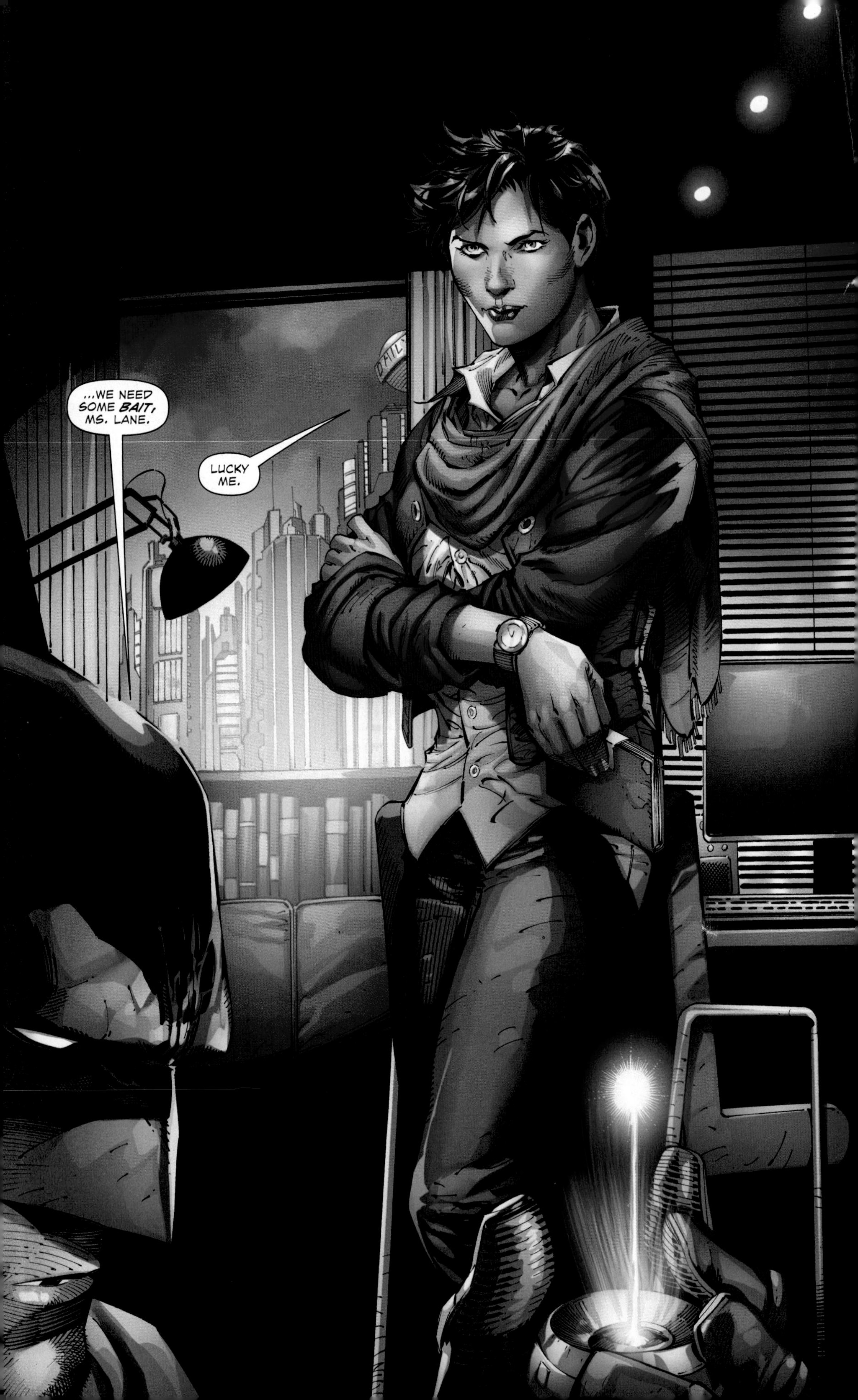
...WE NEED SOME BAIT, MS. LANE.
LUCKY ME.

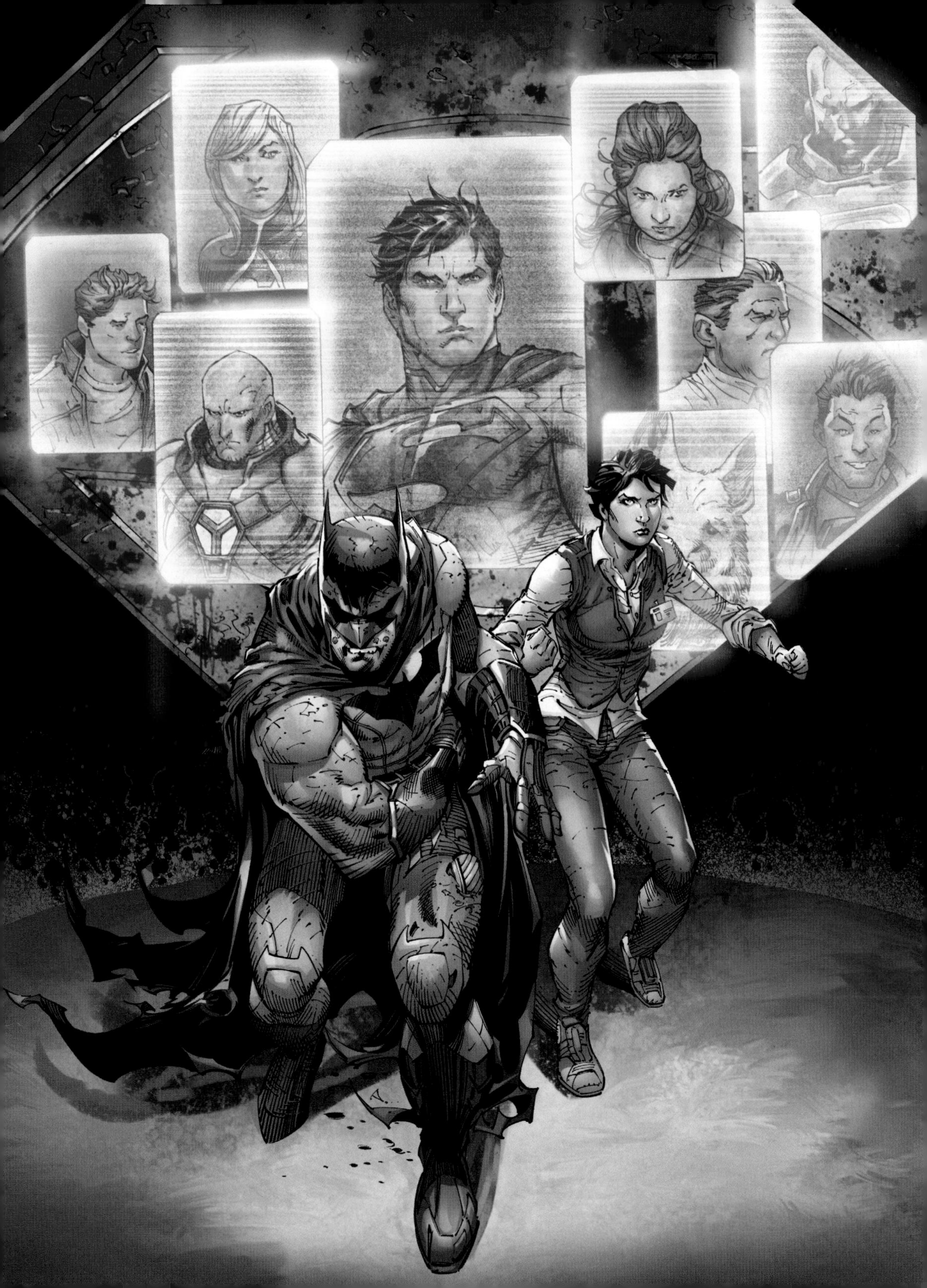

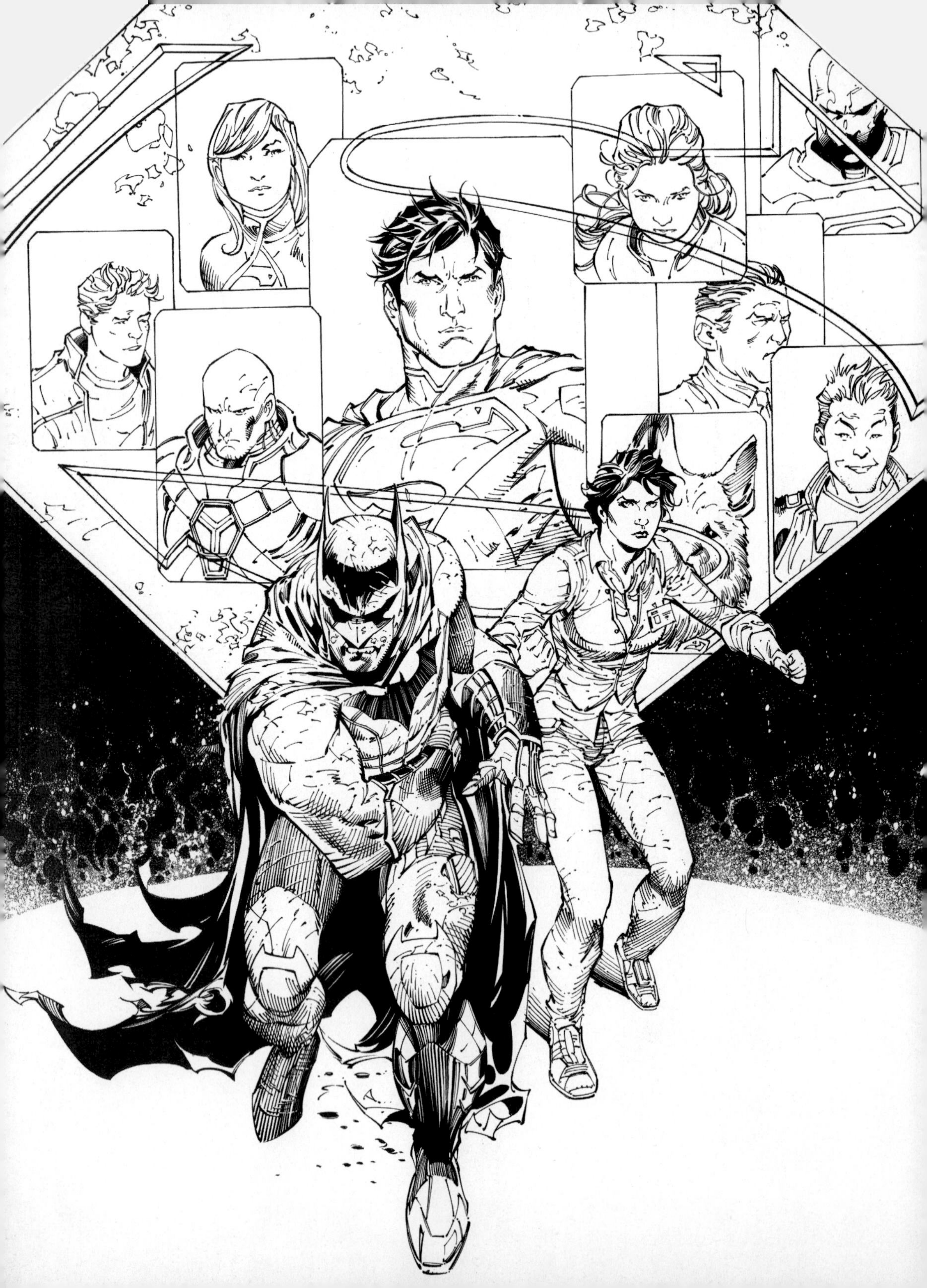

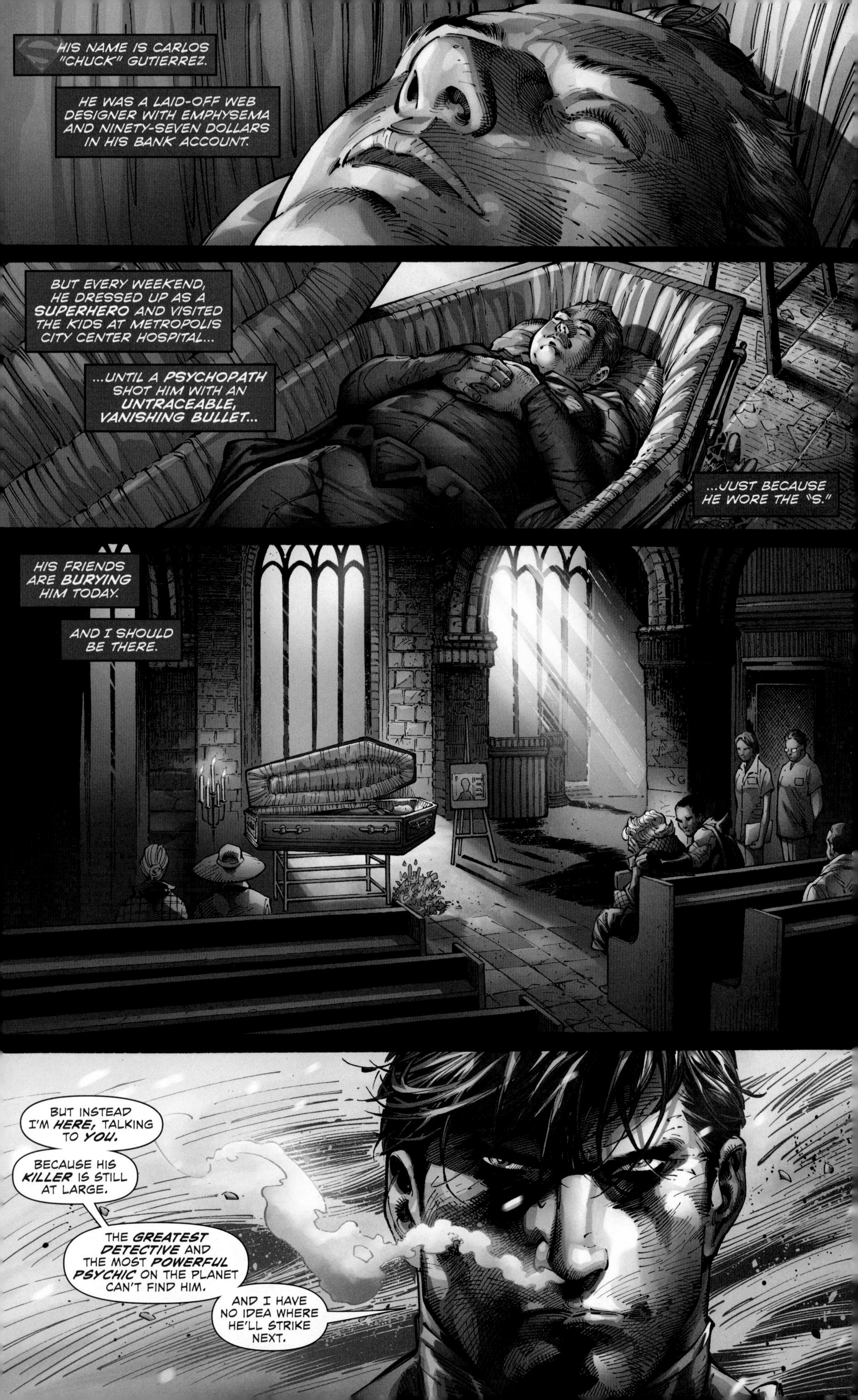
HIS NAME IS CARLOS "CHUCK" GUTIERREZ.
HE WAS A LAID-OFF WEB DESIGNER WITH EMPHYSEMA AND NINETY-SEVEN DOLLARS IN HIS BANK ACCOUNT.
BUT EVERY WEEKEND, HE DRESSED UP AS A SUPERHERO AND VISITED THE KIDS AT METROPOLIS CITY CENTER HOSPITAL...
...UNTIL A PSYCHOPATH SHOT HIM WITH AN UNTRACEABLE, VANISHING BULLET...
...JUST BECAUSE HE WORE THE "S."
HIS FRIENDS ARE BURYING HIM TODAY.
AND I SHOULD BE THERE.
BUT INSTEAD I'M HERE, TALKING TO YOU.
BECAUSE HIS KILLER IS STILL AT LARGE.
THE GREATEST DETECTIVE AND THE MOST POWERFUL PSYCHIC ON THE PLANET CAN'T FIND HIM.
AND I HAVE NO IDEA WHERE HE'LL STRIKE NEXT.

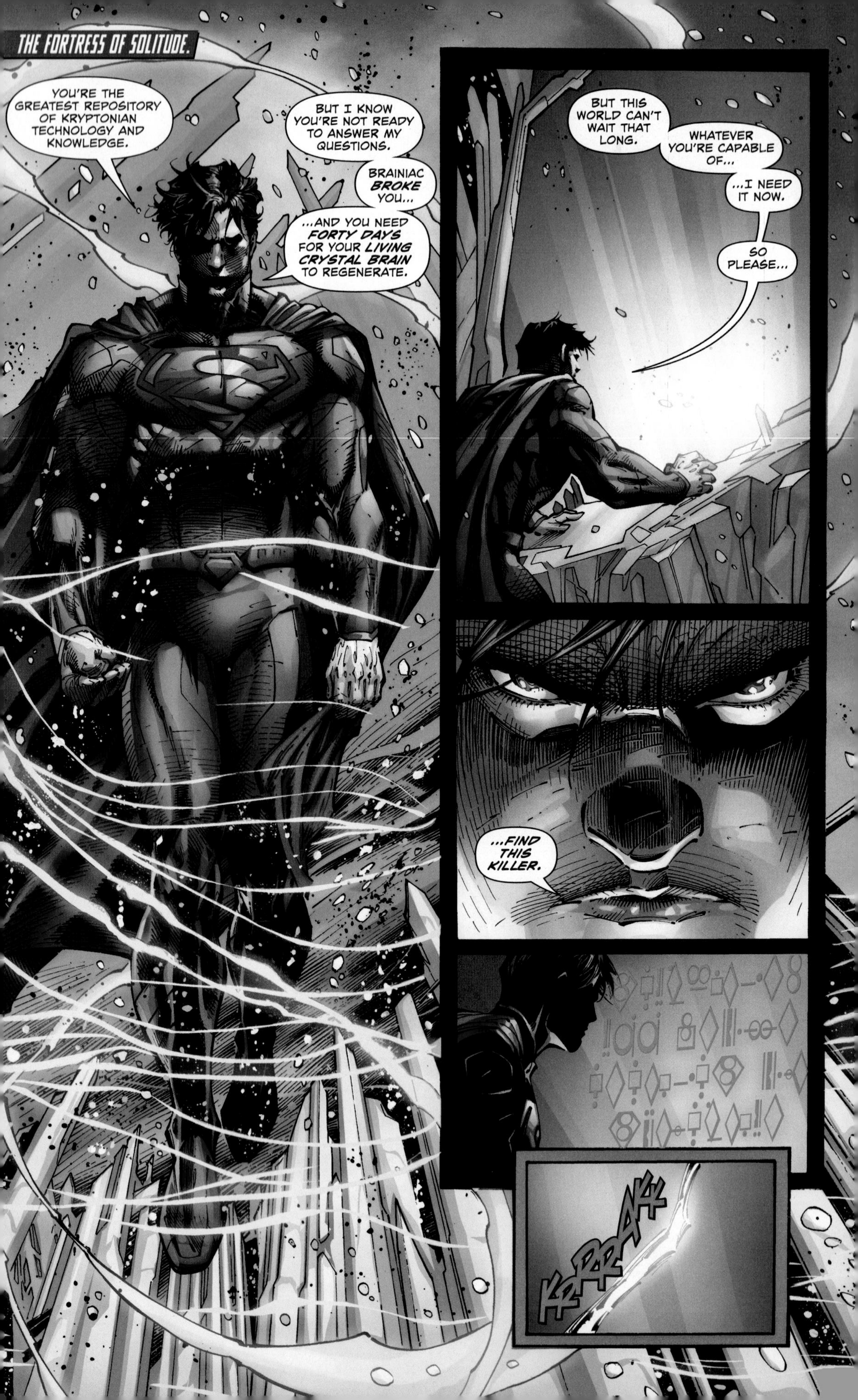

THE FORTRESS OF SOLITUDE.
YOU'RE THE GREATEST REPOSITORY OF KRYPTONIAN TECHNOLOGY AND KNOWLEDGE.
BUT I KNOW YOU'RE NOT READY TO ANSWER MY QUESTIONS.
BRAINIAC BROKE YOU...
...AND YOU NEED FORTY DAYS FOR YOUR LIVING CRYSTAL BRAIN TO REGENERATE.
BUT THIS WORLD CAN'T WAIT THAT LONG.
WHATEVER YOU'RE CAPABLE OF...
...I NEED IT NOW.
SO PLEASE...
...FIND THIS KILLER.
KRRRAKK

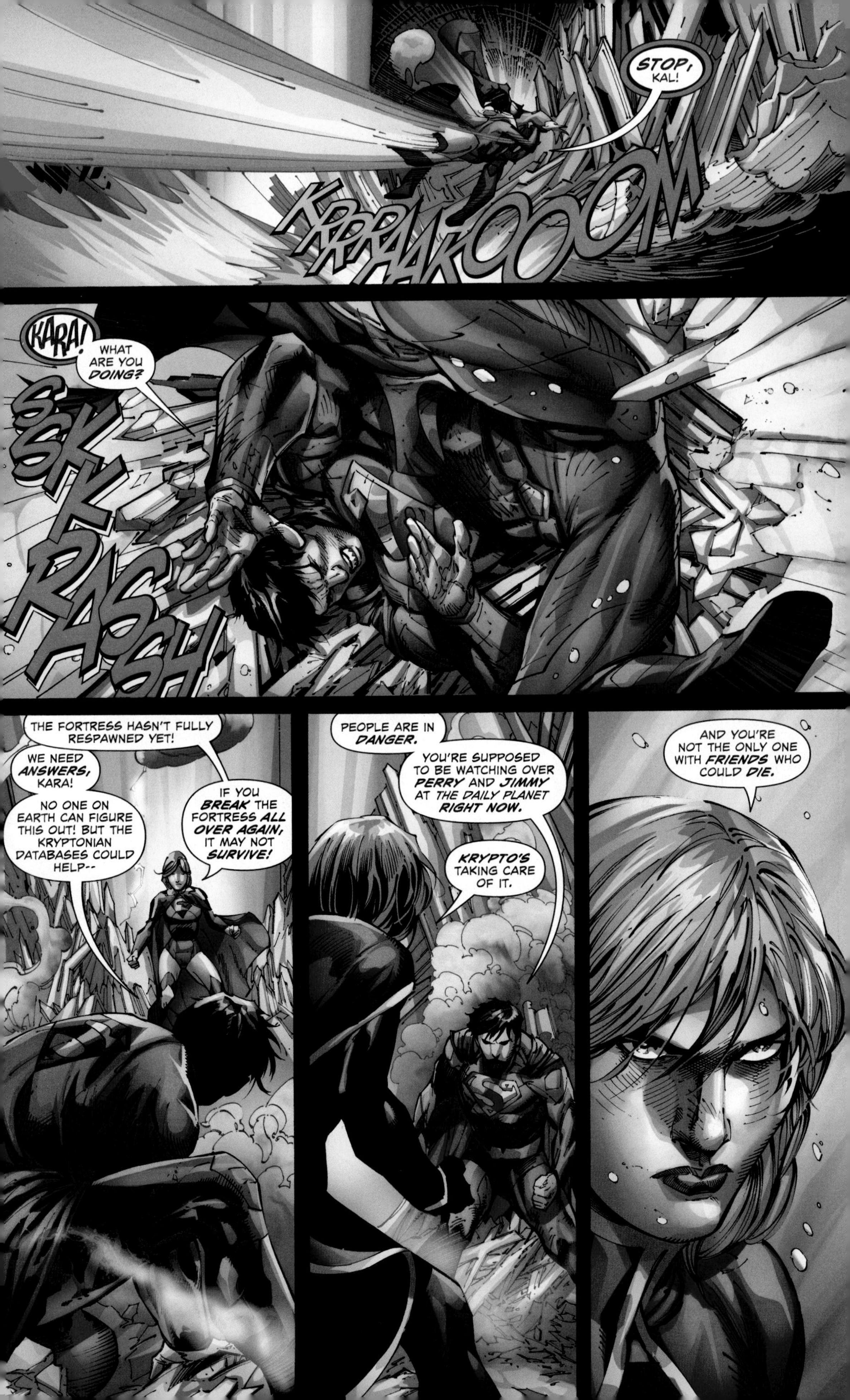
STOP, KAL!
KRRRAAKOOOM
KARA!
WHAT ARE YOU DOING?
SSKKRASSHH
THE FORTRESS HASN'T FULLY RESPAWNED YET!
WE NEED ANSWERS, KARA!
NO ONE ON EARTH CAN FIGURE THIS OUT! BUT THE KRYPTONIAN DATABASES COULD HELP--
IF YOU BREAK THE FORTRESS ALL OVER AGAIN, IT MAY NOT SURVIVE!
PEOPLE ARE IN DANGER.
YOU'RE SUPPOSED TO BE WATCHING OVER PERRY AND JIMMY AT THE DAILY PLANET RIGHT NOW.
KRYPTO'S TAKING CARE OF IT.
AND YOU'RE NOT THE ONLY ONE WITH FRIENDS WHO COULD DIE.

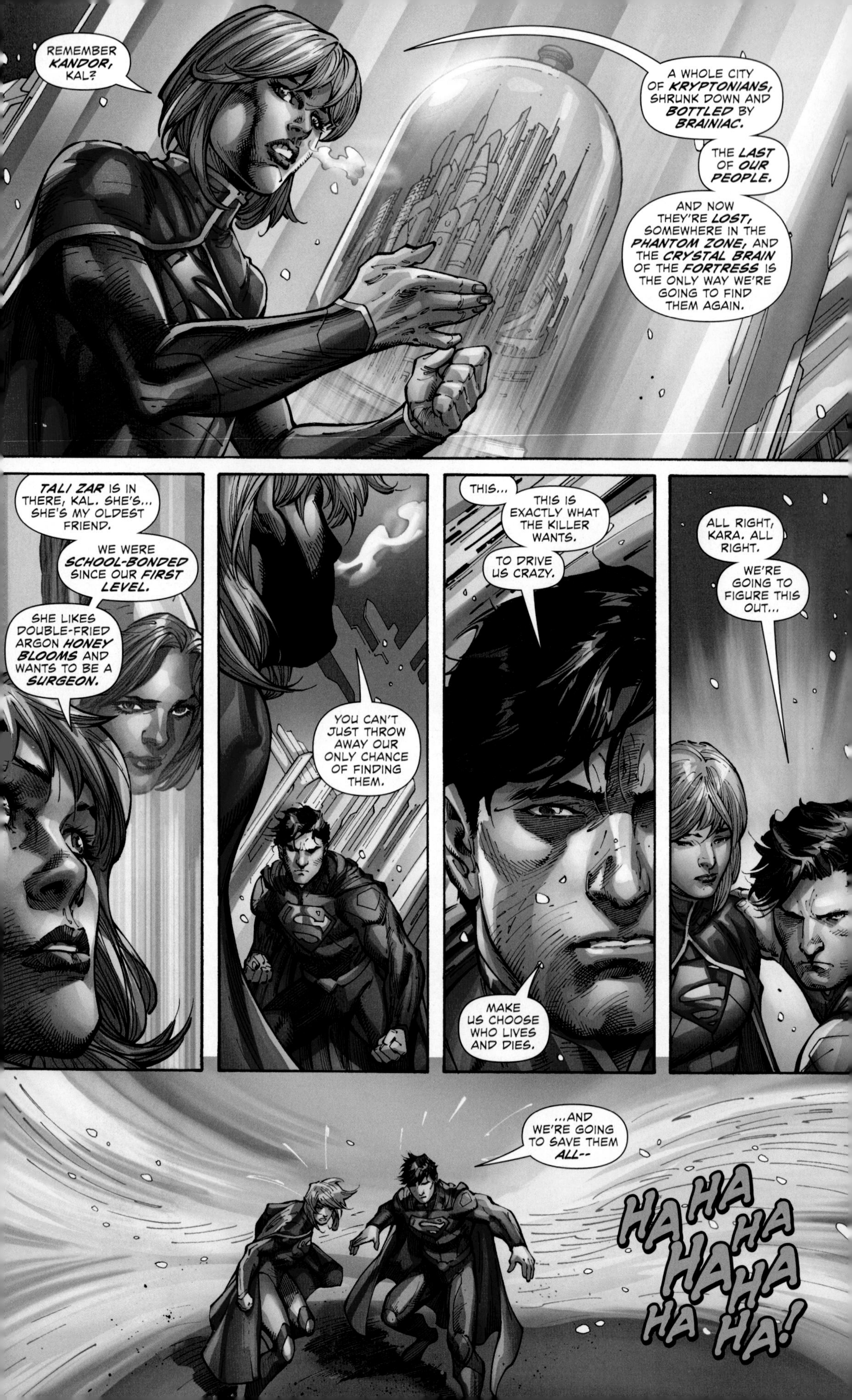
REMEMBER KANDOR, KAL?
A WHOLE CITY OF KRYPTONIANS, SHRUNK DOWN AND BOTTLED BY BRAINIAC.
THE LAST OF OUR PEOPLE.
AND NOW THEY'RE LOST, SOMEWHERE IN THE PHANTOM ZONE; AND THE CRYSTAL BRAIN OF THE FORTRESS IS THE ONLY WAY WE'RE GOING TO FIND THEM AGAIN.
TALI ZAR IS IN THERE, KAL. SHE'S... SHE'S MY OLDEST FRIEND.
WE WERE SCHOOL-BONDED SINCE OUR FIRST LEVEL.
SHE LIKES DOUBLE-FRIED ARGON HONEY BLOOMS AND WANTS TO BE A SURGEON.
YOU CAN'T JUST THROW AWAY OUR ONLY CHANCE OF FINDING THEM.
THIS...
THIS IS EXACTLY WHAT THE KILLER WANTS.
TO DRIVE US CRAZY.
MAKE US CHOOSE WHO LIVES AND DIES.
ALL RIGHT, KARA. ALL RIGHT.
WE'RE GOING TO FIGURE THIS OUT...
...AND WE'RE GOING TO SAVE THEM ALL--
HA HA HA HA HA HA HA HA HA!

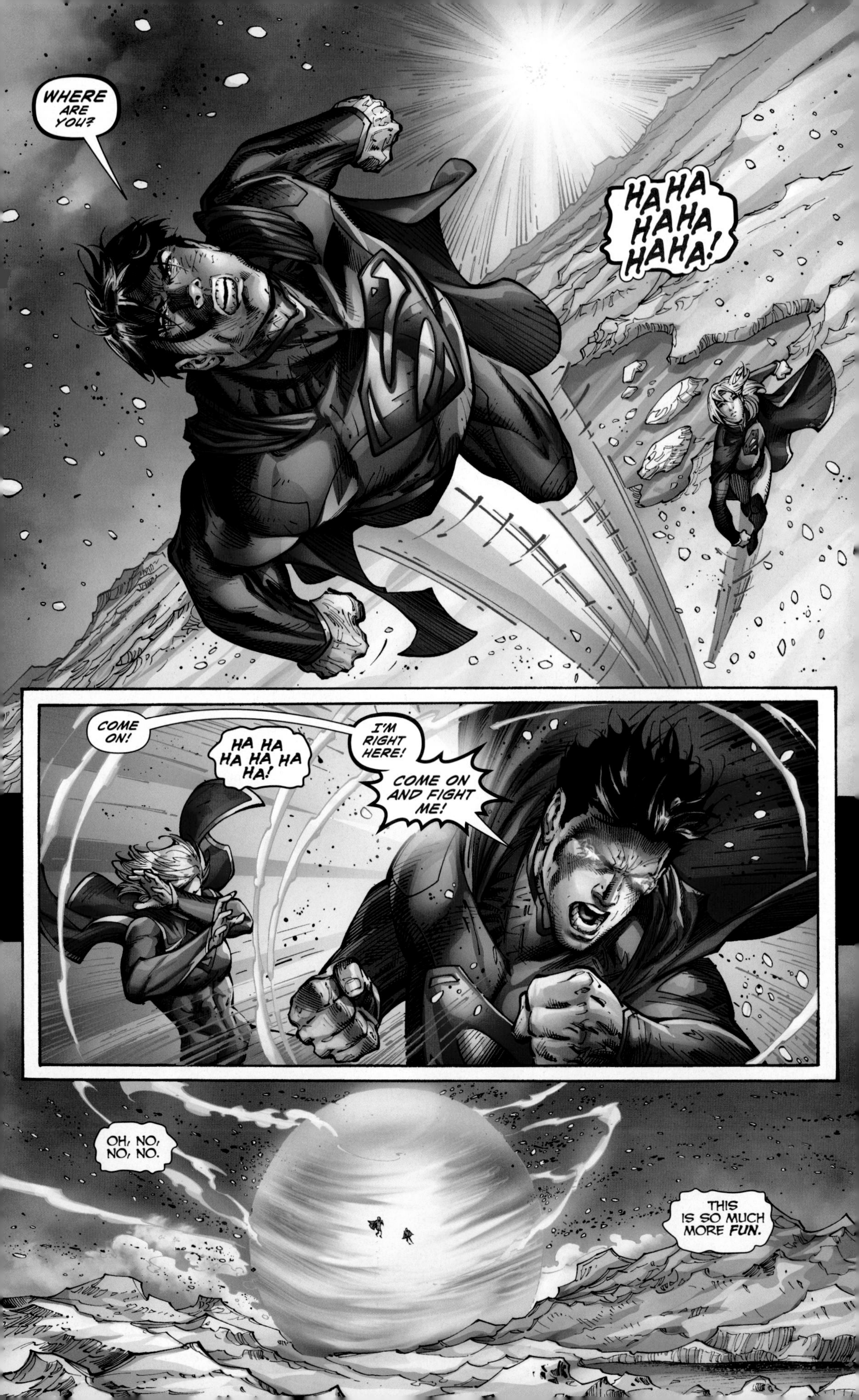
WHERE ARE YOU?
HAHA HAHA HAHA!
COME ON!
HA HA HA HA HA HA!
I'M RIGHT HERE!
COME ON AND FIGHT ME!
OH, NO, NO, NO.
THIS IS SO MUCH MORE FUN.

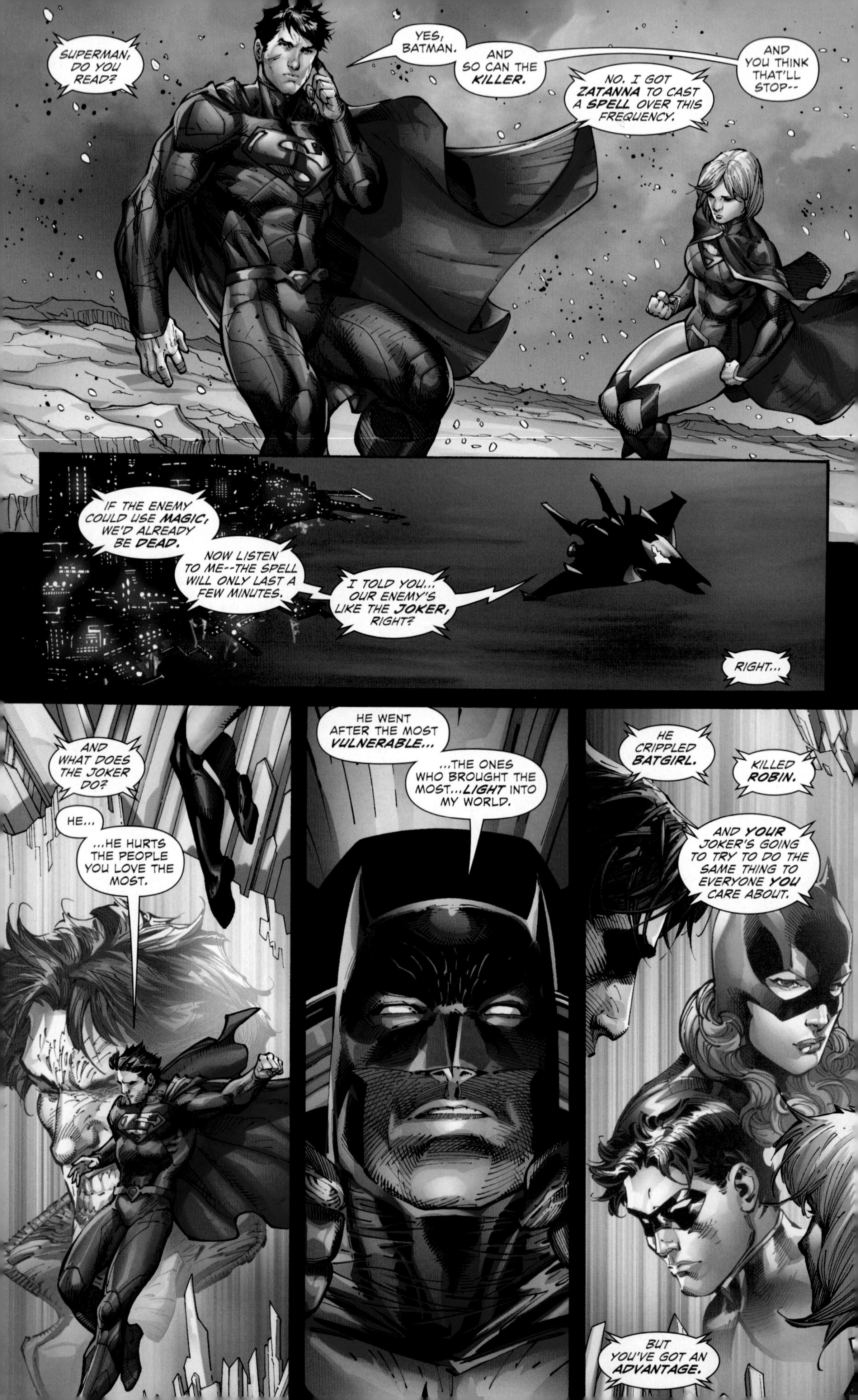
SUPERMAN, DO YOU READ?
YES, BATMAN.
AND SO CAN THE KILLER.
NO. I GOT ZATANNA TO CAST A SPELL OVER THIS FREQUENCY.
AND YOU THINK THAT'LL STOP--
IF THE ENEMY COULD USE MAGIC, WE'D ALREADY BE DEAD.
NOW LISTEN TO ME--THE SPELL WILL ONLY LAST A FEW MINUTES.
I TOLD YOU... OUR ENEMY'S LIKE THE JOKER, RIGHT?
RIGHT...
AND WHAT DOES THE JOKER DO?
HE...
...HE HURTS THE PEOPLE YOU LOVE THE MOST.
HE WENT AFTER THE MOST VULNERABLE...
...THE ONES WHO BROUGHT THE MOST...LIGHT INTO MY WORLD.
HE CRIPPLED BATGIRL.
KILLED ROBIN.
AND YOUR JOKER'S GOING TO TRY TO DO THE SAME THING TO EVERYONE YOU CARE ABOUT.
BUT YOU'VE GOT AN ADVANTAGE.

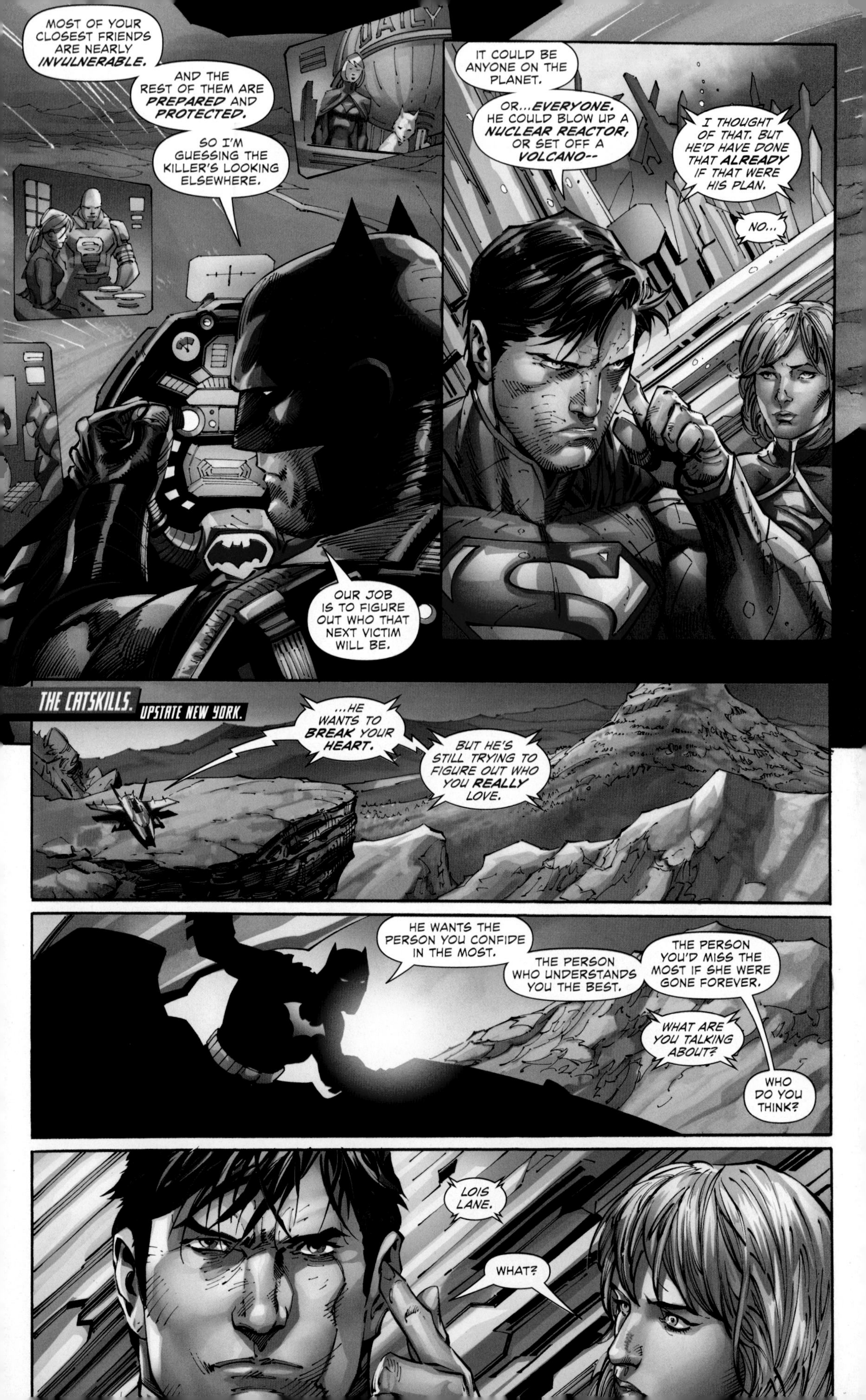

MOST OF YOUR CLOSEST FRIENDS ARE NEARLY INVULNERABLE.
AND THE REST OF THEM ARE PREPARED AND PROTECTED.
SO I'M GUESSING THE KILLER'S LOOKING ELSEWHERE.
OUR JOB IS TO FIGURE OUT WHO THAT NEXT VICTIM WILL BE.
IT COULD BE ANYONE ON THE PLANET.
OR...EVERYONE. HE COULD BLOW UP A NUCLEAR REACTOR, OR SET OFF A VOLCANO--
I THOUGHT OF THAT. BUT HE'D HAVE DONE THAT ALREADY IF THAT WERE HIS PLAN.
NO...
THE CATSKILLS. UPSTATE NEW YORK.
...HE WANTS TO BREAK YOUR HEART.
BUT HE'S STILL TRYING TO FIGURE OUT WHO YOU REALLY LOVE.
HE WANTS THE PERSON YOU CONFIDE IN THE MOST.
THE PERSON WHO UNDERSTANDS YOU THE BEST.
THE PERSON YOU'D MISS THE MOST IF SHE WERE GONE FOREVER.
WHAT ARE YOU TALKING ABOUT?
WHO DO YOU THINK?
LOIS LANE.
WHAT?

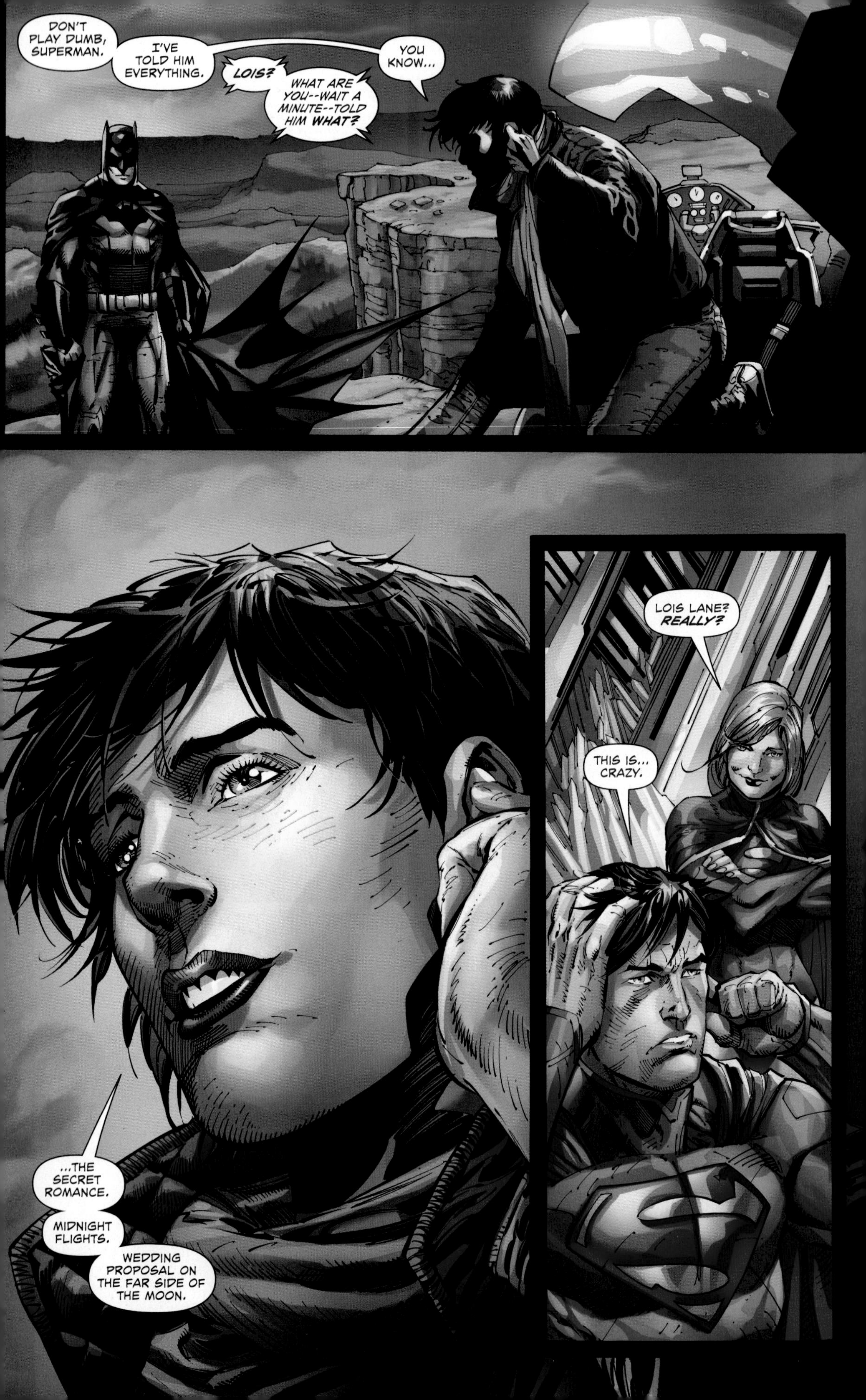
DON'T PLAY DUMB, SUPERMAN.
I'VE TOLD HIM EVERYTHING.
LOIS?
WHAT ARE YOU--WAIT A MINUTE--TOLD HIM WHAT?
YOU KNOW...
...THE SECRET ROMANCE.
MIDNIGHT FLIGHTS.
WEDDING PROPOSAL ON THE FAR SIDE OF THE MOON.
LOIS LANE? REALLY?
THIS IS... CRAZY.

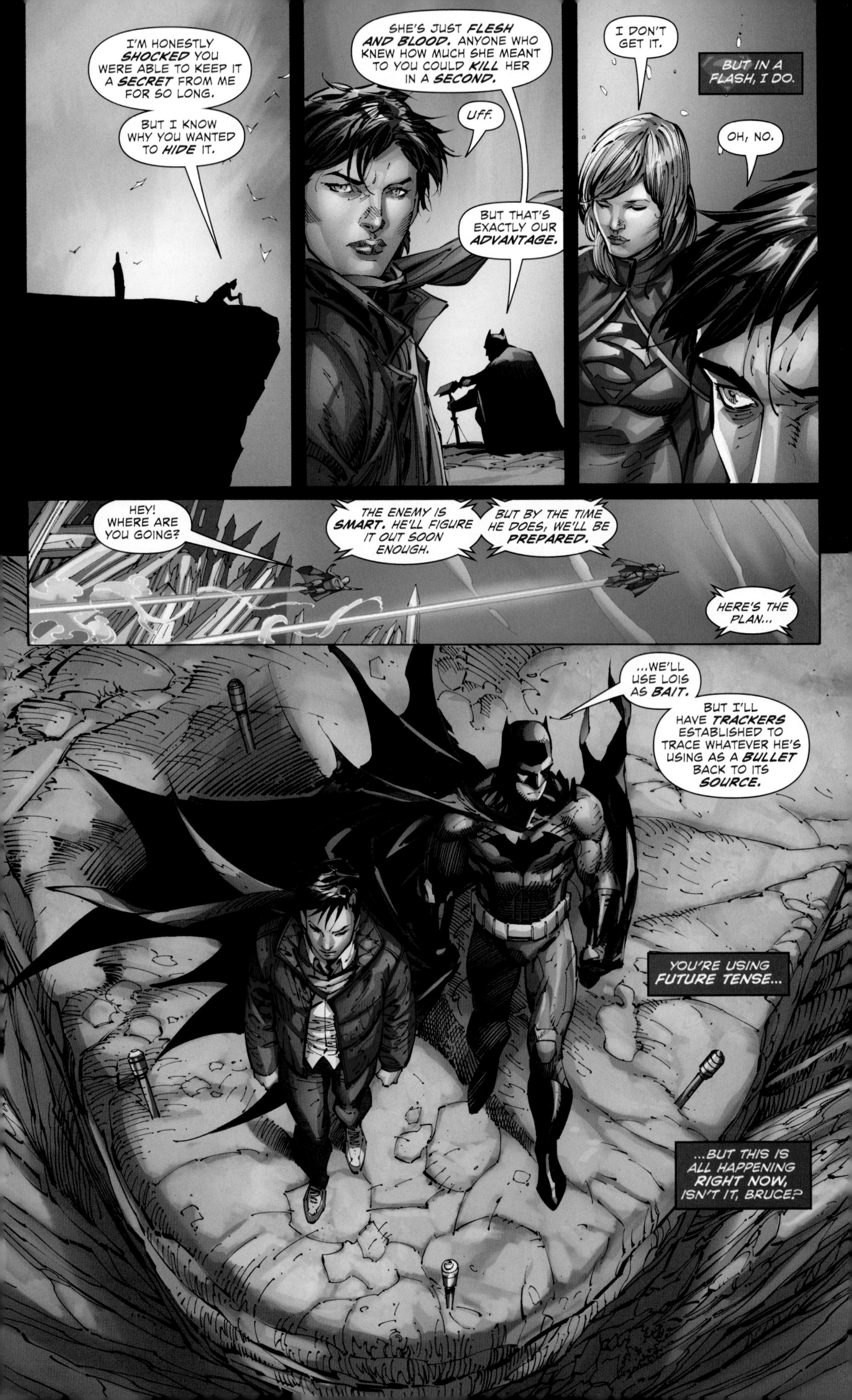
I'M HONESTLY SHOCKED YOU WERE ABLE TO KEEP IT A SECRET FROM ME FOR SO LONG.
BUT I KNOW WHY YOU WANTED TO HIDE IT.
SHE'S JUST FLESH AND BLOOD. ANYONE WHO KNEW HOW MUCH SHE MEANT TO YOU COULD KILL HER IN A SECOND.
UFF.
BUT THAT'S EXACTLY OUR ADVANTAGE.
I DON'T GET IT.
BUT IN A FLASH, I DO.
OH, NO.
HEY! WHERE ARE YOU GOING?
THE ENEMY IS SMART. HE'LL FIGURE IT OUT SOON ENOUGH.
BUT BY THE TIME HE DOES, WE'LL BE PREPARED.
HERE'S THE PLAN...
...WE'LL USE LOIS AS BAIT.
BUT I'LL HAVE TRACKERS ESTABLISHED TO TRACE WHATEVER HE'S USING AS A BULLET BACK TO ITS SOURCE.
YOU'RE USING FUTURE TENSE...
...BUT THIS IS ALL HAPPENING RIGHT NOW, ISN'T IT, BRUCE?

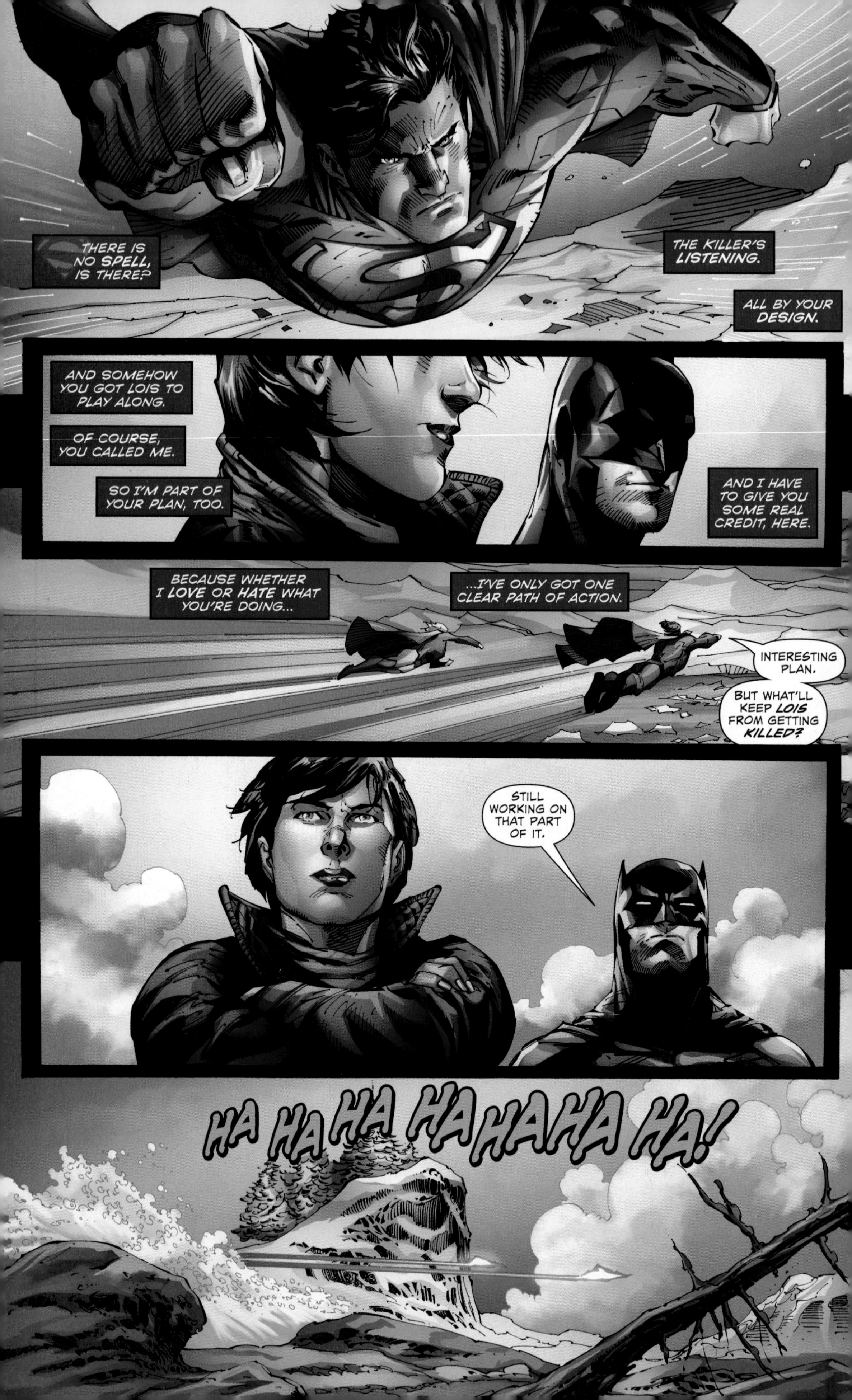
THERE IS NO SPELL, IS THERE?
THE KILLER'S LISTENING.
ALL BY YOUR DESIGN.
AND SOMEHOW YOU GOT LOIS TO PLAY ALONG.
OF COURSE, YOU CALLED ME.
SO I'M PART OF YOUR PLAN, TOO.
AND I HAVE TO GIVE YOU SOME REAL CREDIT, HERE.
BECAUSE WHETHER I LOVE OR HATE WHAT YOU'RE DOING...
...I'VE ONLY GOT ONE CLEAR PATH OF ACTION.
INTERESTING PLAN.
BUT WHAT'LL KEEP LOIS FROM GETTING KILLED?
STILL WORKING ON THAT PART OF IT.
HA HA HA HA HAHAHA HA!

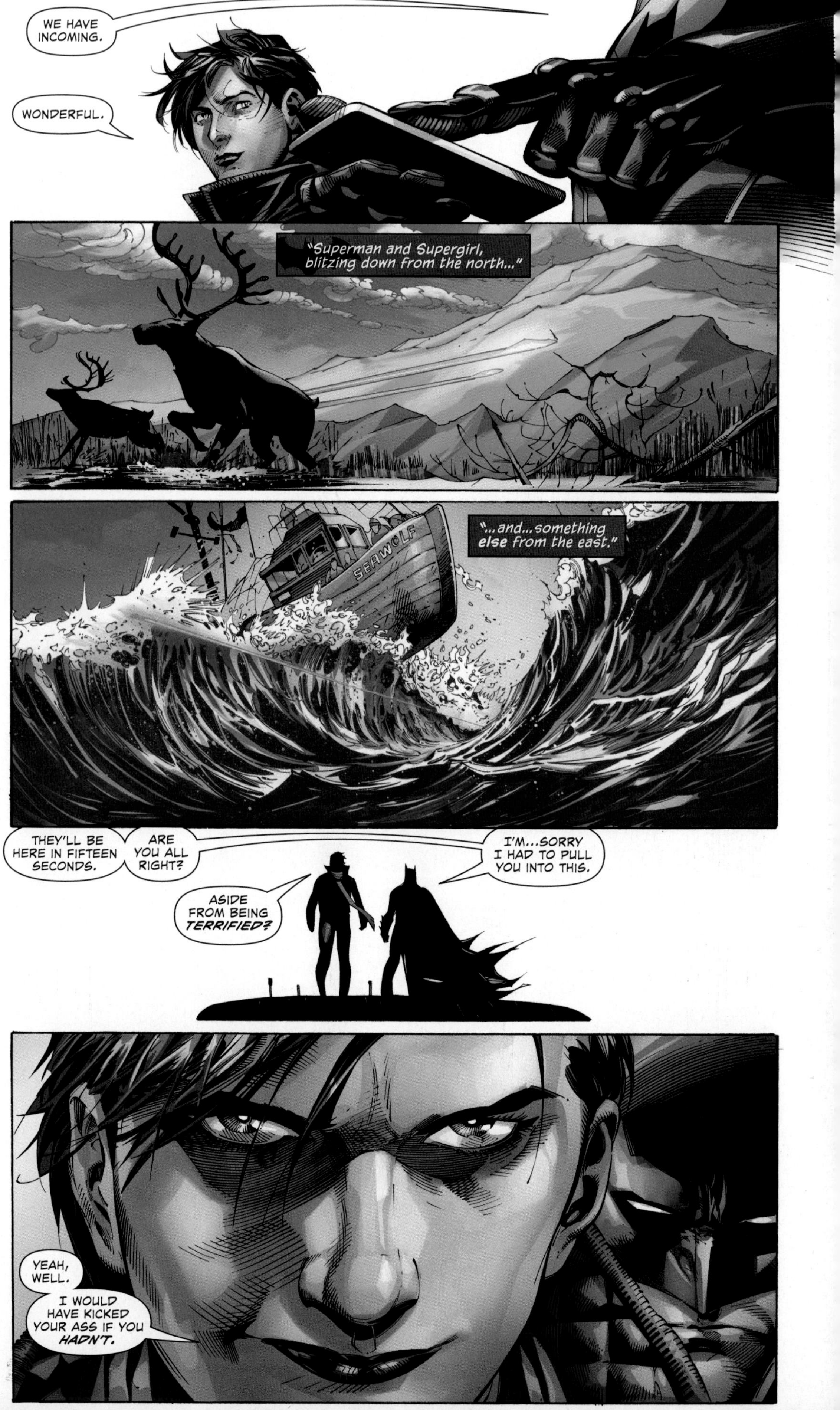
WE HAVE INCOMING.
WONDERFUL.
"Superman and Supergirl, blitzing down from the north..."
"...and...something else from the east."
SEAWOLF
THEY'LL BE HERE IN FIFTEEN SECONDS.
ARE YOU ALL RIGHT?
I'M...SORRY I HAD TO PULL YOU INTO THIS.
ASIDE FROM BEING TERRIFIED?
YEAH, WELL.
I WOULD HAVE KICKED YOUR ASS IF YOU HADN'T.

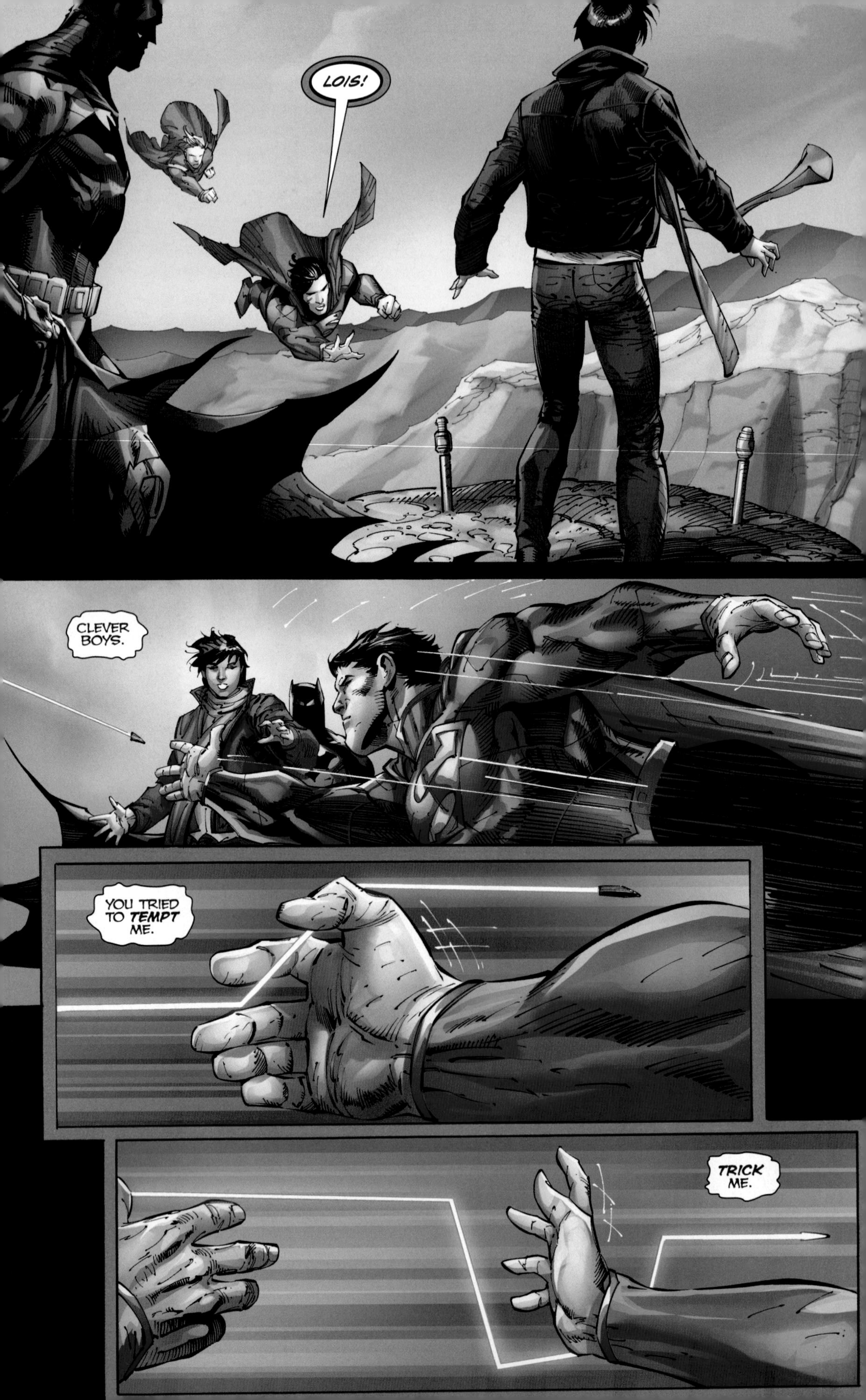
LOIS!
CLEVER BOYS.
YOU TRIED TO TEMPT ME.
TRICK ME.

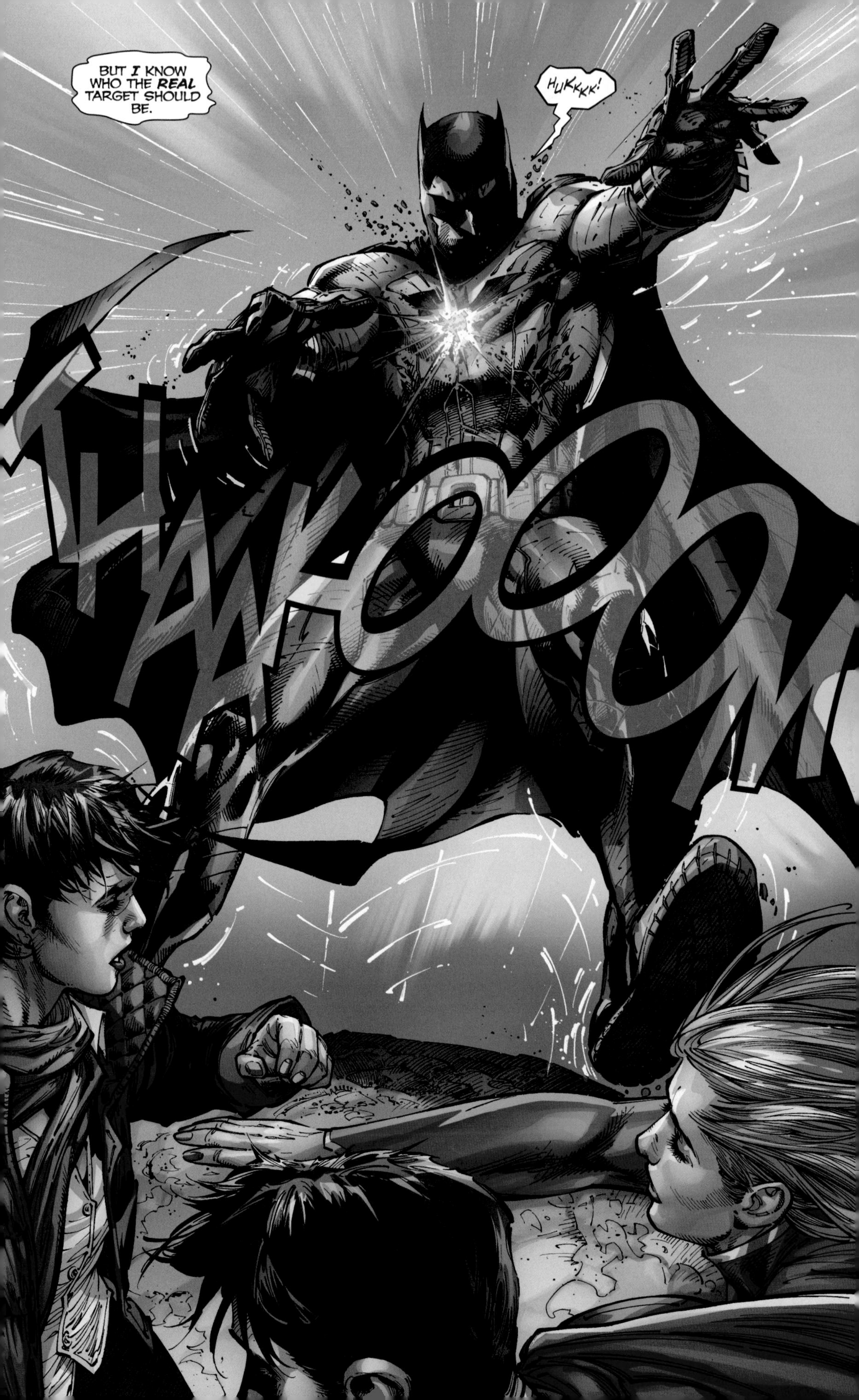

BUT I KNOW WHO THE REAL TARGET SHOULD BE.
HUKKKK!

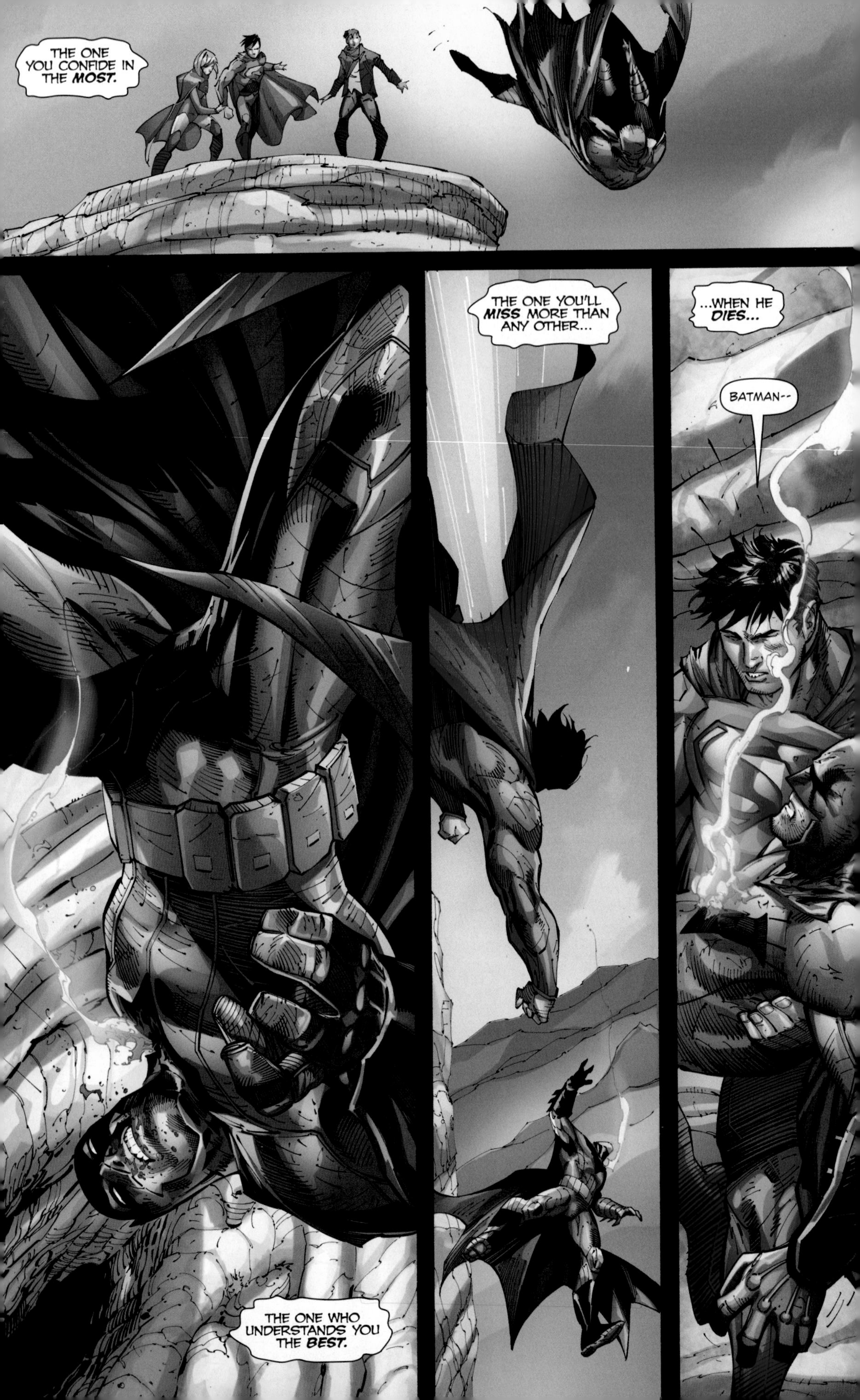
THE ONE YOU CONFIDE IN THE MOST.
THE ONE WHO UNDERSTANDS YOU THE BEST.
THE ONE YOU'LL MISS MORE THAN ANY OTHER...
...WHEN HE DIES...
BATMAN--

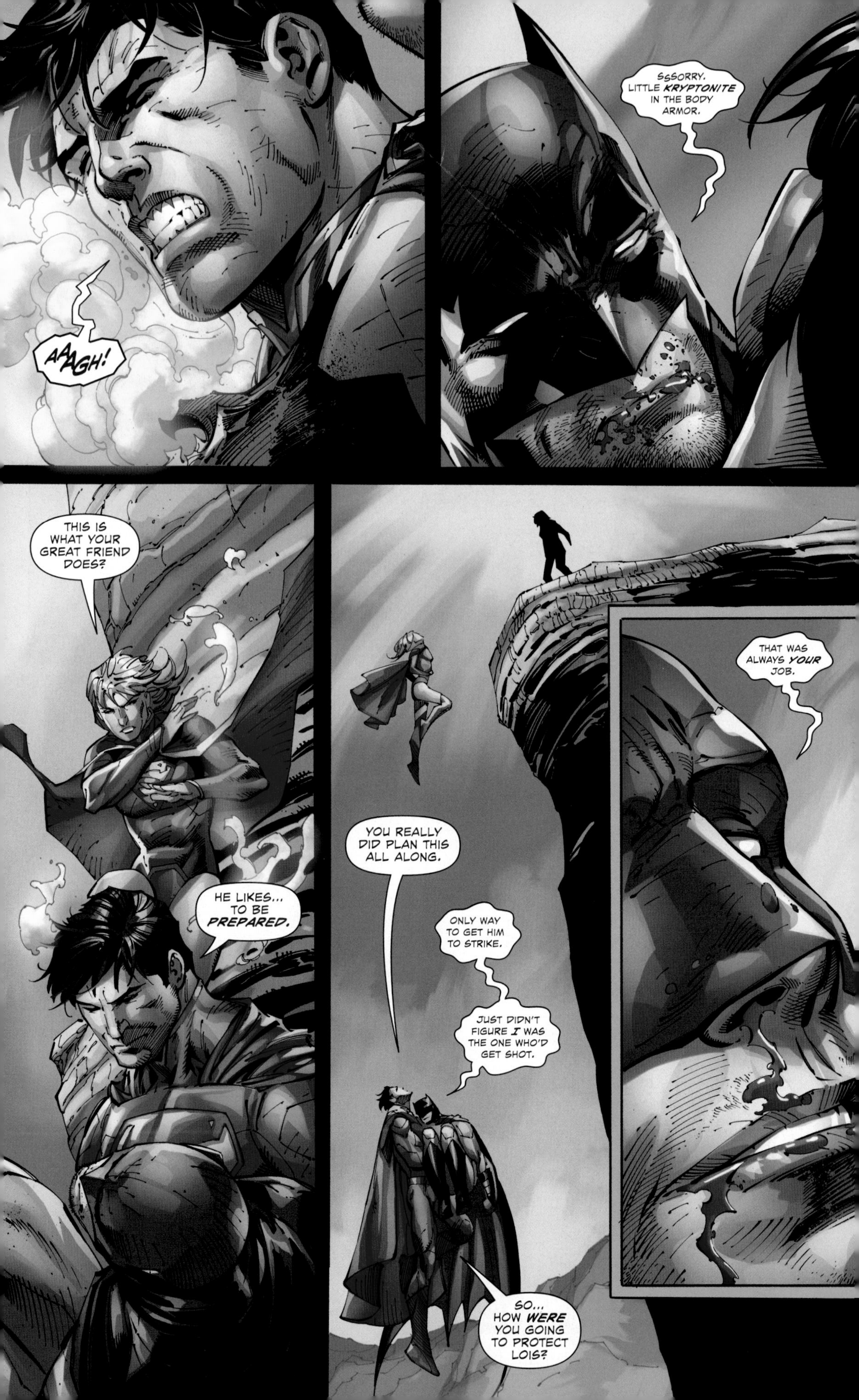
AAAGH!
SSSORRY. LITTLE KRYPTONITE IN THE BODY ARMOR.
THIS IS WHAT YOUR GREAT FRIEND DOES?
HE LIKES... TO BE PREPARED.
YOU REALLY DID PLAN THIS ALL ALONG.
ONLY WAY TO GET HIM TO STRIKE.
JUST DIDN'T FIGURE I WAS THE ONE WHO'D GET SHOT.
SO... HOW WERE YOU GOING TO PROTECT LOIS?
THAT WAS ALWAYS YOUR JOB.

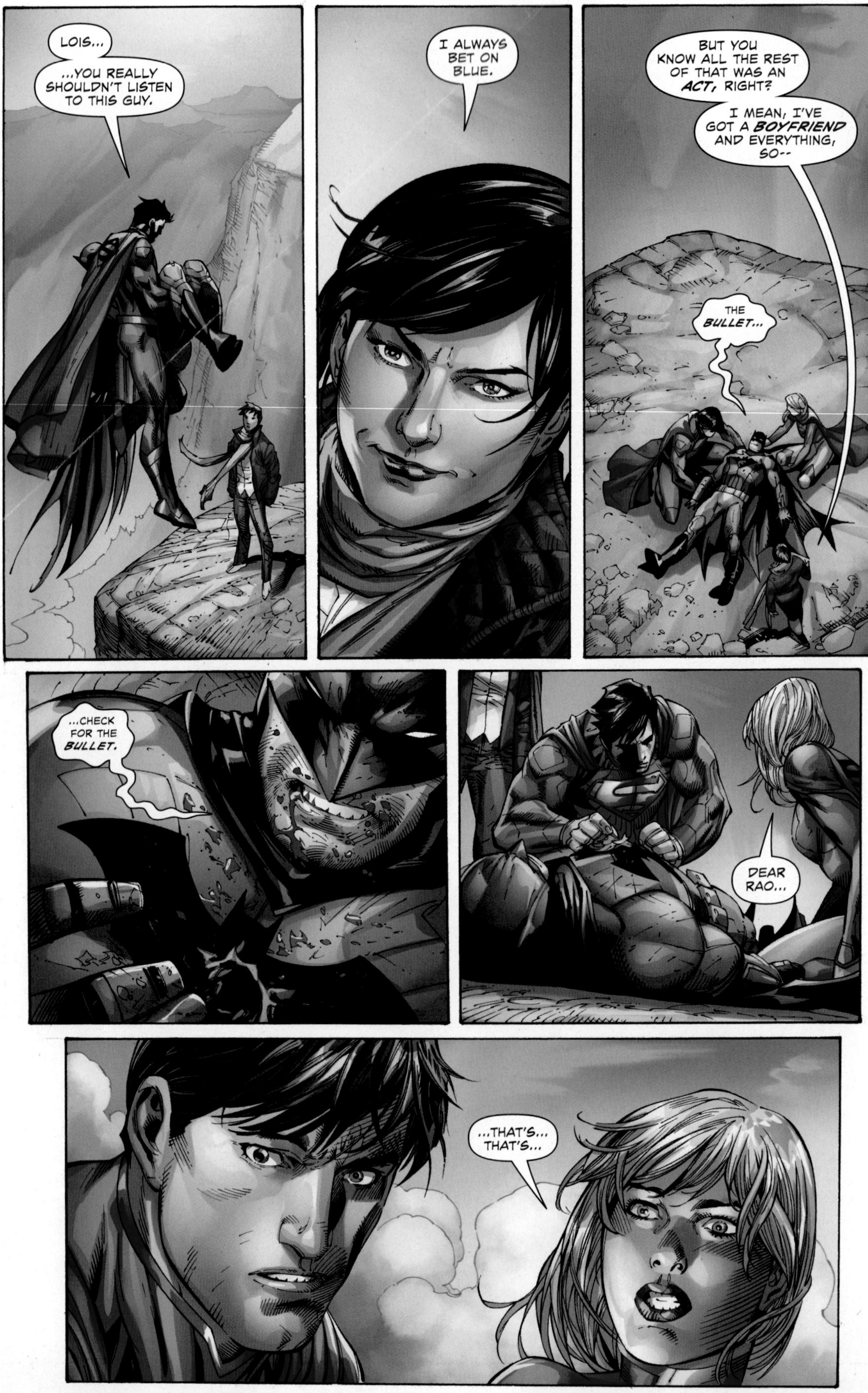
LOIS...
...YOU REALLY SHOULDN'T LISTEN TO THIS GUY.
I ALWAYS BET ON BLUE.
BUT YOU KNOW ALL THE REST OF THAT WAS AN ACT, RIGHT?
I MEAN, I'VE GOT A BOYFRIEND AND EVERYTHING, SO--
THE BULLET...
...CHECK FOR THE BULLET.
DEAR RAO...
...THAT'S... THAT'S...

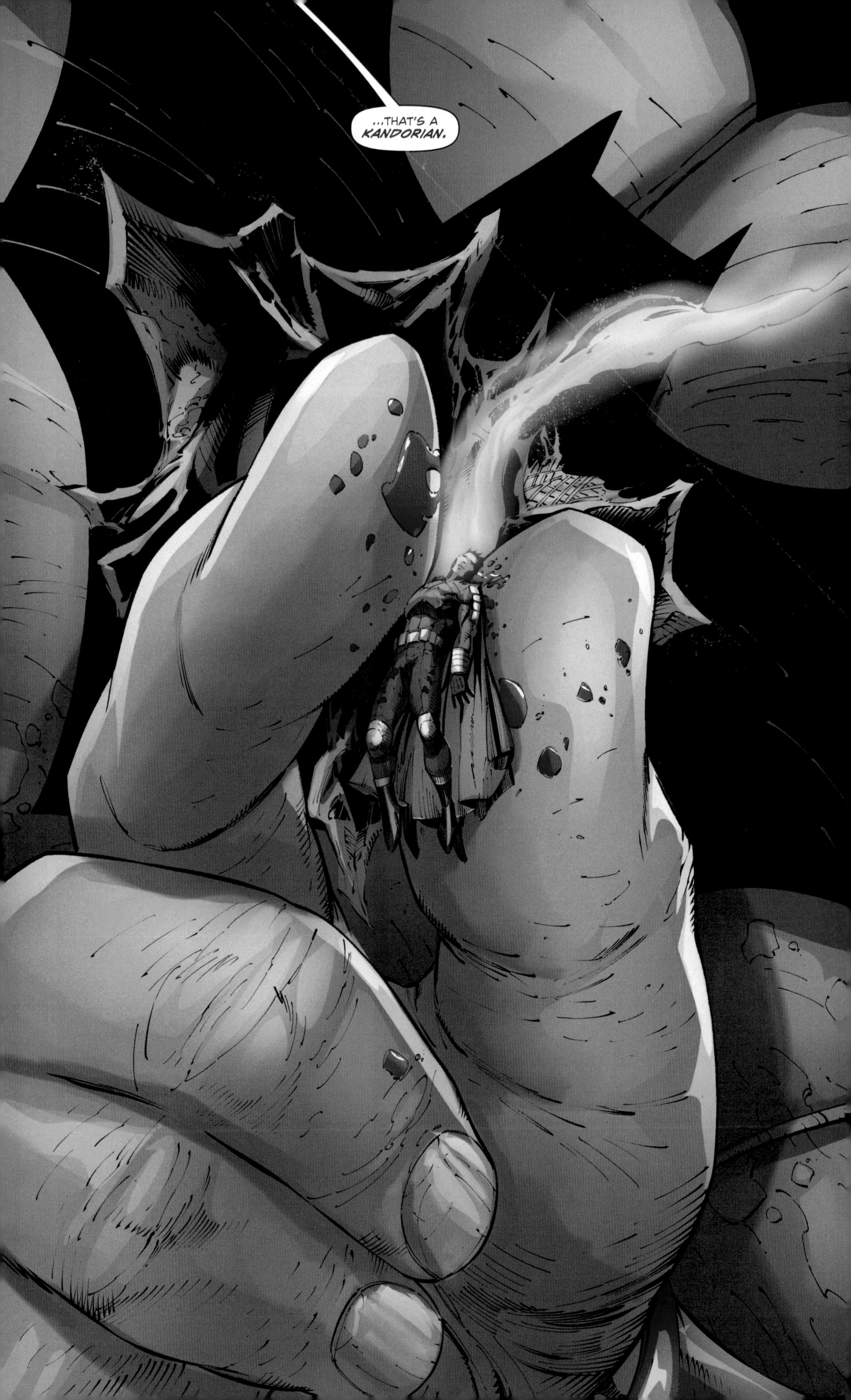
...THAT'S A KANDORIAN.

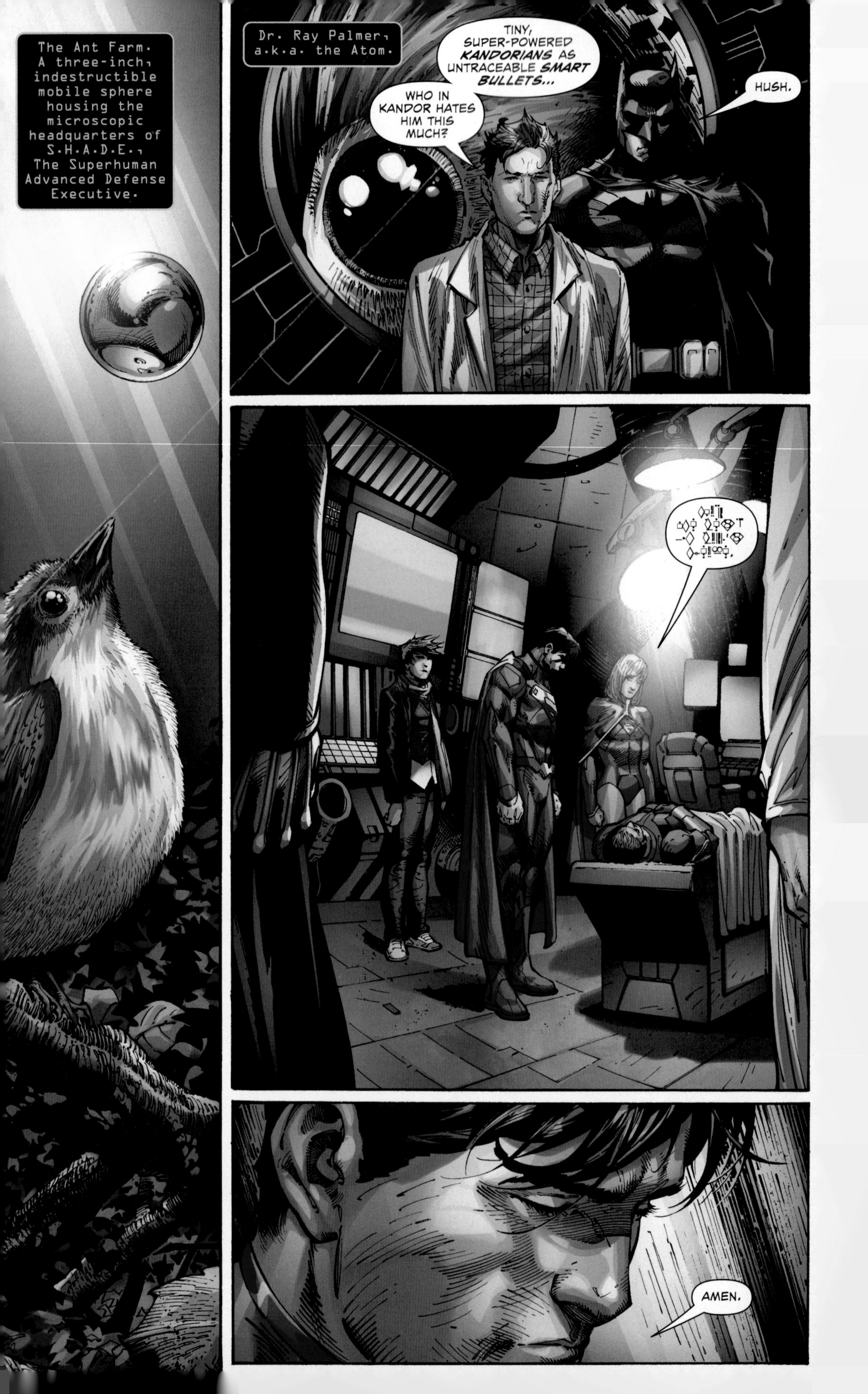
The Ant Farm. A three-inch, indestructible mobile sphere housing the microscopic headquarters of S.H.A.D.E., The Superhuman Advanced Defense Executive.
Dr. Ray Palmer, a.k.a. the Atom.
TINY, SUPER-POWERED KANDORIANS AS UNTRACEABLE SMART BULLETS...
WHO IN KANDOR HATES HIM THIS MUCH?
HUSH.
AMEN.

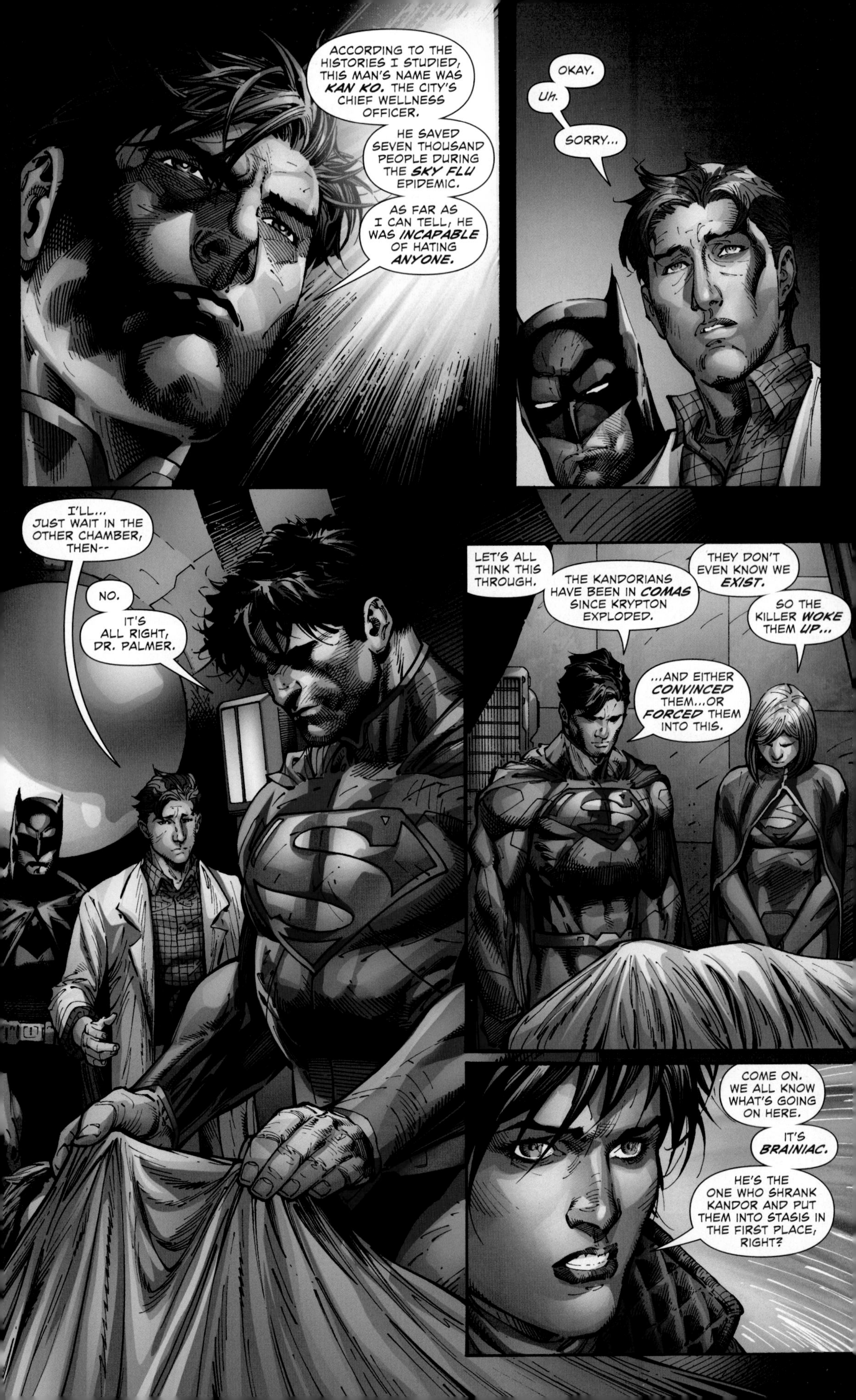
ACCORDING TO THE HISTORIES I STUDIED, THIS MAN'S NAME WAS KAN KO. THE CITY'S CHIEF WELLNESS OFFICER.
HE SAVED SEVEN THOUSAND PEOPLE DURING THE SKY FLU EPIDEMIC.
AS FAR AS I CAN TELL, HE WAS INCAPABLE OF HATING ANYONE.
OKAY.
Uh.
SORRY...
I'LL... JUST WAIT IN THE OTHER CHAMBER, THEN--
NO.
IT'S ALL RIGHT, DR. PALMER.
LET'S ALL THINK THIS THROUGH.
THE KANDORIANS HAVE BEEN IN COMAS SINCE KRYPTON EXPLODED.
THEY DON'T EVEN KNOW WE EXIST.
SO THE KILLER WOKE THEM UP...
...AND EITHER CONVINCED THEM...OR FORCED THEM INTO THIS.
COME ON. WE ALL KNOW WHAT'S GOING ON HERE.
IT'S BRAINIAC.
HE'S THE ONE WHO SHRANK KANDOR AND PUT THEM INTO STASIS IN THE FIRST PLACE, RIGHT?

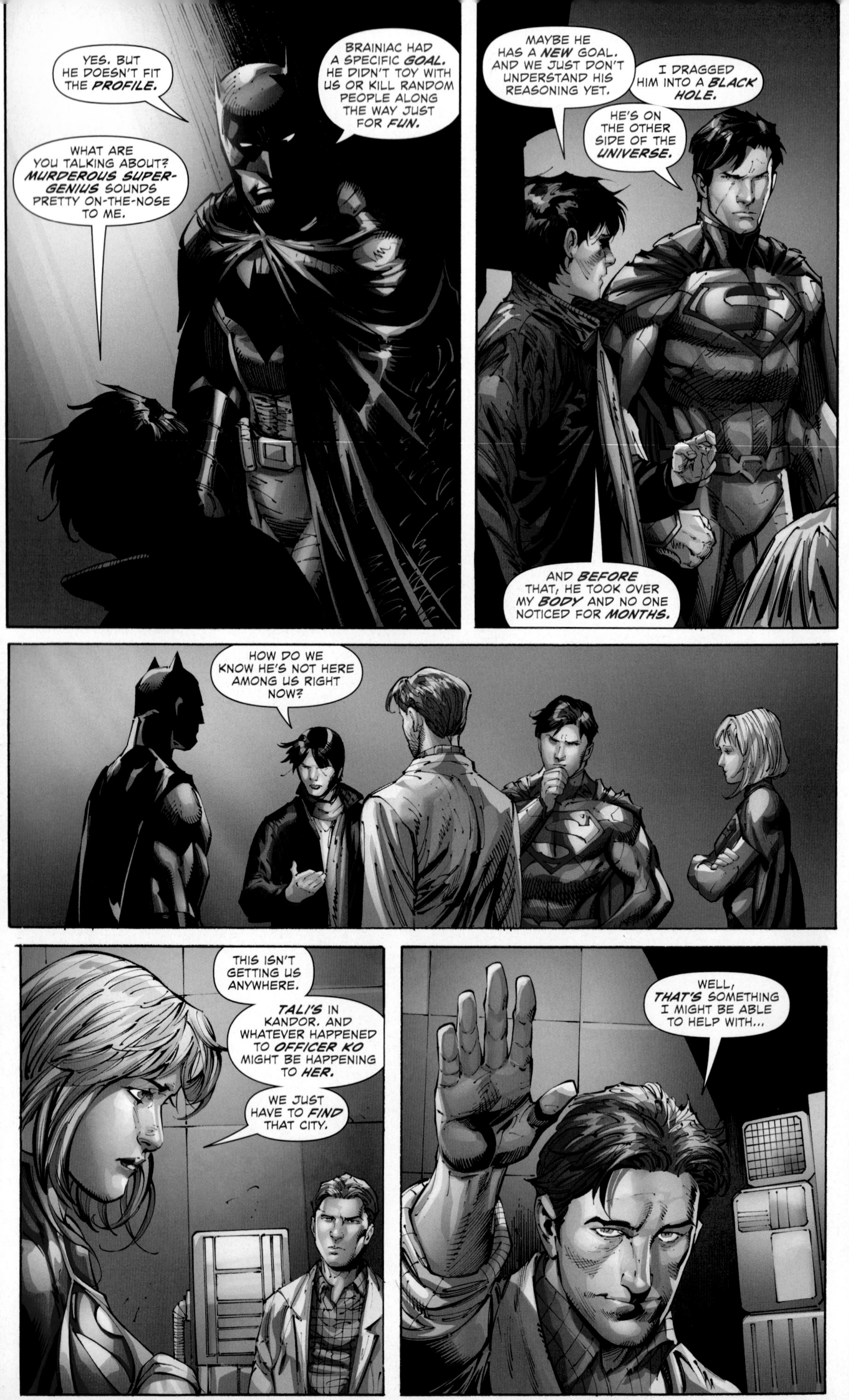
YES. BUT HE DOESN'T FIT THE PROFILE.
WHAT ARE YOU TALKING ABOUT? MURDEROUS SUPER-GENIUS SOUNDS PRETTY ON-THE-NOSE TO ME.
BRAINIAC HAD A SPECIFIC GOAL. HE DIDN'T TOY WITH US OR KILL RANDOM PEOPLE ALONG THE WAY JUST FOR FUN.
MAYBE HE HAS A NEW GOAL. AND WE JUST DON'T UNDERSTAND HIS REASONING YET.
I DRAGGED HIM INTO A BLACK HOLE.
HE'S ON THE OTHER SIDE OF THE UNIVERSE.
AND BEFORE THAT, HE TOOK OVER MY BODY AND NO ONE NOTICED FOR MONTHS.
HOW DO WE KNOW HE'S NOT HERE AMONG US RIGHT NOW?
THIS ISN'T GETTING US ANYWHERE.
TALI'S IN KANDOR. AND WHATEVER HAPPENED TO OFFICER KO MIGHT BE HAPPENING TO HER.
WE JUST HAVE TO FIND THAT CITY.
WELL, THAT'S SOMETHING I MIGHT BE ABLE TO HELP WITH...

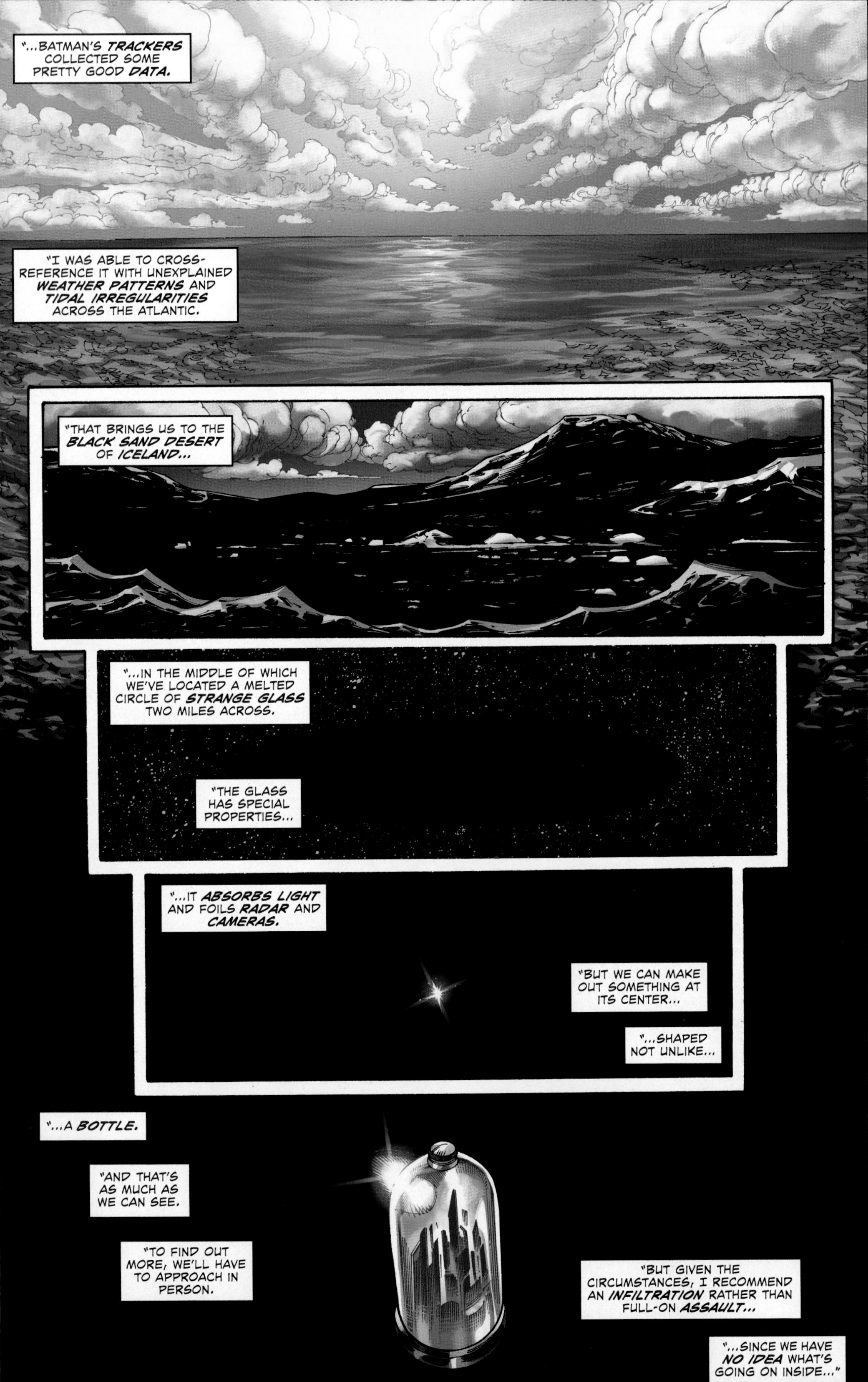
"...BATMAN'S TRACKERS COLLECTED SOME PRETTY GOOD DATA.
"I WAS ABLE TO CROSS-REFERENCE IT WITH UNEXPLAINED WEATHER PATTERNS AND TIDAL IRREGULARITIES ACROSS THE ATLANTIC.
"THAT BRINGS US TO THE BLACK SAND DESERT OF ICELAND...
"...IN THE MIDDLE OF WHICH WE'VE LOCATED A MELTED CIRCLE OF STRANGE GLASS TWO MILES ACROSS.
"THE GLASS HAS SPECIAL PROPERTIES...
"...IT ABSORBS LIGHT AND FOILS RADAR AND CAMERAS.
"BUT WE CAN MAKE OUT SOMETHING AT ITS CENTER...
"...SHAPED NOT UNLIKE...
"...A BOTTLE.
"AND THAT'S AS MUCH AS WE CAN SEE.
"TO FIND OUT MORE, WE'LL HAVE TO APPROACH IN PERSON.
"BUT GIVEN THE CIRCUMSTANCES, I RECOMMEND AN INFILTRATION RATHER THAN FULL-ON ASSAULT...
"...SINCE WE HAVE NO IDEA WHAT'S GOING ON INSIDE..."

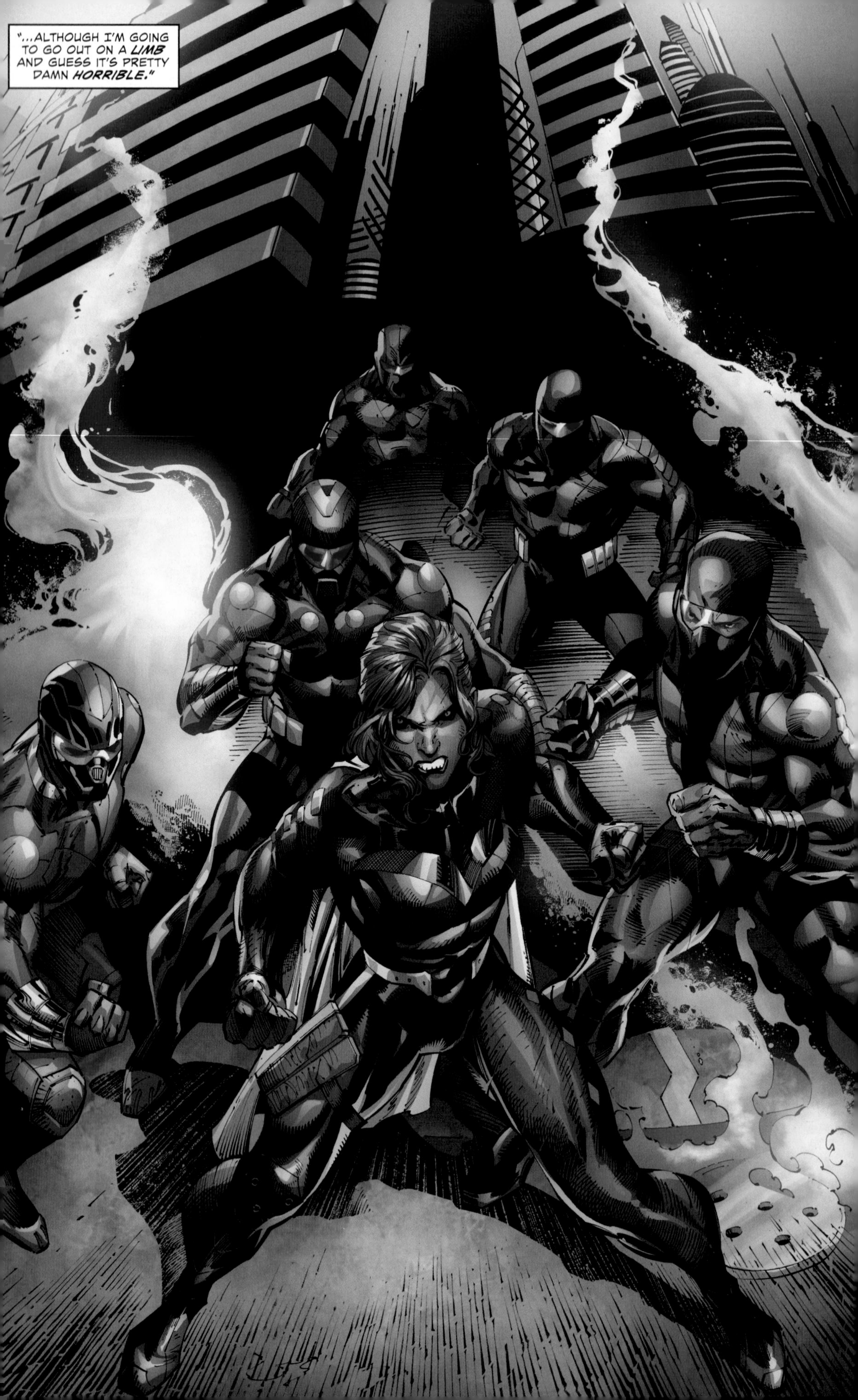
"...ALTHOUGH I'M GOING TO GO OUT ON A *LIMB* AND GUESS IT'S PRETTY DAMN *HORRIBLE.*"

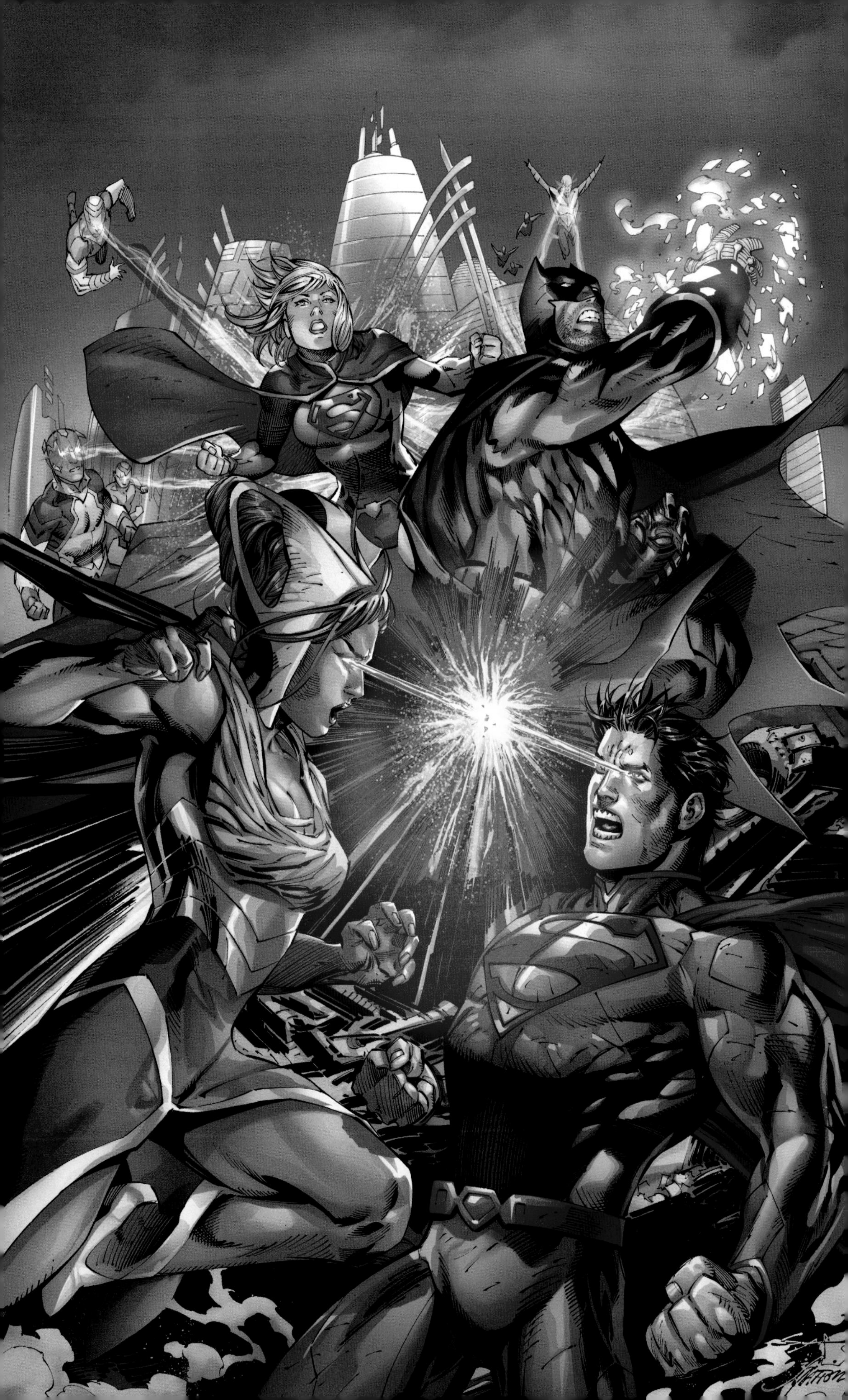

GREG PAK writer ARDIAN SYAF penciller MARK MORALES, JAIME MENDOZA, DON HO, VICENTE CIFUENTES inkers ULISES ARREOLA colorist ROB LEIGH letterer
cover by ARDIAN SYAF, JONATHAN GLAPION and ULISES ARREOLA

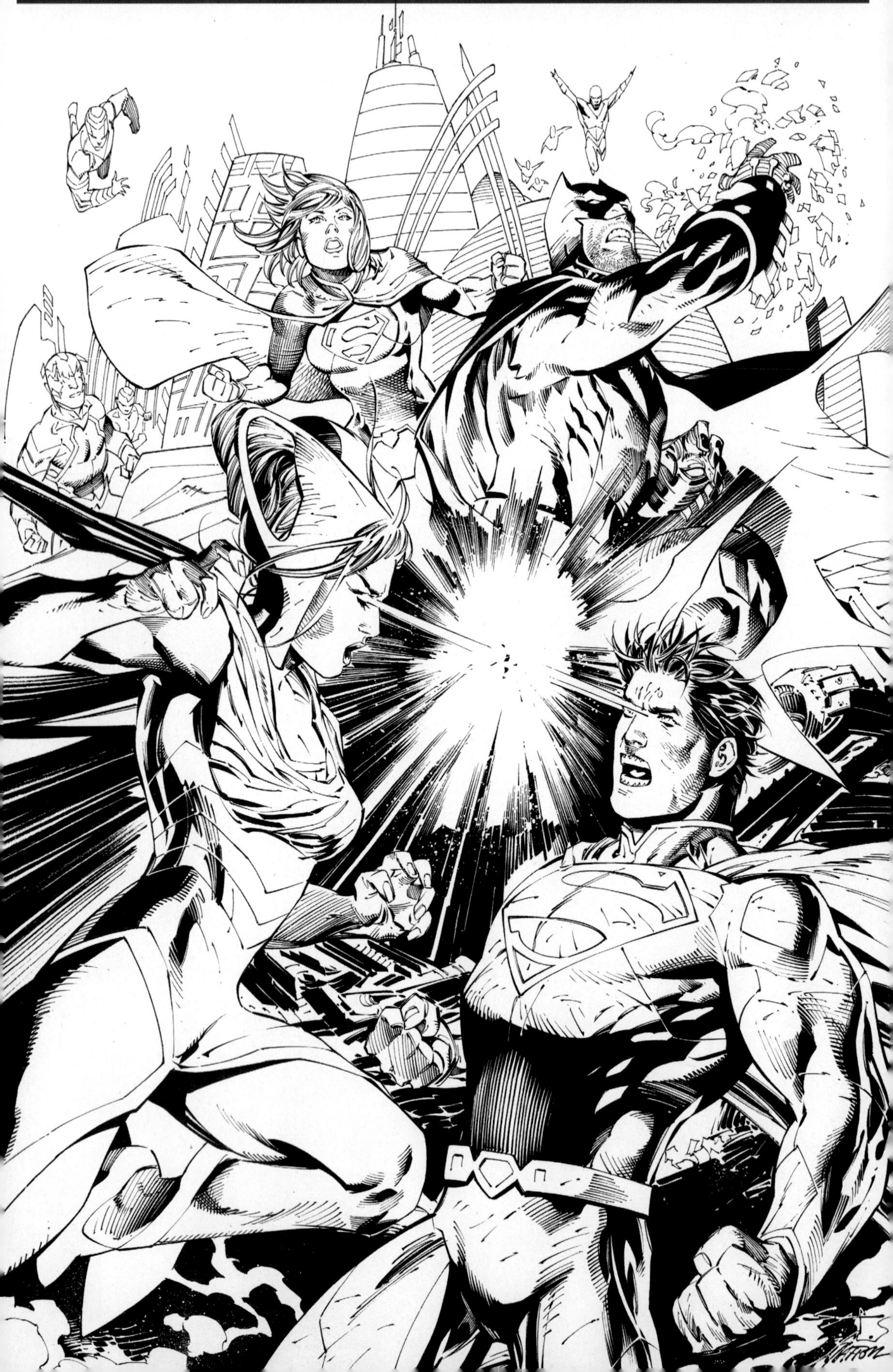

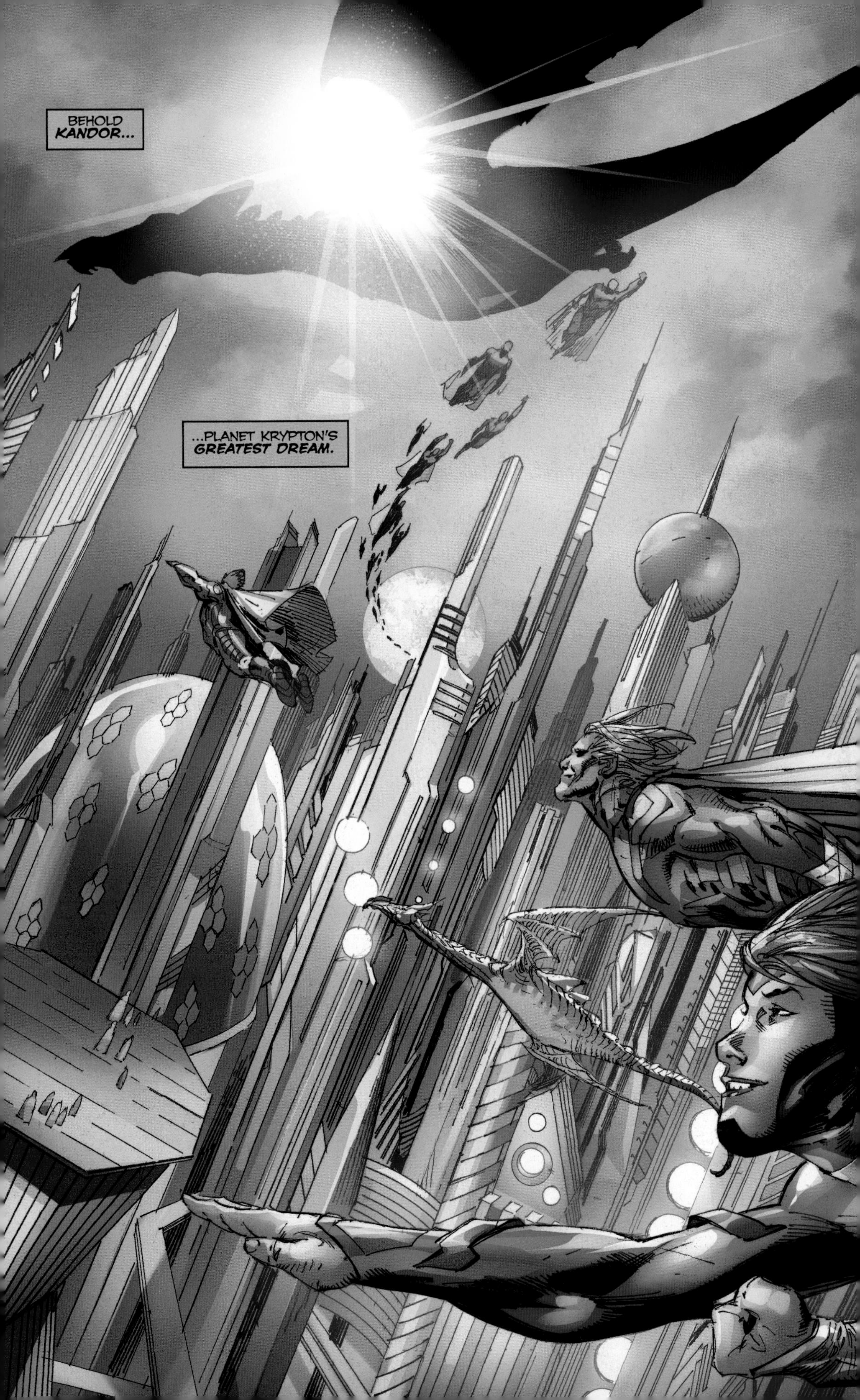
BEHOLD KANDOR...
...PLANET KRYPTON'S GREATEST DREAM.

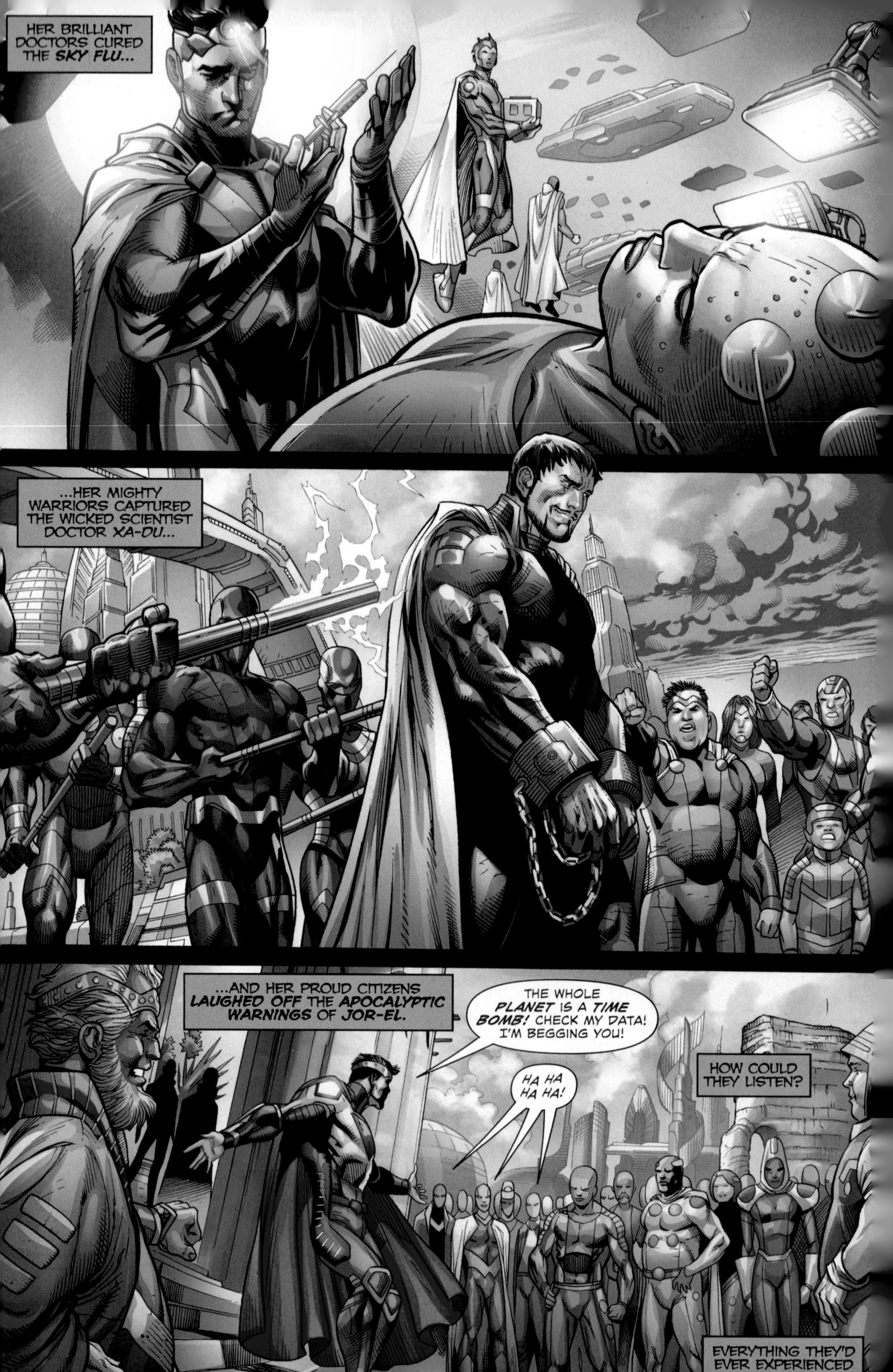
HER BRILLIANT DOCTORS CURED THE SKY FLU...
...HER MIGHTY WARRIORS CAPTURED THE WICKED SCIENTIST DOCTOR XA-DU...
...AND HER PROUD CITIZENS LAUGHED OFF THE APOCALYPTIC WARNINGS OF JOR-EL.
THE WHOLE PLANET IS A TIME BOMB! CHECK MY DATA! I'M BEGGING YOU!
HA HA HA HA!
HOW COULD THEY LISTEN?
EVERYTHING THEY'D EVER EXPERIENCED TOLD THEM...

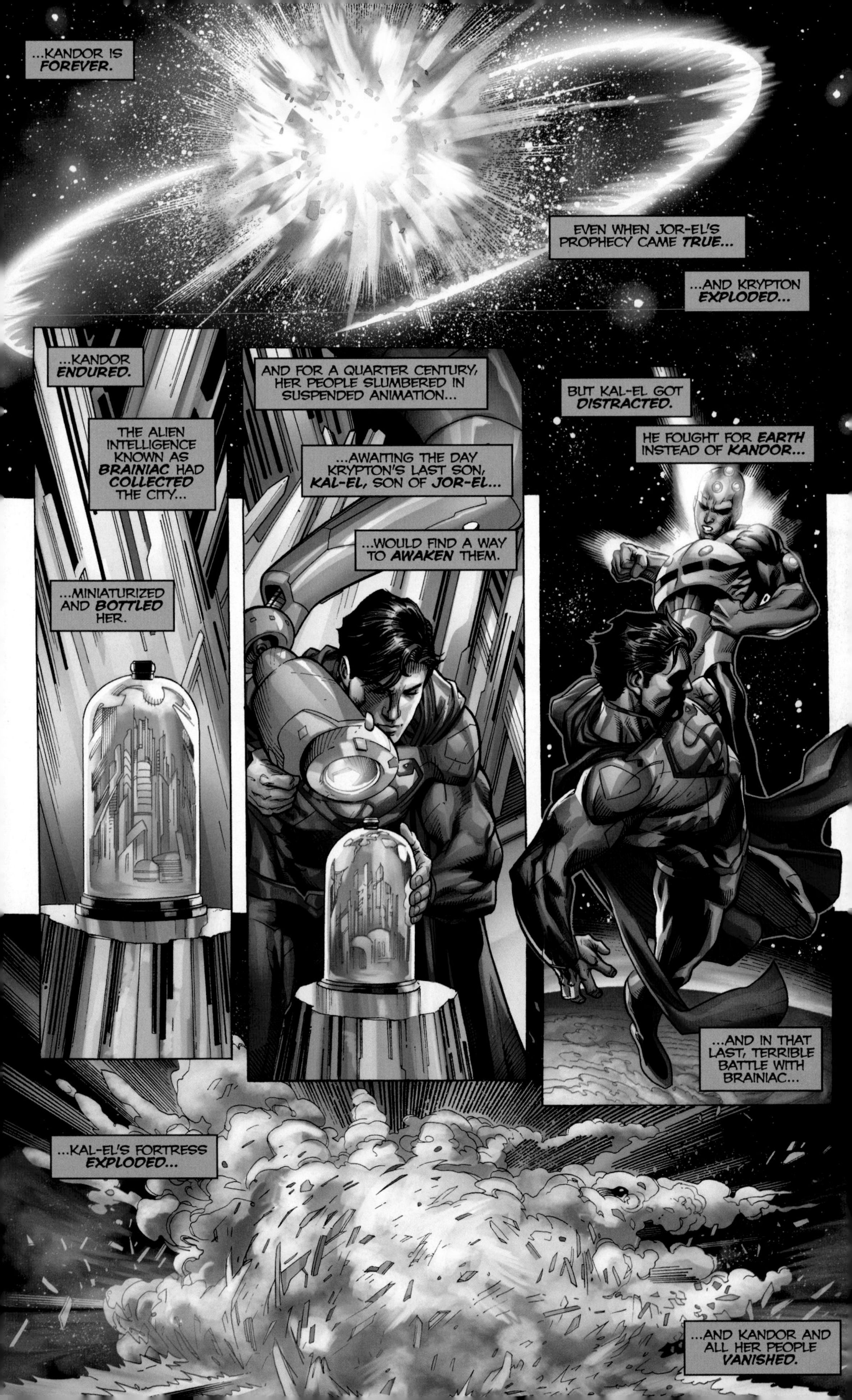

...KANDOR IS FOREVER.
EVEN WHEN JOR-EL'S PROPHECY CAME TRUE...
...AND KRYPTON EXPLODED...
...KANDOR ENDURED.
THE ALIEN INTELLIGENCE KNOWN AS BRAINIAC HAD COLLECTED THE CITY...
...MINIATURIZED AND BOTTLED HER.
AND FOR A QUARTER CENTURY, HER PEOPLE SLUMBERED IN SUSPENDED ANIMATION...
...AWAITING THE DAY KRYPTON'S LAST SON, KAL-EL, SON OF JOR-EL...
...WOULD FIND A WAY TO AWAKEN THEM.
BUT KAL-EL GOT DISTRACTED.
HE FOUGHT FOR EARTH INSTEAD OF KANDOR...
...AND IN THAT LAST, TERRIBLE BATTLE WITH BRAINIAC...
...KAL-EL'S FORTRESS EXPLODED...
...AND KANDOR AND ALL HER PEOPLE VANISHED.

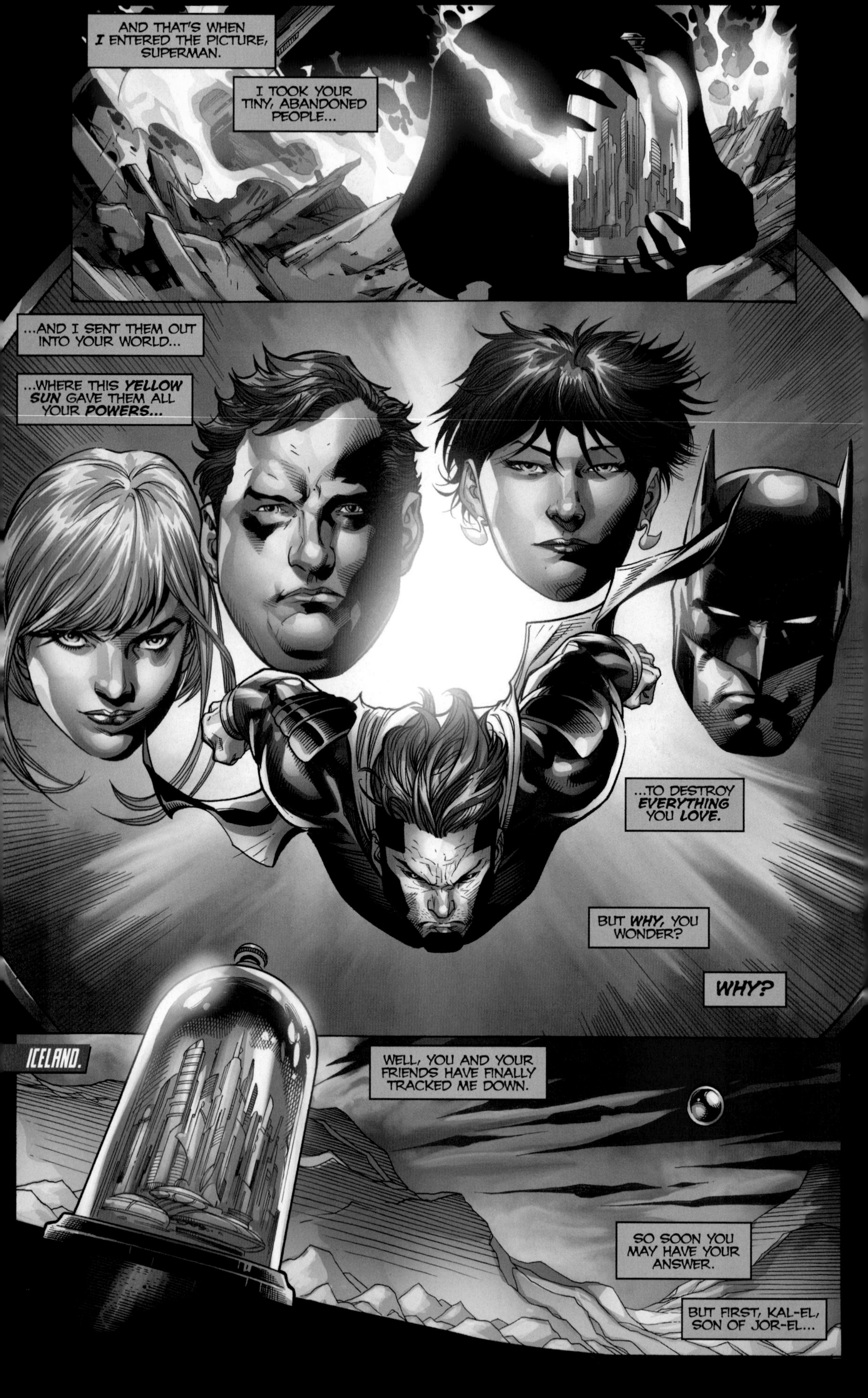
AND THAT'S WHEN *I* ENTERED THE PICTURE, SUPERMAN.
I TOOK YOUR TINY, ABANDONED PEOPLE...
...AND I SENT THEM OUT INTO YOUR WORLD...
...WHERE THIS ***YELLOW SUN*** GAVE THEM ALL YOUR ***POWERS...***
...TO DESTROY ***EVERYTHING*** YOU ***LOVE.***
BUT ***WHY,*** YOU WONDER?
WHY?
ICELAND.
WELL, YOU AND YOUR FRIENDS HAVE FINALLY TRACKED ME DOWN.
SO SOON YOU MAY HAVE YOUR ANSWER.
BUT FIRST, KAL-EL, SON OF JOR-EL...

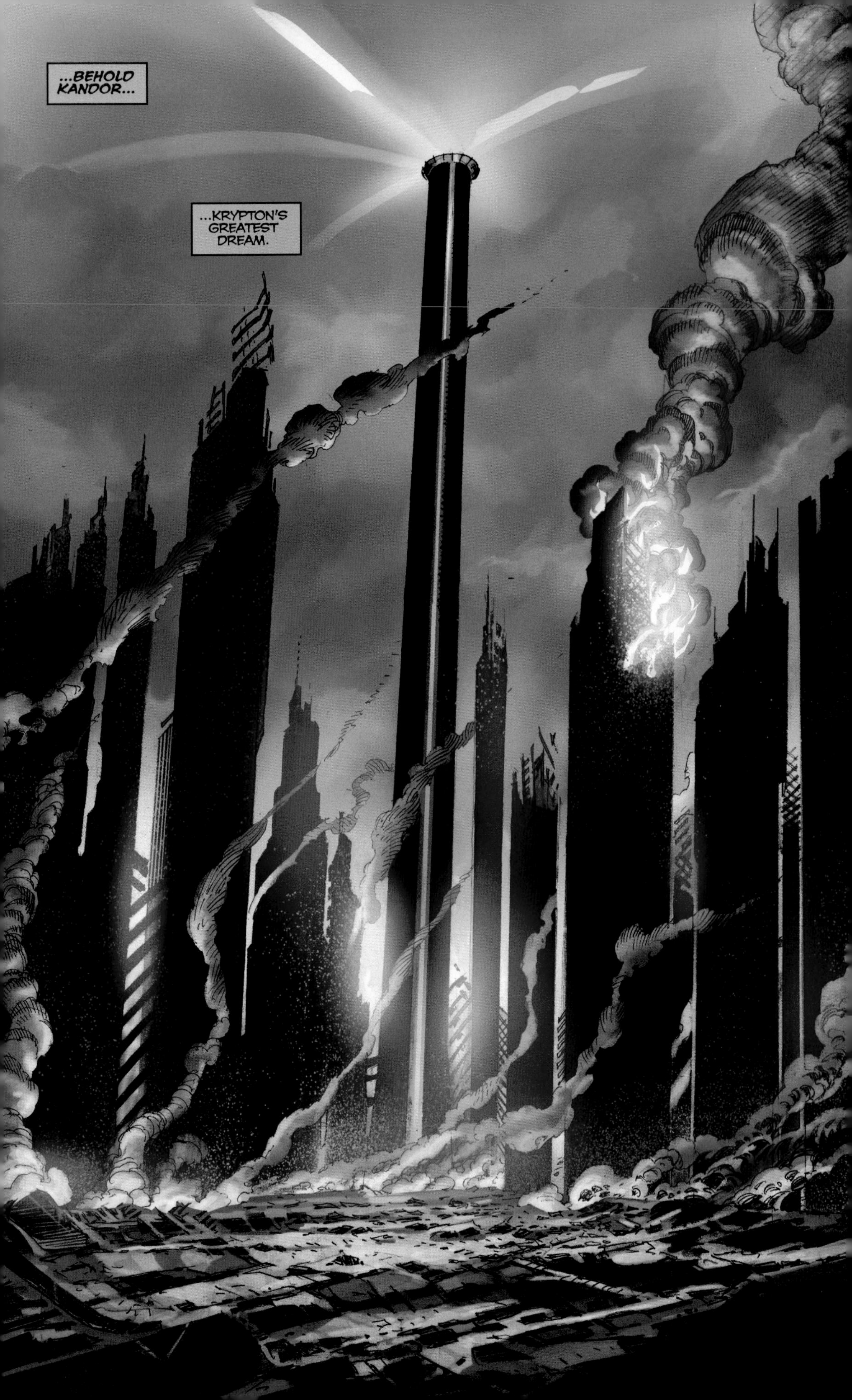
...BEHOLD KANDOR...
...KRYPTON'S GREATEST DREAM.

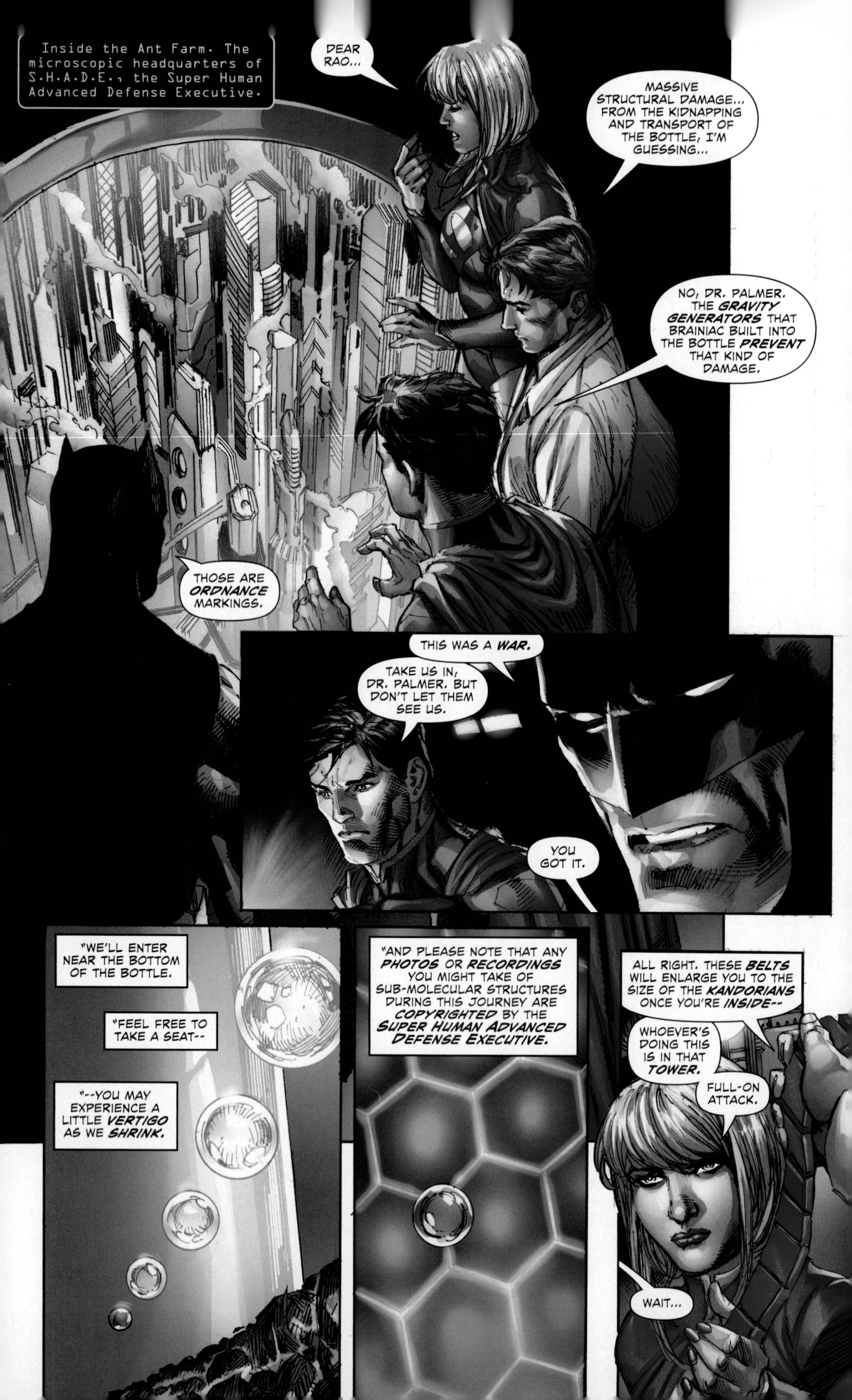

Inside the Ant Farm. The microscopic headquarters of S.H.A.D.E., the Super Human Advanced Defense Executive.
DEAR RAO...
MASSIVE STRUCTURAL DAMAGE... FROM THE KIDNAPPING AND TRANSPORT OF THE BOTTLE, I'M GUESSING...
NO, DR. PALMER. THE GRAVITY GENERATORS THAT BRAINIAC BUILT INTO THE BOTTLE PREVENT THAT KIND OF DAMAGE.
THOSE ARE ORDNANCE MARKINGS.
THIS WAS A WAR.
TAKE US IN, DR. PALMER. BUT DON'T LET THEM SEE US.
YOU GOT IT.
"WE'LL ENTER NEAR THE BOTTOM OF THE BOTTLE.
"FEEL FREE TO TAKE A SEAT--
"--YOU MAY EXPERIENCE A LITTLE VERTIGO AS WE SHRINK.
"AND PLEASE NOTE THAT ANY PHOTOS OR RECORDINGS YOU MIGHT TAKE OF SUB-MOLECULAR STRUCTURES DURING THIS JOURNEY ARE COPYRIGHTED BY THE SUPER HUMAN ADVANCED DEFENSE EXECUTIVE.
ALL RIGHT. THESE BELTS WILL ENLARGE YOU TO THE SIZE OF THE KANDORIANS ONCE YOU'RE INSIDE--
WHOEVER'S DOING THIS IS IN THAT TOWER.
FULL-ON ATTACK.
WAIT...

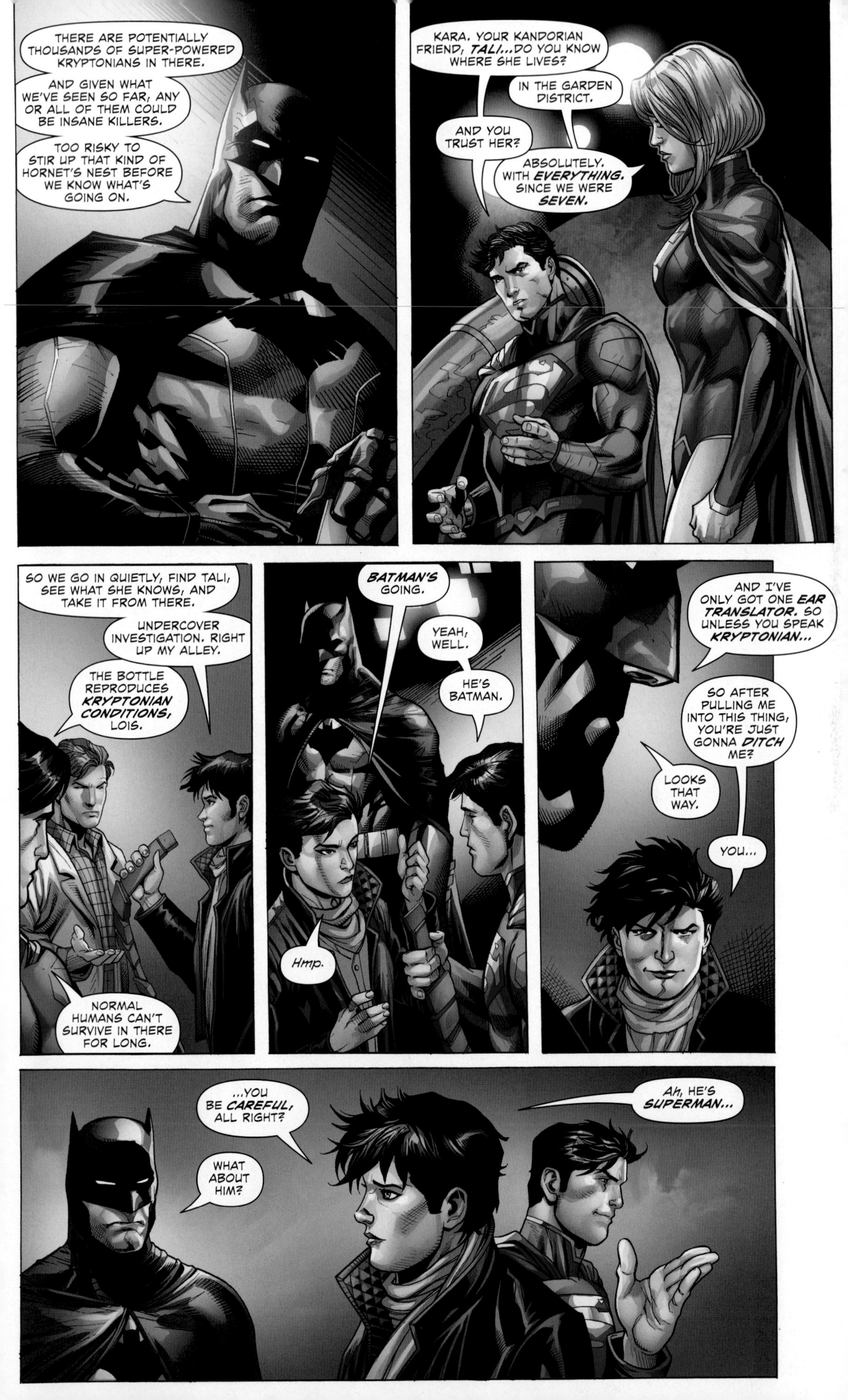

THERE ARE POTENTIALLY THOUSANDS OF SUPER-POWERED KRYPTONIANS IN THERE.
AND GIVEN WHAT WE'VE SEEN SO FAR, ANY OR ALL OF THEM COULD BE INSANE KILLERS.
TOO RISKY TO STIR UP THAT KIND OF HORNET'S NEST BEFORE WE KNOW WHAT'S GOING ON.
KARA. YOUR KANDORIAN FRIEND, TALI...DO YOU KNOW WHERE SHE LIVES?
IN THE GARDEN DISTRICT.
AND YOU TRUST HER?
ABSOLUTELY. WITH EVERYTHING. SINCE WE WERE SEVEN.
SO WE GO IN QUIETLY, FIND TALI, SEE WHAT SHE KNOWS, AND TAKE IT FROM THERE.
UNDERCOVER INVESTIGATION. RIGHT UP MY ALLEY.
THE BOTTLE REPRODUCES KRYPTONIAN CONDITIONS, LOIS.
NORMAL HUMANS CAN'T SURVIVE IN THERE FOR LONG.
BATMAN'S GOING.
YEAH, WELL.
HE'S BATMAN.
Hmp.
AND I'VE ONLY GOT ONE EAR TRANSLATOR. SO UNLESS YOU SPEAK KRYPTONIAN...
SO AFTER PULLING ME INTO THIS THING, YOU'RE JUST GONNA DITCH ME?
LOOKS THAT WAY.
YOU...
...YOU BE CAREFUL, ALL RIGHT?
WHAT ABOUT HIM?
Ah, HE'S SUPERMAN...

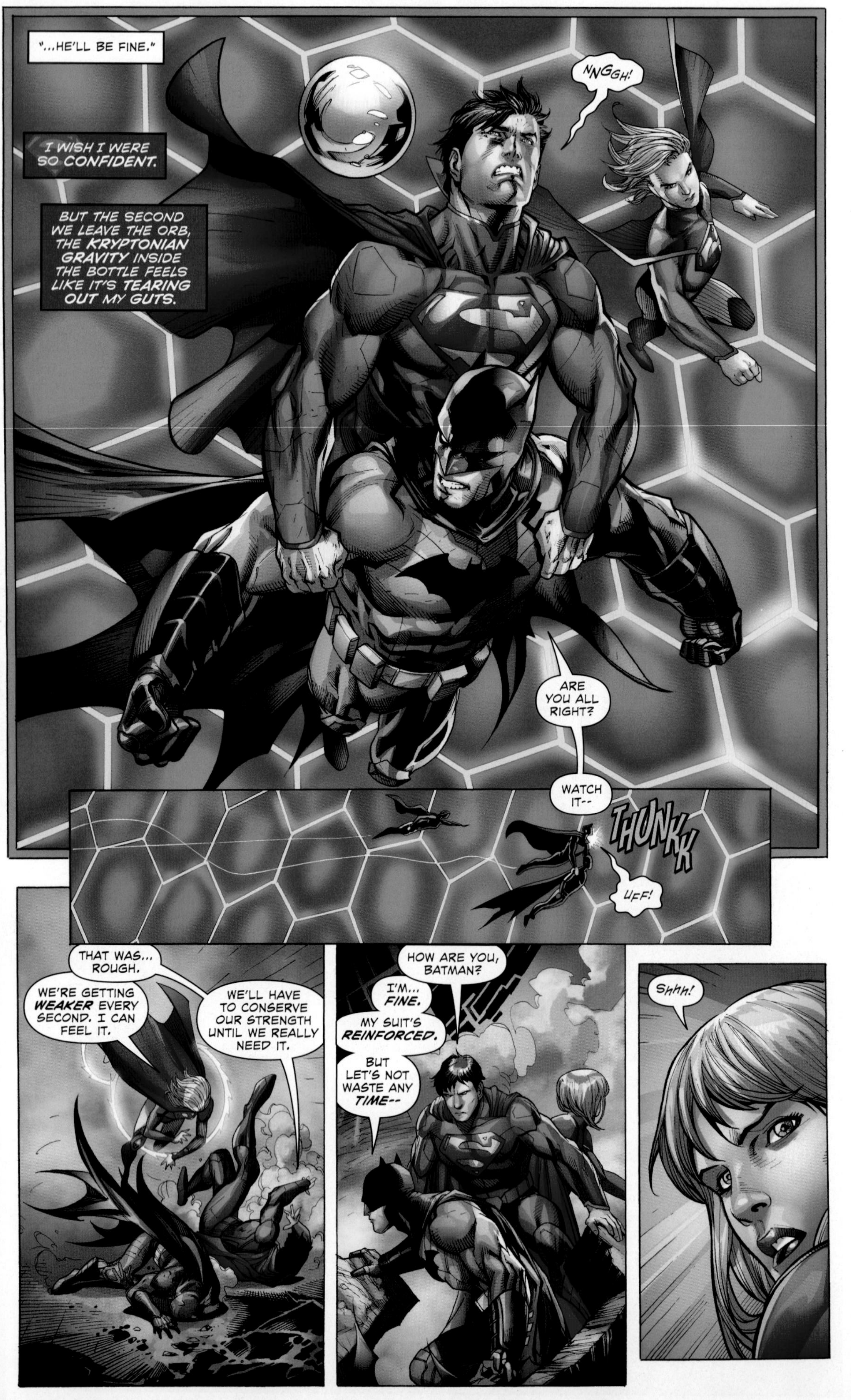
"...HE'LL BE FINE."
I WISH I WERE SO CONFIDENT.
BUT THE SECOND WE LEAVE THE ORB, THE KRYPTONIAN GRAVITY INSIDE THE BOTTLE FEELS LIKE IT'S TEARING OUT MY GUTS.
NNGGH!
ARE YOU ALL RIGHT?
WATCH IT--
THUNKK
UFF!
THAT WAS... ROUGH.
WE'RE GETTING WEAKER EVERY SECOND. I CAN FEEL IT.
WE'LL HAVE TO CONSERVE OUR STRENGTH UNTIL WE REALLY NEED IT.
HOW ARE YOU, BATMAN?
I'M... FINE.
MY SUIT'S REINFORCED.
BUT LET'S NOT WASTE ANY TIME--
Shhh!

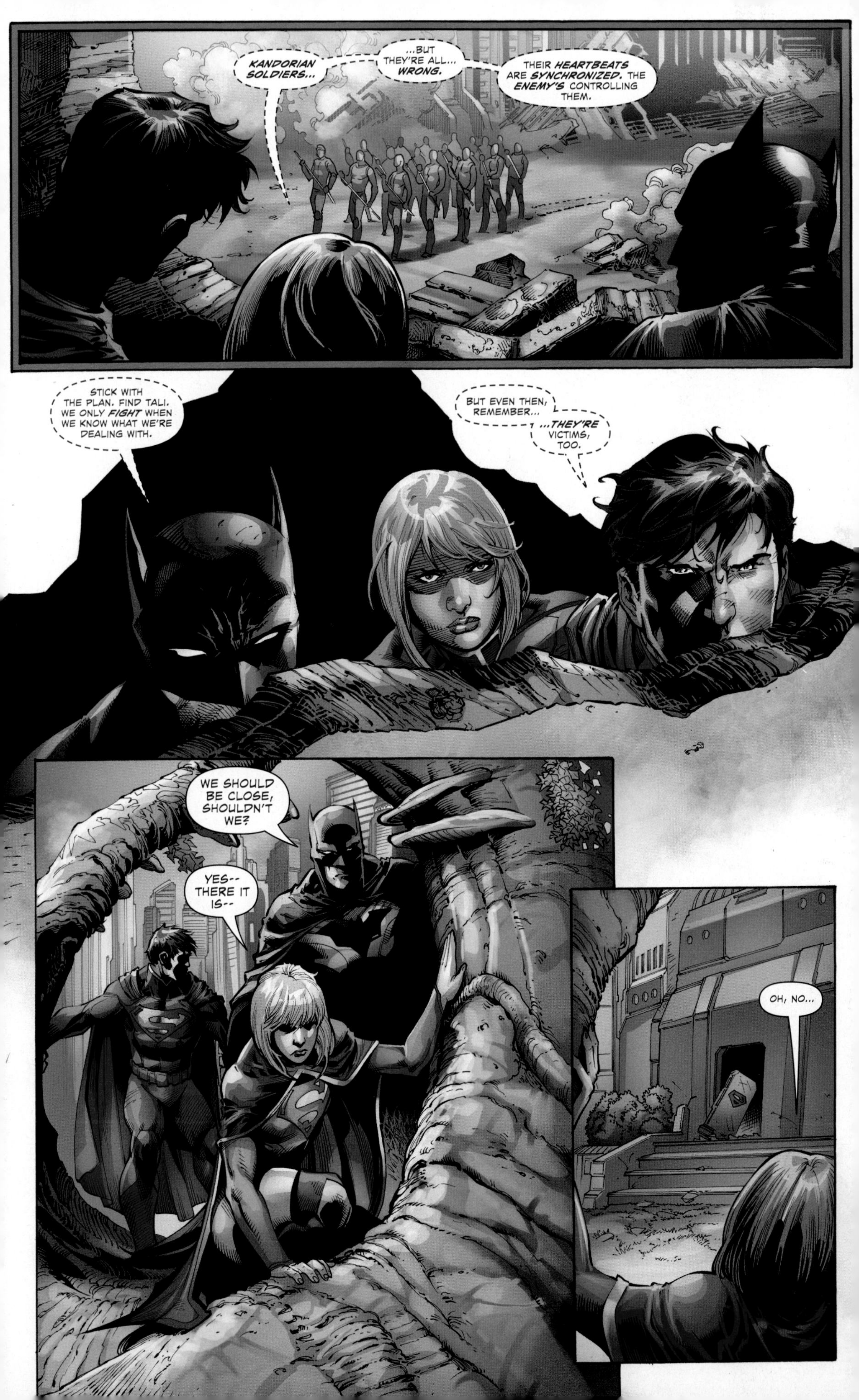
KANDORIAN SOLDIERS...
...BUT THEY'RE ALL... WRONG.
THEIR HEARTBEATS ARE SYNCHRONIZED. THE ENEMY'S CONTROLLING THEM.
STICK WITH THE PLAN. FIND TALI. WE ONLY FIGHT WHEN WE KNOW WHAT WE'RE DEALING WITH.
BUT EVEN THEN, REMEMBER...
...THEY'RE VICTIMS, TOO.
WE SHOULD BE CLOSE, SHOULDN'T WE?
YES-- THERE IT IS--
OH, NO...

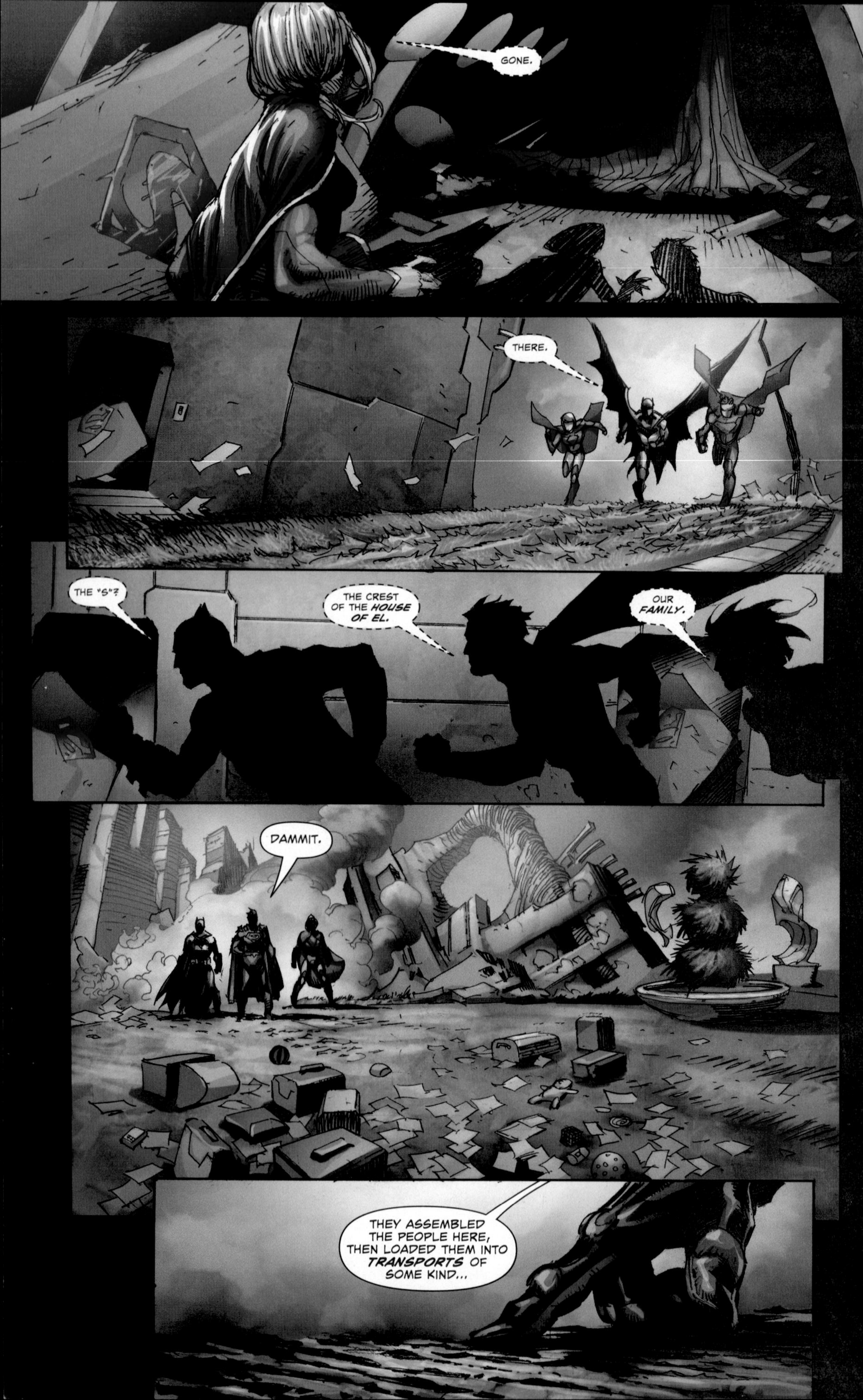
GONE.
THERE.
THE "S"?
THE CREST OF THE *HOUSE OF EL.*
OUR *FAMILY.*
DAMMIT.
THEY ASSEMBLED THE PEOPLE HERE, THEN LOADED THEM INTO *TRANSPORTS* OF SOME KIND...

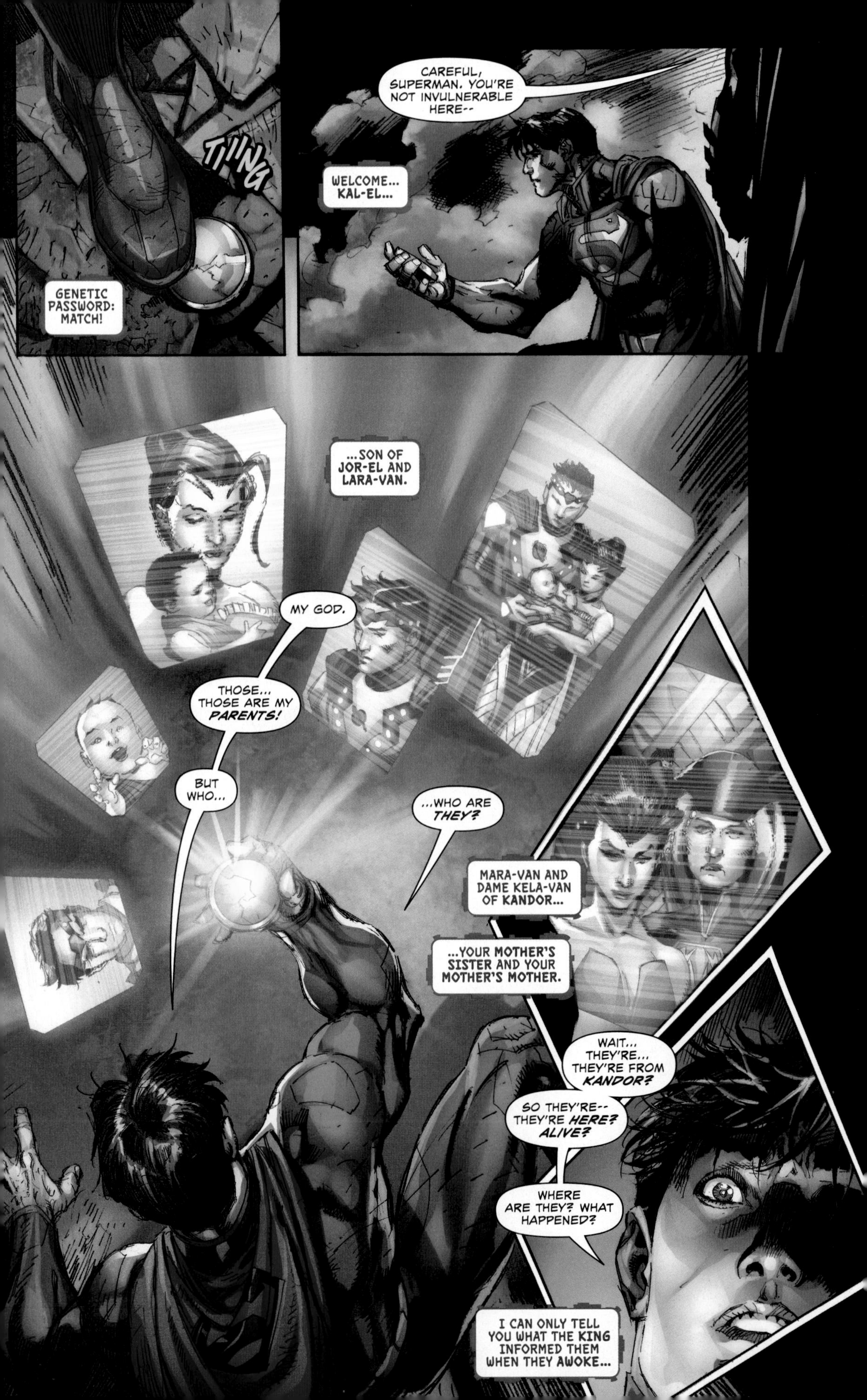
TIIING
GENETIC PASSWORD: MATCH!
CAREFUL, SUPERMAN. YOU'RE NOT INVULNERABLE HERE--
WELCOME... KAL-EL...
...SON OF JOR-EL AND LARA-VAN.
MY GOD.
THOSE... THOSE ARE MY *PARENTS!*
BUT WHO...
...WHO ARE *THEY?*
MARA-VAN AND DAME KELA-VAN OF KANDOR...
...YOUR MOTHER'S SISTER AND YOUR MOTHER'S MOTHER.
WAIT... THEY'RE... THEY'RE FROM *KANDOR?*
SO THEY'RE-- THEY'RE *HERE? ALIVE?*
WHERE ARE THEY? WHAT HAPPENED?
I CAN ONLY TELL YOU WHAT THE KING INFORMED THEM WHEN THEY AWOKE...

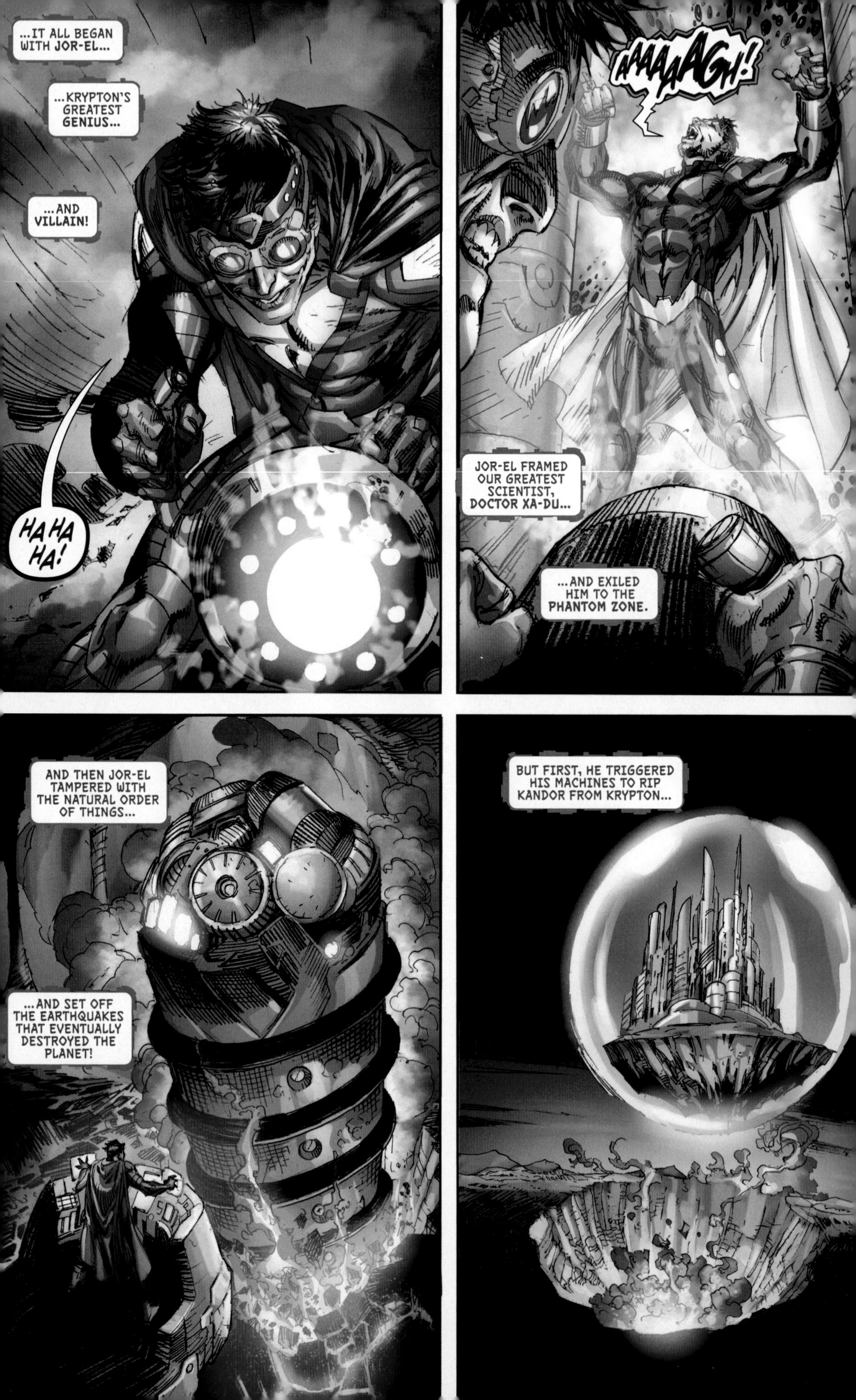
...IT ALL BEGAN WITH JOR-EL...
...KRYPTON'S GREATEST GENIUS...
...AND VILLAIN!
HA HA HA!
AAAAAAGH!
JOR-EL FRAMED OUR GREATEST SCIENTIST, DOCTOR XA-DU...
...AND EXILED HIM TO THE PHANTOM ZONE.
AND THEN JOR-EL TAMPERED WITH THE NATURAL ORDER OF THINGS...
...AND SET OFF THE EARTHQUAKES THAT EVENTUALLY DESTROYED THE PLANET!
BUT FIRST, HE TRIGGERED HIS MACHINES TO RIP KANDOR FROM KRYPTON...

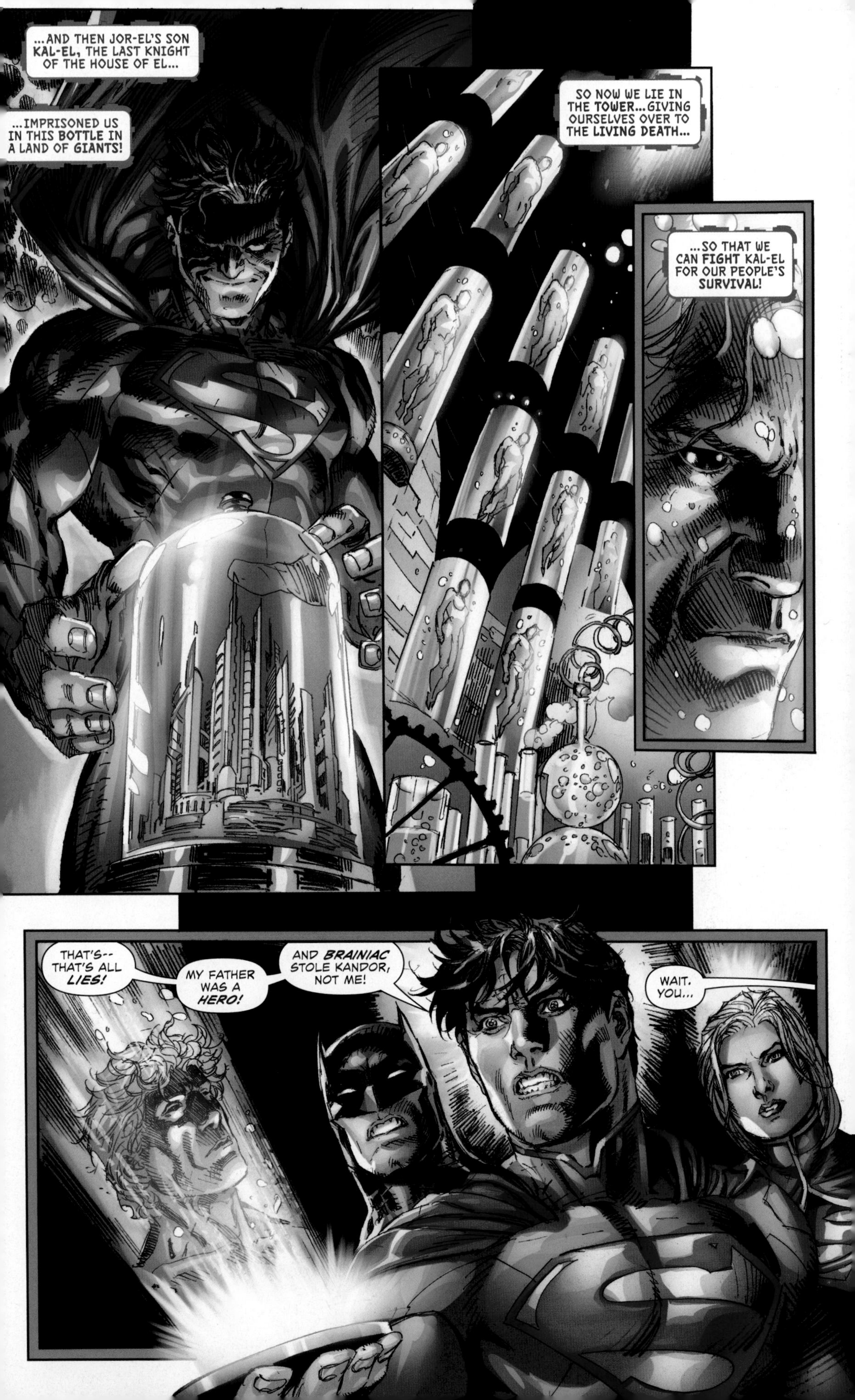
...AND THEN JOR-EL'S SON KAL-EL, THE LAST KNIGHT OF THE HOUSE OF EL...
...IMPRISONED US IN THIS BOTTLE IN A LAND OF GIANTS!
SO NOW WE LIE IN THE TOWER...GIVING OURSELVES OVER TO THE LIVING DEATH...
...SO THAT WE CAN FIGHT KAL-EL FOR OUR PEOPLE'S SURVIVAL!
THAT'S-- THAT'S ALL LIES!
MY FATHER WAS A HERO!
AND BRAINIAC STOLE KANDOR, NOT ME!
WAIT. YOU...

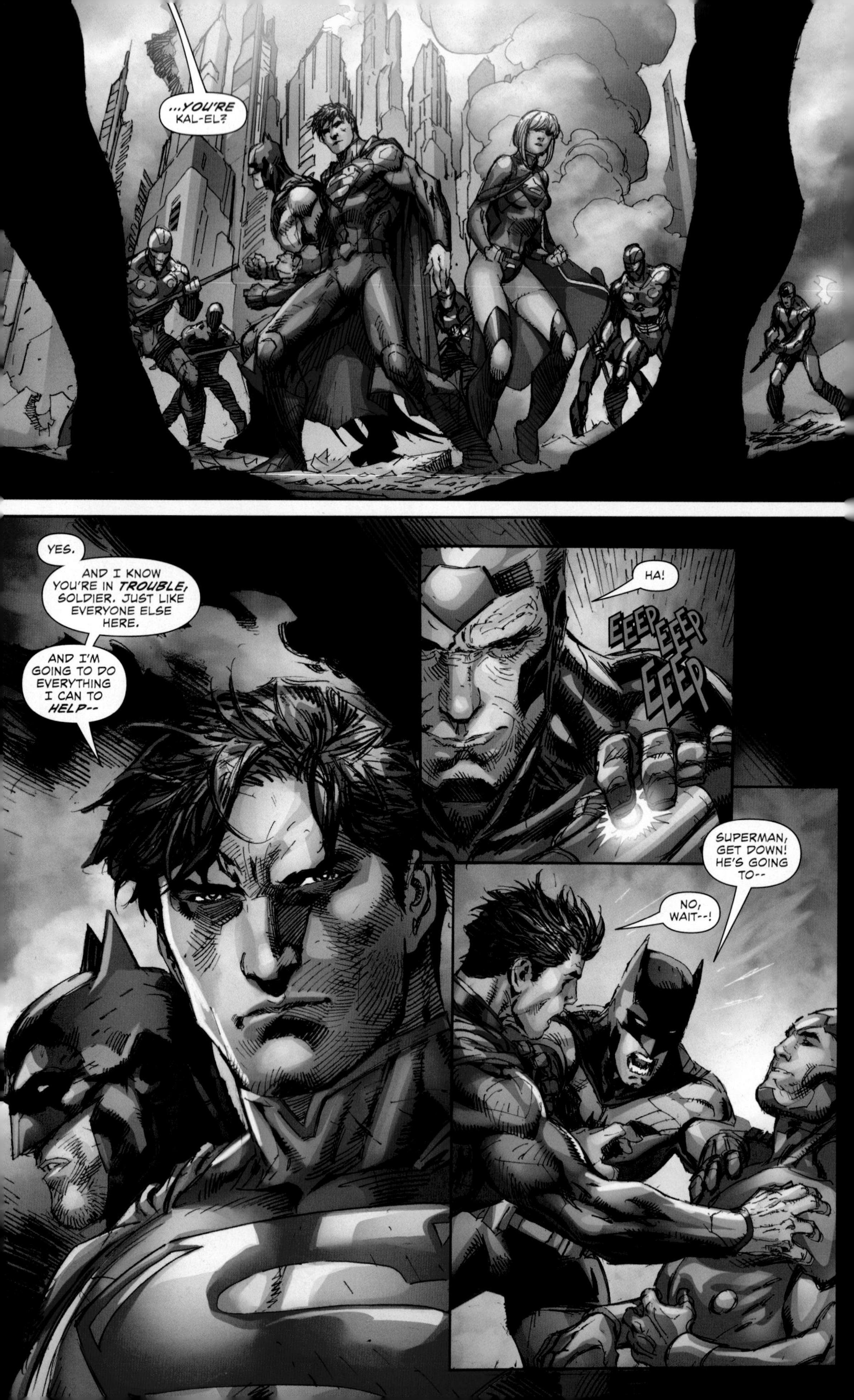
...YOU'RE KAL-EL?
YES.
AND I KNOW YOU'RE IN *TROUBLE*, SOLDIER. JUST LIKE EVERYONE ELSE HERE.
AND I'M GOING TO DO EVERYTHING I CAN TO *HELP*--
HA!
EEEP EEEP EEEP
SUPERMAN, GET DOWN! HE'S GOING TO--
NO, WAIT--!

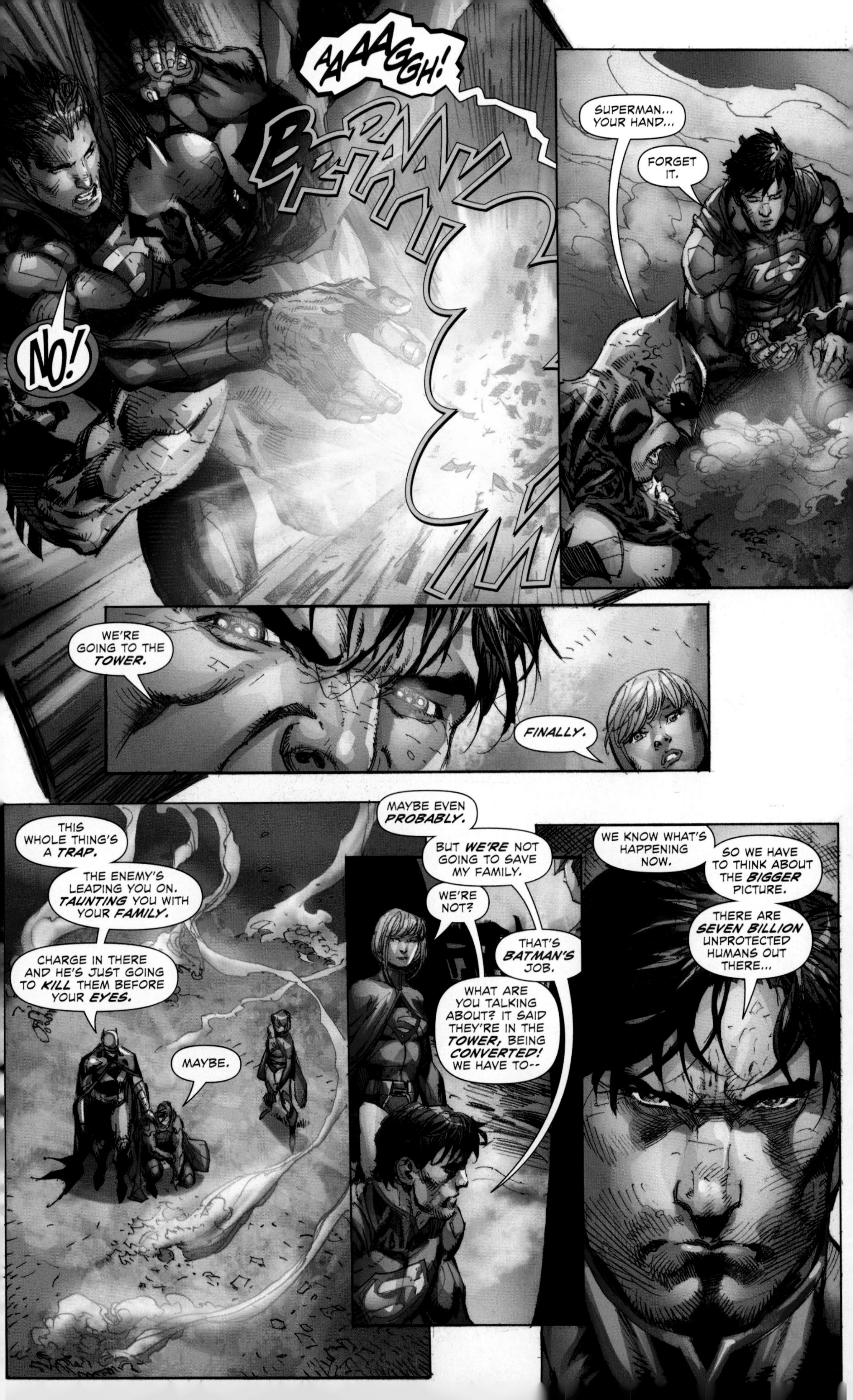
AAAAGGH!
BRRRAAKK
NO!
SUPERMAN... YOUR HAND...
FORGET IT.
WE'RE GOING TO THE TOWER.
FINALLY.
THIS WHOLE THING'S A TRAP.
THE ENEMY'S LEADING YOU ON. TAUNTING YOU WITH YOUR FAMILY.
CHARGE IN THERE AND HE'S JUST GOING TO KILL THEM BEFORE YOUR EYES.
MAYBE.
MAYBE EVEN PROBABLY.
BUT WE'RE NOT GOING TO SAVE MY FAMILY.
WE'RE NOT?
THAT'S BATMAN'S JOB.
WHAT ARE YOU TALKING ABOUT? IT SAID THEY'RE IN THE TOWER, BEING CONVERTED! WE HAVE TO--
WE KNOW WHAT'S HAPPENING NOW.
SO WE HAVE TO THINK ABOUT THE BIGGER PICTURE.
THERE ARE SEVEN BILLION UNPROTECTED HUMANS OUT THERE...

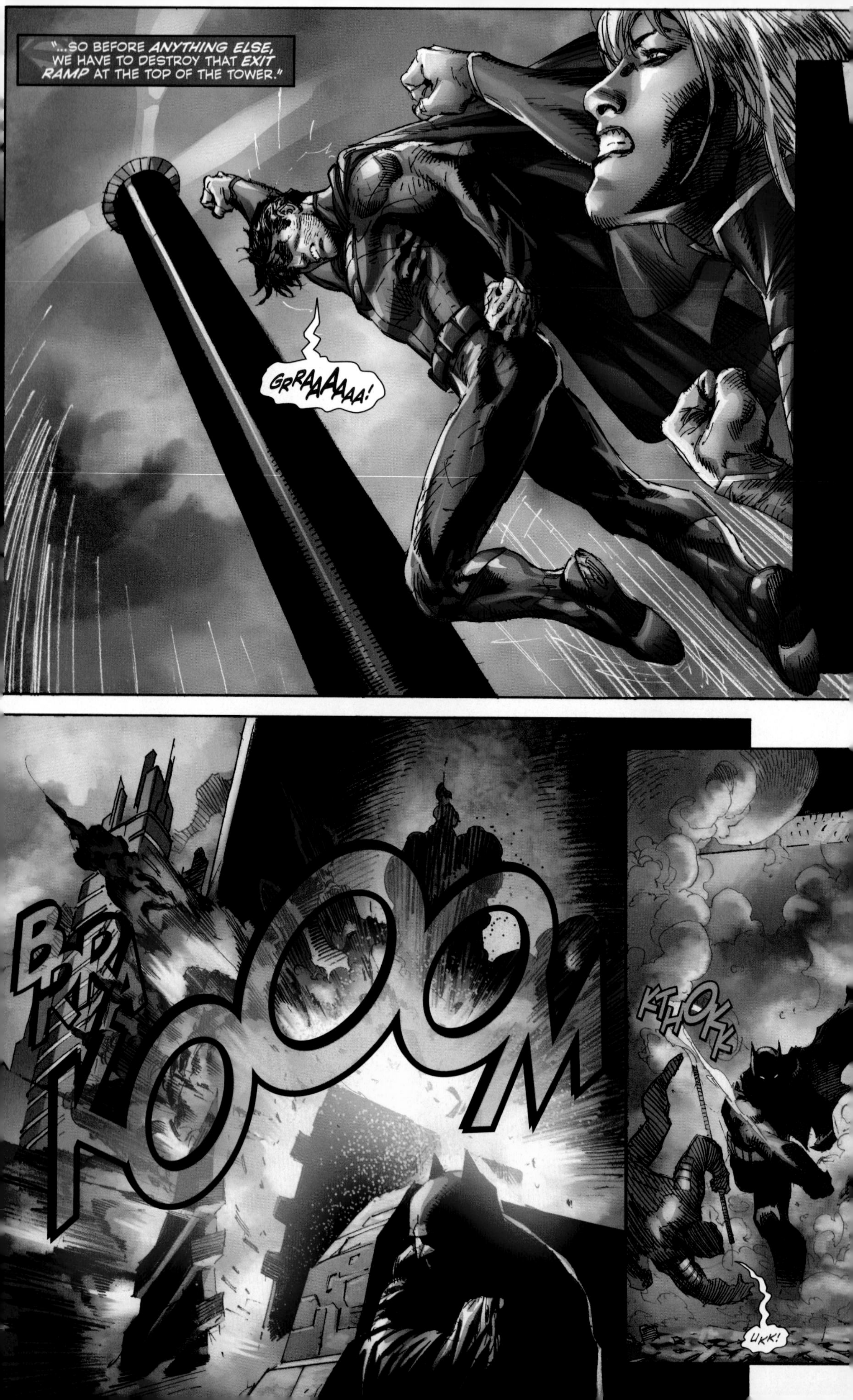
"...SO BEFORE ANYTHING ELSE, WE HAVE TO DESTROY THAT EXIT RAMP AT THE TOP OF THE TOWER."
GRRAAAAAA!
B-DA-DA-BOOOOM
KTHOKK
UKK!

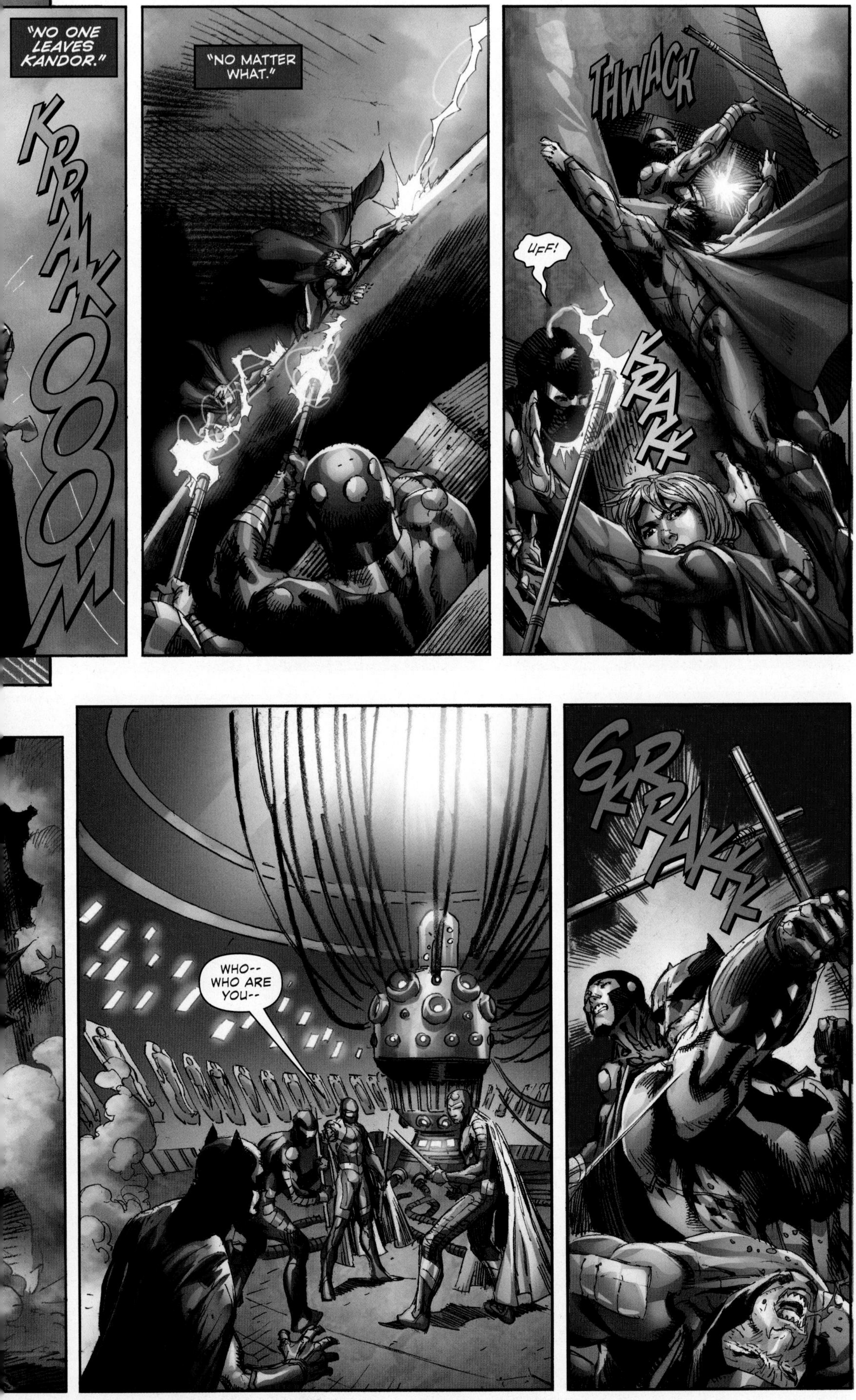
"NO ONE LEAVES KANDOR."
KRRAKOOOM
"NO MATTER WHAT."
THWACK
UFF!
KRAKK
WHO-- WHO ARE YOU--
SKRRAKKK

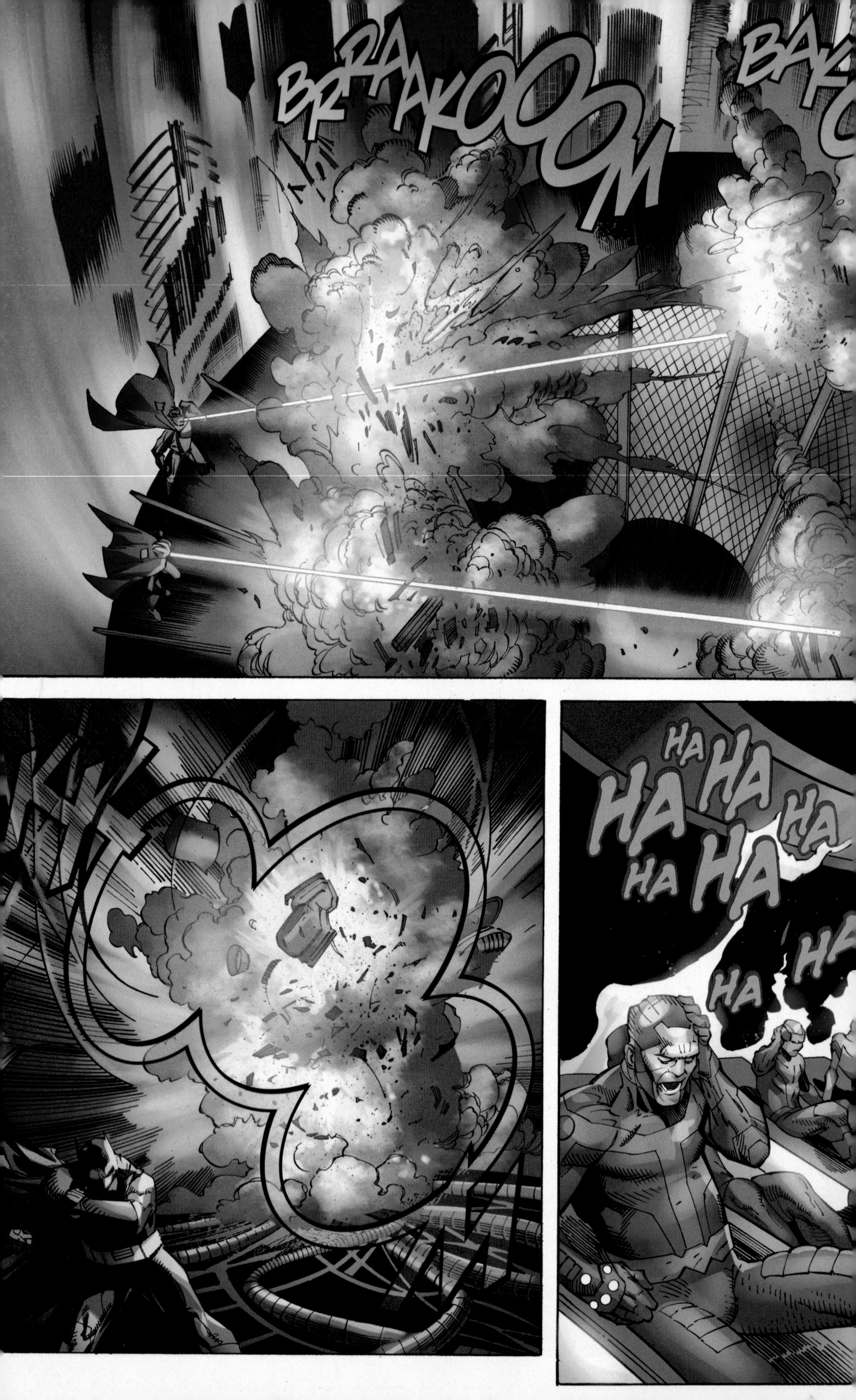
BRRAAKOOOOM
BAK
HA HA HA HA HA HA HA
HA HA

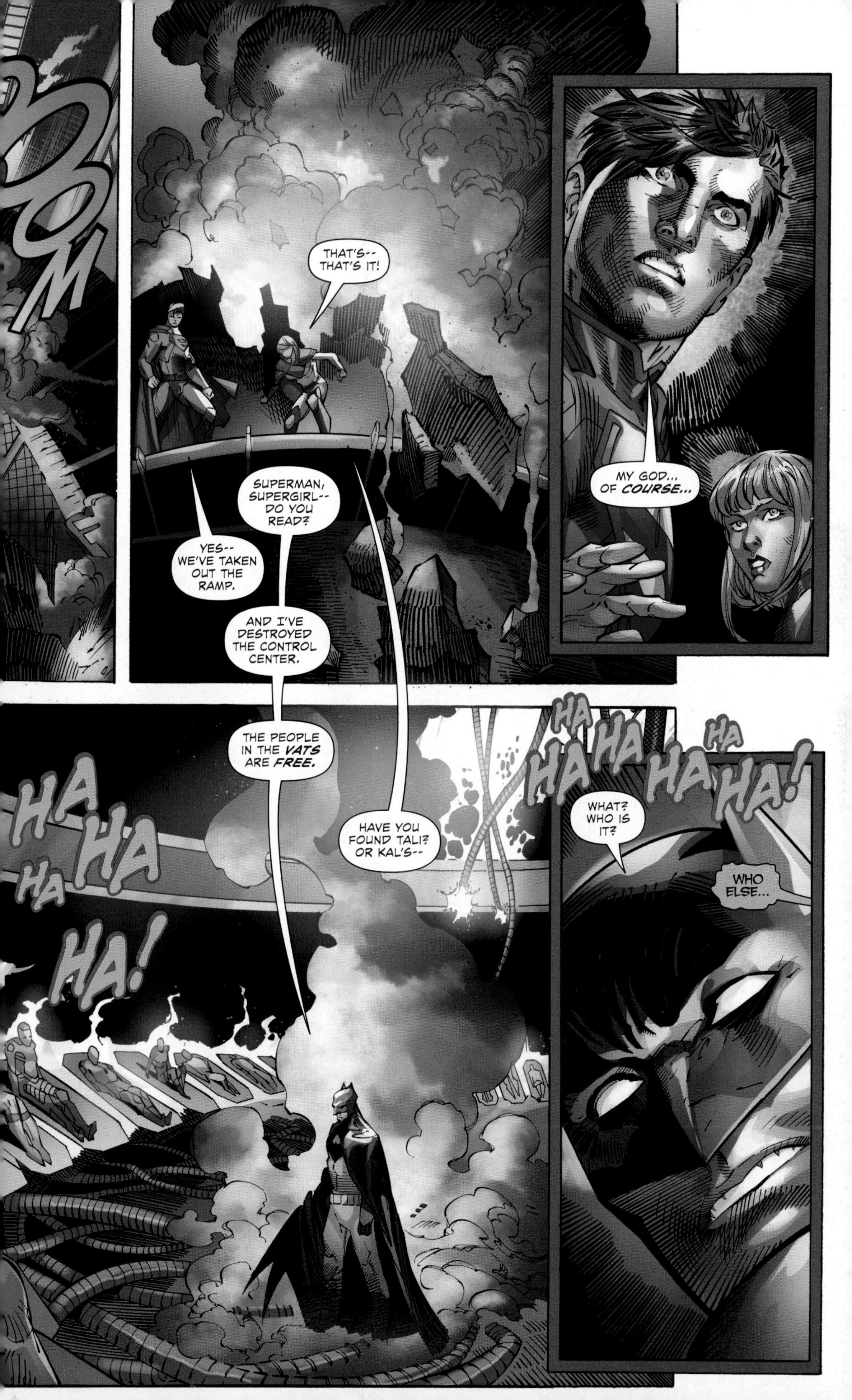
BOOM
THAT'S--
THAT'S IT!
MY GOD...
OF COURSE...
SUPERMAN, SUPERGIRL--
DO YOU READ?
YES--
WE'VE TAKEN OUT THE RAMP.
AND I'VE DESTROYED THE CONTROL CENTER.
THE PEOPLE IN THE VATS ARE FREE.
HAVE YOU FOUND TALI? OR KAL'S--
HA HA HA HA HA HA HA HA HA!
HA HA HA HA HA!
WHAT? WHO IS IT?
WHO ELSE...

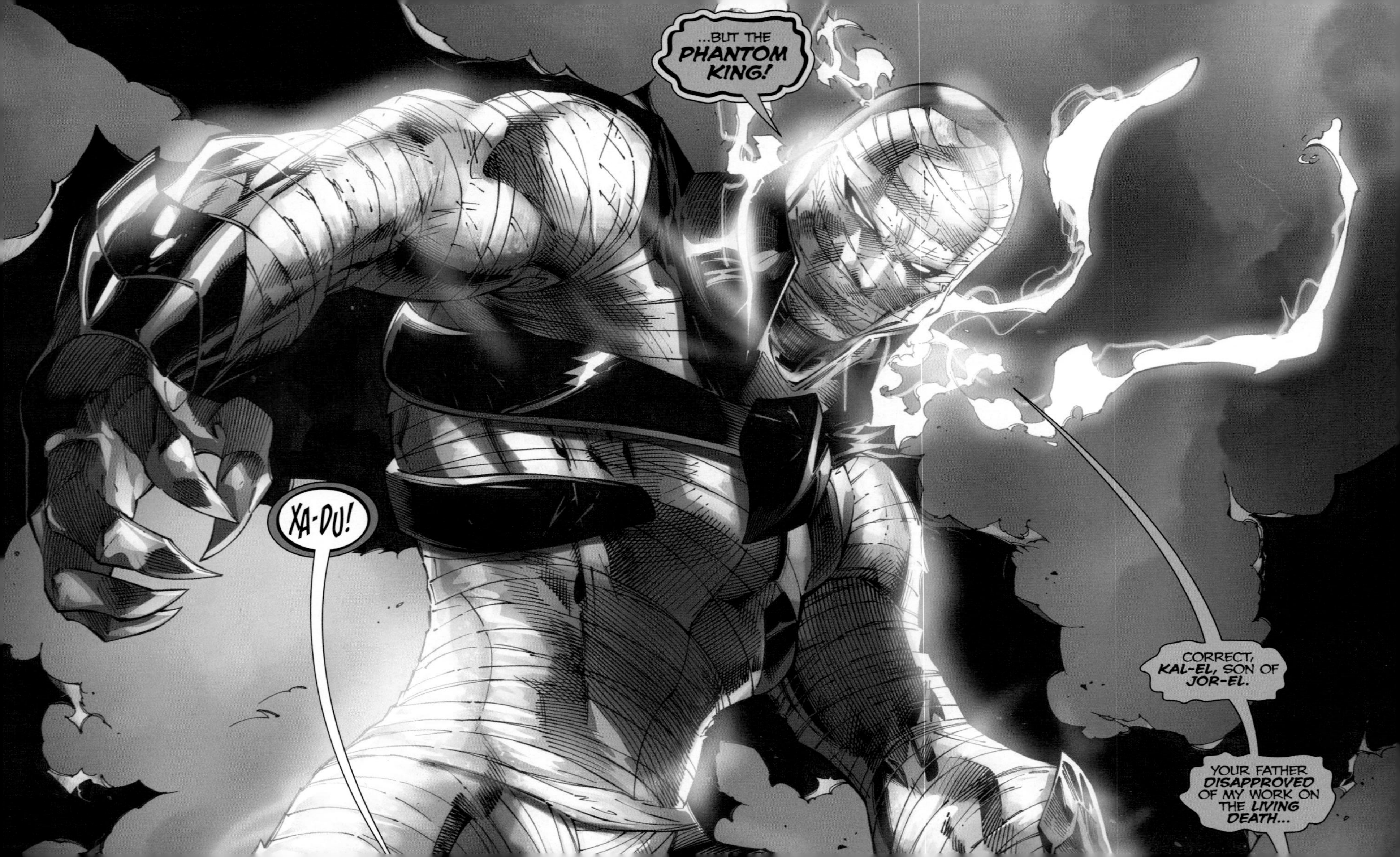
...BUT THE *PHANTOM KING!*
XA-DU!
CORRECT, *KAL-EL*, SON OF *JOR-EL*.
YOUR FATHER *DISAPPROVED* OF MY WORK ON THE *LIVING DEATH*...

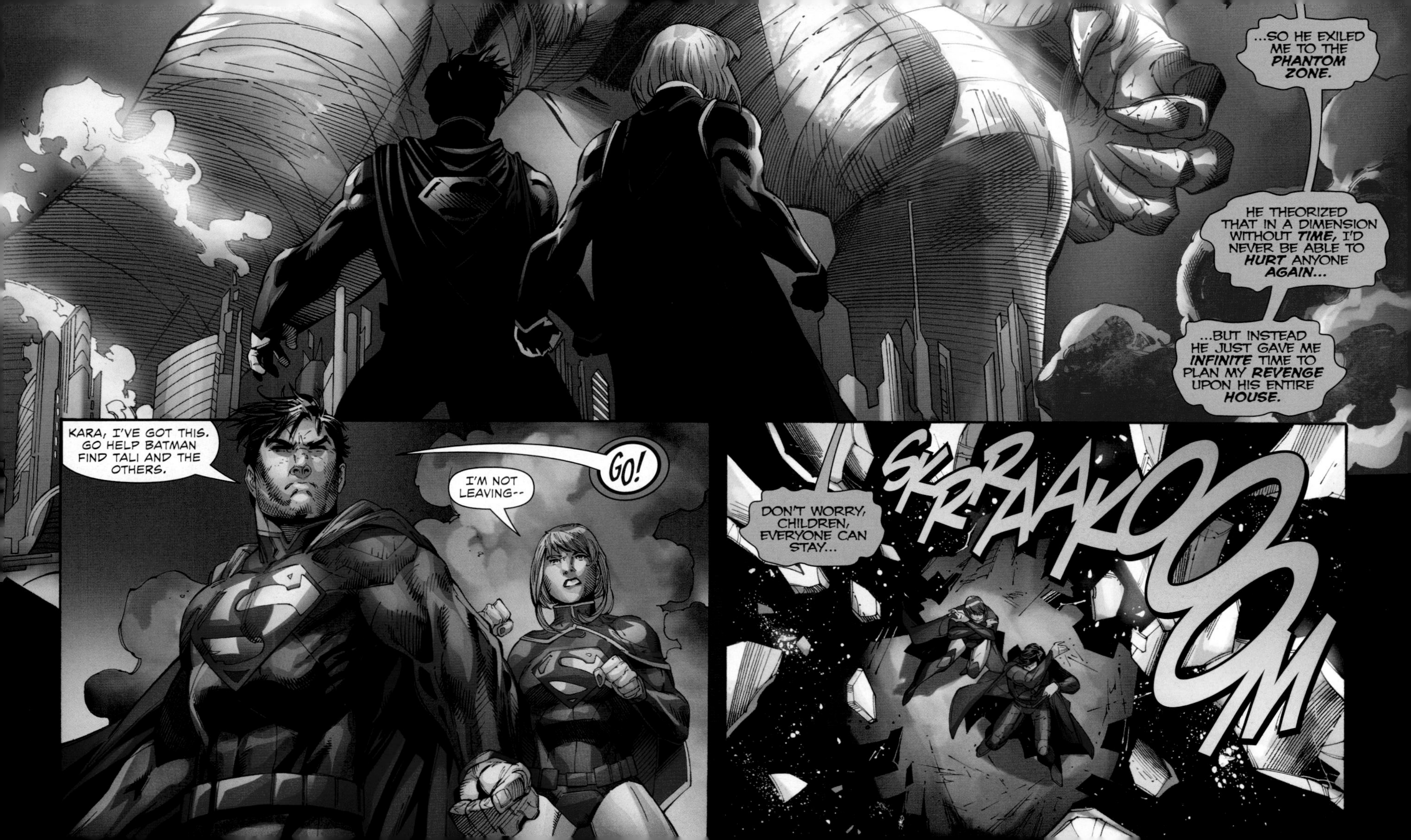
...SO HE EXILED ME TO THE *PHANTOM ZONE.*
HE THEORIZED THAT IN A DIMENSION WITHOUT *TIME,* I'D NEVER BE ABLE TO *HURT* ANYONE *AGAIN...*
...BUT INSTEAD HE JUST GAVE ME *INFINITE* TIME TO PLAN MY *REVENGE* UPON HIS ENTIRE *HOUSE.*
KARA, I'VE GOT THIS. GO HELP BATMAN FIND TALI AND THE OTHERS.
I'M NOT LEAVING--
GO!
DON'T WORRY, CHILDREN, EVERYONE CAN STAY...
SKRRAAKOOOM

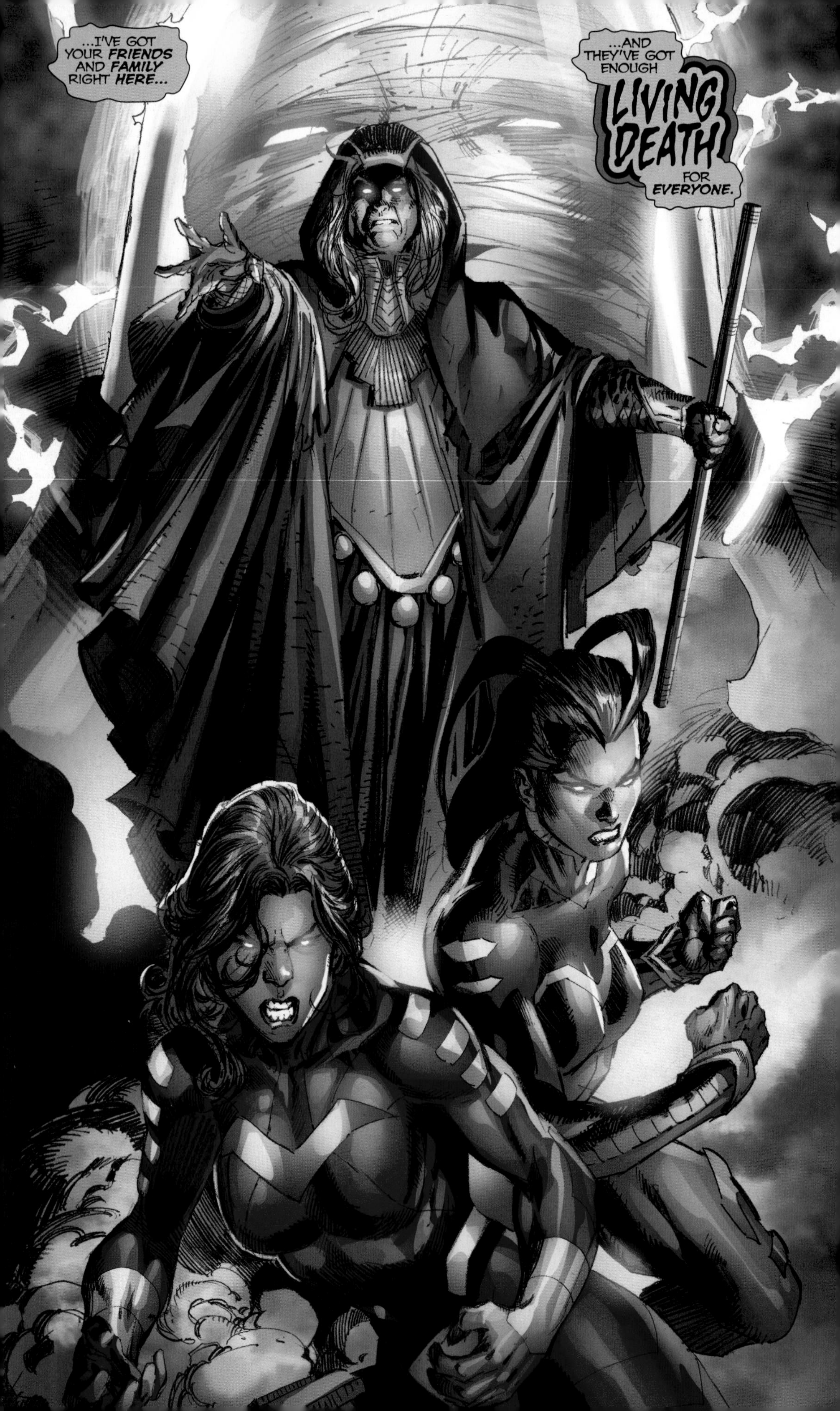
...I'VE GOT YOUR FRIENDS AND FAMILY RIGHT HERE...
...AND THEY'VE GOT ENOUGH LIVING DEATH FOR EVERYONE.

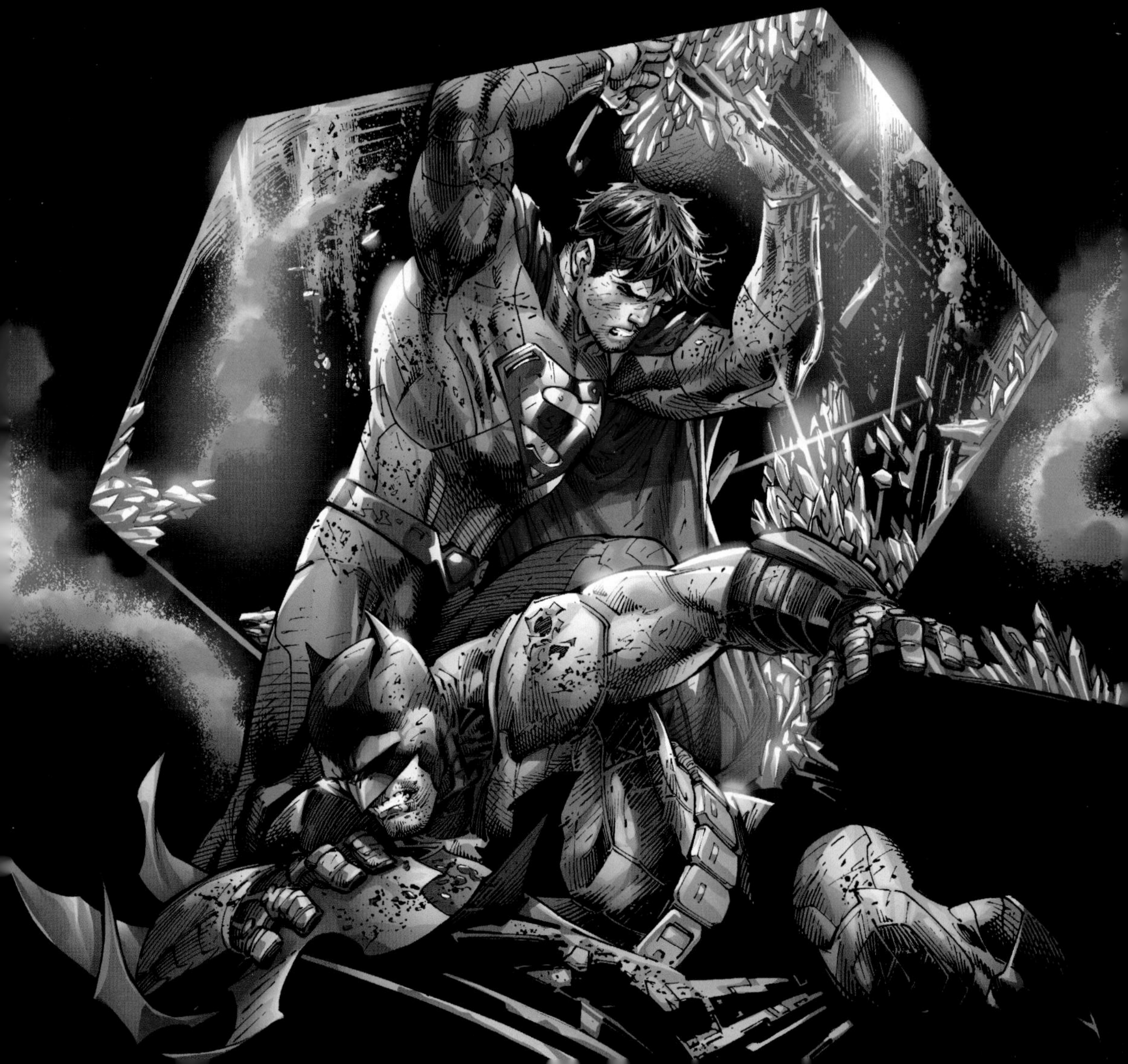

FAMILY MATTERS

GREG PAK writer **ARDIAN SYAF** penciller **VICENTE CIFUENTES, MARK MORALES** inkers **ULISES ARREOLA** colorist **ROB LEIGH** letterer
cover by **ARDIAN SYAF, SANDRA HOPE ARCHER** and **ULISES ARREOLA**

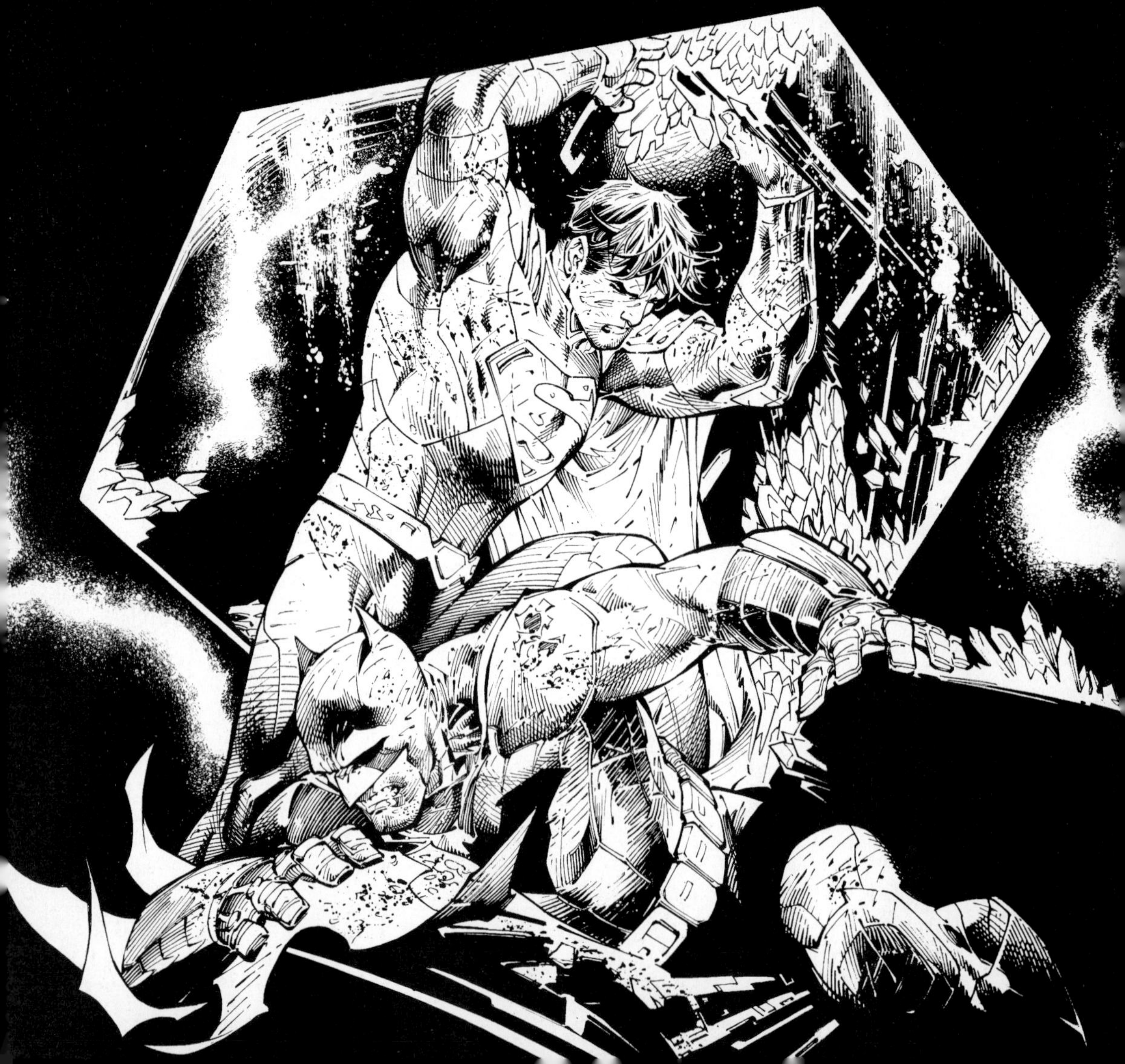

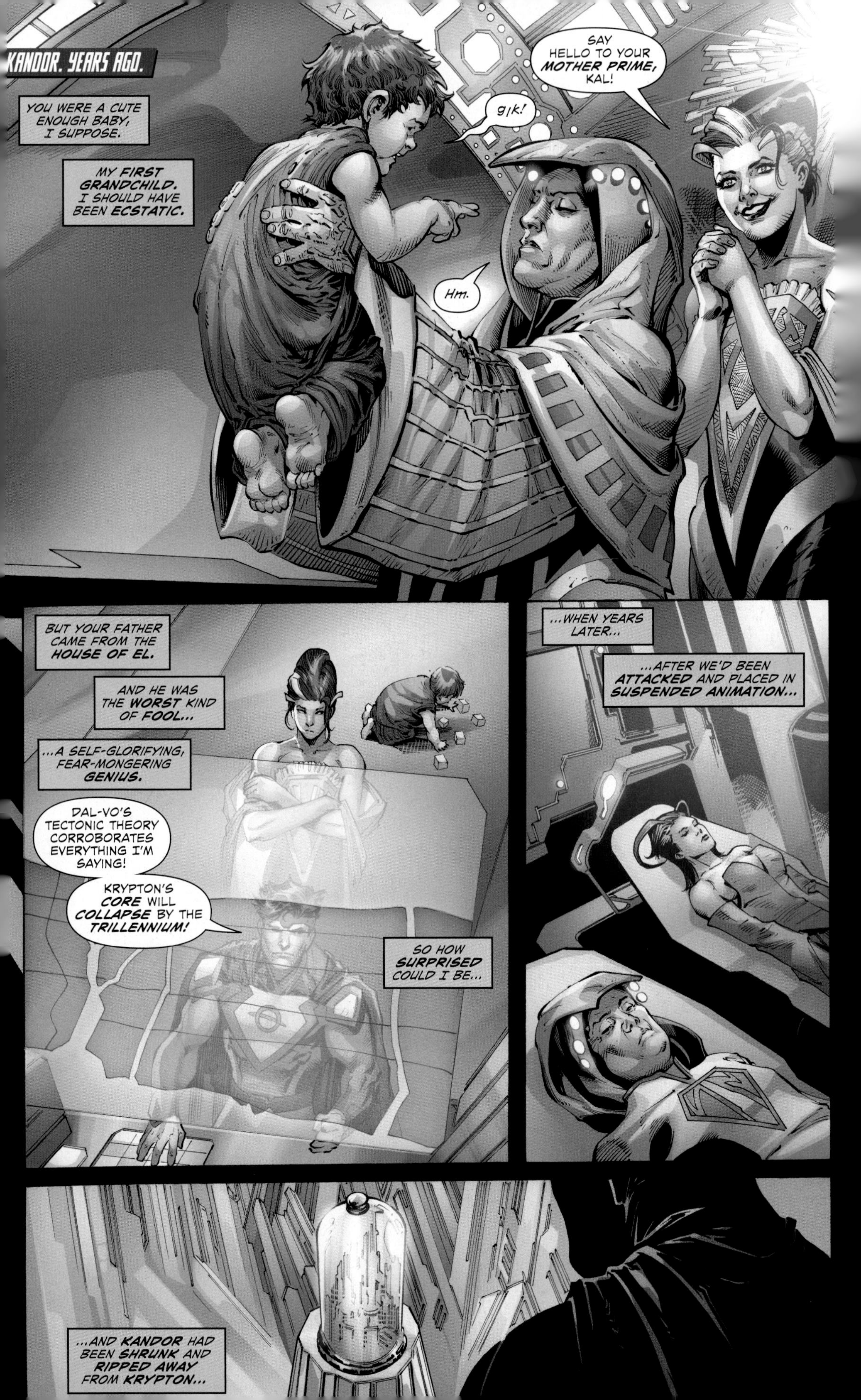

KANDOR. YEARS AGO.
YOU WERE A CUTE ENOUGH BABY, I SUPPOSE.
MY FIRST GRANDCHILD. I SHOULD HAVE BEEN ECSTATIC.
SAY HELLO TO YOUR MOTHER PRIME, KAL!
gik!
Hm.
BUT YOUR FATHER CAME FROM THE HOUSE OF EL.
AND HE WAS THE WORST KIND OF FOOL...
...A SELF-GLORIFYING, FEAR-MONGERING GENIUS.
DAL-VO'S TECTONIC THEORY CORROBORATES EVERYTHING I'M SAYING!
KRYPTON'S CORE WILL COLLAPSE BY THE TRILLENNIUM!
SO HOW SURPRISED COULD I BE...
...WHEN YEARS LATER...
...AFTER WE'D BEEN ATTACKED AND PLACED IN SUSPENDED ANIMATION...
...AND KANDOR HAD BEEN SHRUNK AND RIPPED AWAY FROM KRYPTON...

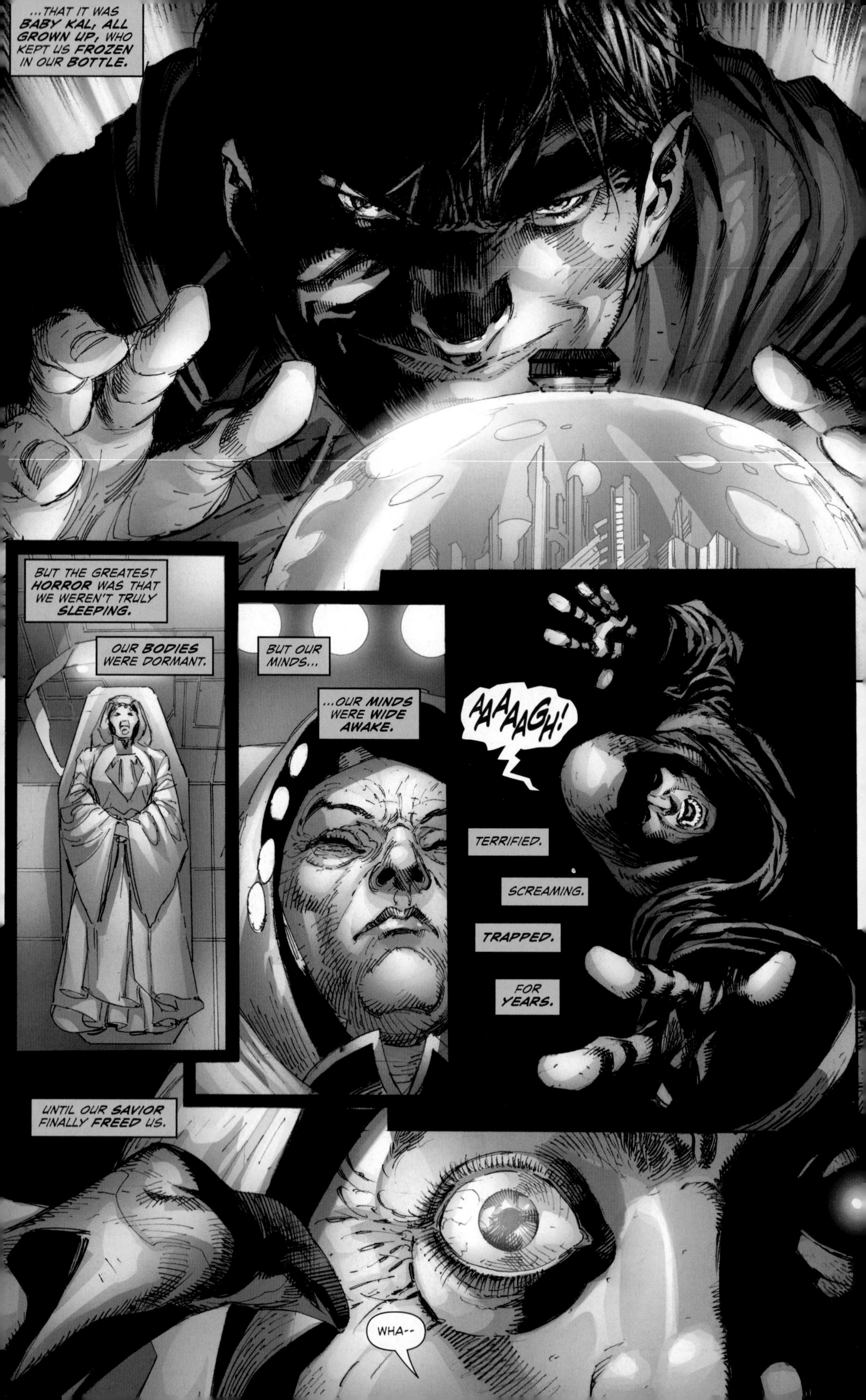
...THAT IT WAS BABY KAL, ALL GROWN UP, WHO KEPT US FROZEN IN OUR BOTTLE.
BUT THE GREATEST HORROR WAS THAT WE WEREN'T TRULY SLEEPING.
OUR BODIES WERE DORMANT.
BUT OUR MINDS...
...OUR MINDS WERE WIDE AWAKE.
AAAAAGH!
TERRIFIED.
SCREAMING.
TRAPPED.
FOR YEARS.
UNTIL OUR SAVIOR FINALLY FREED US.
WHA--

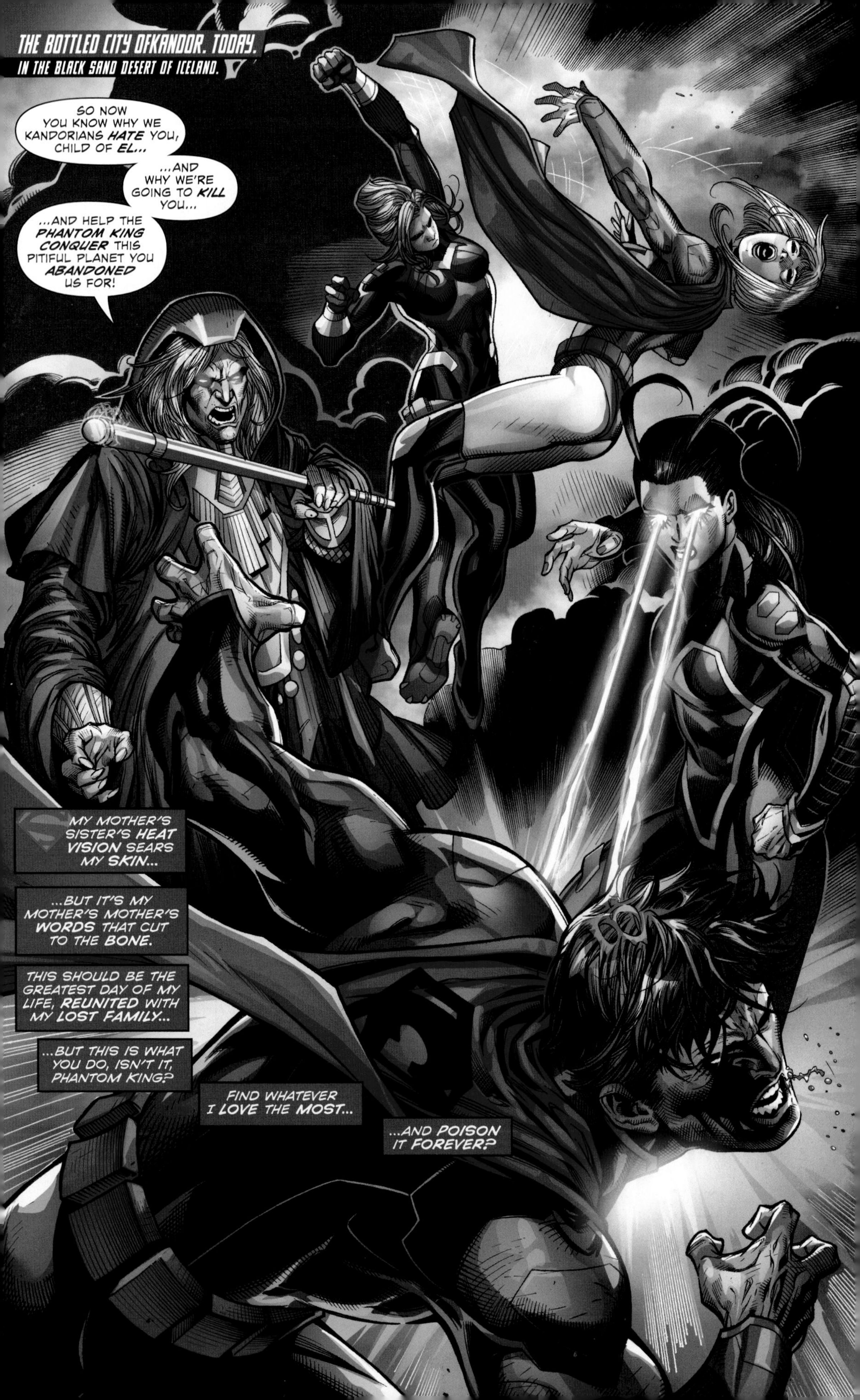
THE BOTTLED CITY OFKANDOR. TODAY.
IN THE BLACK SAND DESERT OF ICELAND.
SO NOW YOU KNOW WHY WE KANDORIANS HATE YOU, CHILD OF EL...
...AND WHY WE'RE GOING TO KILL YOU...
...AND HELP THE PHANTOM KING CONQUER THIS PITIFUL PLANET YOU ABANDONED US FOR!
MY MOTHER'S SISTER'S HEAT VISION SEARS MY SKIN...
...BUT IT'S MY MOTHER'S MOTHER'S WORDS THAT CUT TO THE BONE.
THIS SHOULD BE THE GREATEST DAY OF MY LIFE, REUNITED WITH MY LOST FAMILY...
...BUT THIS IS WHAT YOU DO, ISN'T IT, PHANTOM KING?
FIND WHATEVER I LOVE THE MOST...
...AND POISON IT FOREVER?

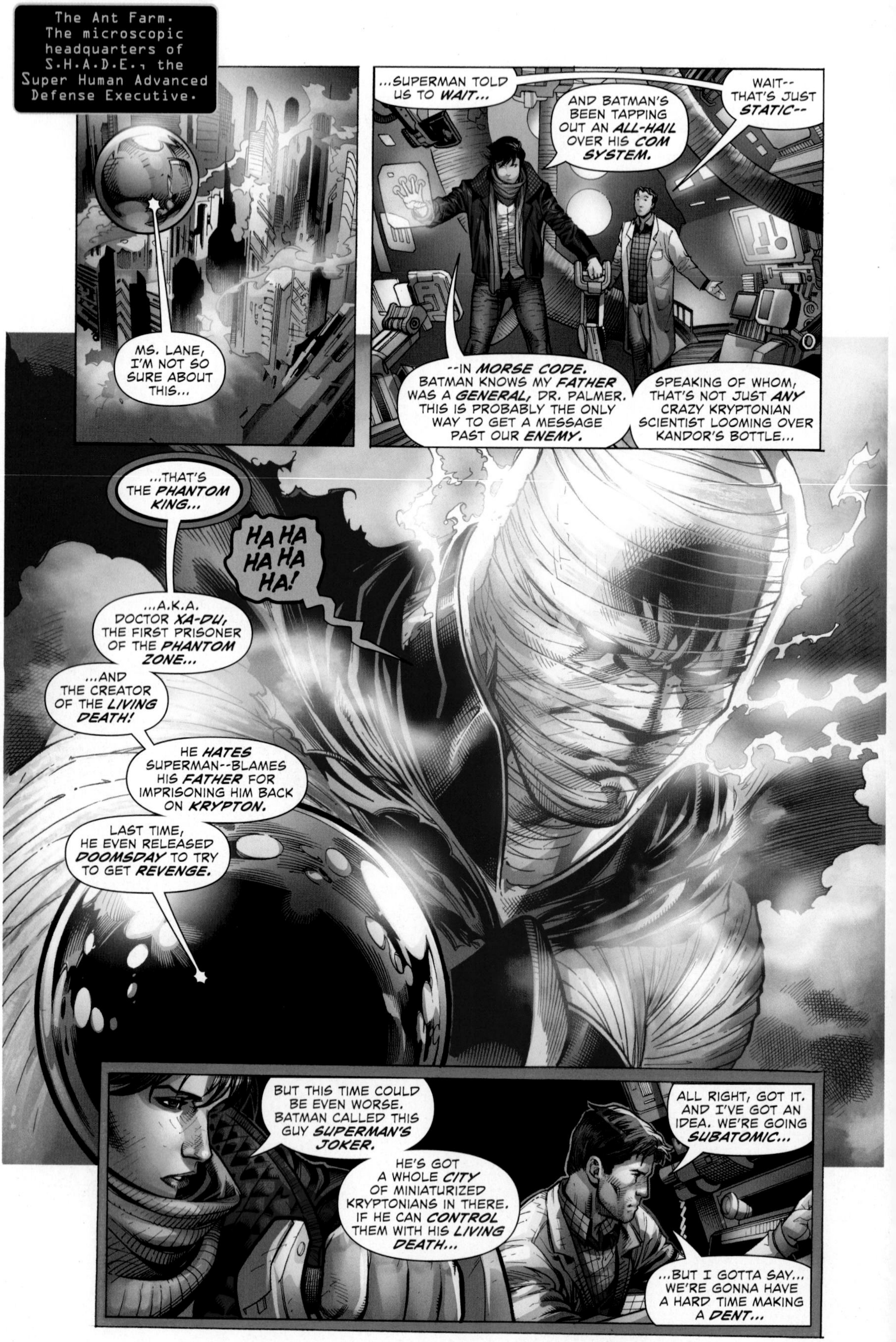
The Ant Farm. The microscopic headquarters of S.H.A.D.E., the Super Human Advanced Defense Executive.
MS. LANE, I'M NOT SO SURE ABOUT THIS...
...SUPERMAN TOLD US TO WAIT...
AND BATMAN'S BEEN TAPPING OUT AN ALL-HAIL OVER HIS COM SYSTEM.
WAIT--THAT'S JUST STATIC--
--IN MORSE CODE. BATMAN KNOWS MY FATHER WAS A GENERAL, DR. PALMER. THIS IS PROBABLY THE ONLY WAY TO GET A MESSAGE PAST OUR ENEMY.
SPEAKING OF WHOM, THAT'S NOT JUST ANY CRAZY KRYPTONIAN SCIENTIST LOOMING OVER KANDOR'S BOTTLE...
...THAT'S THE PHANTOM KING...
HA HA HA HA HA!
...A.K.A. DOCTOR XA-DU, THE FIRST PRISONER OF THE PHANTOM ZONE...
...AND THE CREATOR OF THE LIVING DEATH!
HE HATES SUPERMAN--BLAMES HIS FATHER FOR IMPRISONING HIM BACK ON KRYPTON.
LAST TIME, HE EVEN RELEASED DOOMSDAY TO TRY TO GET REVENGE.
BUT THIS TIME COULD BE EVEN WORSE. BATMAN CALLED THIS GUY SUPERMAN'S JOKER.
HE'S GOT A WHOLE CITY OF MINIATURIZED KRYPTONIANS IN THERE. IF HE CAN CONTROL THEM WITH HIS LIVING DEATH...
ALL RIGHT, GOT IT. AND I'VE GOT AN IDEA. WE'RE GOING SUBATOMIC...
...BUT I GOTTA SAY... WE'RE GONNA HAVE A HARD TIME MAKING A DENT...

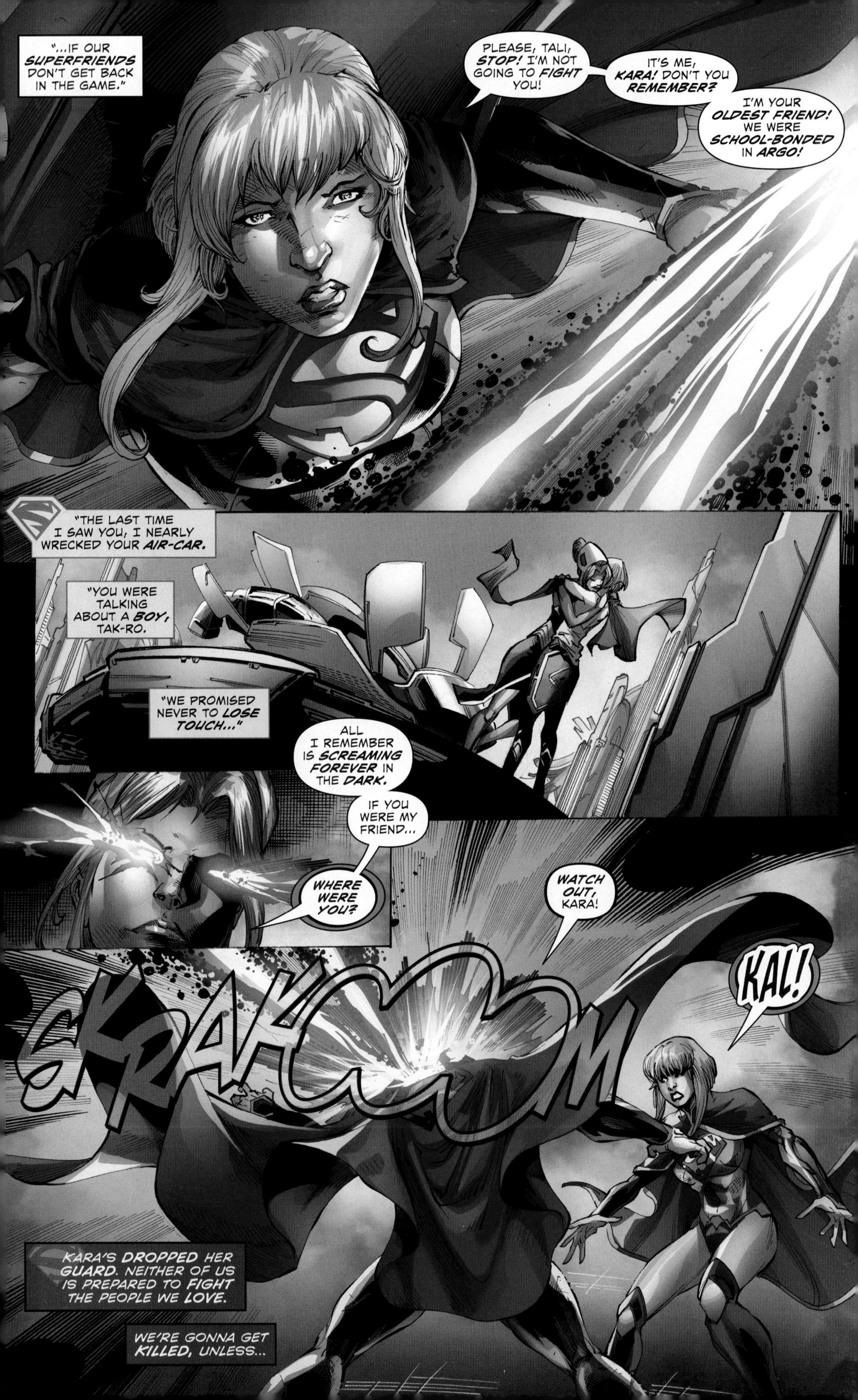
"...IF OUR SUPERFRIENDS DON'T GET BACK IN THE GAME."
PLEASE, TALI, STOP! I'M NOT GOING TO FIGHT YOU!
IT'S ME, KARA! DON'T YOU REMEMBER?
I'M YOUR OLDEST FRIEND! WE WERE SCHOOL-BONDED IN ARGO!
"THE LAST TIME I SAW YOU, I NEARLY WRECKED YOUR AIR-CAR.
"YOU WERE TALKING ABOUT A BOY, TAK-RO.
"WE PROMISED NEVER TO LOSE TOUCH..."
ALL I REMEMBER IS SCREAMING FOREVER IN THE DARK.
IF YOU WERE MY FRIEND...
WHERE WERE YOU?
WATCH OUT, KARA!
SKRAKOOM
KAL!
KARA'S DROPPED HER GUARD. NEITHER OF US IS PREPARED TO FIGHT THE PEOPLE WE LOVE.
WE'RE GONNA GET KILLED, UNLESS...

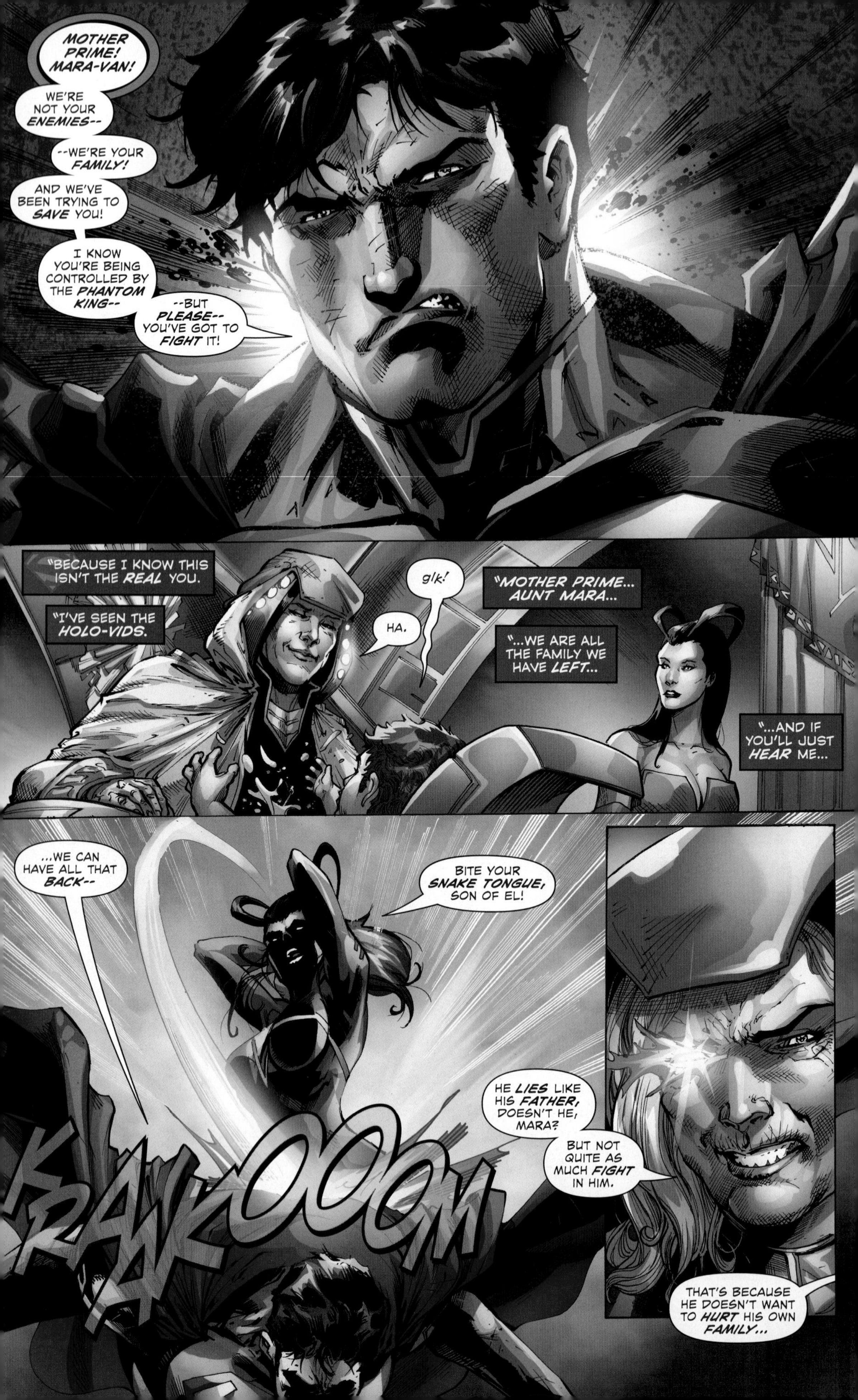
MOTHER PRIME! MARA-VAN!
WE'RE NOT YOUR ENEMIES--
--WE'RE YOUR FAMILY!
AND WE'VE BEEN TRYING TO SAVE YOU!
I KNOW YOU'RE BEING CONTROLLED BY THE PHANTOM KING--
--BUT PLEASE-- YOU'VE GOT TO FIGHT IT!
"BECAUSE I KNOW THIS ISN'T THE REAL YOU.
"I'VE SEEN THE HOLO-VIDS.
HA.
glk!
"MOTHER PRIME... AUNT MARA...
"...WE ARE ALL THE FAMILY WE HAVE LEFT...
"...AND IF YOU'LL JUST HEAR ME...
...WE CAN HAVE ALL THAT BACK--
BITE YOUR SNAKE TONGUE, SON OF EL!
KRAKOOOOM
HE LIES LIKE HIS FATHER, DOESN'T HE, MARA?
BUT NOT QUITE AS MUCH FIGHT IN HIM.
THAT'S BECAUSE HE DOESN'T WANT TO HURT HIS OWN FAMILY...

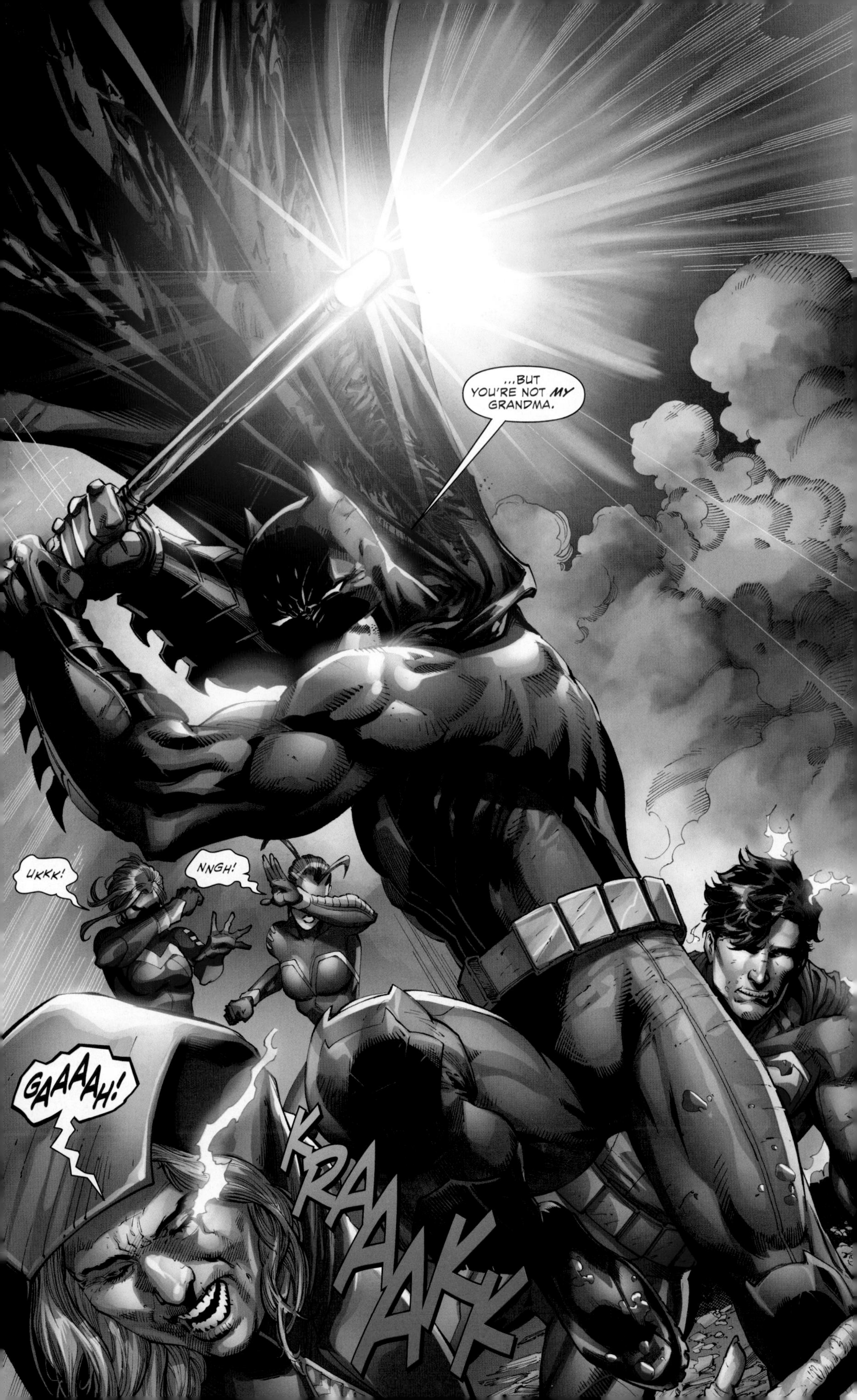
...BUT YOU'RE NOT MY GRANDMA.
UKKK!
NNGH!
GAAAAH!
KRAAAKK

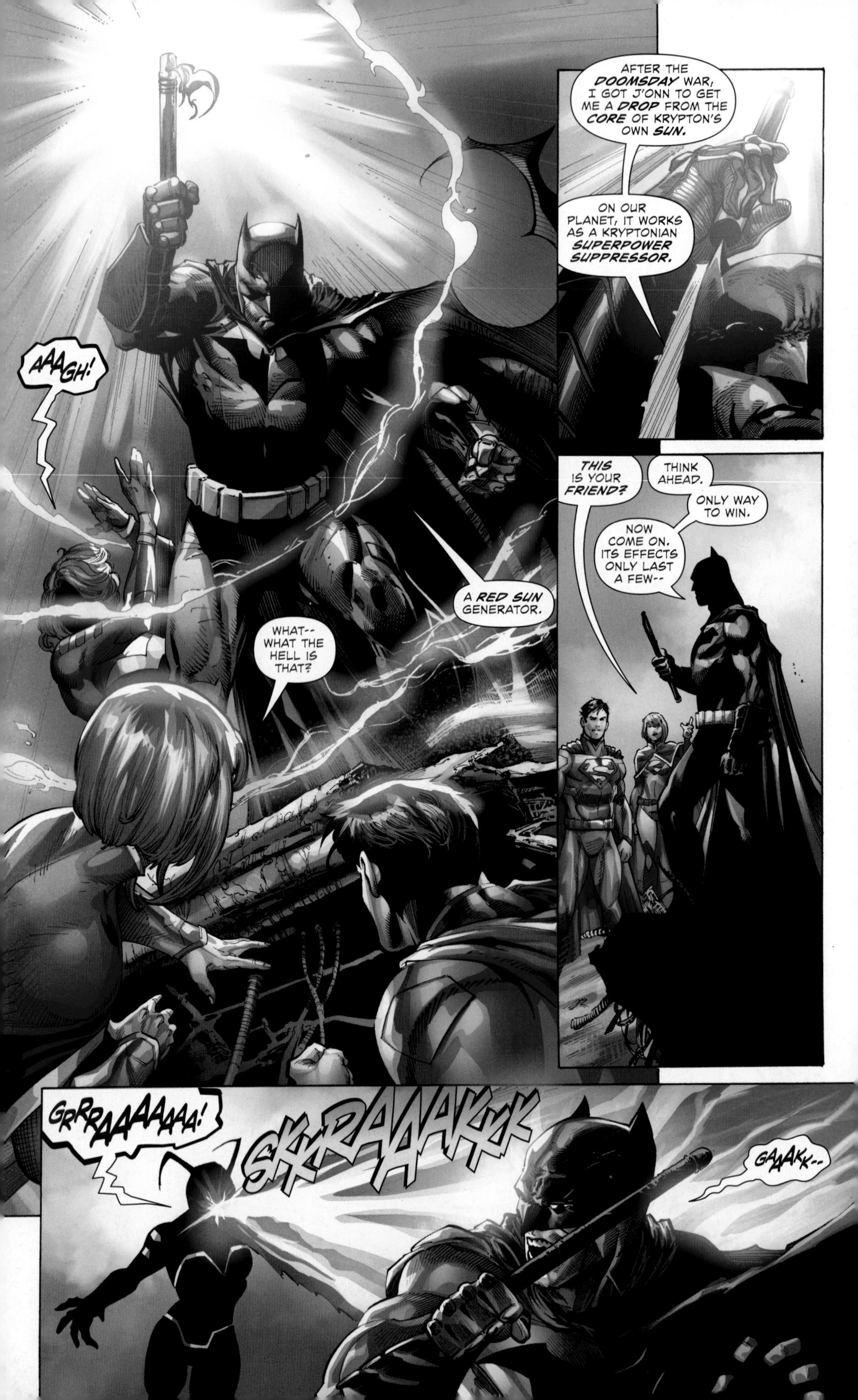
AAAGH!
WHAT--
WHAT THE
HELL IS
THAT?
A RED SUN
GENERATOR.
AFTER THE DOOMSDAY WAR, I GOT J'ONN TO GET ME A DROP FROM THE CORE OF KRYPTON'S OWN SUN.
ON OUR PLANET, IT WORKS AS A KRYPTONIAN SUPERPOWER SUPPRESSOR.
THIS IS YOUR FRIEND?
THINK AHEAD.
ONLY WAY TO WIN.
NOW COME ON. ITS EFFECTS ONLY LAST A FEW--
GRRRAAAAAAA!
SKKRAAAKKK
GAAAKK--

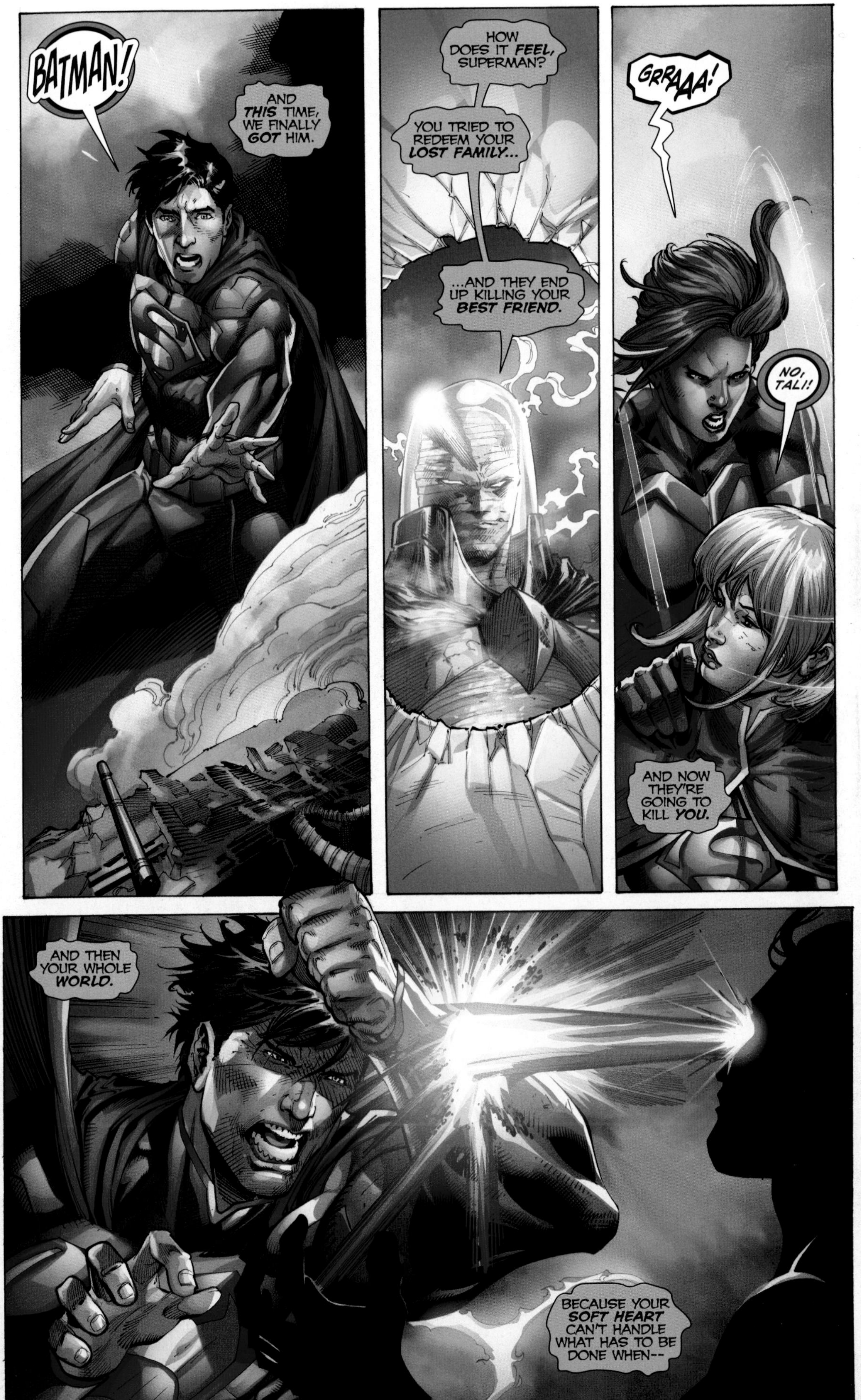
BATMAN!
AND THIS TIME, WE FINALLY GOT HIM.
HOW DOES IT FEEL, SUPERMAN?
YOU TRIED TO REDEEM YOUR LOST FAMILY...
...AND THEY END UP KILLING YOUR BEST FRIEND.
GRRAAA!
NO, TALI!
AND NOW THEY'RE GOING TO KILL YOU.
AND THEN YOUR WHOLE WORLD.
BECAUSE YOUR SOFT HEART CAN'T HANDLE WHAT HAS TO BE DONE WHEN--

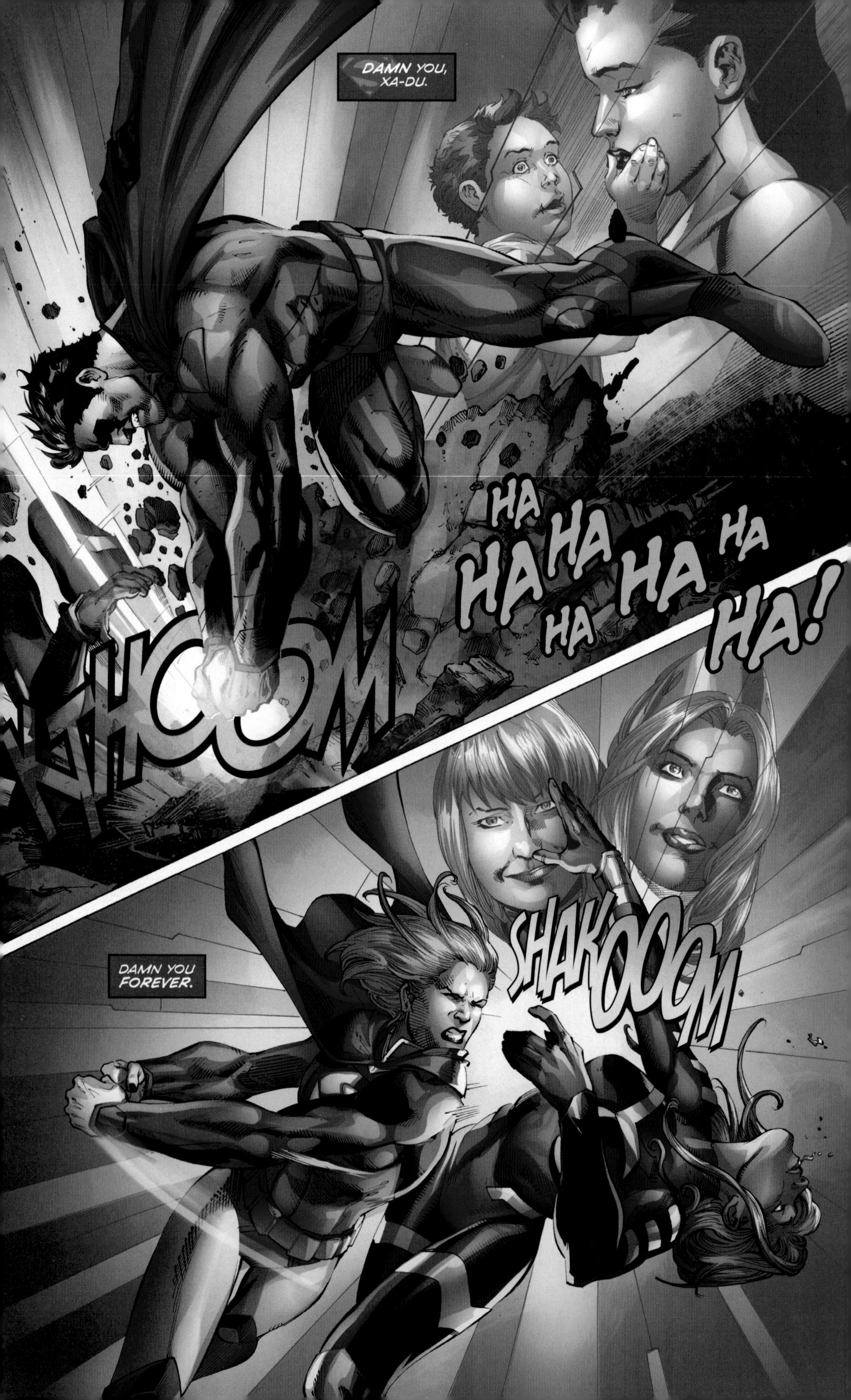
DAMN YOU, XA-DU.
HA HA HA HA HA HA HA HA!
THOOOM
DAMN YOU FOREVER.
SHAKOOOM

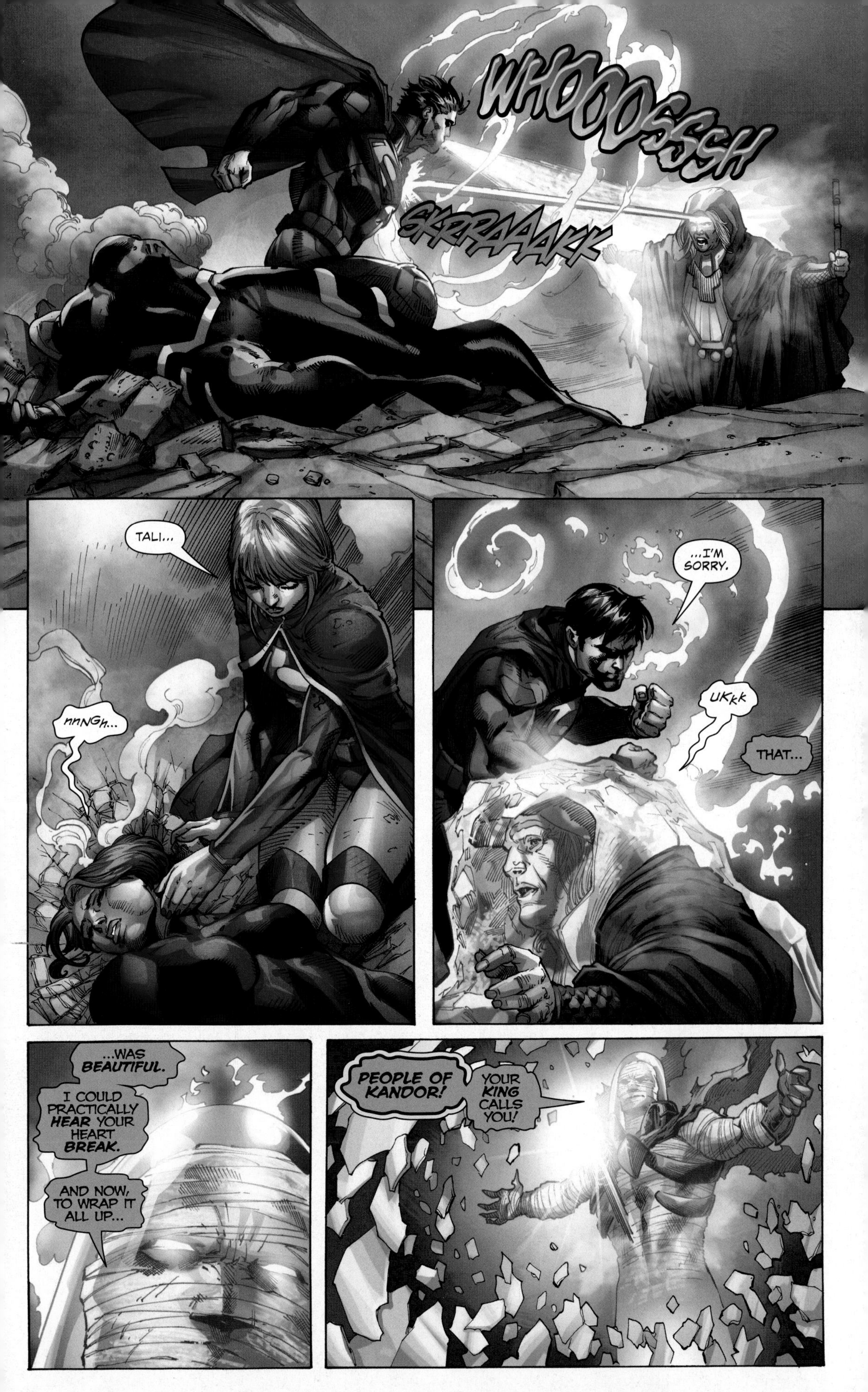
WHOOOOSSSH
SKRRAAAKK
TALI...
nnNGh...
...I'M SORRY.
UKkk
THAT...
...WAS BEAUTIFUL.
I COULD PRACTICALLY HEAR YOUR HEART BREAK.
AND NOW, TO WRAP IT ALL UP...
PEOPLE OF KANDOR!
YOUR KING CALLS YOU!

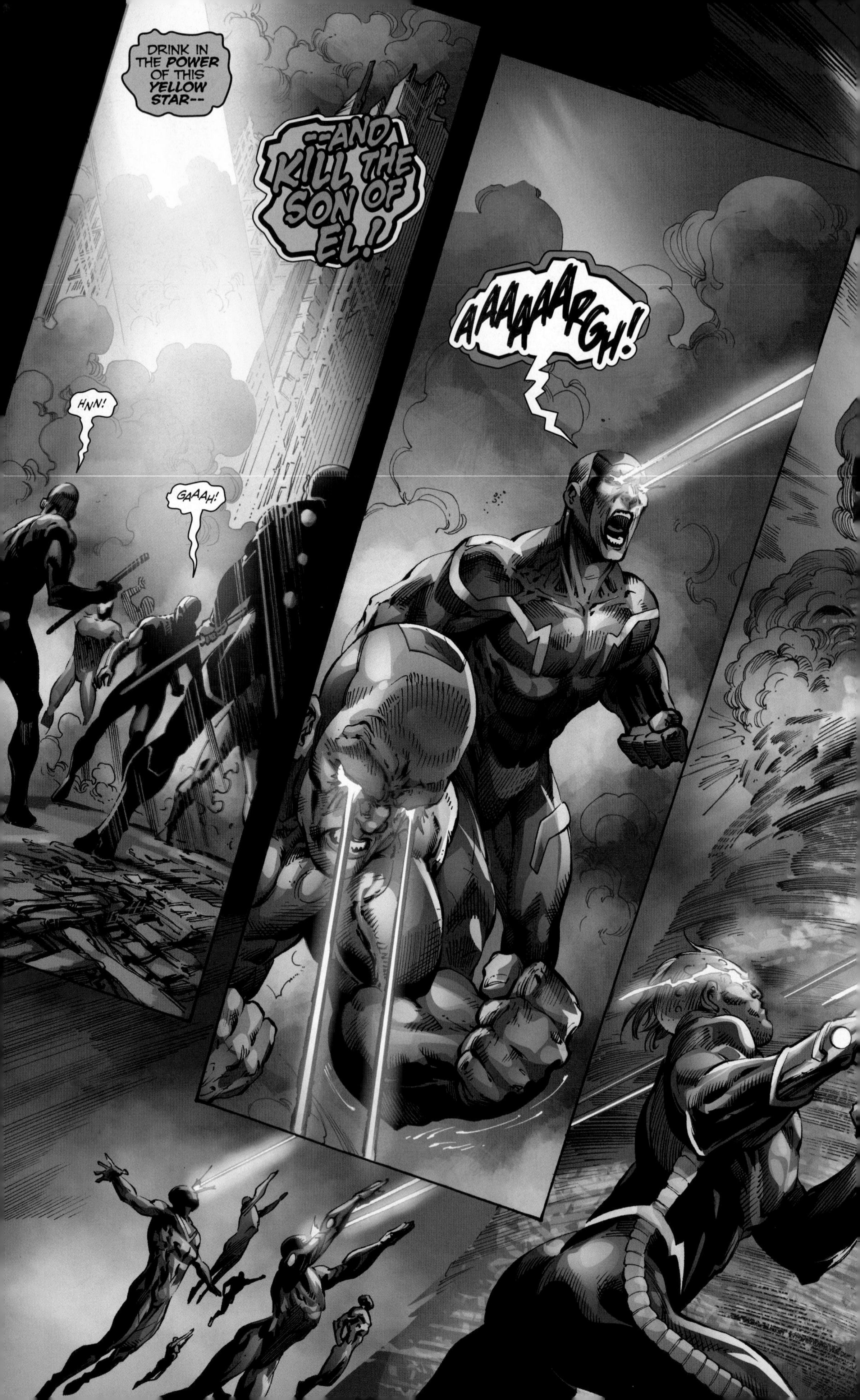
DRINK IN THE POWER OF THIS YELLOW STAR--
--AND KILL THE SON OF EL!
HNN!
GAAAH!
AAAAAAARGH!

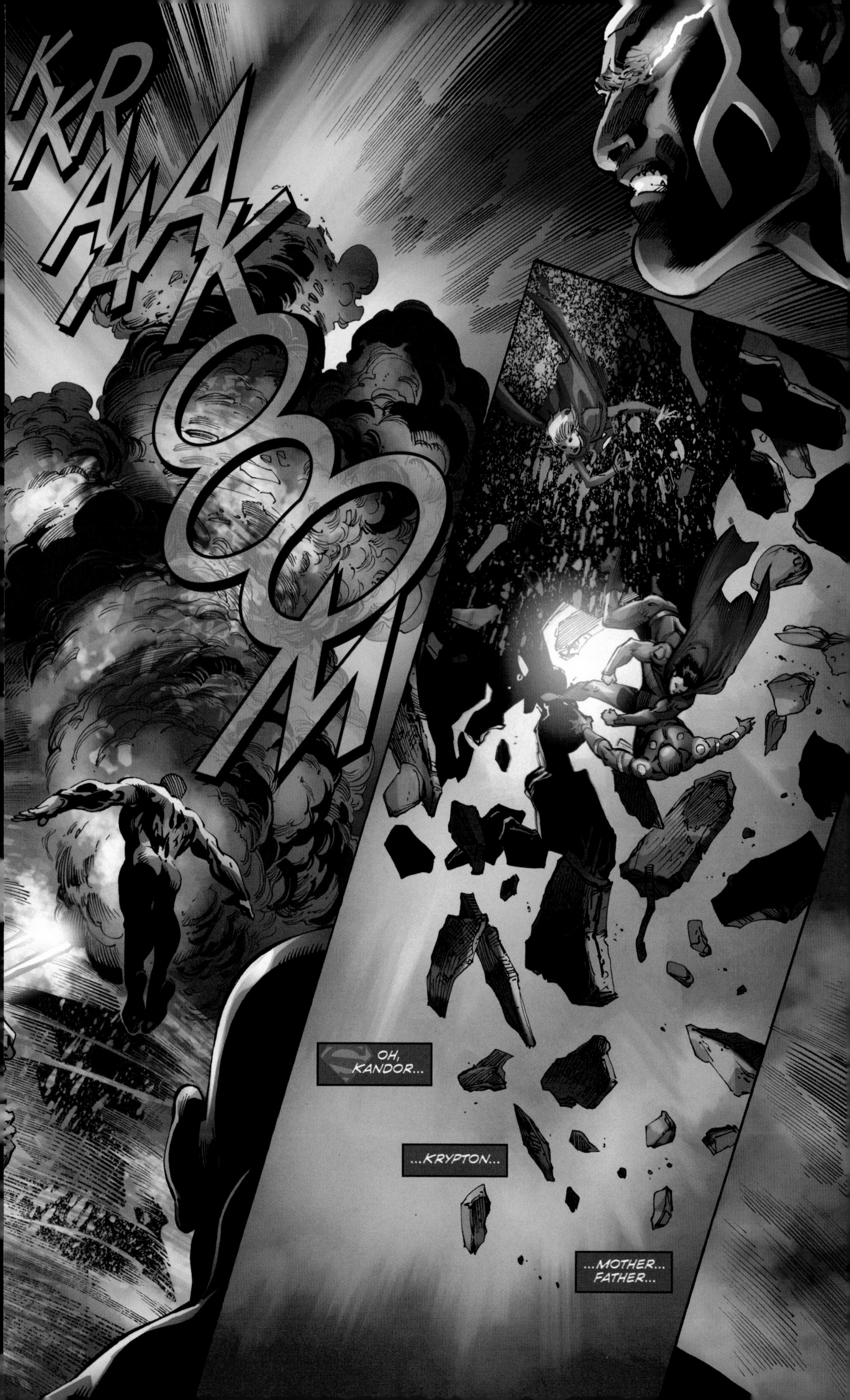

KRAKAKABOOM
OH, KANDOR...
...KRYPTON...
...MOTHER... FATHER...

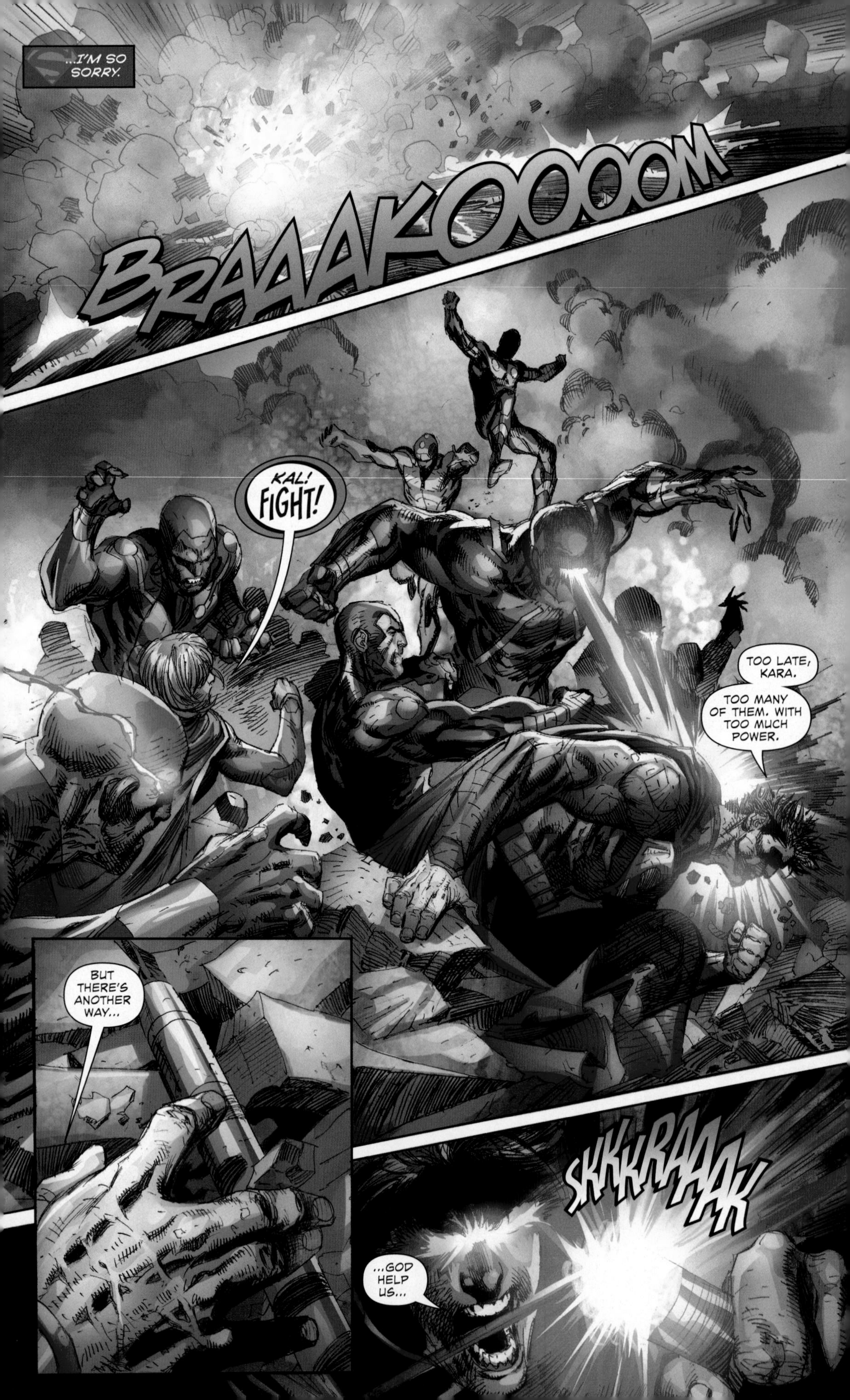
...I'M SO SORRY.
BRAAAKOOOOM
KAL! FIGHT!
TOO LATE, KARA.
TOO MANY OF THEM. WITH TOO MUCH POWER.
BUT THERE'S ANOTHER WAY...
SKKKRAAAAK
...GOD HELP US...

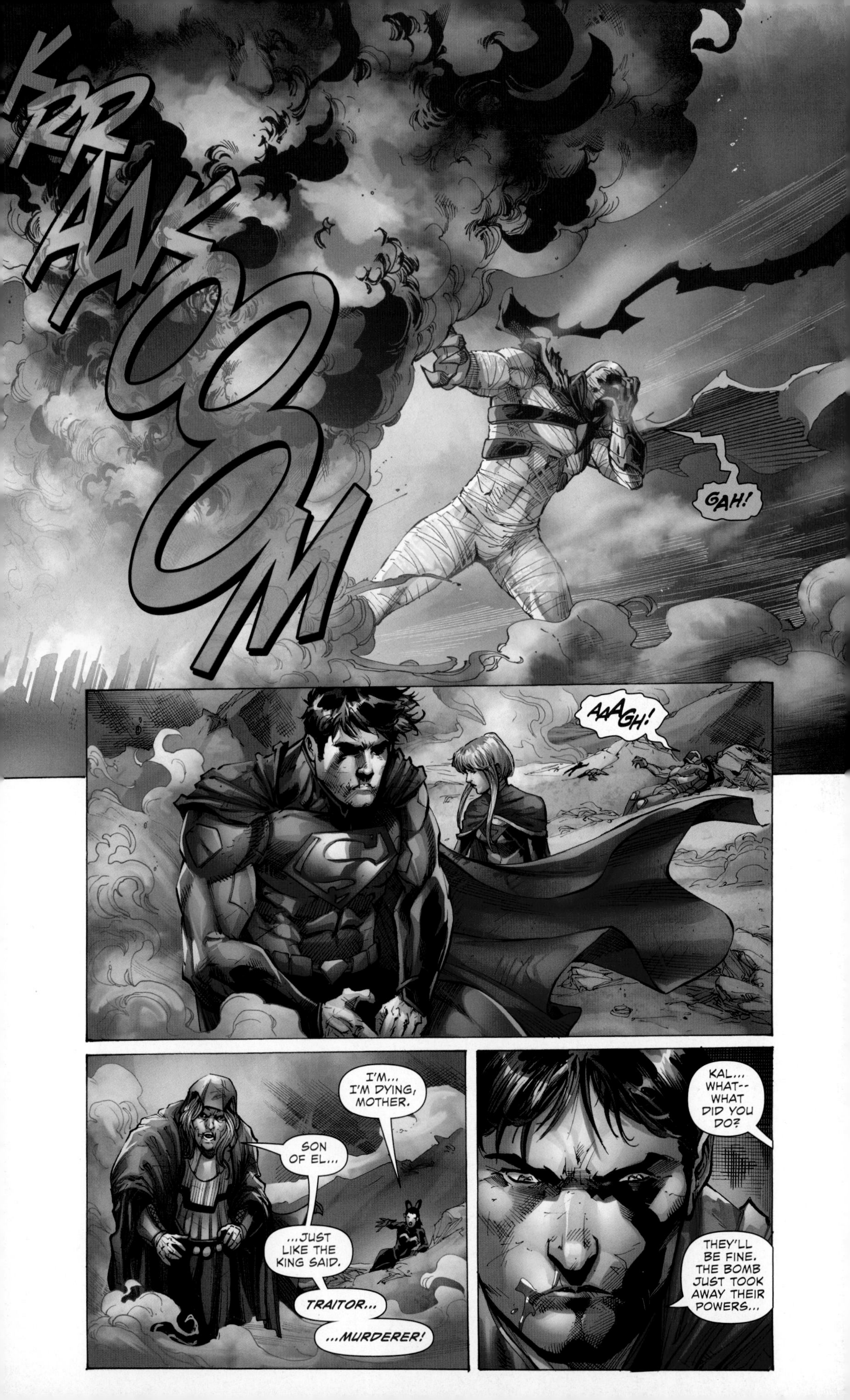
KRRRAAKOOOOM
GAH!
AAAGH!
I'M... I'M DYING, MOTHER.
SON OF EL...
...JUST LIKE THE KING SAID.
TRAITOR...
...MURDERER!
KAL... WHAT--WHAT DID YOU DO?
THEY'LL BE FINE. THE BOMB JUST TOOK AWAY THEIR POWERS...

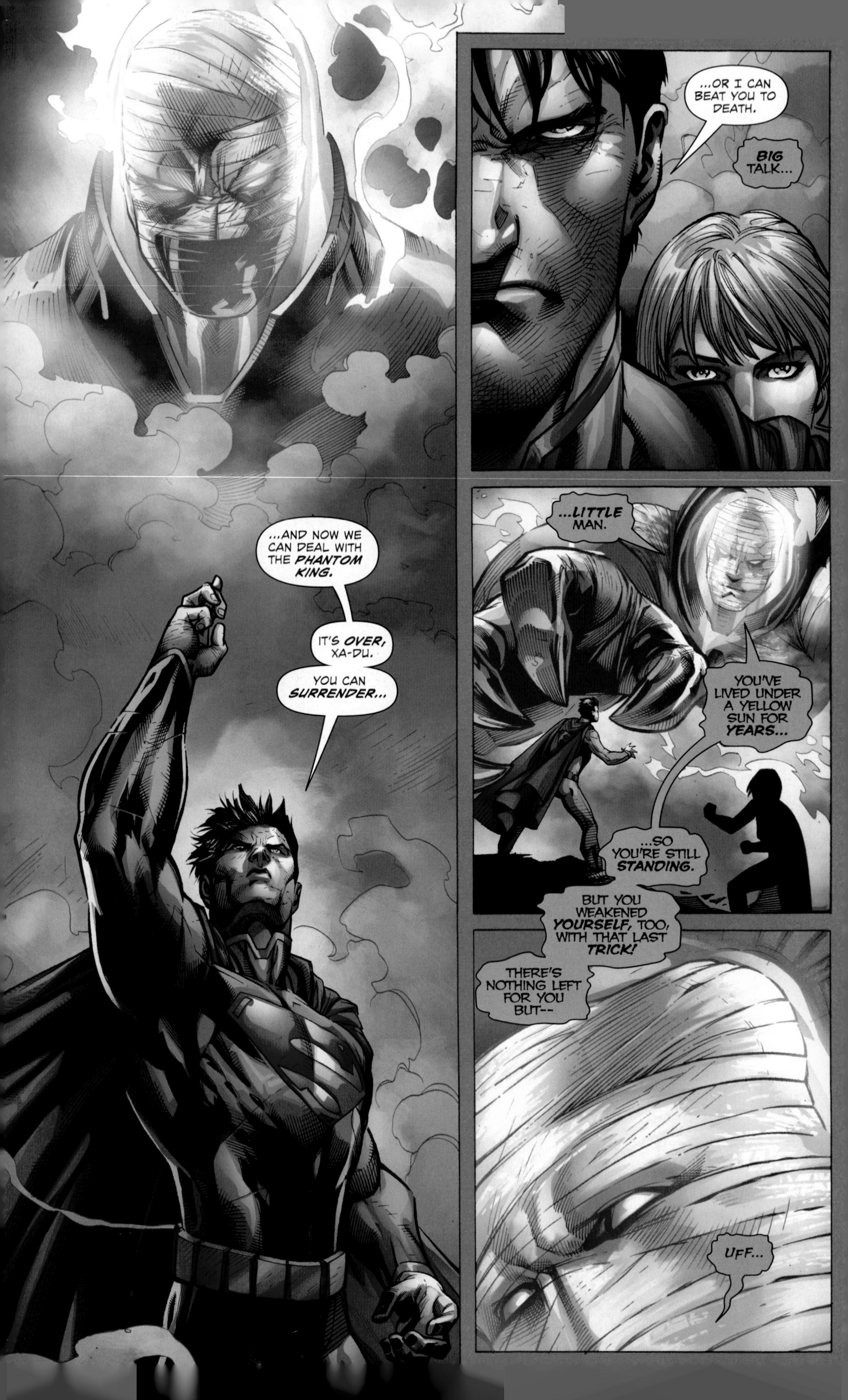
...OR I CAN BEAT YOU TO DEATH.
BIG TALK...
...AND NOW WE CAN DEAL WITH THE PHANTOM KING.
IT'S OVER, XA-DU.
YOU CAN SURRENDER...
...LITTLE MAN.
YOU'VE LIVED UNDER A YELLOW SUN FOR YEARS...
...SO YOU'RE STILL STANDING.
BUT YOU WEAKENED YOURSELF, TOO, WITH THAT LAST TRICK!
THERE'S NOTHING LEFT FOR YOU BUT--
UFF...

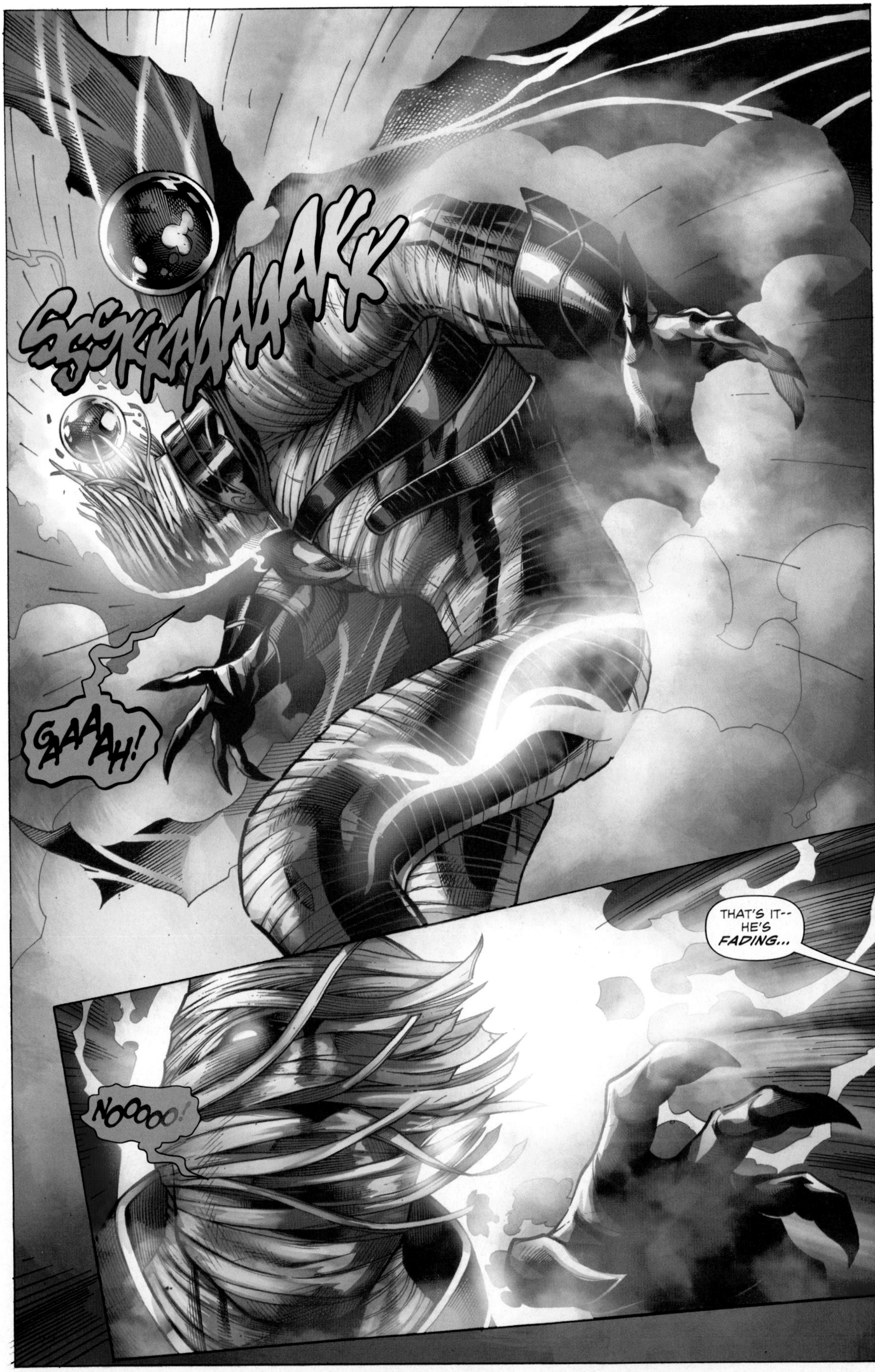
SSSKRAAAAAKK
GAAAAH!
THAT'S IT--
HE'S
FADING...
NOOOOO!

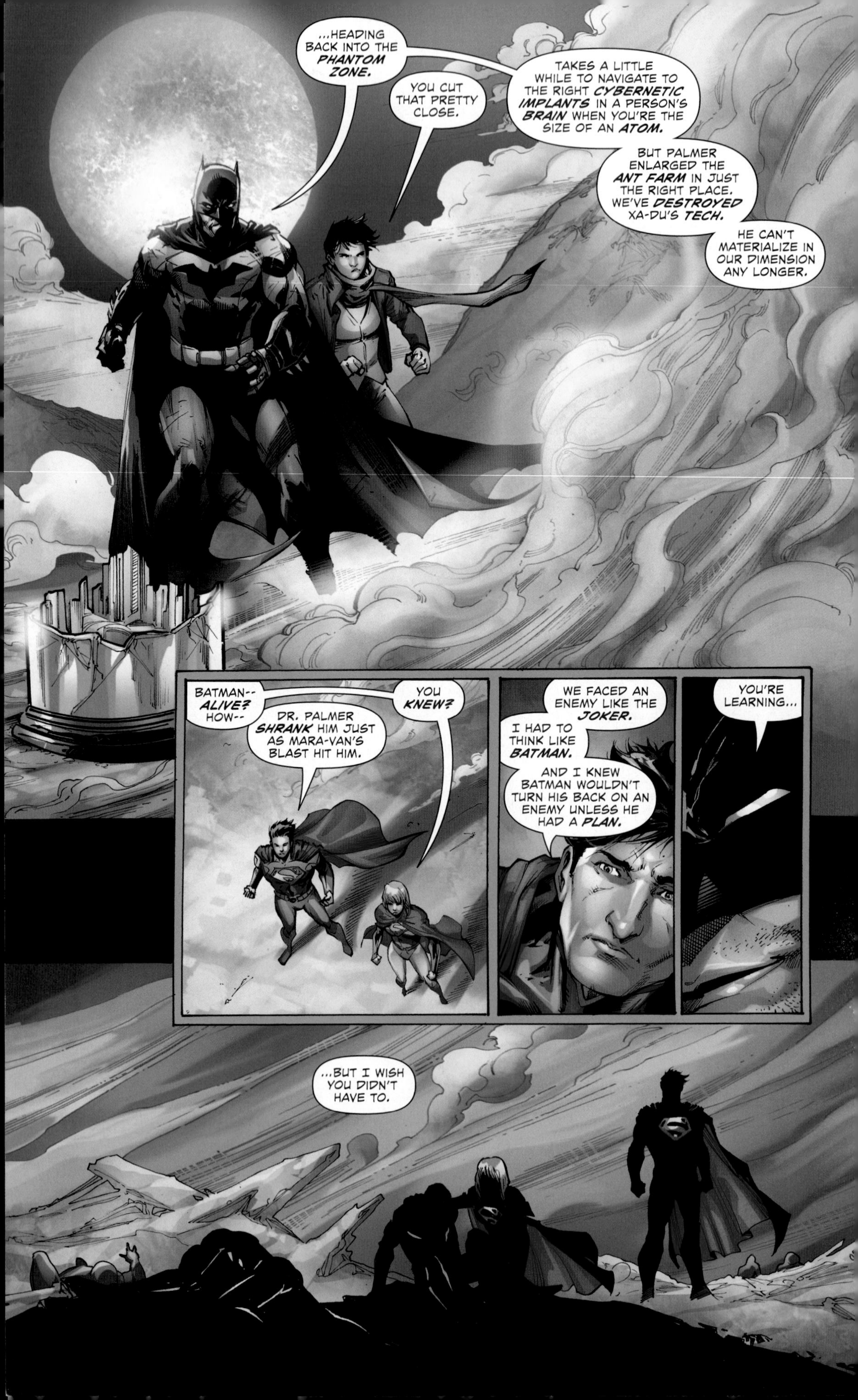

...HEADING BACK INTO THE PHANTOM ZONE.
YOU CUT THAT PRETTY CLOSE.
TAKES A LITTLE WHILE TO NAVIGATE TO THE RIGHT CYBERNETIC IMPLANTS IN A PERSON'S BRAIN WHEN YOU'RE THE SIZE OF AN ATOM.
BUT PALMER ENLARGED THE ANT FARM IN JUST THE RIGHT PLACE. WE'VE DESTROYED XA-DU'S TECH.
HE CAN'T MATERIALIZE IN OUR DIMENSION ANY LONGER.
BATMAN-- ALIVE? HOW--
DR. PALMER SHRANK HIM JUST AS MARA-VAN'S BLAST HIT HIM.
YOU KNEW?
WE FACED AN ENEMY LIKE THE JOKER.
I HAD TO THINK LIKE BATMAN.
AND I KNEW BATMAN WOULDN'T TURN HIS BACK ON AN ENEMY UNLESS HE HAD A PLAN.
YOU'RE LEARNING...
...BUT I WISH YOU DIDN'T HAVE TO.

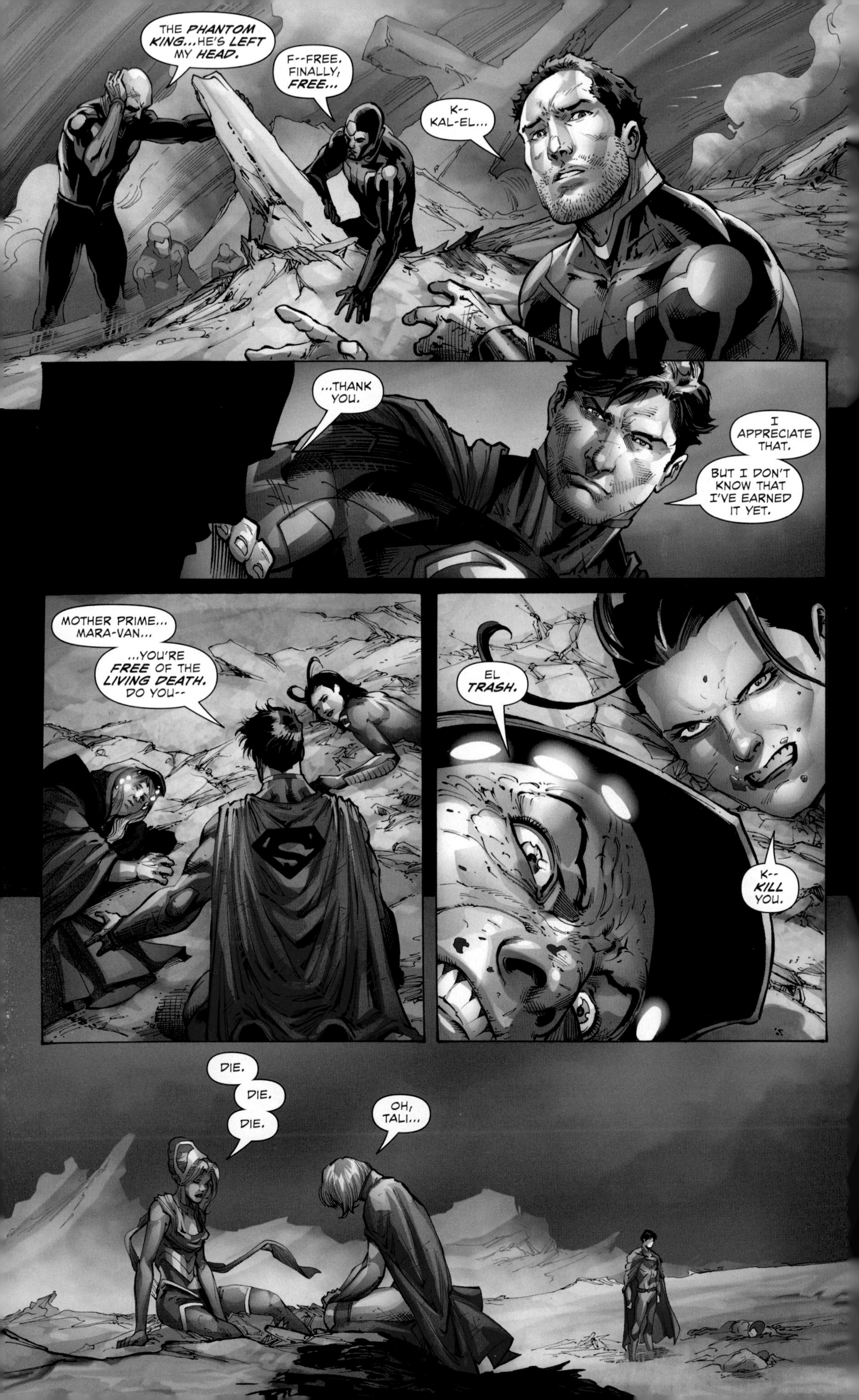
THE PHANTOM KING...HE'S LEFT MY HEAD.
F--FREE. FINALLY, FREE...
K-- KAL-EL...
...THANK YOU.
I APPRECIATE THAT.
BUT I DON'T KNOW THAT I'VE EARNED IT YET.
MOTHER PRIME... MARA-VAN...
...YOU'RE FREE OF THE LIVING DEATH. DO YOU--
EL TRASH.
K-- KILL YOU.
DIE.
DIE.
DIE.
OH, TALI...

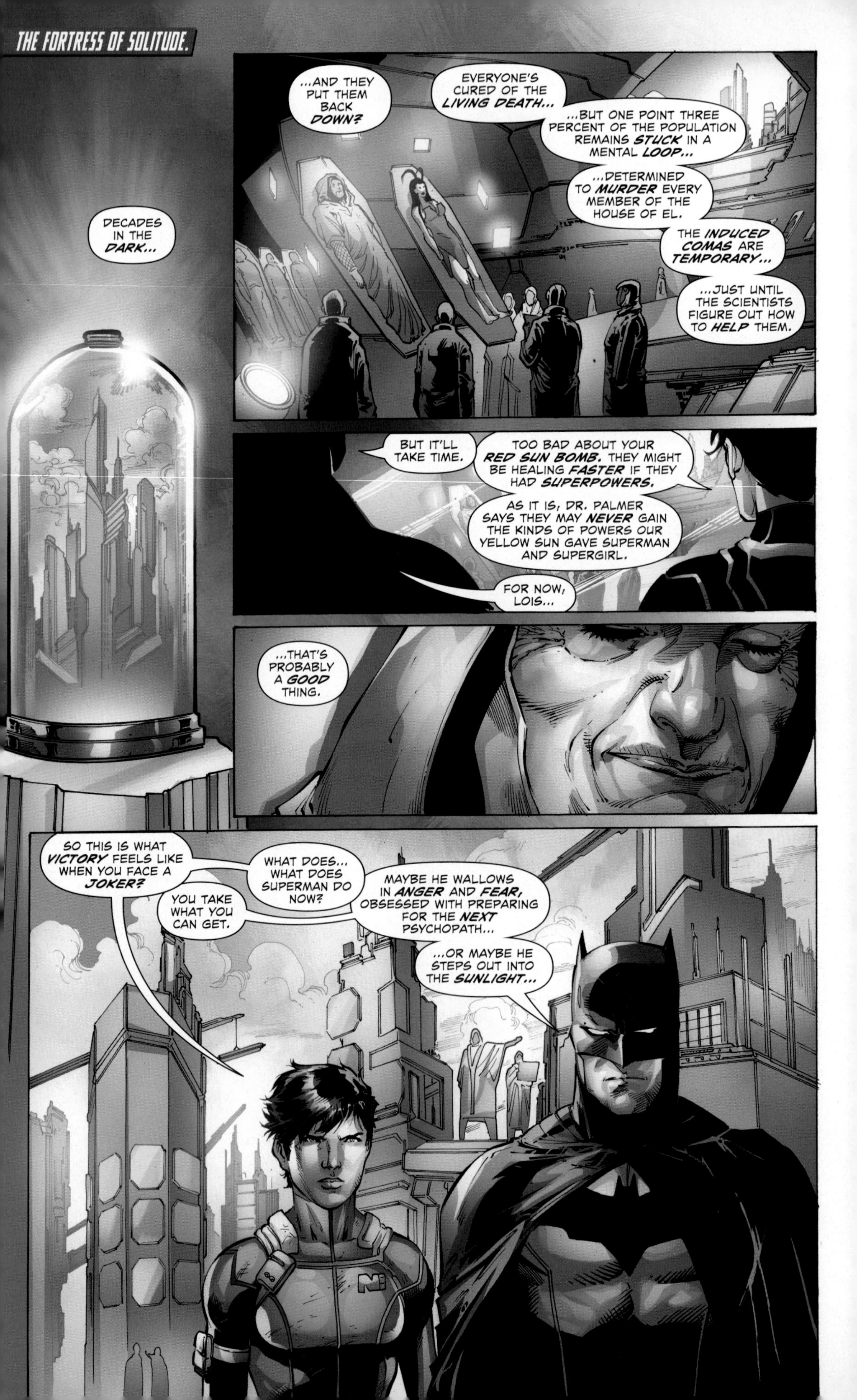
THE FORTRESS OF SOLITUDE.
...AND THEY PUT THEM BACK DOWN?
EVERYONE'S CURED OF THE LIVING DEATH...
...BUT ONE POINT THREE PERCENT OF THE POPULATION REMAINS STUCK IN A MENTAL LOOP...
...DETERMINED TO MURDER EVERY MEMBER OF THE HOUSE OF EL.
THE INDUCED COMAS ARE TEMPORARY...
...JUST UNTIL THE SCIENTISTS FIGURE OUT HOW TO HELP THEM.
DECADES IN THE DARK...
BUT IT'LL TAKE TIME.
TOO BAD ABOUT YOUR RED SUN BOMB. THEY MIGHT BE HEALING FASTER IF THEY HAD SUPERPOWERS.
AS IT IS, DR. PALMER SAYS THEY MAY NEVER GAIN THE KINDS OF POWERS OUR YELLOW SUN GAVE SUPERMAN AND SUPERGIRL.
FOR NOW, LOIS...
...THAT'S PROBABLY A GOOD THING.
SO THIS IS WHAT VICTORY FEELS LIKE WHEN YOU FACE A JOKER?
YOU TAKE WHAT YOU CAN GET.
WHAT DOES... WHAT DOES SUPERMAN DO NOW?
MAYBE HE WALLOWS IN ANGER AND FEAR, OBSESSED WITH PREPARING FOR THE NEXT PSYCHOPATH...
...OR MAYBE HE STEPS OUT INTO THE SUNLIGHT...

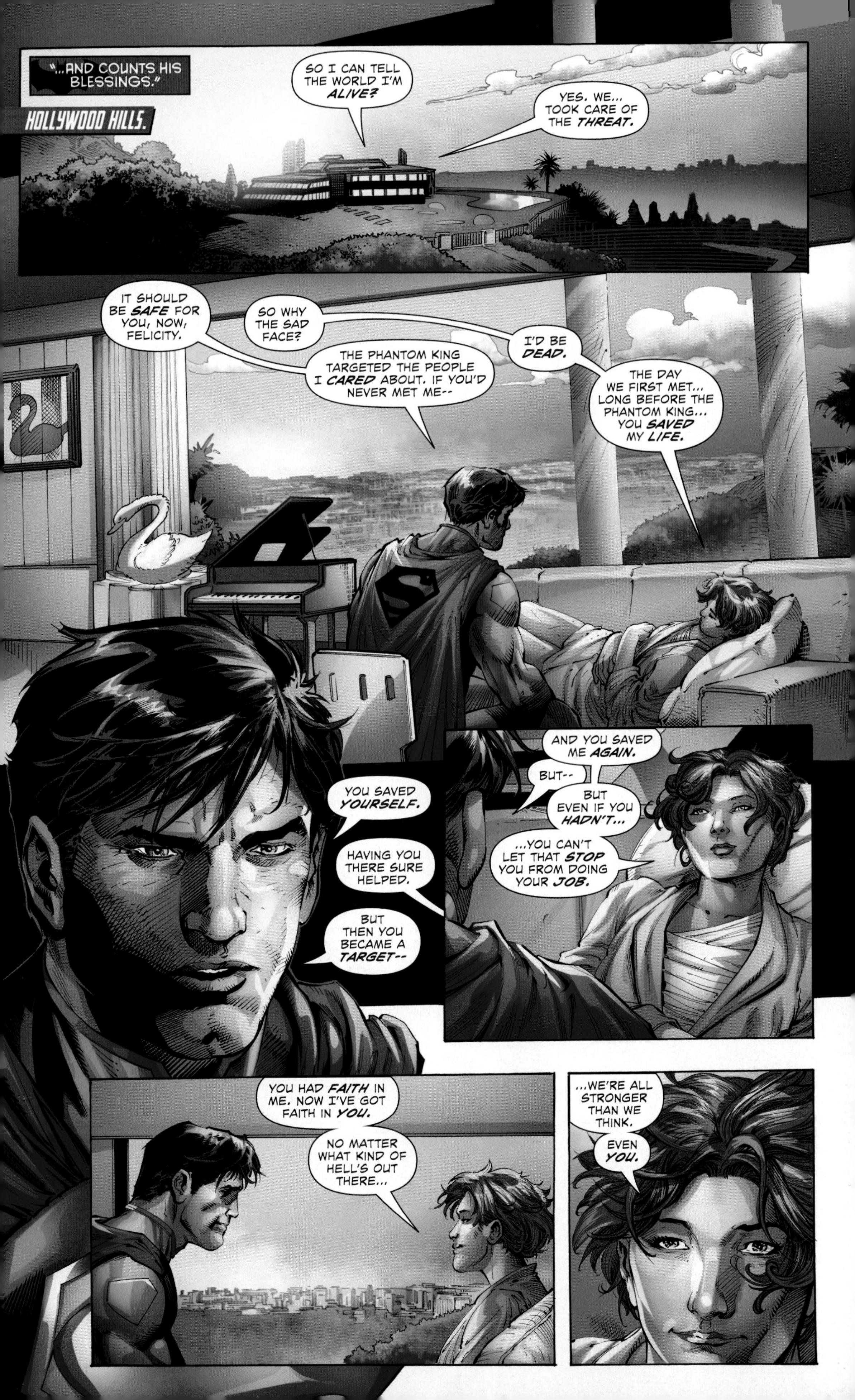
"...AND COUNTS HIS BLESSINGS."
HOLLYWOOD HILLS.
SO I CAN TELL THE WORLD I'M ALIVE?
YES. WE... TOOK CARE OF THE THREAT.
IT SHOULD BE SAFE FOR YOU, NOW, FELICITY.
SO WHY THE SAD FACE?
THE PHANTOM KING TARGETED THE PEOPLE I CARED ABOUT. IF YOU'D NEVER MET ME--
I'D BE DEAD.
THE DAY WE FIRST MET... LONG BEFORE THE PHANTOM KING... YOU SAVED MY LIFE.
YOU SAVED YOURSELF.
HAVING YOU THERE SURE HELPED.
BUT THEN YOU BECAME A TARGET--
AND YOU SAVED ME AGAIN.
BUT--
BUT EVEN IF YOU HADN'T...
...YOU CAN'T LET THAT STOP YOU FROM DOING YOUR JOB.
YOU HAD FAITH IN ME. NOW I'VE GOT FAITH IN YOU.
NO MATTER WHAT KIND OF HELL'S OUT THERE...
...WE'RE ALL STRONGER THAN WE THINK.
EVEN YOU.

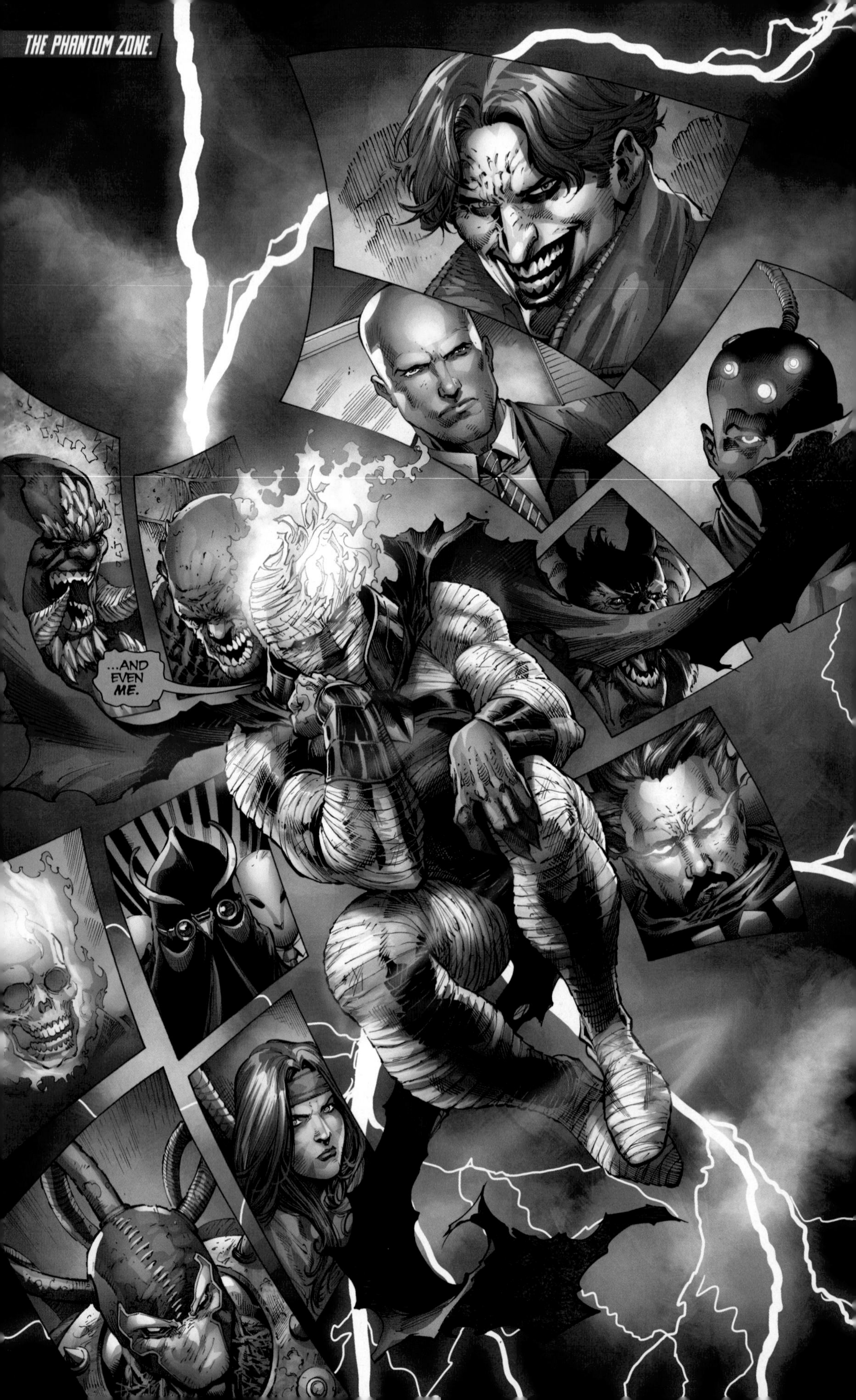
THE PHANTOM ZONE.
...AND EVEN ME.

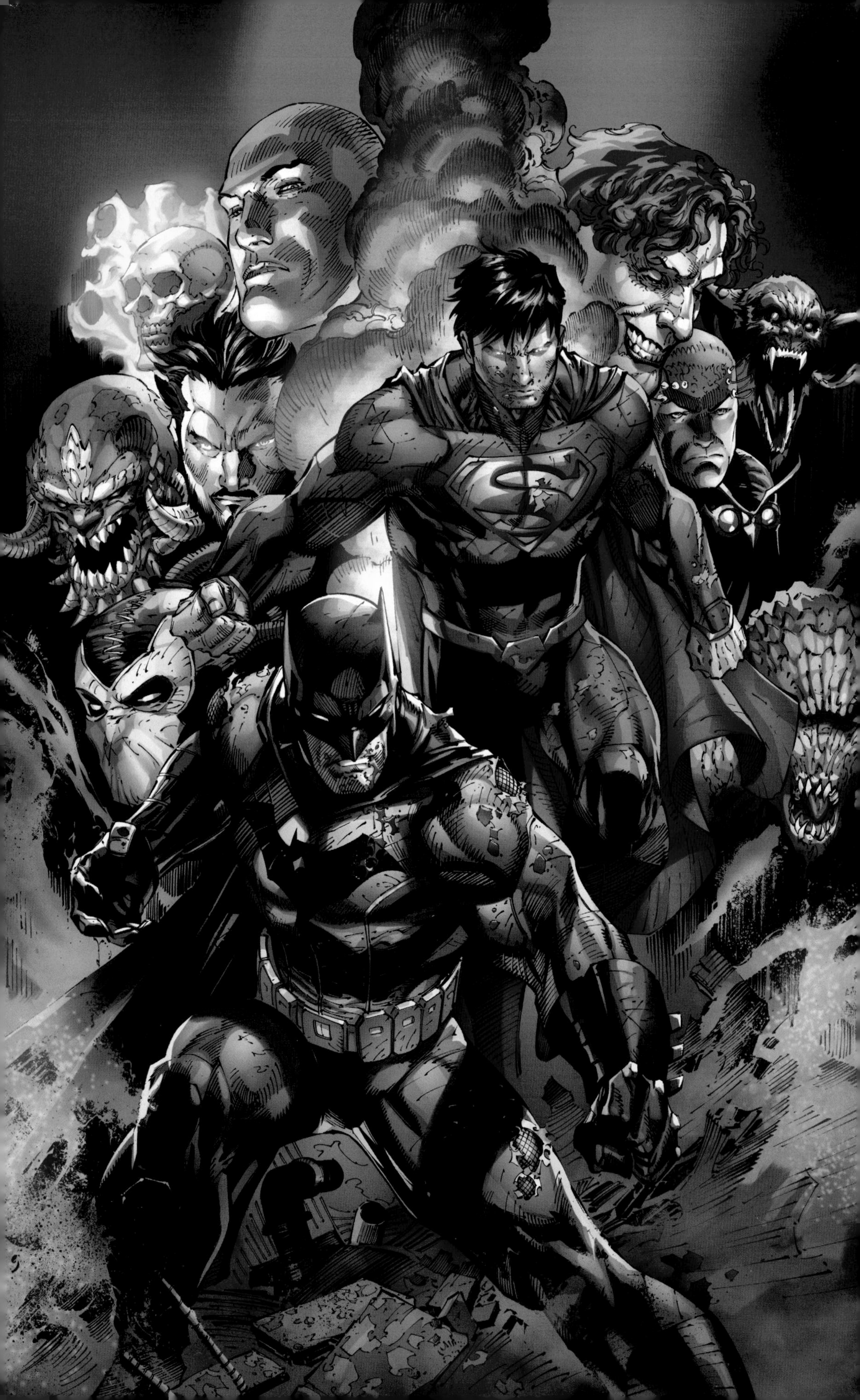

GREG PAK writer TOM DERENICK, TYLER KIRKHAM, IAN CHURCHILL, ARDIAN SYAF, EMANUELA LUPACCHINO pencillers
VICENTE CIFUENTES, TYLER KIRKHAM, MARK MORALES, JAIME MENDOZA, RAY MCCARTHY inkers ARIF PRIANTO, FAHRIZA KAMAPUTRA, JESSICA KHOLINNE, GLORIA CAELI colorists
ROB LEIGH letterer cover by ARDIAN SYAF, JONATHAN GLAPION and ULISES ARREOLA

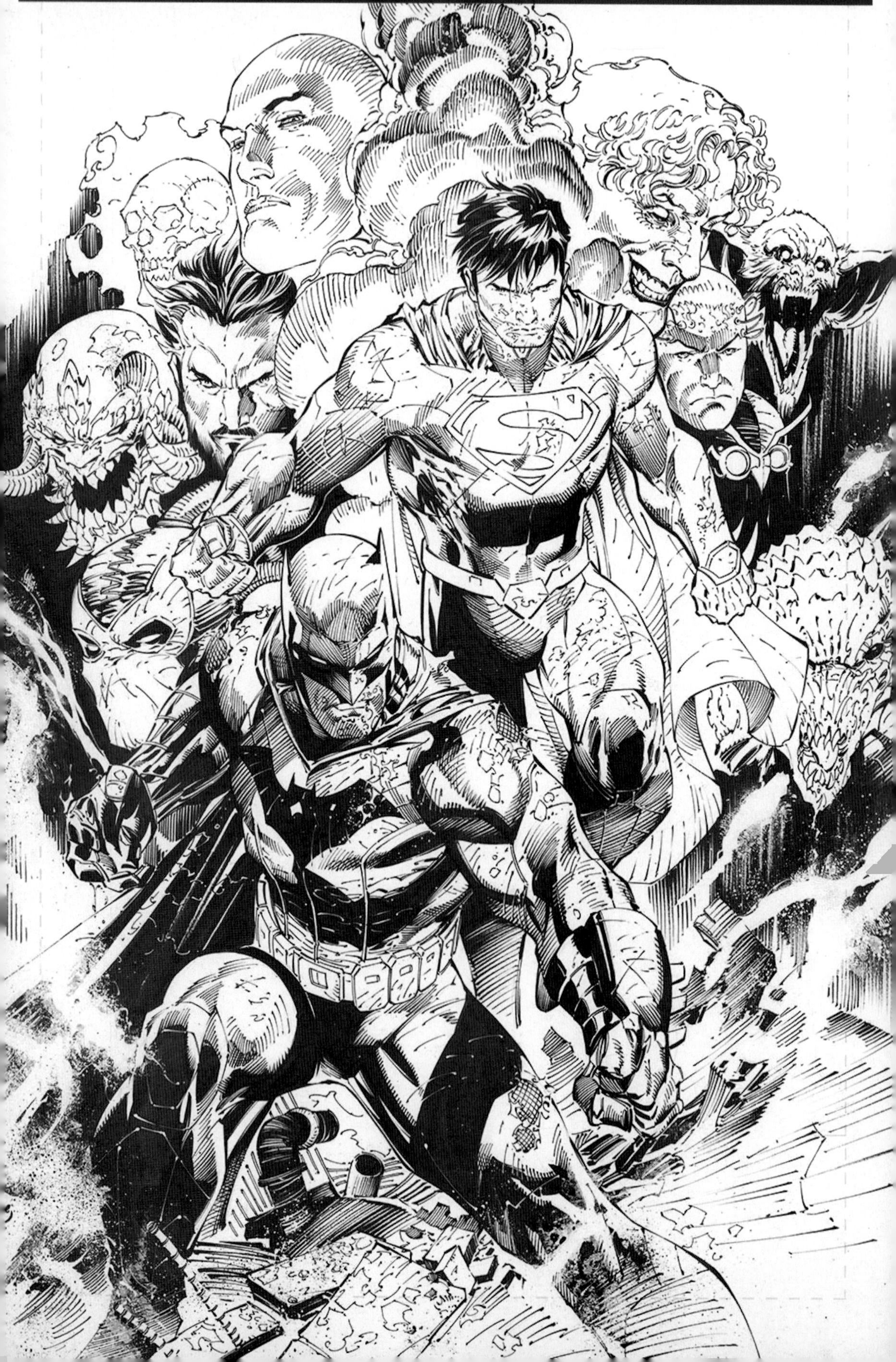

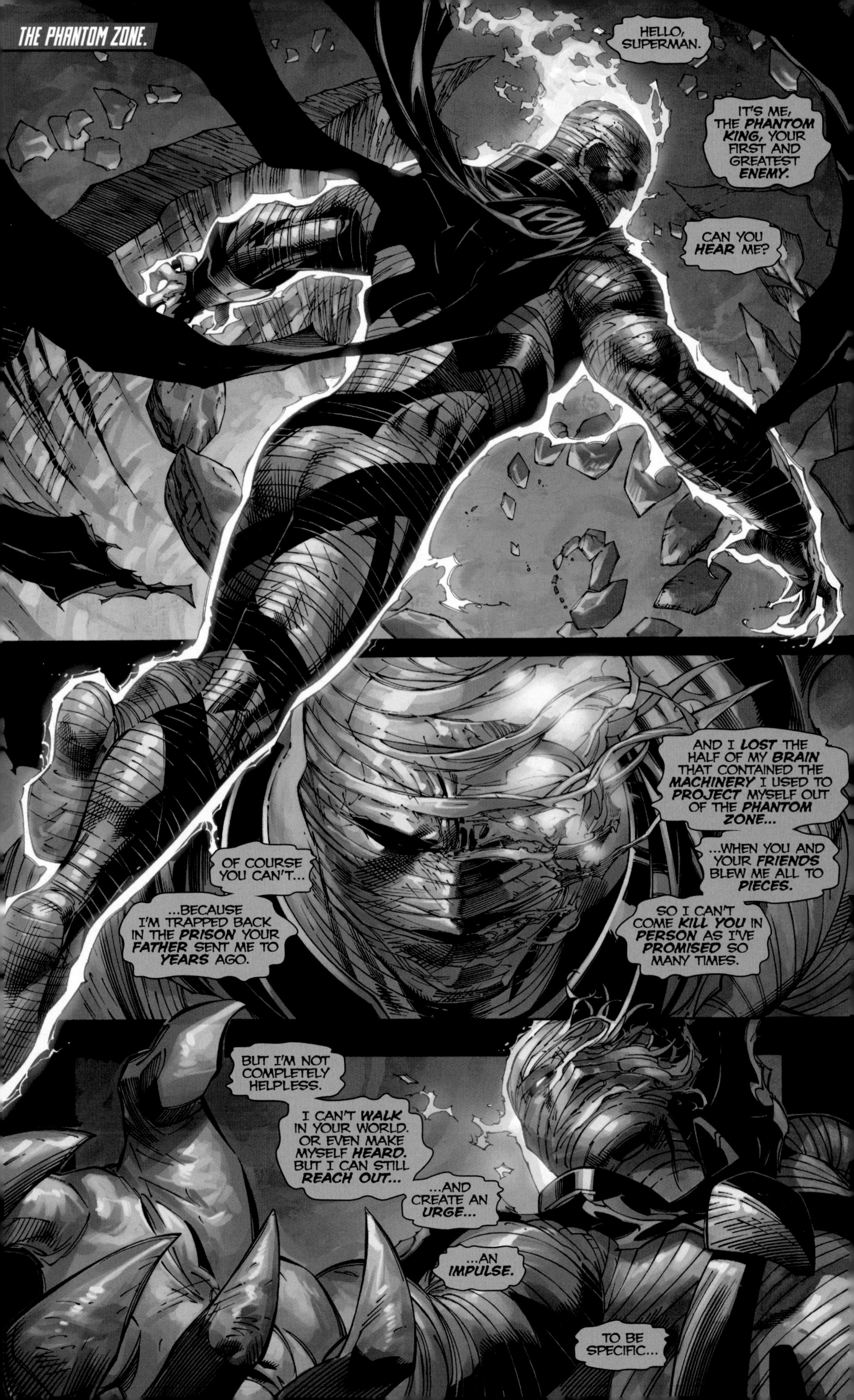
THE PHANTOM ZONE.
HELLO, SUPERMAN.
IT'S ME, THE PHANTOM KING, YOUR FIRST AND GREATEST ENEMY.
CAN YOU HEAR ME?
OF COURSE YOU CAN'T...
...BECAUSE I'M TRAPPED BACK IN THE PRISON YOUR FATHER SENT ME TO YEARS AGO.
AND I LOST THE HALF OF MY BRAIN THAT CONTAINED THE MACHINERY I USED TO PROJECT MYSELF OUT OF THE PHANTOM ZONE...
...WHEN YOU AND YOUR FRIENDS BLEW ME ALL TO PIECES.
SO I CAN'T COME KILL YOU IN PERSON AS I'VE PROMISED SO MANY TIMES.
BUT I'M NOT COMPLETELY HELPLESS.
I CAN'T WALK IN YOUR WORLD. OR EVEN MAKE MYSELF HEARD. BUT I CAN STILL REACH OUT...
...AND CREATE AN URGE...
...AN IMPULSE.
TO BE SPECIFIC...

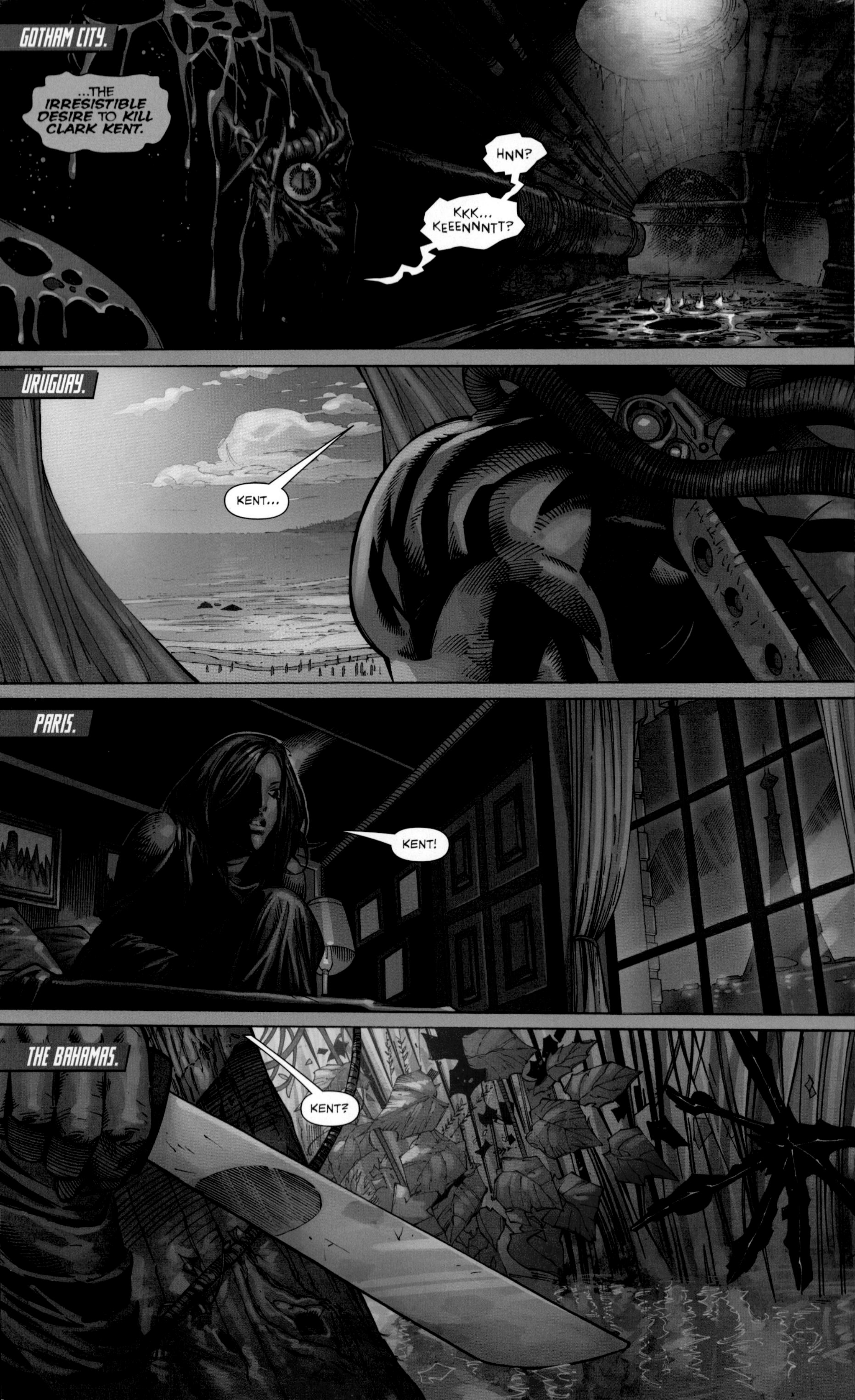
GOTHAM CITY.
...THE IRRESISTIBLE DESIRE TO KILL CLARK KENT.
HNN?
KKK... KEEENNNTT?
URUGUAY.
KENT...
PARIS.
KENT!
THE BAHAMAS.
KENT?

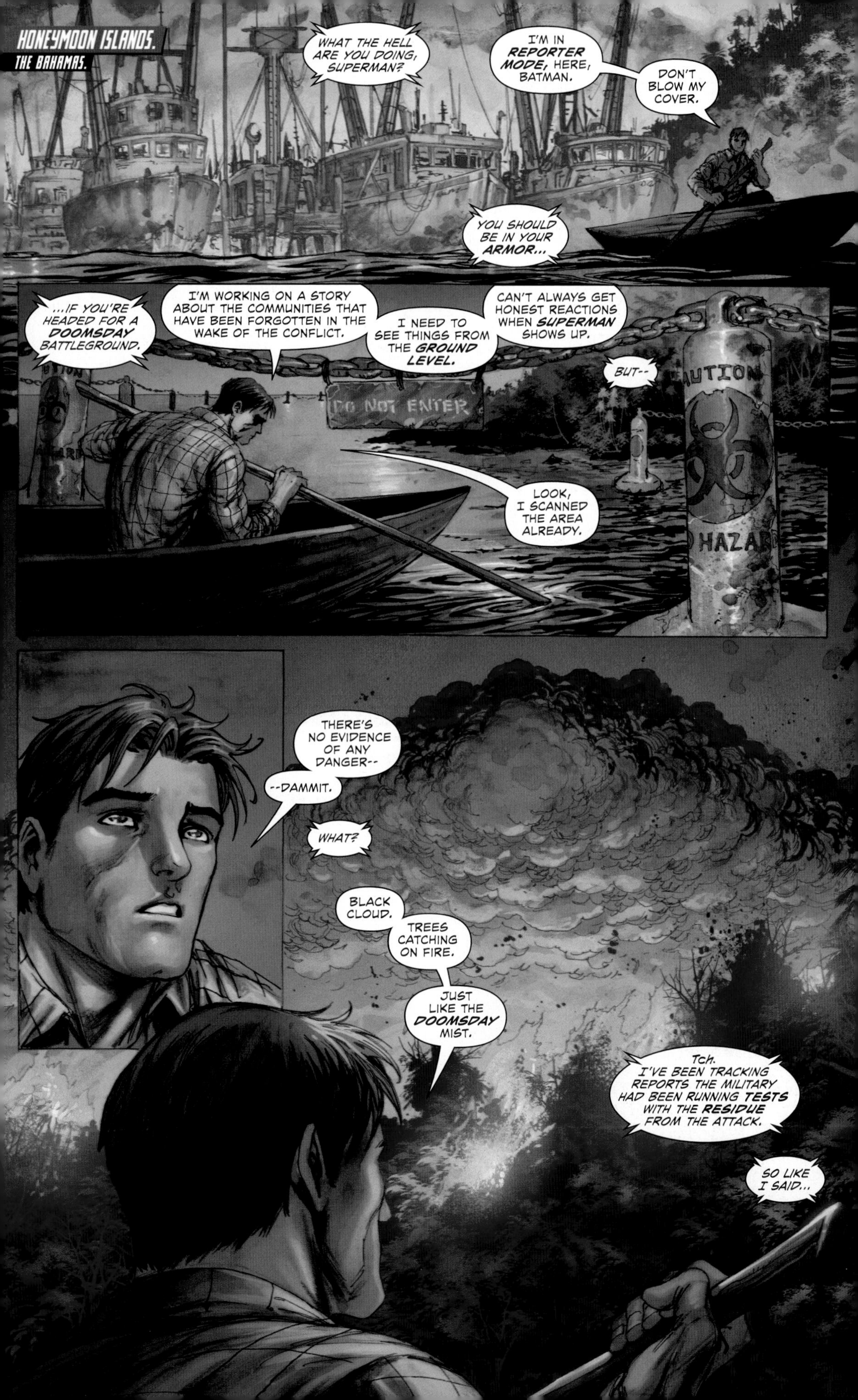
HONEYMOON ISLANDS.
THE BAHAMAS.
WHAT THE HELL ARE YOU DOING, SUPERMAN?
I'M IN REPORTER MODE, HERE, BATMAN.
DON'T BLOW MY COVER.
YOU SHOULD BE IN YOUR ARMOR...
...IF YOU'RE HEADED FOR A DOOMSDAY BATTLEGROUND.
I'M WORKING ON A STORY ABOUT THE COMMUNITIES THAT HAVE BEEN FORGOTTEN IN THE WAKE OF THE CONFLICT.
I NEED TO SEE THINGS FROM THE GROUND LEVEL.
CAN'T ALWAYS GET HONEST REACTIONS WHEN SUPERMAN SHOWS UP.
BUT--
DO NOT ENTER
LOOK, I SCANNED THE AREA ALREADY.
THERE'S NO EVIDENCE OF ANY DANGER--
--DAMMIT.
WHAT?
BLACK CLOUD.
TREES CATCHING ON FIRE.
JUST LIKE THE DOOMSDAY MIST.
Tch. I'VE BEEN TRACKING REPORTS THE MILITARY HAD BEEN RUNNING TESTS WITH THE RESIDUE FROM THE ATTACK.
SO LIKE I SAID...

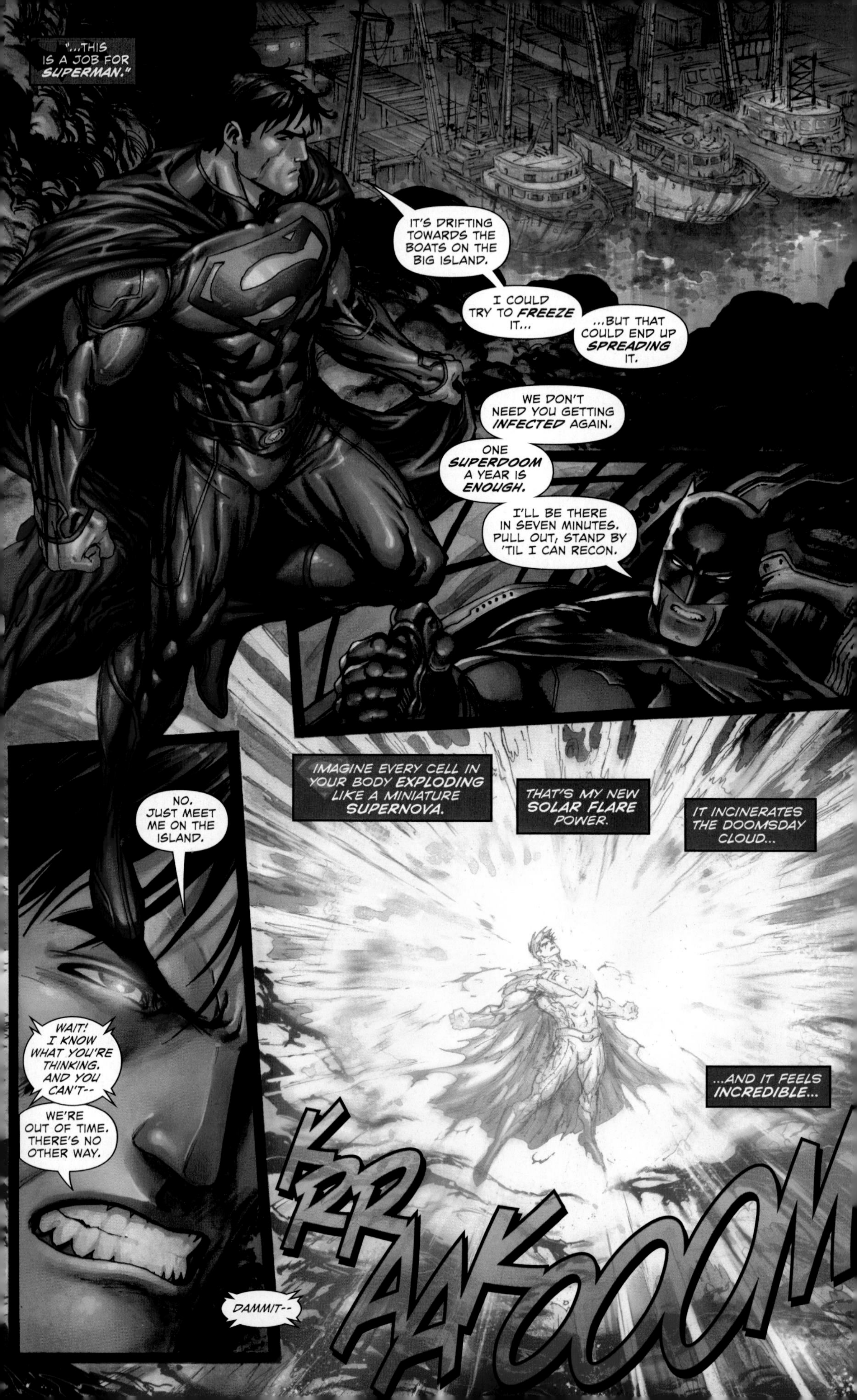
"...THIS IS A JOB FOR SUPERMAN."
IT'S DRIFTING TOWARDS THE BOATS ON THE BIG ISLAND.
I COULD TRY TO FREEZE IT...
...BUT THAT COULD END UP SPREADING IT.
WE DON'T NEED YOU GETTING INFECTED AGAIN.
ONE SUPERDOOM A YEAR IS ENOUGH.
I'LL BE THERE IN SEVEN MINUTES. PULL OUT, STAND BY 'TIL I CAN RECON.
NO. JUST MEET ME ON THE ISLAND.
WAIT! I KNOW WHAT YOU'RE THINKING. AND YOU CAN'T--
WE'RE OUT OF TIME. THERE'S NO OTHER WAY.
DAMMIT--
IMAGINE EVERY CELL IN YOUR BODY EXPLODING LIKE A MINIATURE SUPERNOVA.
THAT'S MY NEW SOLAR FLARE POWER.
IT INCINERATES THE DOOMSDAY CLOUD...
...AND IT FEELS INCREDIBLE...
KRRAKOOOOM

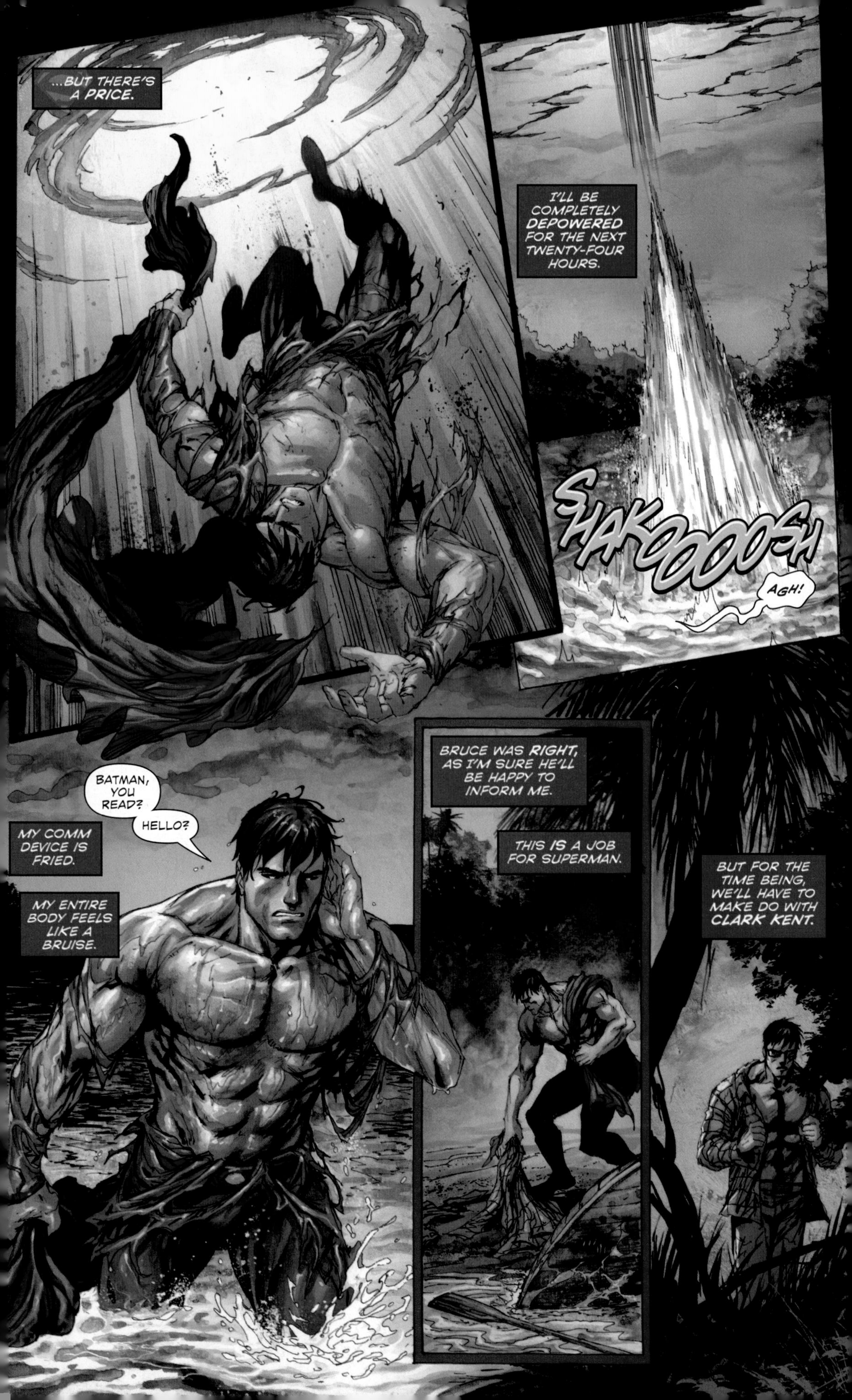
...BUT THERE'S A PRICE.
I'LL BE COMPLETELY DEPOWERED FOR THE NEXT TWENTY-FOUR HOURS.
SHAKOOOOOSH
AGH!
BATMAN, YOU READ?
HELLO?
MY COMM DEVICE IS FRIED.
MY ENTIRE BODY FEELS LIKE A BRUISE.
BRUCE WAS RIGHT, AS I'M SURE HE'LL BE HAPPY TO INFORM ME.
THIS IS A JOB FOR SUPERMAN.
BUT FOR THE TIME BEING, WE'LL HAVE TO MAKE DO WITH CLARK KENT.

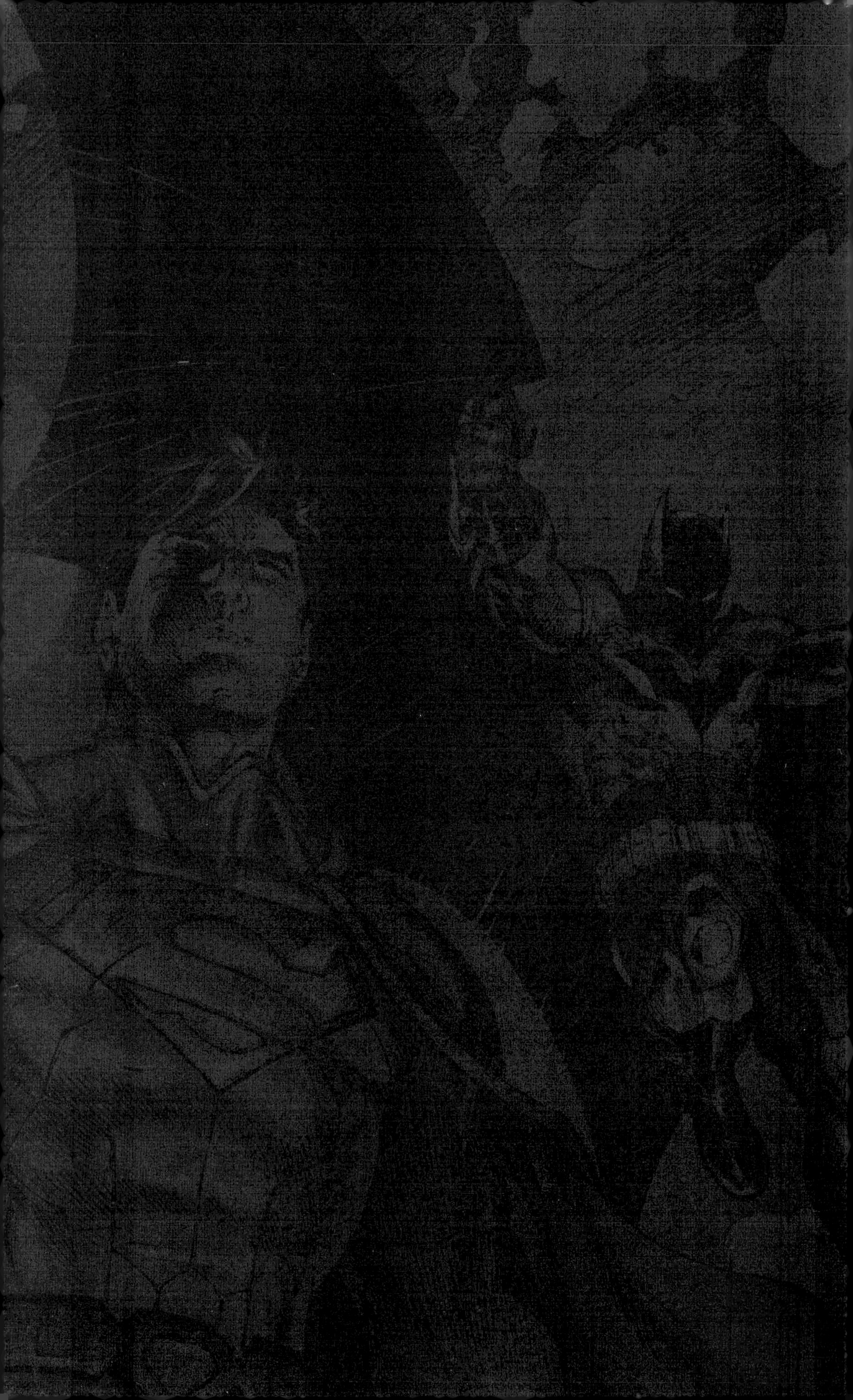

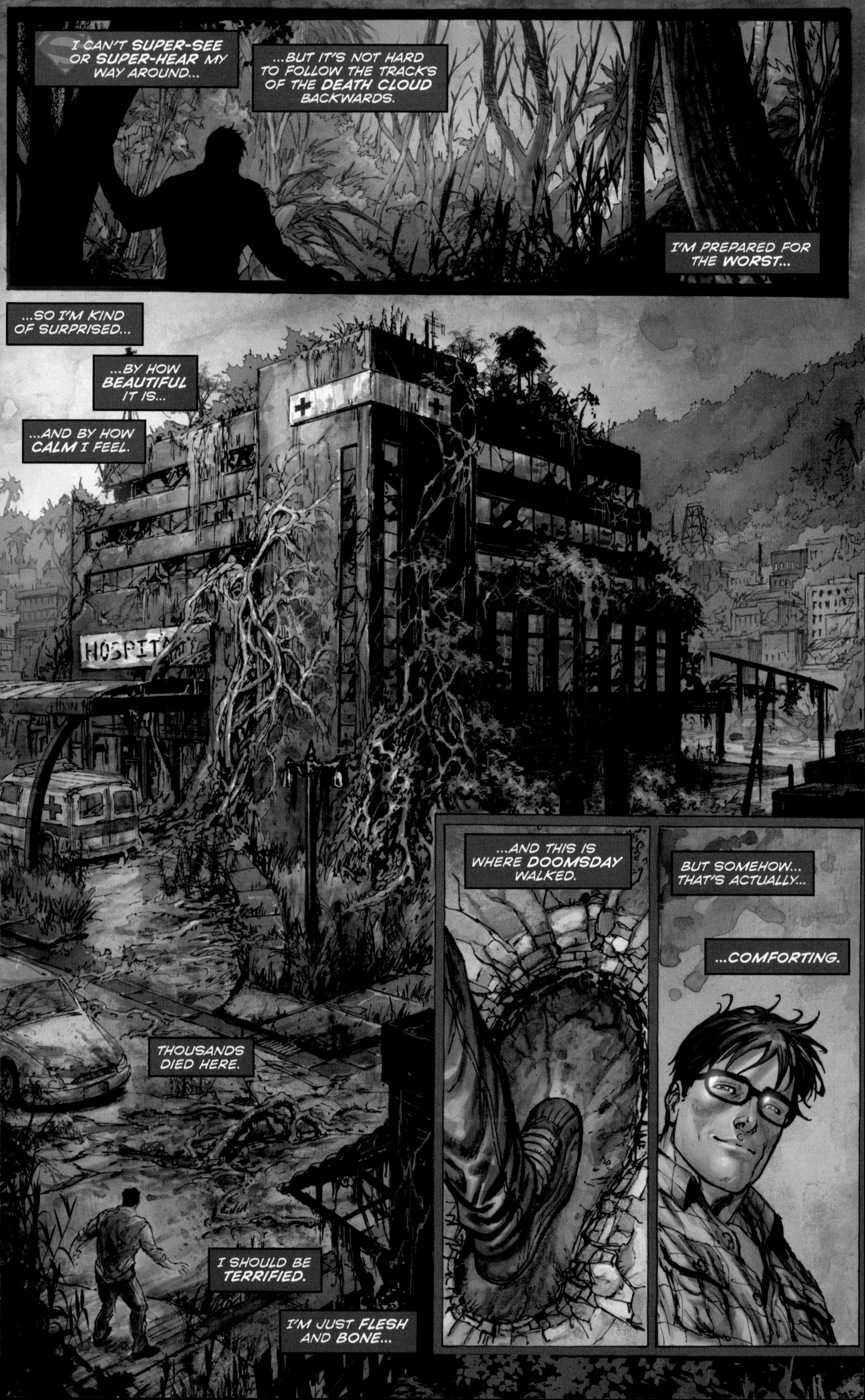
I CAN'T SUPER-SEE OR SUPER-HEAR MY WAY AROUND...
...BUT IT'S NOT HARD TO FOLLOW THE TRACKS OF THE DEATH CLOUD BACKWARDS.
I'M PREPARED FOR THE WORST...
...SO I'M KIND OF SURPRISED...
...BY HOW BEAUTIFUL IT IS...
...AND BY HOW CALM I FEEL.
HOSPIT
THOUSANDS DIED HERE.
I SHOULD BE TERRIFIED.
I'M JUST FLESH AND BONE...
...AND THIS IS WHERE DOOMSDAY WALKED.
BUT SOMEHOW... THAT'S ACTUALLY...
...COMFORTING.

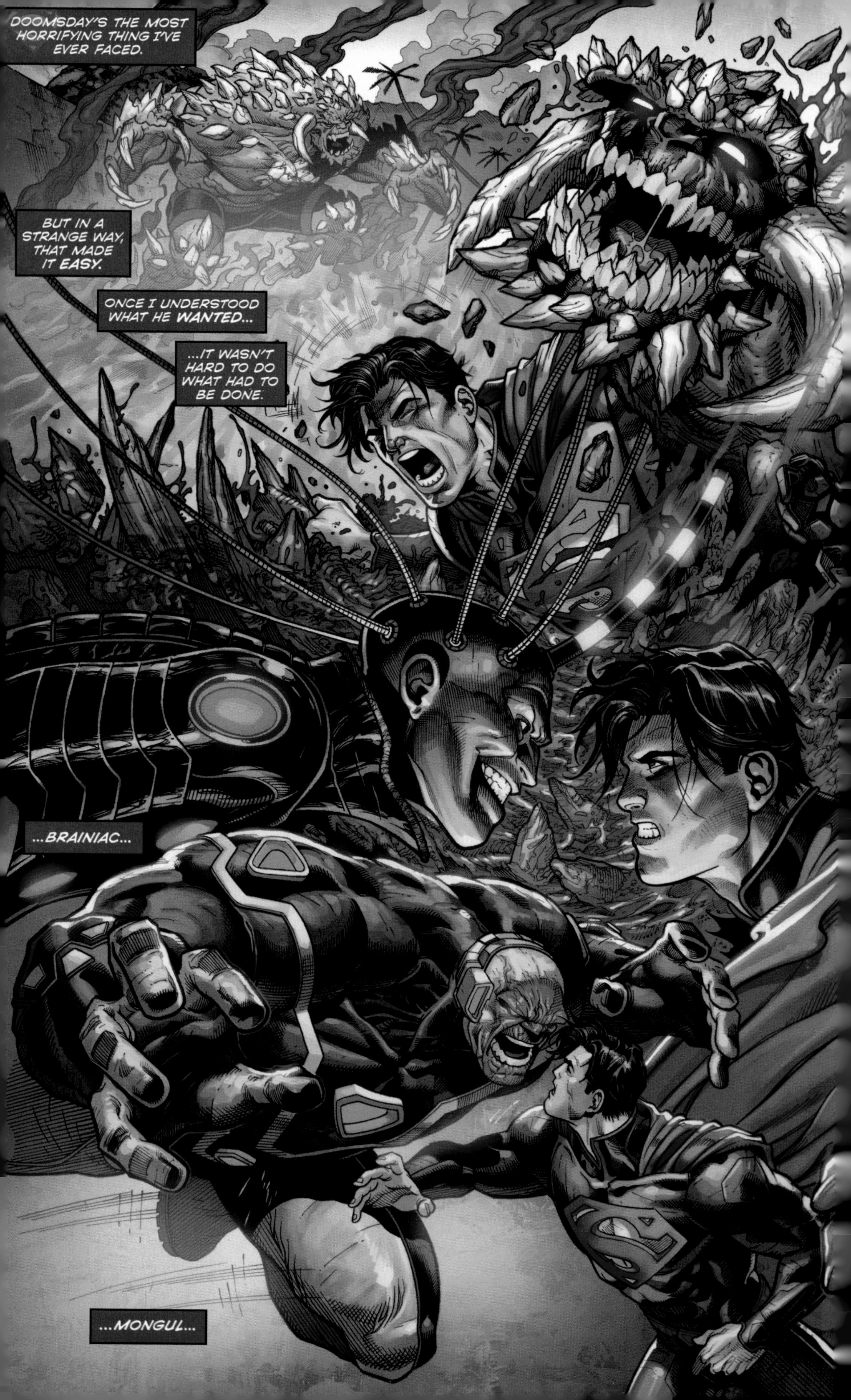
DOOMSDAY'S THE MOST HORRIFYING THING I'VE EVER FACED.
BUT IN A STRANGE WAY, THAT MADE IT EASY.
ONCE I UNDERSTOOD WHAT HE WANTED...
...IT WASN'T HARD TO DO WHAT HAD TO BE DONE.
...BRAINIAC...
...MONGUL...

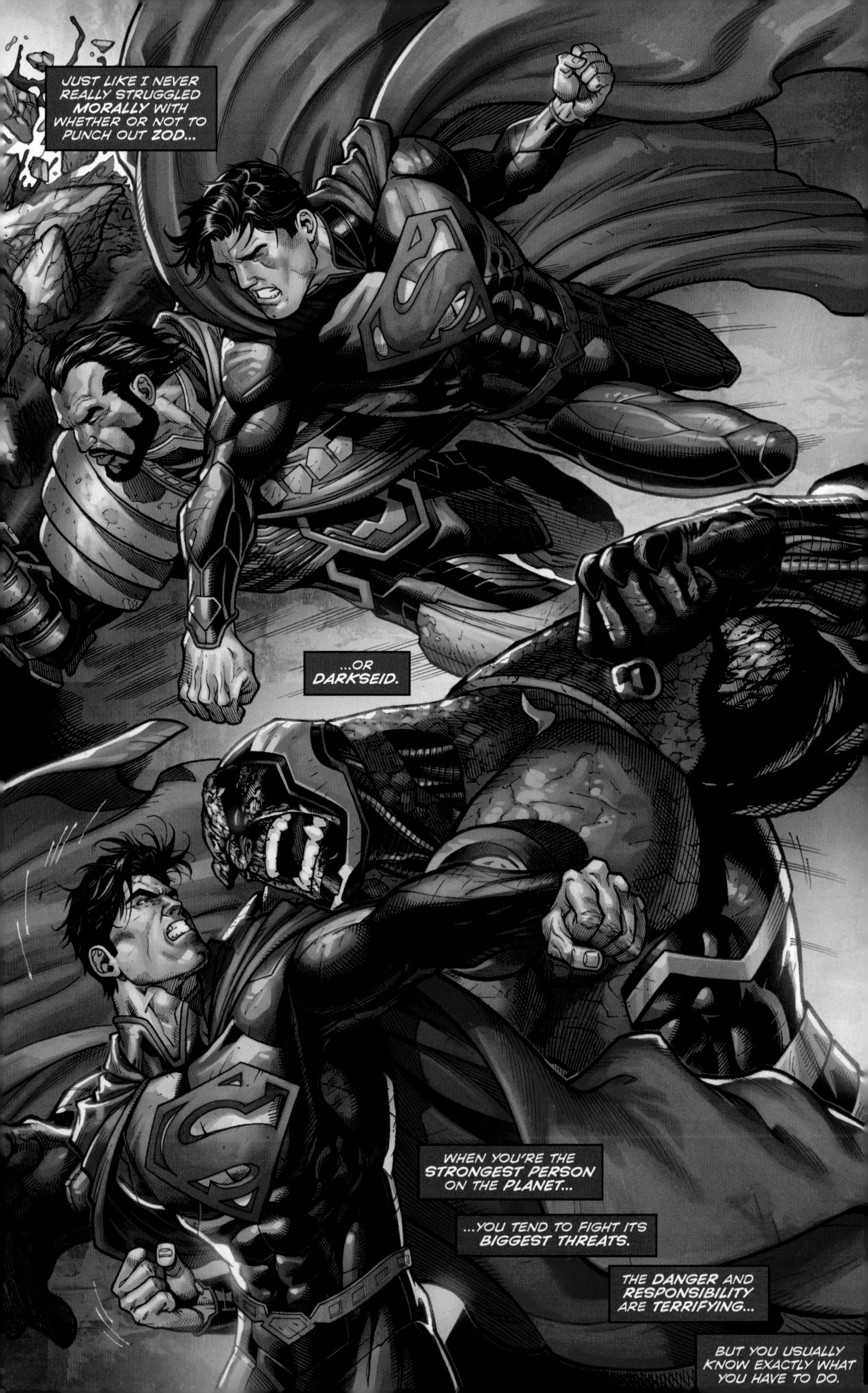
JUST LIKE I NEVER REALLY STRUGGLED MORALLY WITH WHETHER OR NOT TO PUNCH OUT ZOD...
...OR DARKSEID.
WHEN YOU'RE THE STRONGEST PERSON ON THE PLANET...
...YOU TEND TO FIGHT ITS BIGGEST THREATS.
THE DANGER AND RESPONSIBILITY ARE TERRIFYING...
BUT YOU USUALLY KNOW EXACTLY WHAT YOU HAVE TO DO.

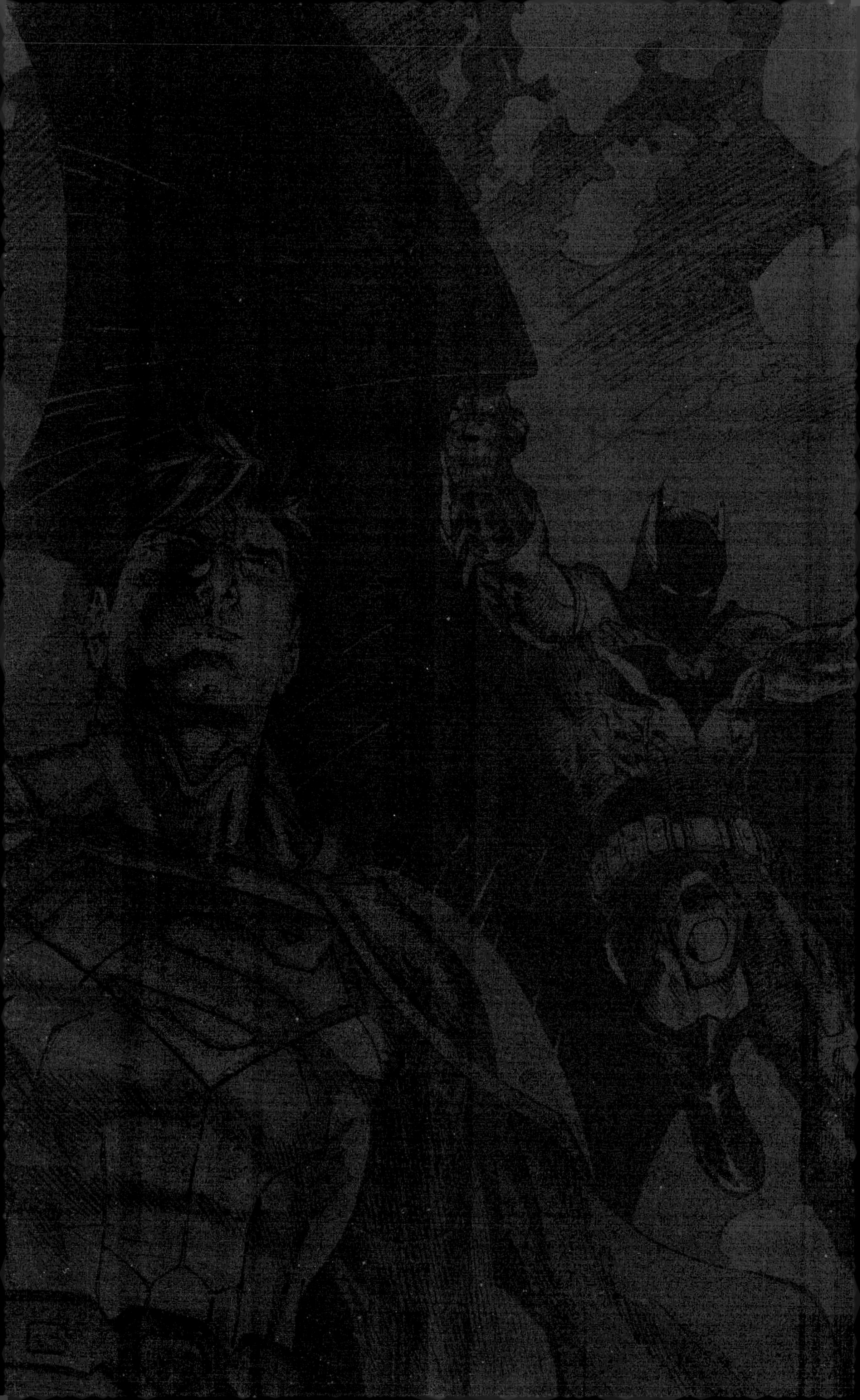

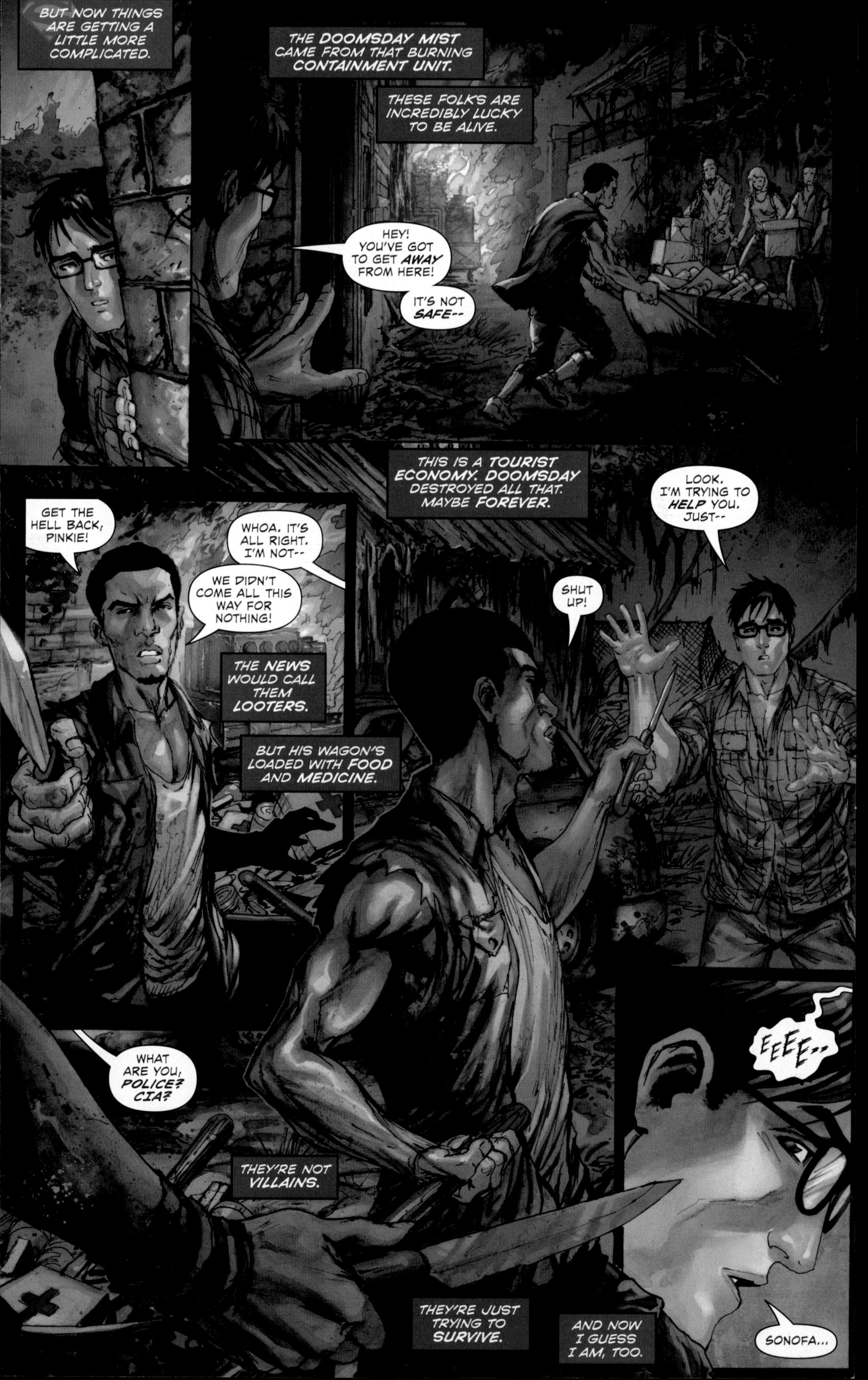

BUT NOW THINGS ARE GETTING A LITTLE MORE COMPLICATED.
THE DOOMSDAY MIST CAME FROM THAT BURNING CONTAINMENT UNIT.
THESE FOLKS ARE INCREDIBLY LUCKY TO BE ALIVE.
HEY! YOU'VE GOT TO GET AWAY FROM HERE!
IT'S NOT SAFE--
THIS IS A TOURIST ECONOMY. DOOMSDAY DESTROYED ALL THAT. MAYBE FOREVER.
GET THE HELL BACK, PINKIE!
WHOA. IT'S ALL RIGHT. I'M NOT--
WE DIDN'T COME ALL THIS WAY FOR NOTHING!
THE NEWS WOULD CALL THEM LOOTERS.
BUT HIS WAGON'S LOADED WITH FOOD AND MEDICINE.
LOOK. I'M TRYING TO HELP YOU. JUST--
SHUT UP!
WHAT ARE YOU, POLICE? CIA?
THEY'RE NOT VILLAINS.
EEEE--
THEY'RE JUST TRYING TO SURVIVE.
AND NOW I GUESS I AM, TOO.
SONOFA...

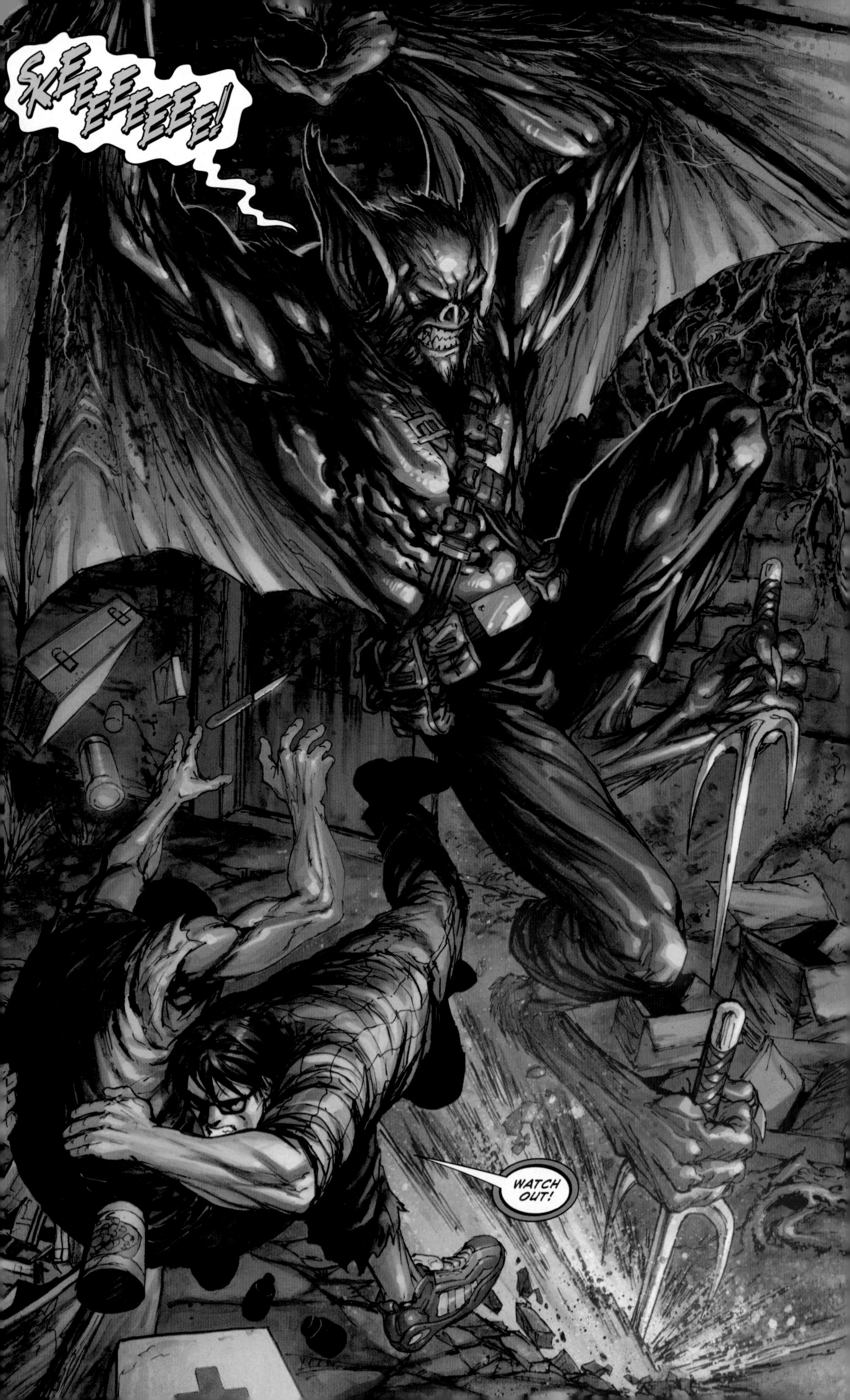
SKEEEEEEEE!
WATCH OUT!

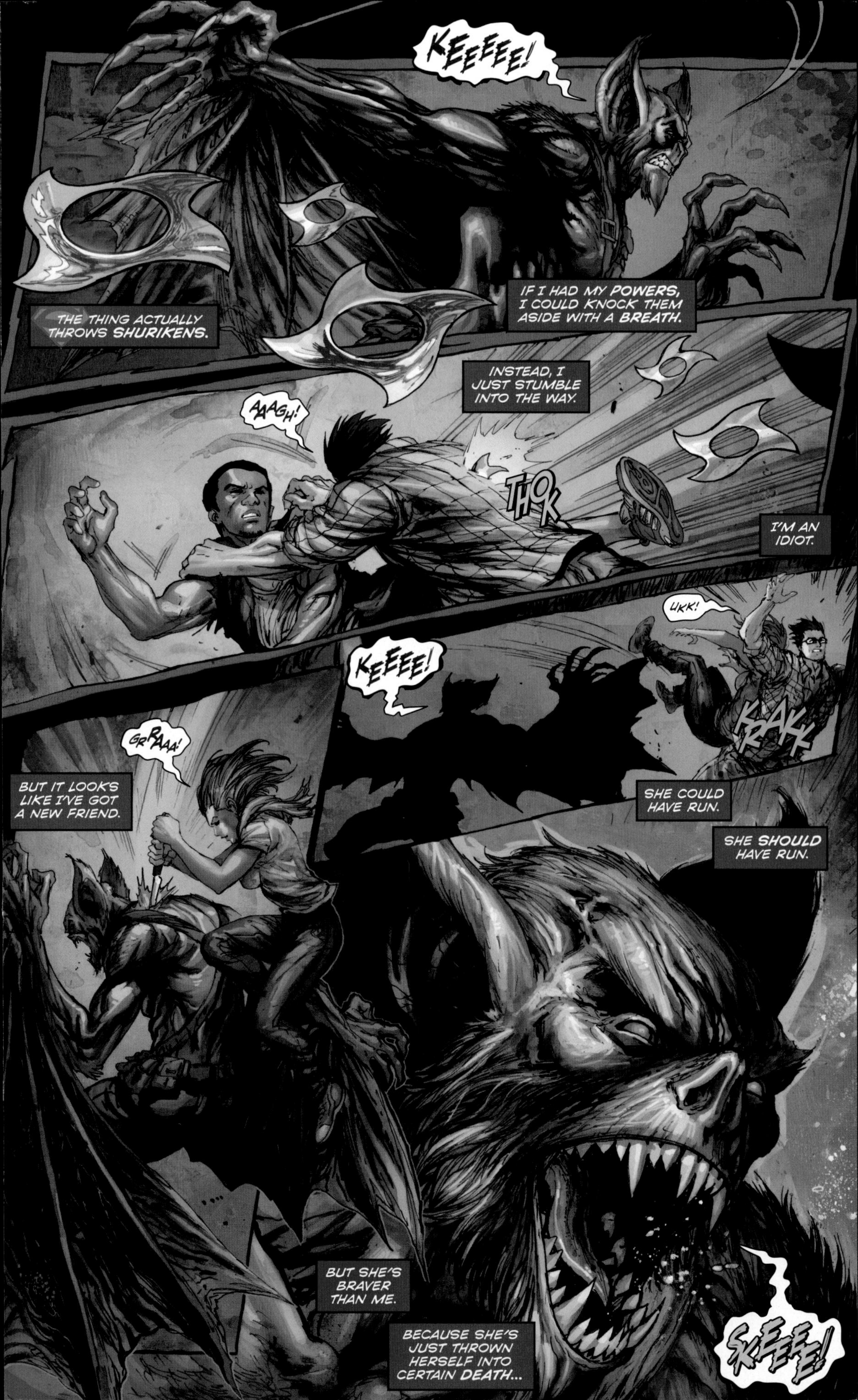

KEEEEE!
THE THING ACTUALLY THROWS SHURIKENS.
IF I HAD MY POWERS, I COULD KNOCK THEM ASIDE WITH A BREATH.
INSTEAD, I JUST STUMBLE INTO THE WAY.
AAAGH!
THOK
I'M AN IDIOT.
UKK!
KEEEE!
KRAKK
GRRAAA!
BUT IT LOOKS LIKE I'VE GOT A NEW FRIEND.
SHE COULD HAVE RUN.
SHE SHOULD HAVE RUN.
BUT SHE'S BRAVER THAN ME.
BECAUSE SHE'S JUST THROWN HERSELF INTO CERTAIN DEATH...
SKEEEE!

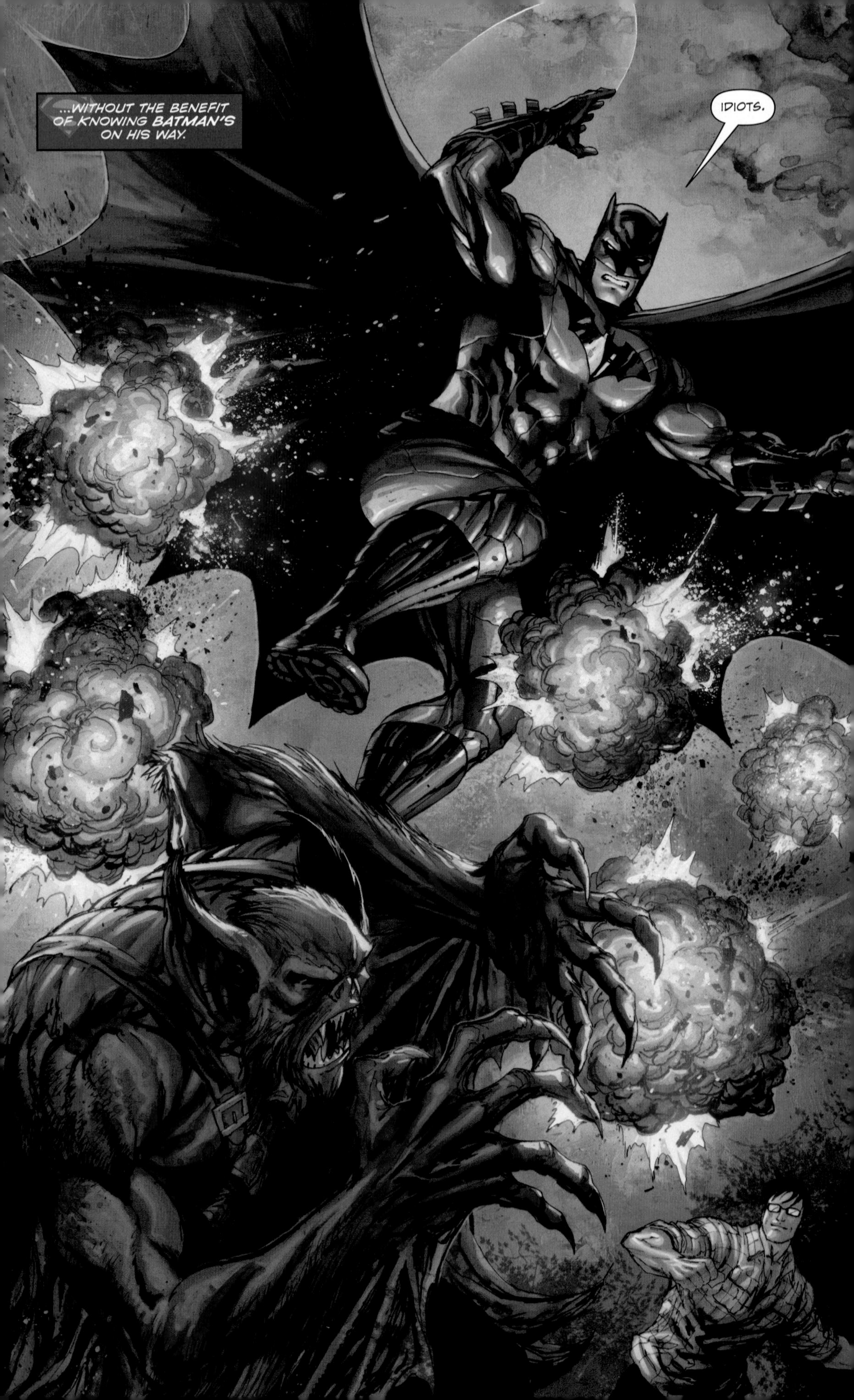
...WITHOUT THE BENEFIT OF KNOWING BATMAN'S ON HIS WAY.
IDIOTS.

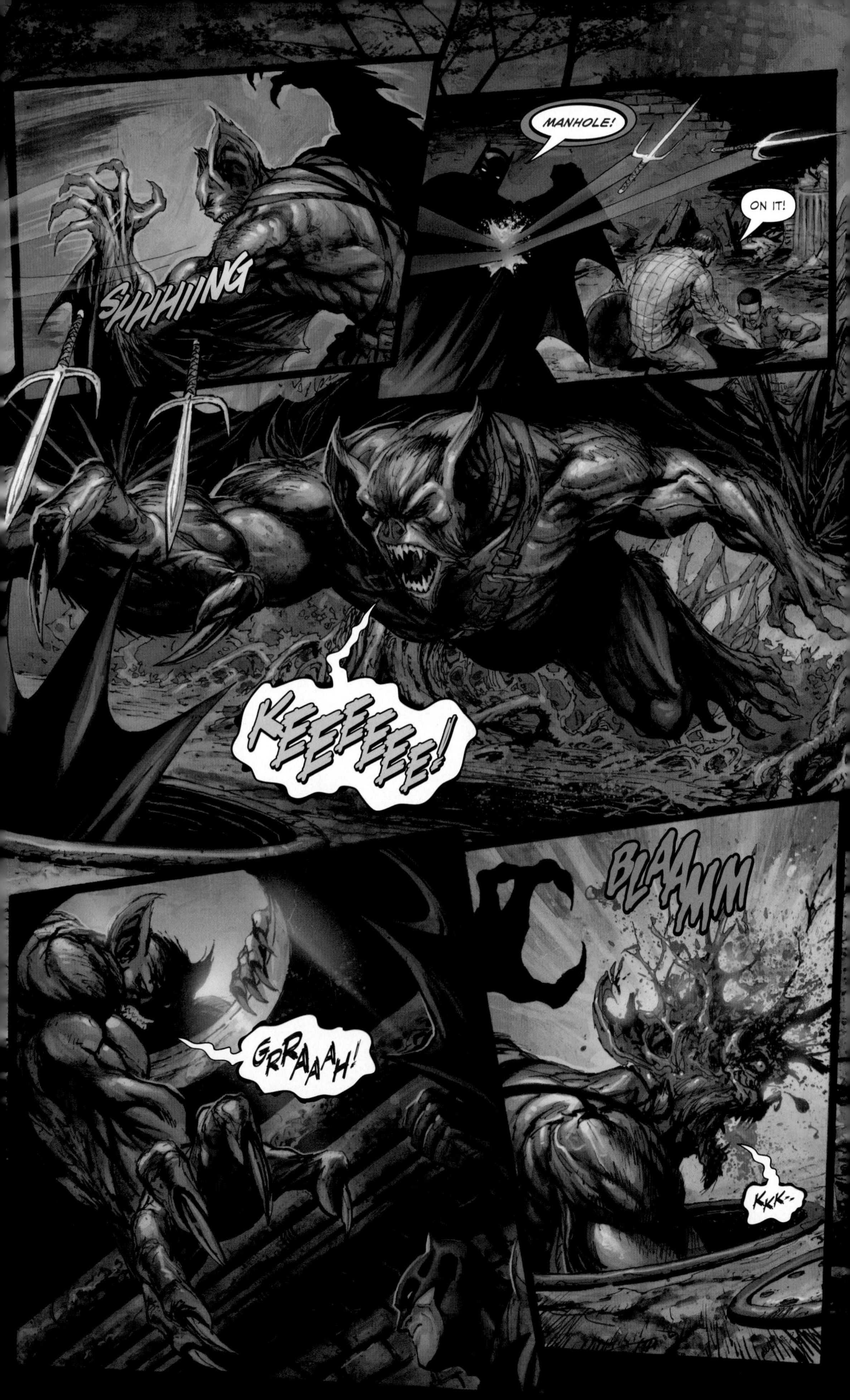
SHHHIING
MANHOLE!
ON IT!
KEEEEEEE!
GRRAAAH!
BLAAMM
KKK--

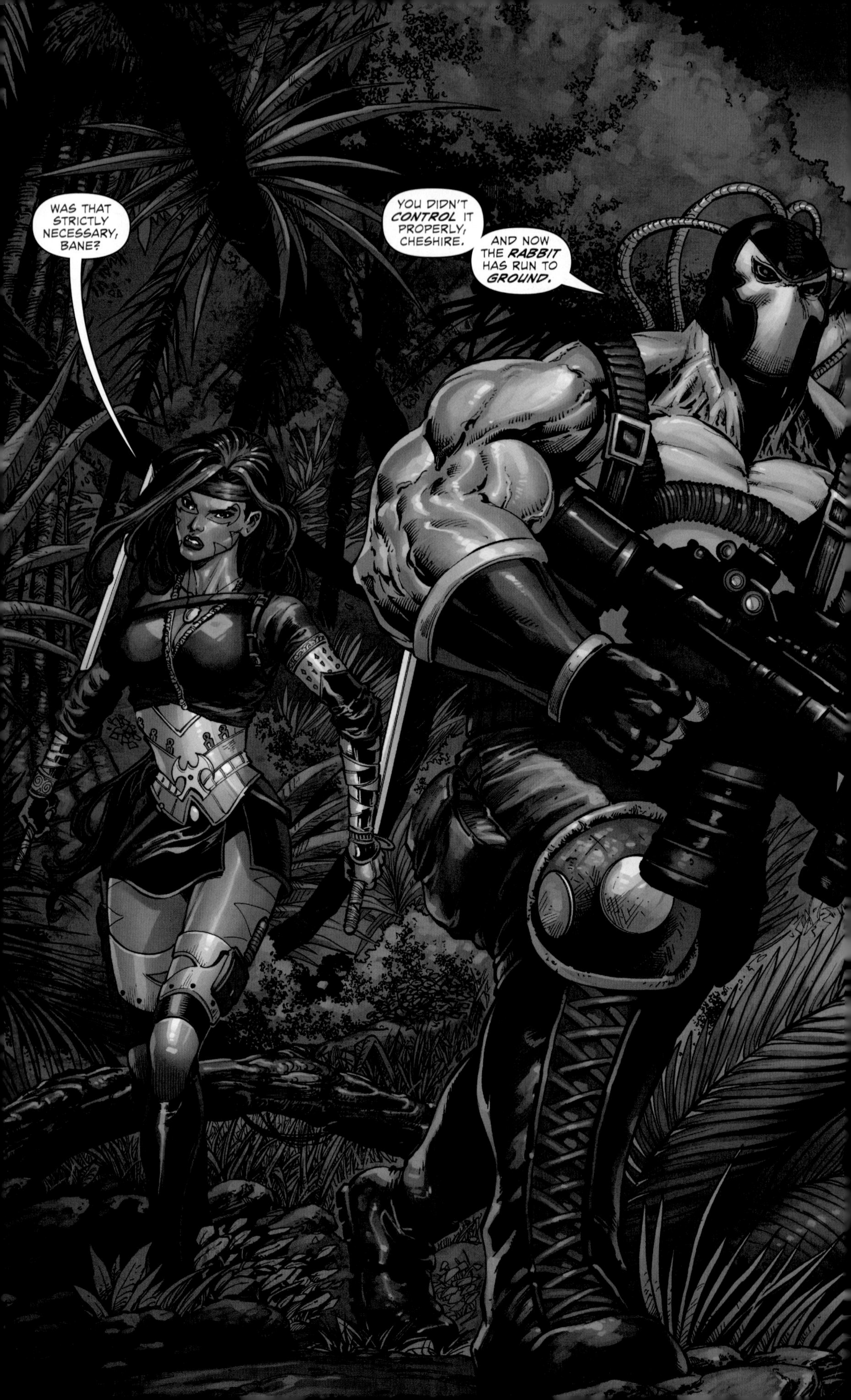
WAS THAT STRICTLY NECESSARY, BANE?
YOU DIDN'T *CONTROL* IT PROPERLY, CHESHIRE.
AND NOW THE *RABBIT* HAS RUN TO *GROUND*.

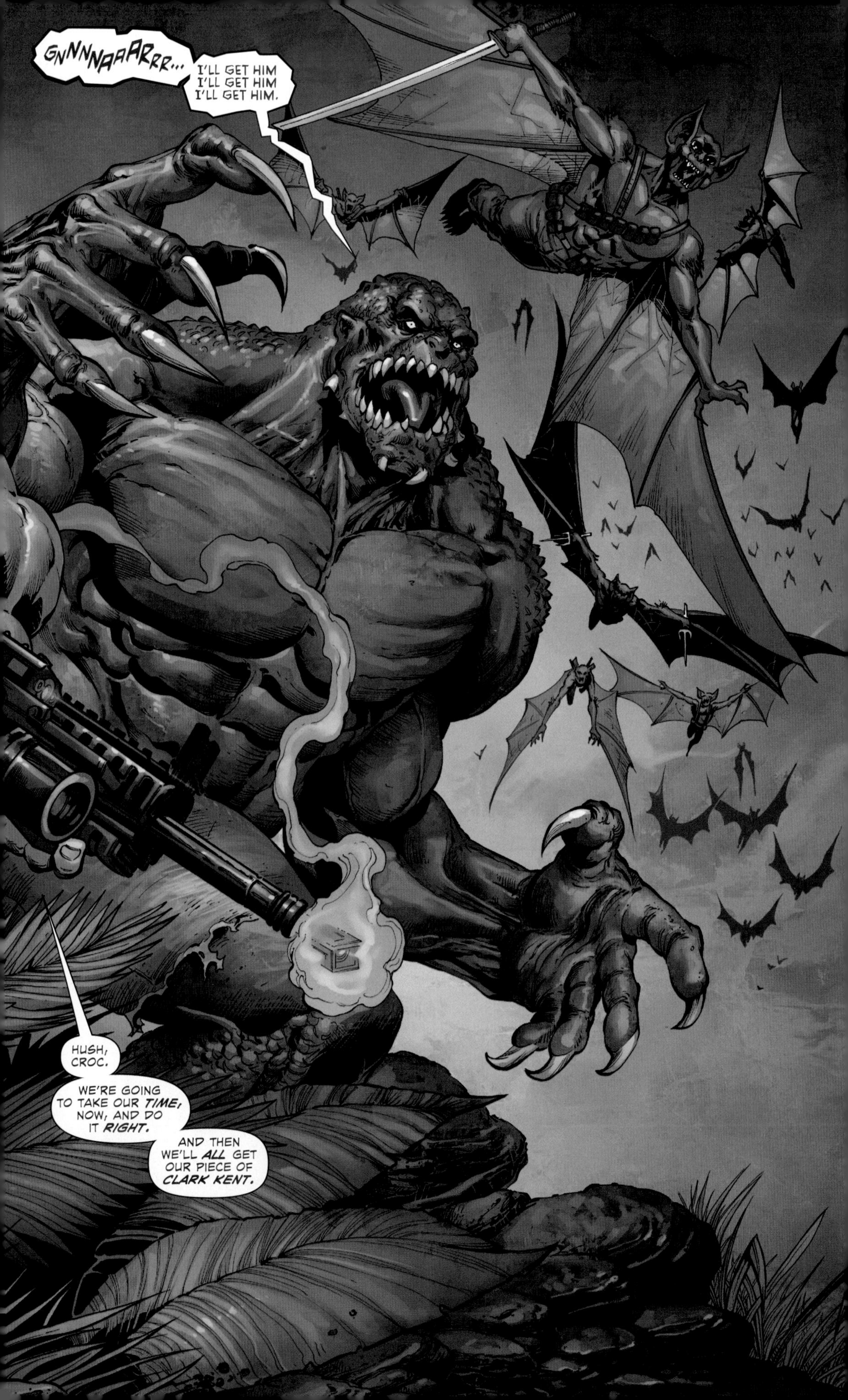
GNNNNAAARRR...
I'LL GET HIM I'LL GET HIM I'LL GET HIM.
HUSH, CROC.
WE'RE GOING TO TAKE OUR TIME, NOW, AND DO IT RIGHT.
AND THEN WE'LL ALL GET OUR PIECE OF CLARK KENT.

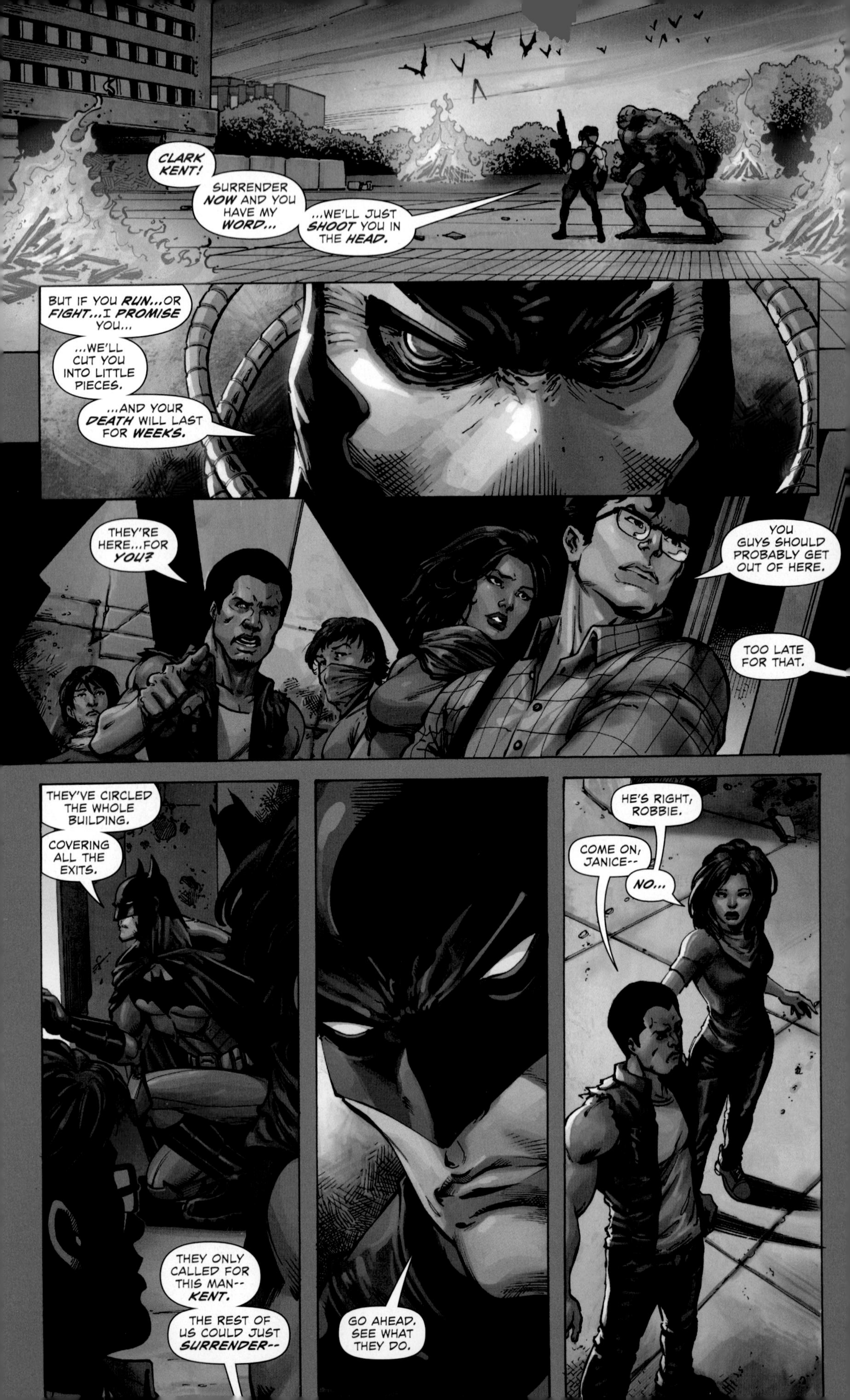
CLARK KENT!
SURRENDER NOW AND YOU HAVE MY WORD...
...WE'LL JUST SHOOT YOU IN THE HEAD.
BUT IF YOU RUN...OR FIGHT...I PROMISE YOU...
...WE'LL CUT YOU INTO LITTLE PIECES.
...AND YOUR DEATH WILL LAST FOR WEEKS.
THEY'RE HERE...FOR YOU?
YOU GUYS SHOULD PROBABLY GET OUT OF HERE.
TOO LATE FOR THAT.
THEY'VE CIRCLED THE WHOLE BUILDING.
COVERING ALL THE EXITS.
THEY ONLY CALLED FOR THIS MAN-- KENT.
THE REST OF US COULD JUST SURRENDER--
GO AHEAD. SEE WHAT THEY DO.
HE'S RIGHT, ROBBIE.
COME ON, JANICE--
NO...

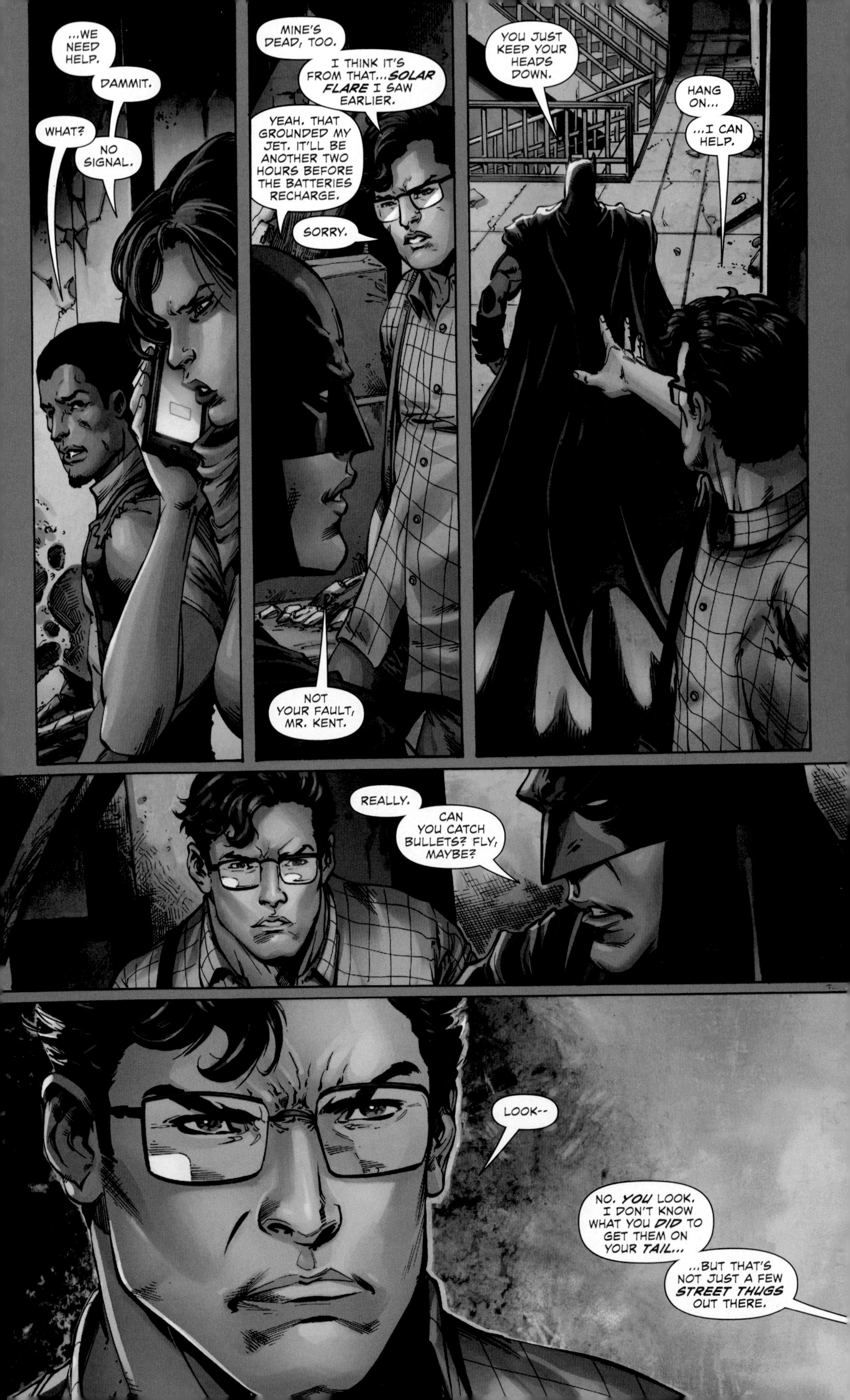

...WE NEED HELP.
DAMMIT.
WHAT?
NO SIGNAL.
MINE'S DEAD, TOO.
I THINK IT'S FROM THAT...SOLAR FLARE I SAW EARLIER.
YEAH. THAT GROUNDED MY JET. IT'LL BE ANOTHER TWO HOURS BEFORE THE BATTERIES RECHARGE.
SORRY.
NOT YOUR FAULT, MR. KENT.
YOU JUST KEEP YOUR HEADS DOWN.
HANG ON...
...I CAN HELP.
REALLY.
CAN YOU CATCH BULLETS? FLY, MAYBE?
LOOK--
NO. YOU LOOK. I DON'T KNOW WHAT YOU DID TO GET THEM ON YOUR TAIL...
...BUT THAT'S NOT JUST A FEW STREET THUGS OUT THERE.

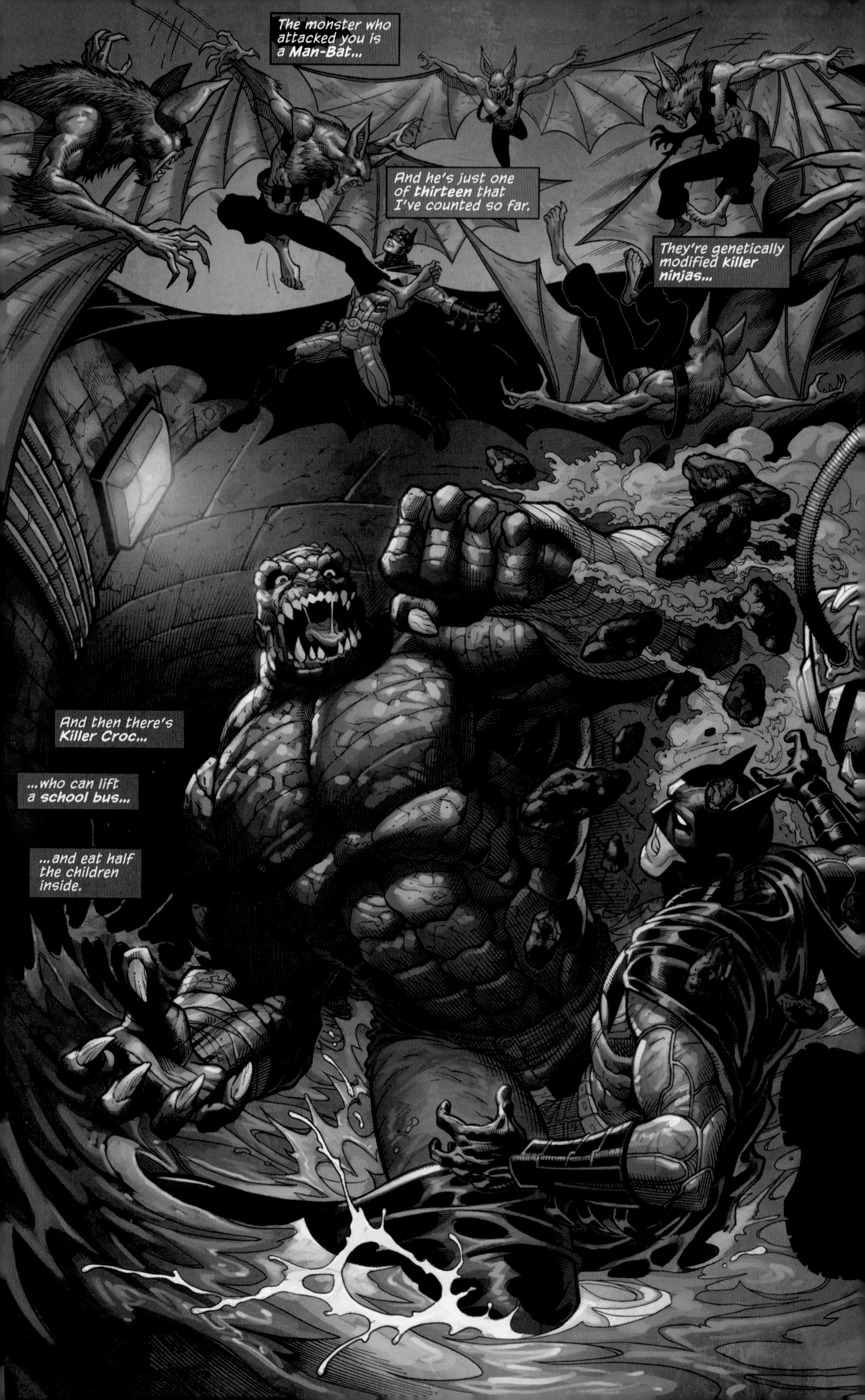
The monster who attacked you is a Man-Bat...
And he's just one of thirteen that I've counted so far.
They're genetically modified killer ninjas...
And then there's Killer Croc...
...who can lift a school bus...
...and eat half the children inside.

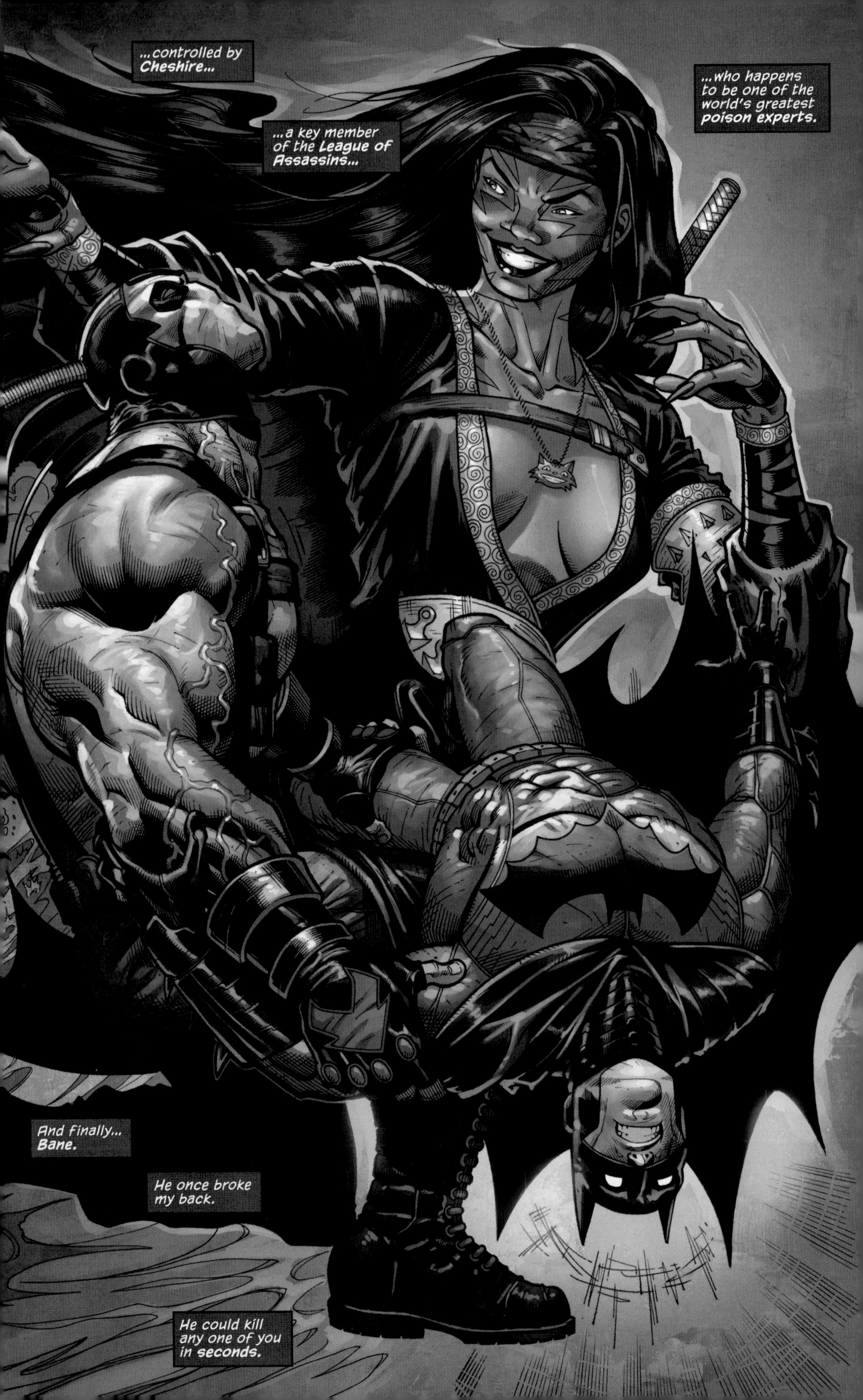
...controlled by Cheshire...
...a key member of the League of Assassins...
...who happens to be one of the world's greatest poison experts.
And finally... Bane.
He once broke my back.
He could kill any one of you in seconds.

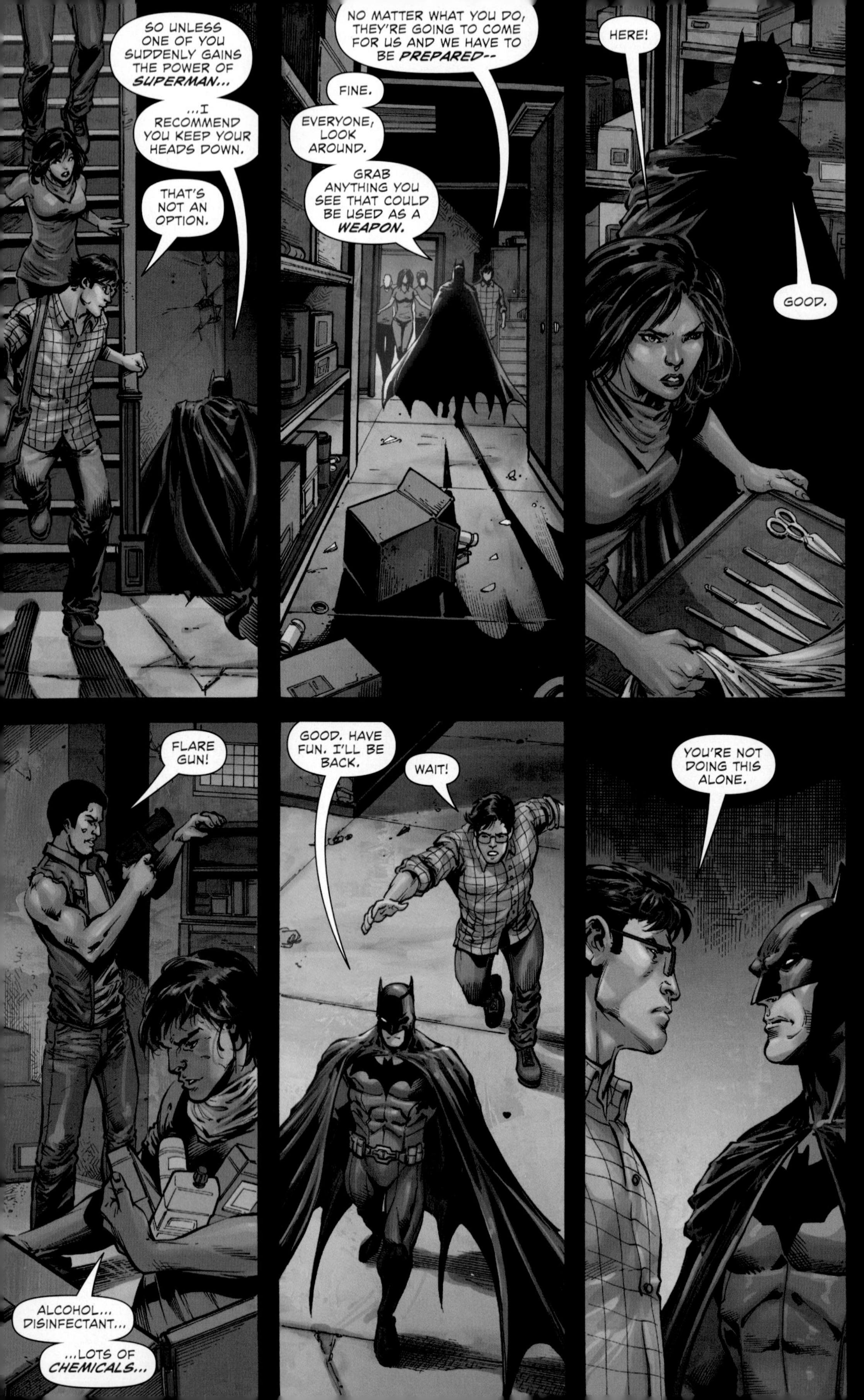
SO UNLESS ONE OF YOU SUDDENLY GAINS THE POWER OF SUPERMAN...
...I RECOMMEND YOU KEEP YOUR HEADS DOWN.
THAT'S NOT AN OPTION.
NO MATTER WHAT YOU DO, THEY'RE GOING TO COME FOR US AND WE HAVE TO BE PREPARED--
FINE.
EVERYONE, LOOK AROUND.
GRAB ANYTHING YOU SEE THAT COULD BE USED AS A WEAPON.
HERE!
GOOD.
FLARE GUN!
ALCOHOL... DISINFECTANT...
...LOTS OF CHEMICALS...
GOOD. HAVE FUN. I'LL BE BACK.
WAIT!
YOU'RE NOT DOING THIS ALONE.

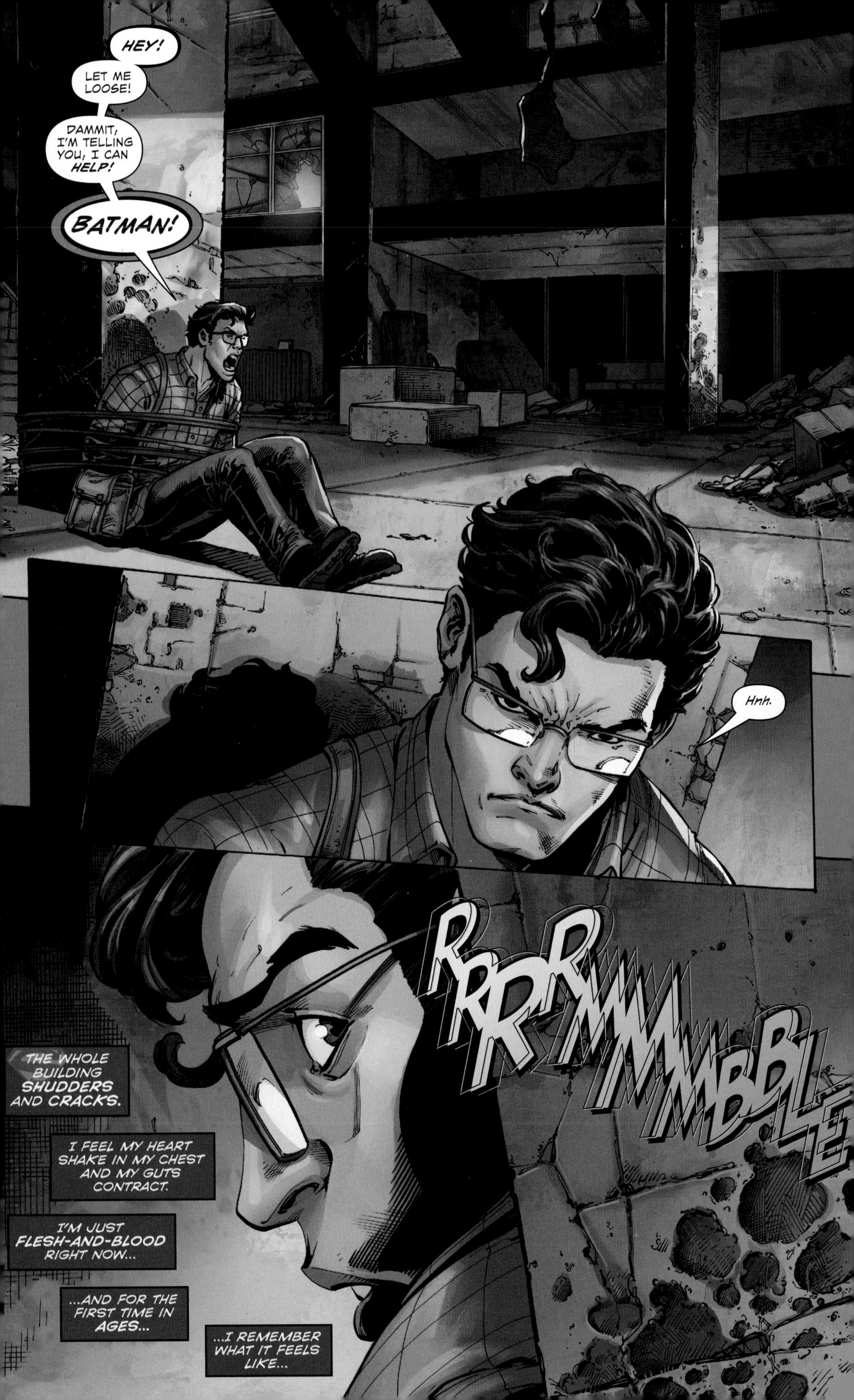
HEY!
LET ME LOOSE!
DAMMIT, I'M TELLING YOU, I CAN HELP!
BATMAN!
Hnh.
RRRRMMMBBLLE
THE WHOLE BUILDING SHUDDERS AND CRACKS.
I FEEL MY HEART SHAKE IN MY CHEST AND MY GUTS CONTRACT.
I'M JUST FLESH-AND-BLOOD RIGHT NOW...
...AND FOR THE FIRST TIME IN AGES...
...I REMEMBER WHAT IT FEELS LIKE...

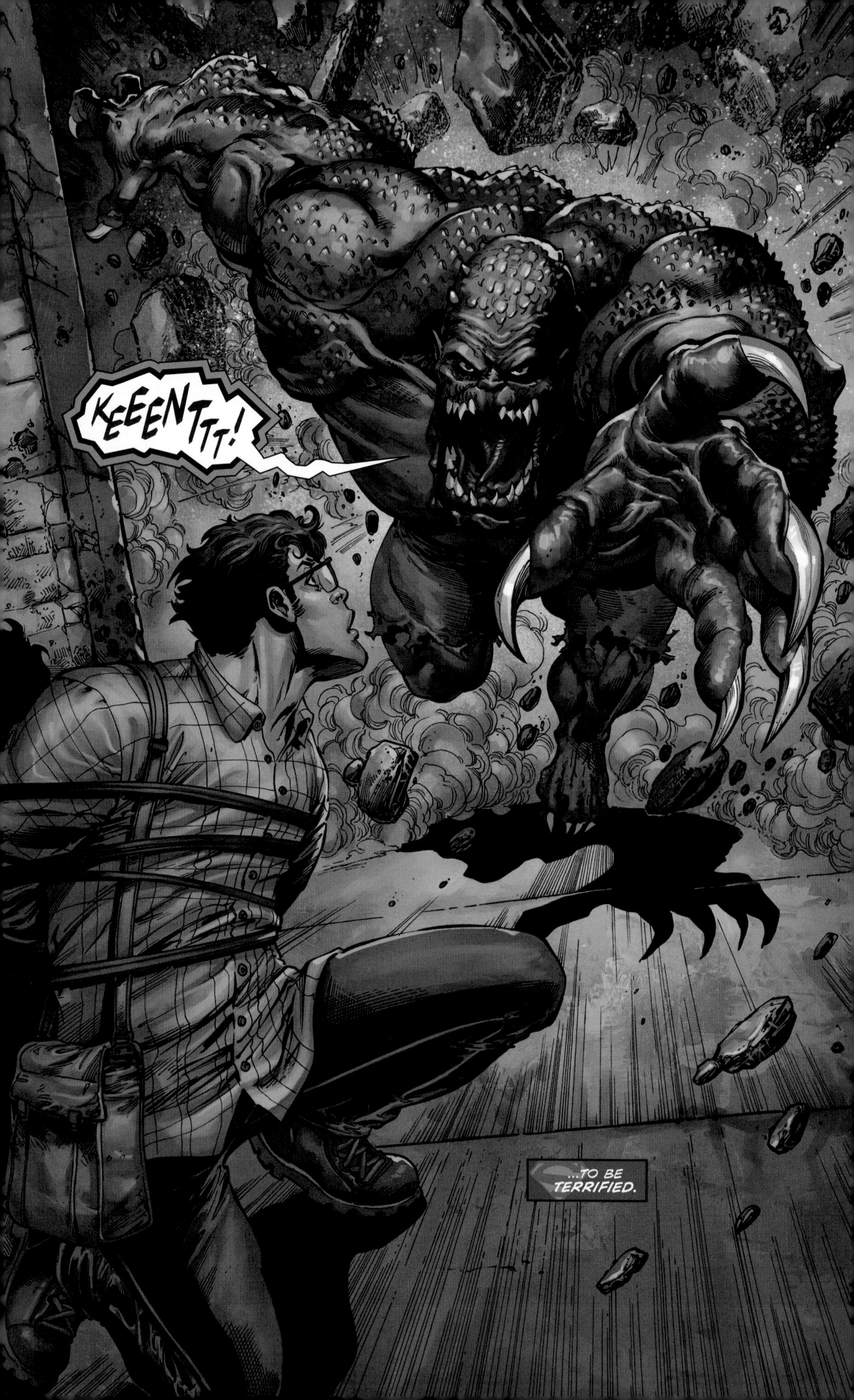
KEEENTTT!
...TO BE TERRIFIED.

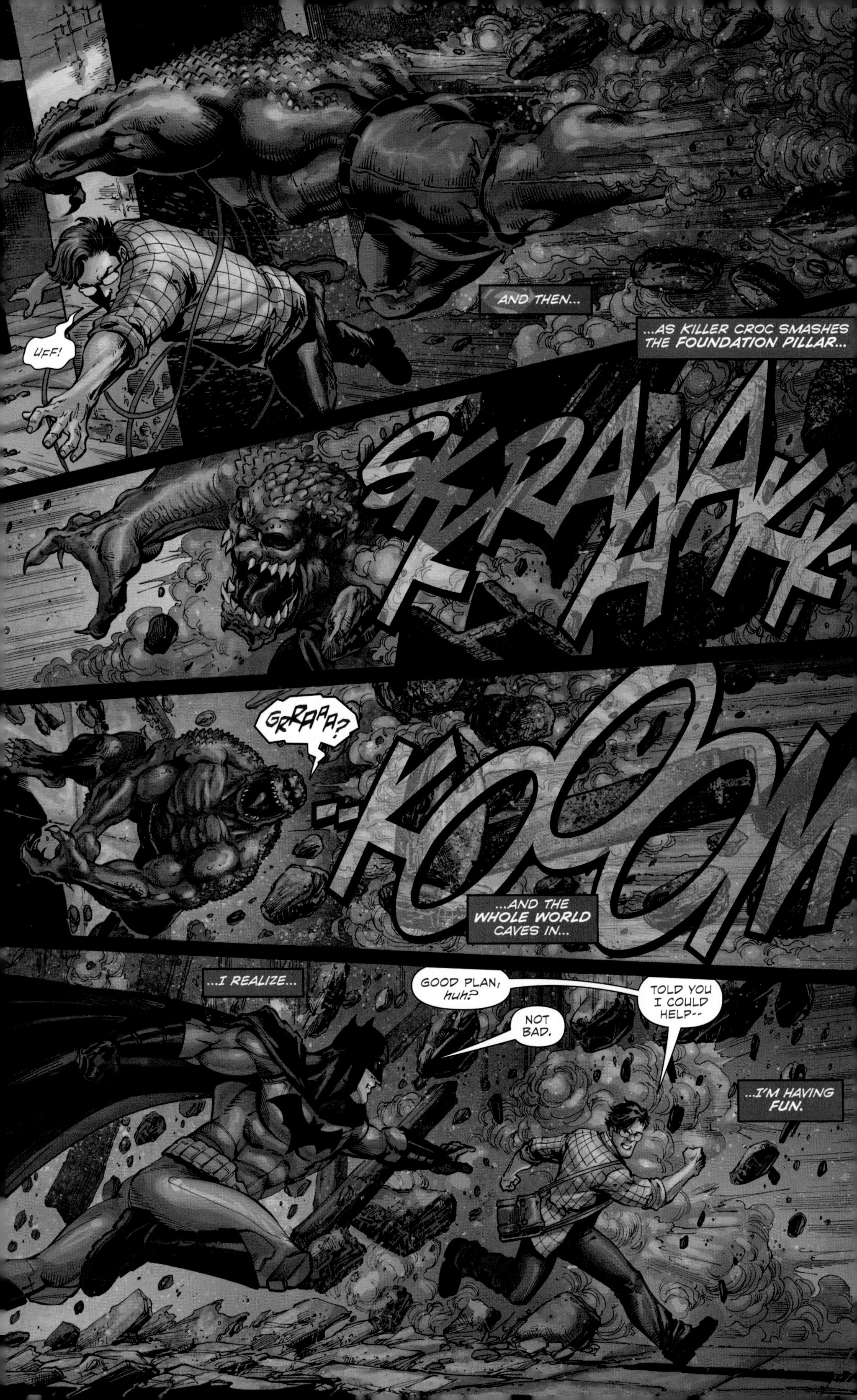
AND THEN...
UFF!
...AS KILLER CROC SMASHES THE FOUNDATION PILLAR...
SKRAVAKK
GRRAAA?
KOOOM
...AND THE WHOLE WORLD CAVES IN...
...I REALIZE...
GOOD PLAN, huh?
NOT BAD.
TOLD YOU I COULD HELP--
...I'M HAVING FUN.

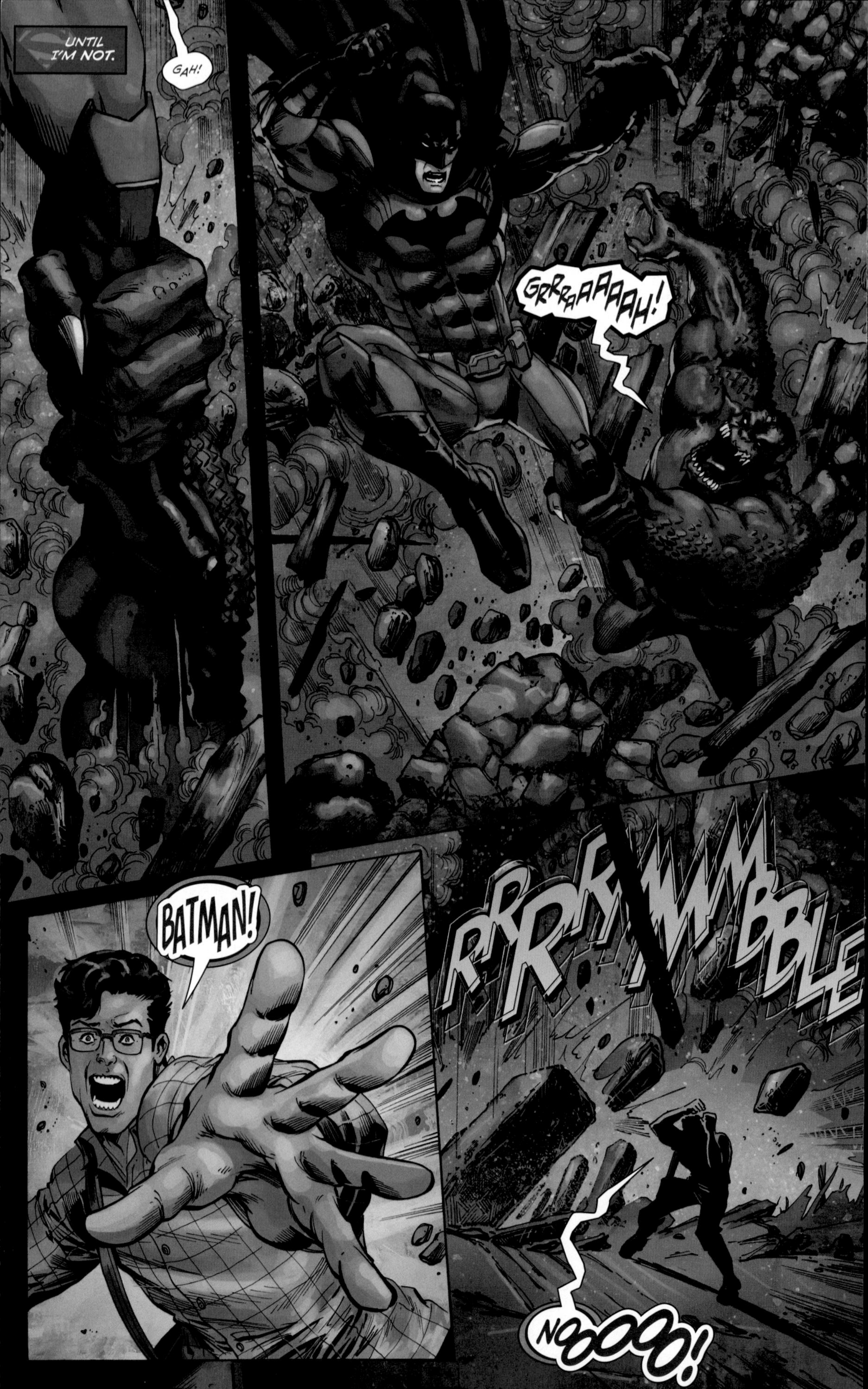
UNTIL I'M NOT.
GAH!
GRRRAAAAAH!
BATMAN!
RRRRUMBBLE
NOOOOO!

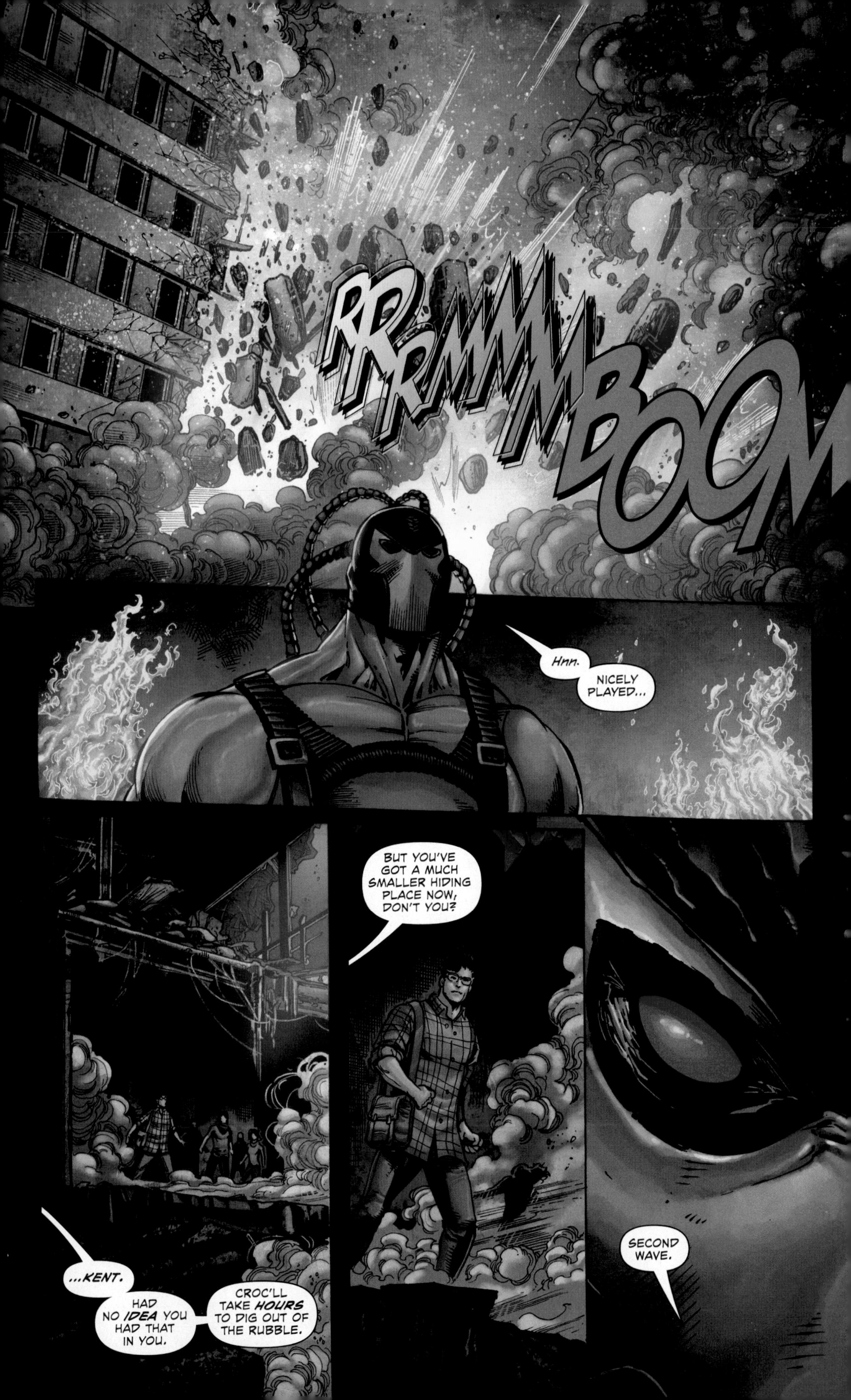
RRRMMMMBOOM
Hnn. NICELY PLAYED...
...KENT.
HAD NO IDEA YOU HAD THAT IN YOU.
CROC'LL TAKE HOURS TO DIG OUT OF THE RUBBLE.
BUT YOU'VE GOT A MUCH SMALLER HIDING PLACE NOW, DON'T YOU?
SECOND WAVE.

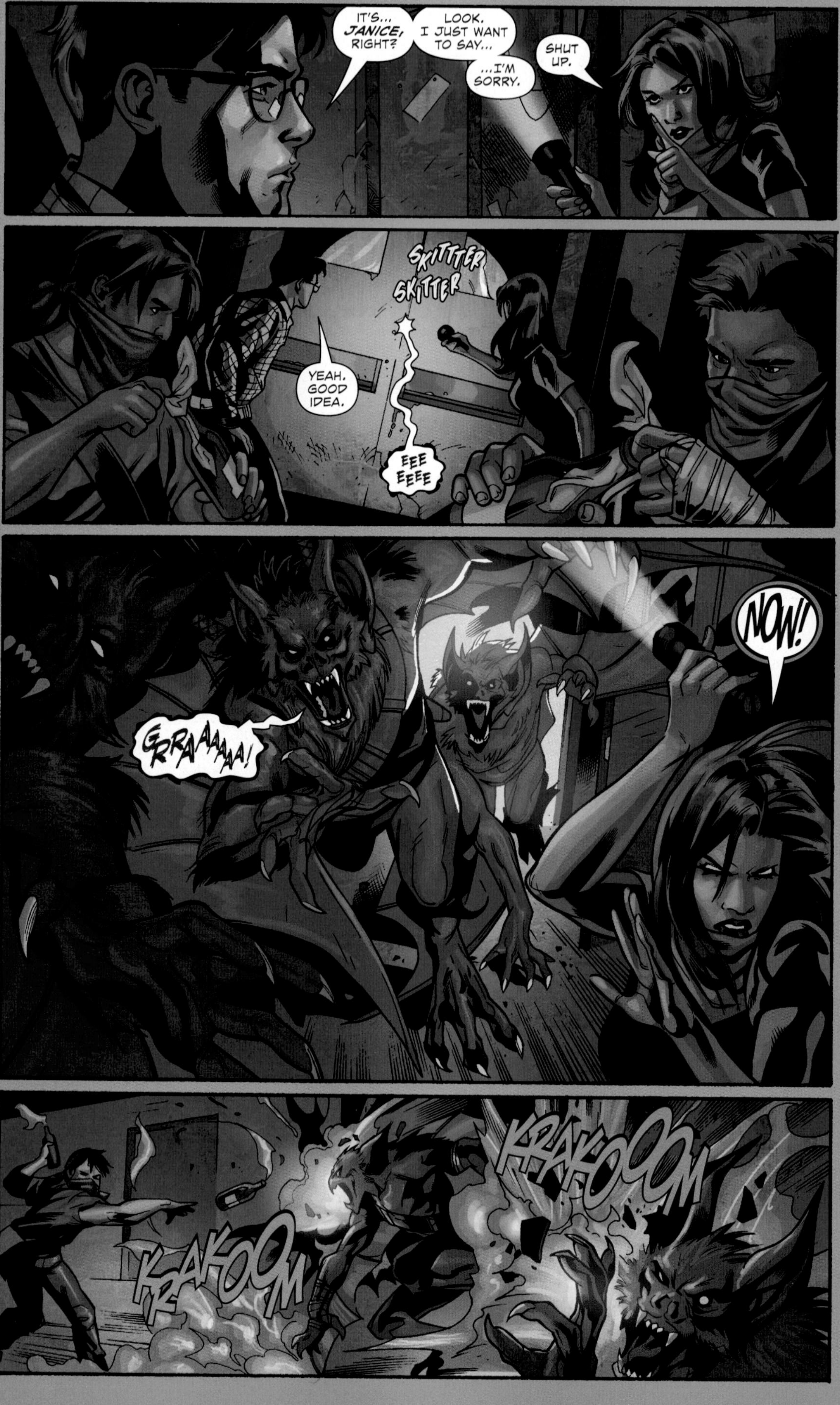
IT'S... JANICE, RIGHT?
LOOK. I JUST WANT TO SAY...
...I'M SORRY.
SHUT UP.
SKITTTER
SKITTER
YEAH. GOOD IDEA.
EEE EEEE
NOW!
GRRAAAAAA!
KRAKOOOM
KRAKOOM

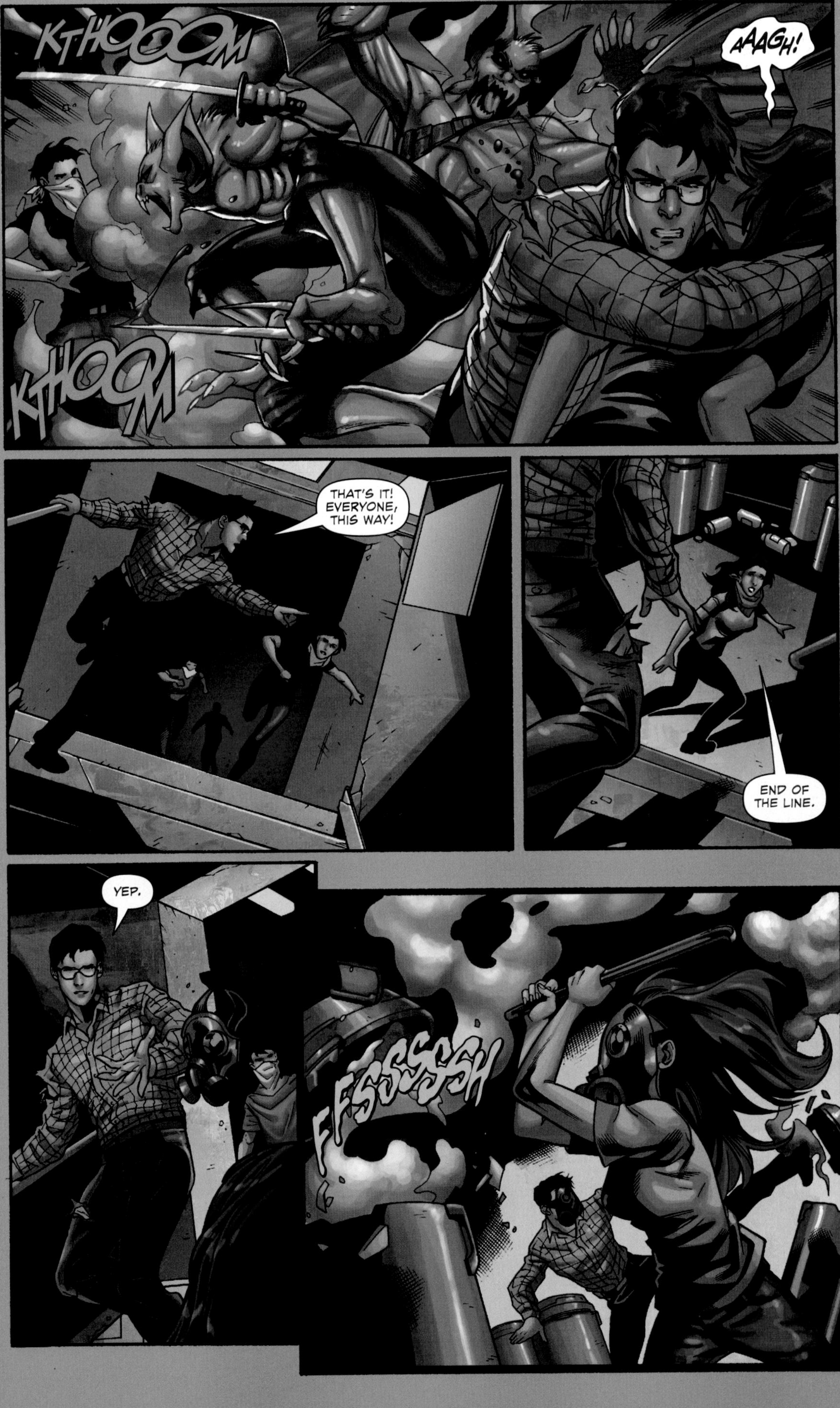
KTHOOOM
AAAGH!
KTHOOM
THAT'S IT! EVERYONE, THIS WAY!
END OF THE LINE.
YEP.
FFSSSSSH

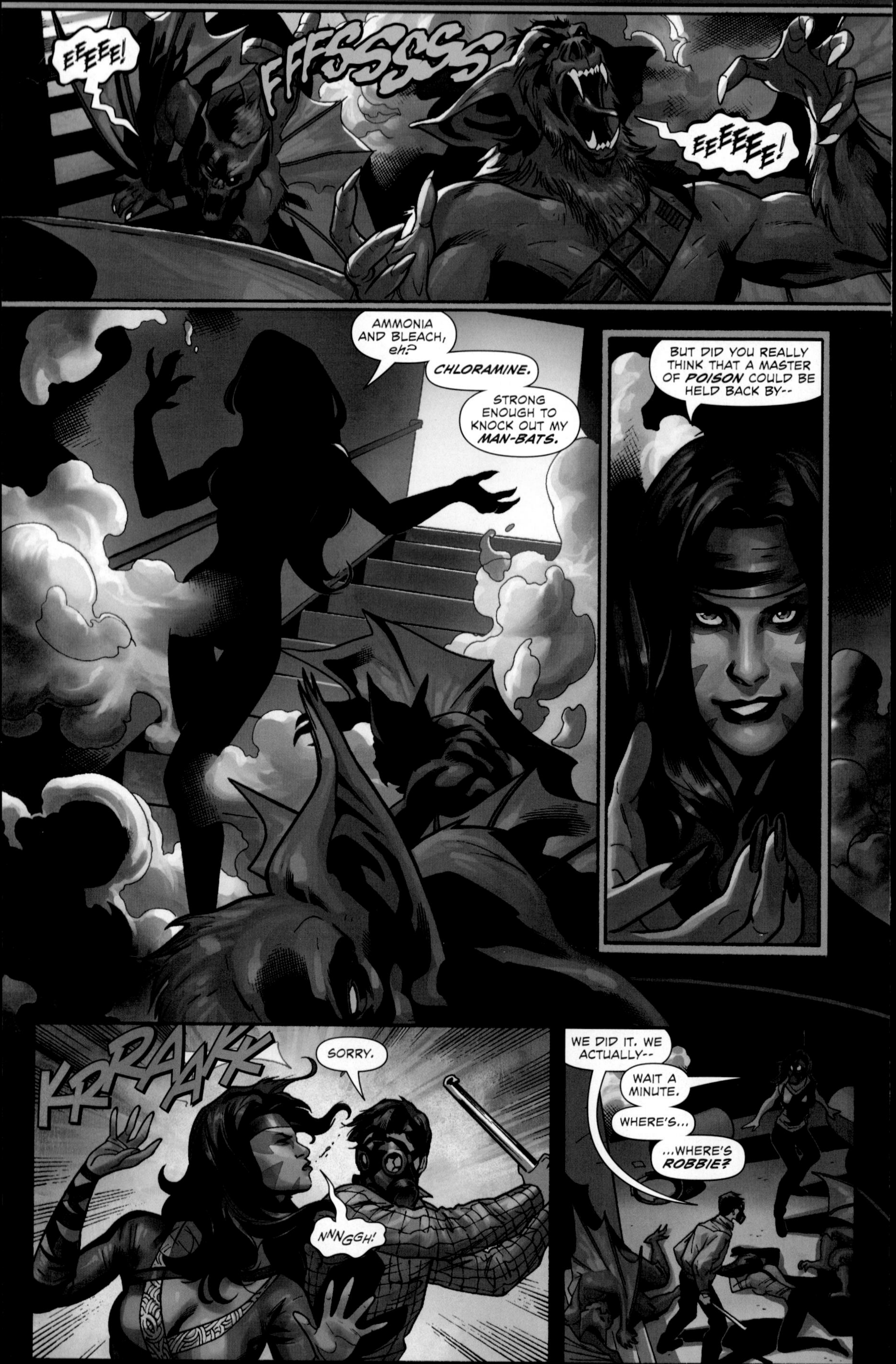
EEEEE!
FFFSSSSS
EEEEEE!
AMMONIA AND BLEACH, eh?
CHLORAMINE.
STRONG ENOUGH TO KNOCK OUT MY MAN-BATS.
BUT DID YOU REALLY THINK THAT A MASTER OF POISON COULD BE HELD BACK BY--
KRAAKK
SORRY.
NNNGGH!
WE DID IT. WE ACTUALLY--
WAIT A MINUTE.
WHERE'S...
...WHERE'S ROBBIE?

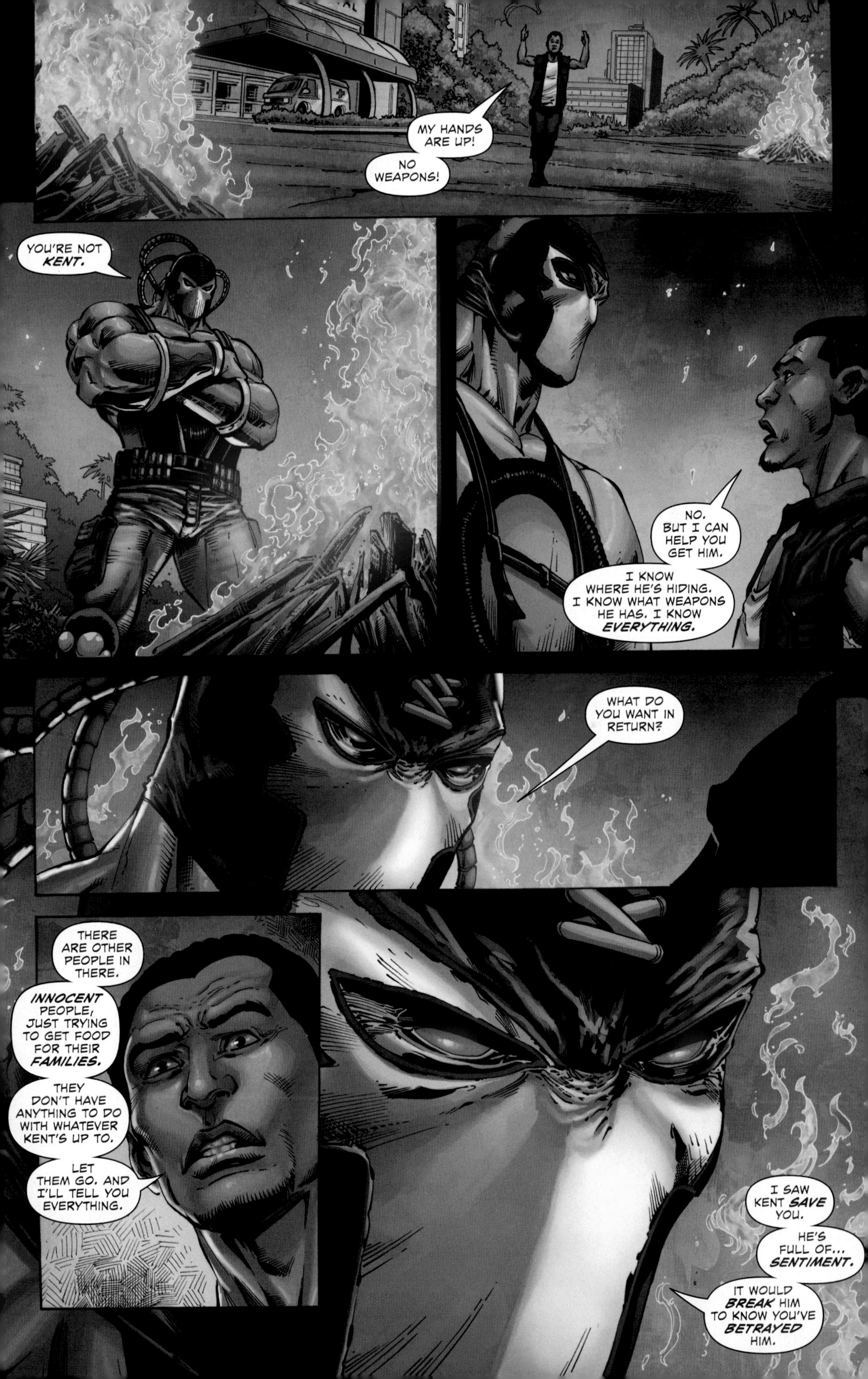
MY HANDS ARE UP!
NO WEAPONS!
YOU'RE NOT KENT.
NO. BUT I CAN HELP YOU GET HIM.
I KNOW WHERE HE'S HIDING. I KNOW WHAT WEAPONS HE HAS. I KNOW EVERYTHING.
WHAT DO YOU WANT IN RETURN?
THERE ARE OTHER PEOPLE IN THERE.
INNOCENT PEOPLE, JUST TRYING TO GET FOOD FOR THEIR FAMILIES.
THEY DON'T HAVE ANYTHING TO DO WITH WHATEVER KENT'S UP TO.
LET THEM GO. AND I'LL TELL YOU EVERYTHING.
I SAW KENT SAVE YOU.
HE'S FULL OF... SENTIMENT.
IT WOULD BREAK HIM TO KNOW YOU'VE BETRAYED HIM.

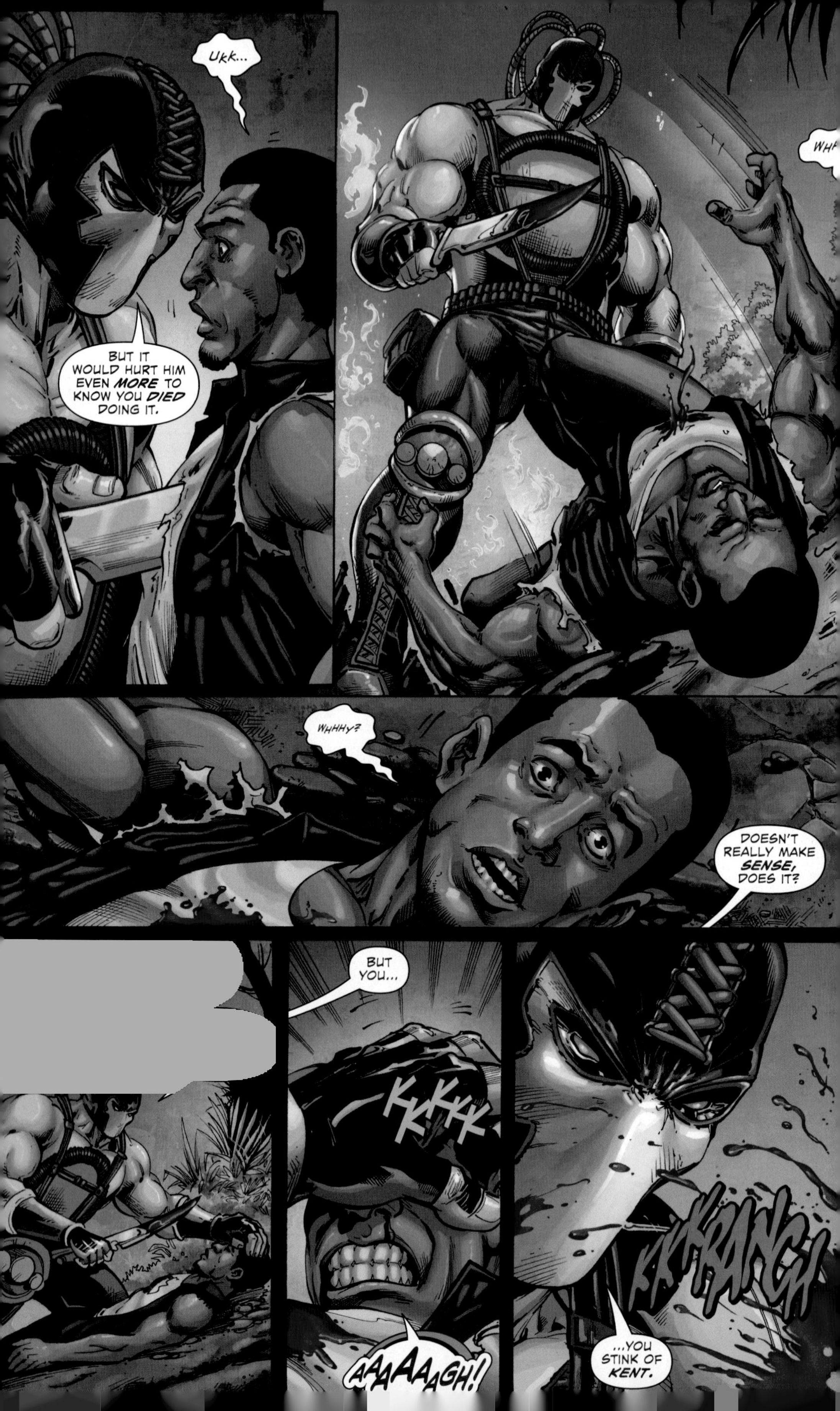
UKK...
BUT IT WOULD HURT HIM EVEN MORE TO KNOW YOU DIED DOING IT.
WHHY?
DOESN'T REALLY MAKE SENSE, DOES IT?
BUT YOU...
KKKKK
AAAAAAGH!
KRANCH
...YOU STINK OF KENT.

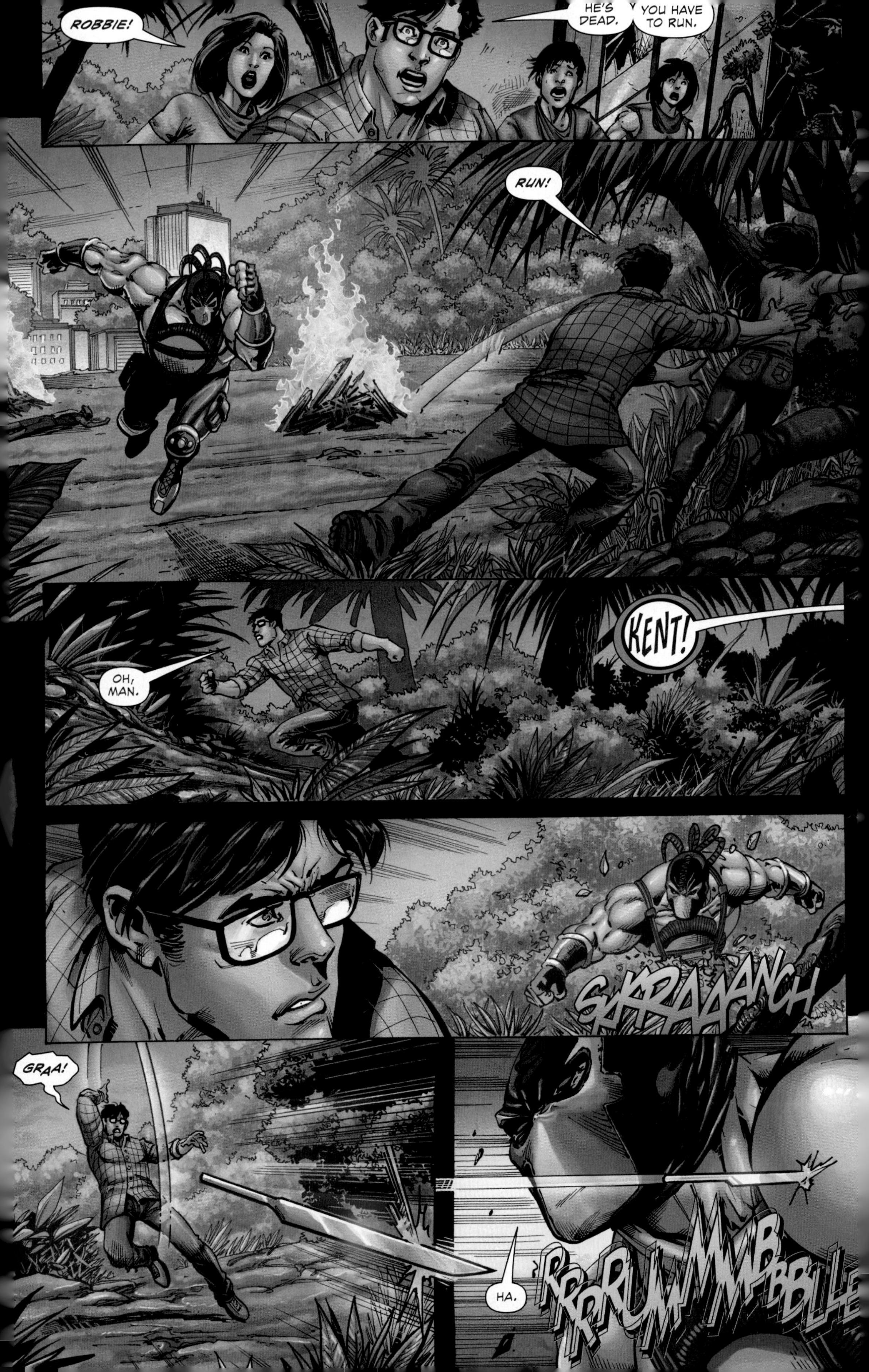
ROBBIE!
HE'S DEAD.
YOU HAVE TO RUN.
RUN!
OH, MAN.
KENT!
SKRAAAANCH
GRAA!
HA.
RRRRUMMBBLLE

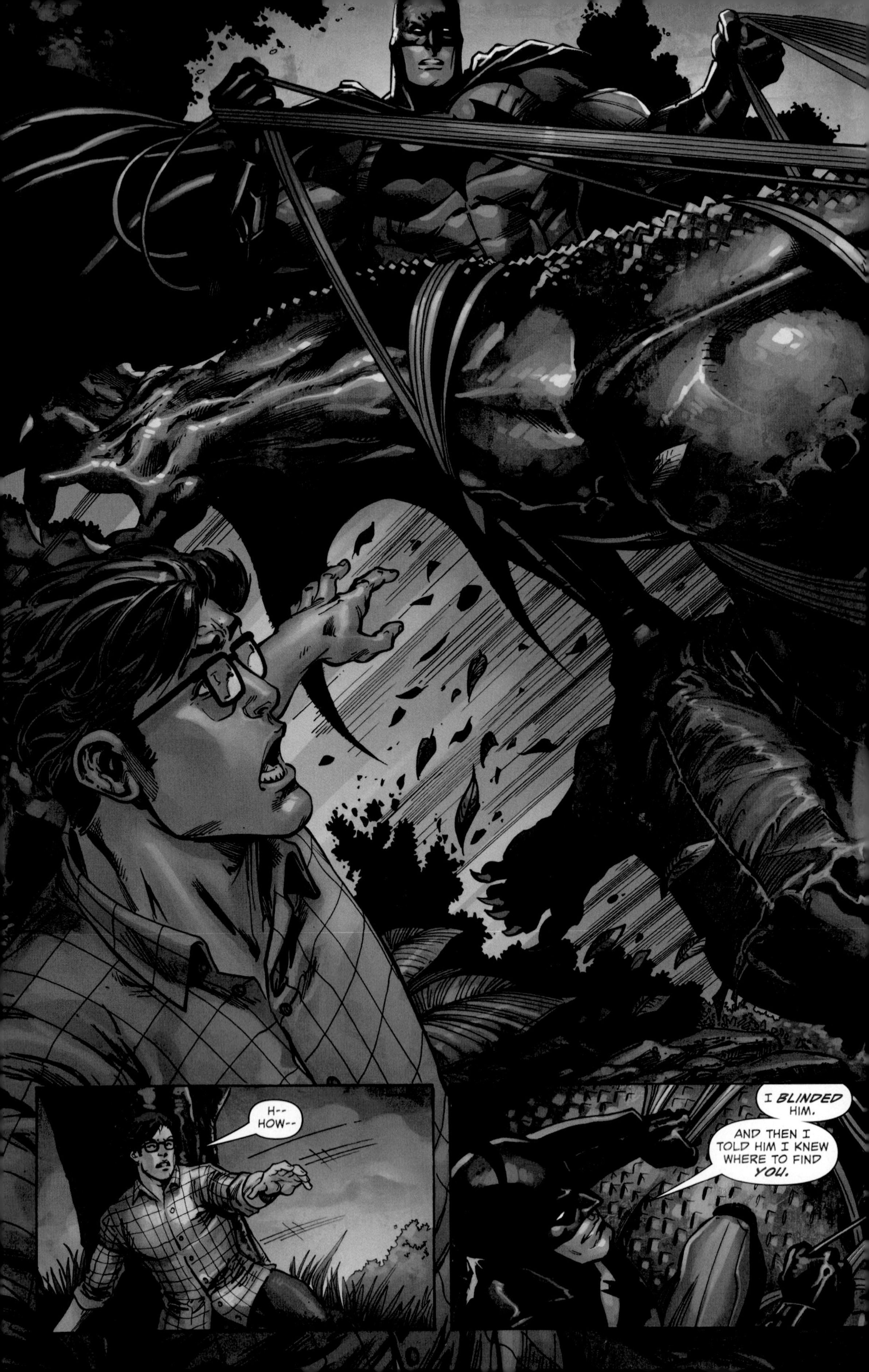
H-- HOW--
I BLINDED HIM.
AND THEN I TOLD HIM I KNEW WHERE TO FIND YOU.

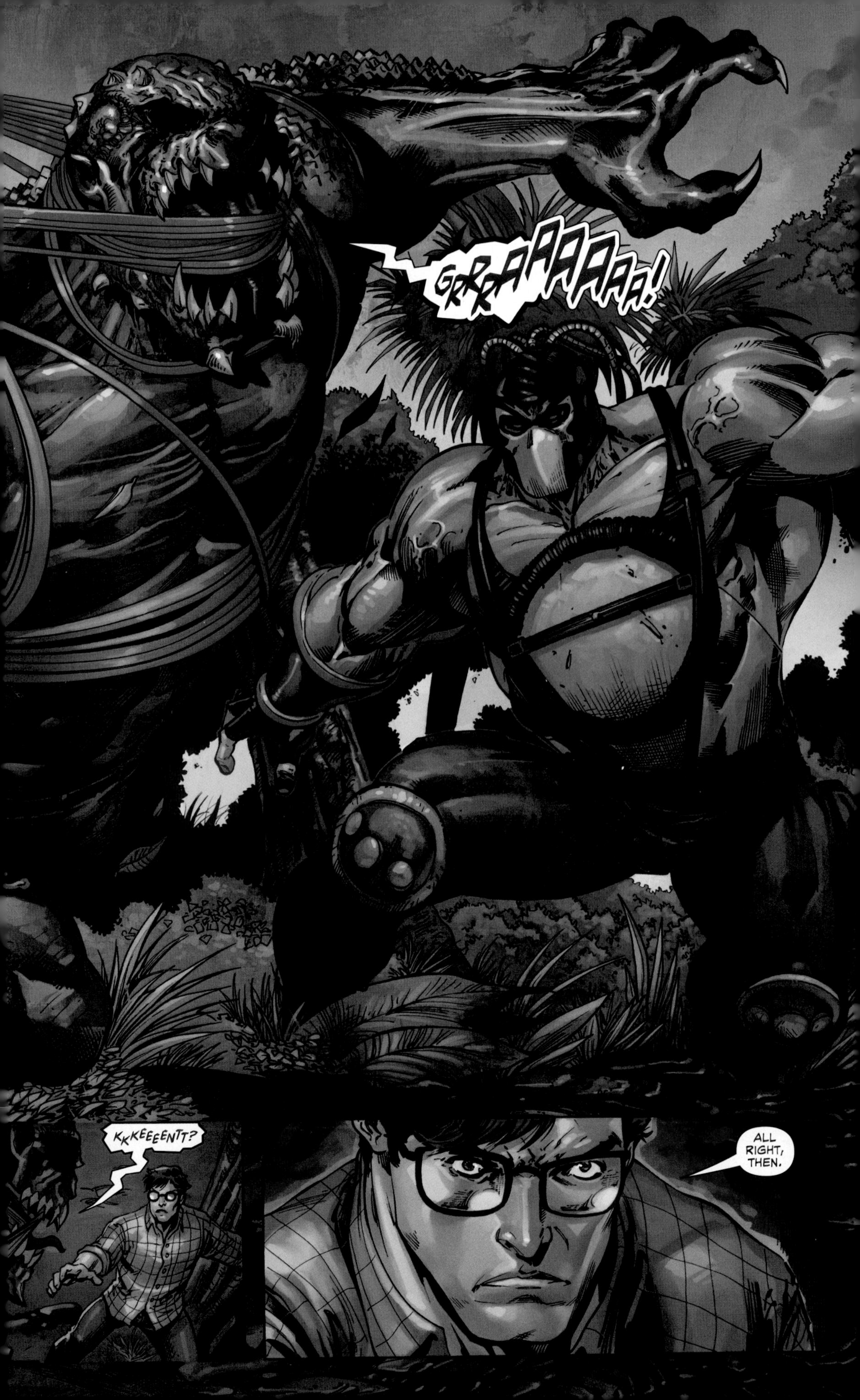
GRRRAAAAAAAA!
KKKEEEEENTT?
ALL RIGHT, THEN.

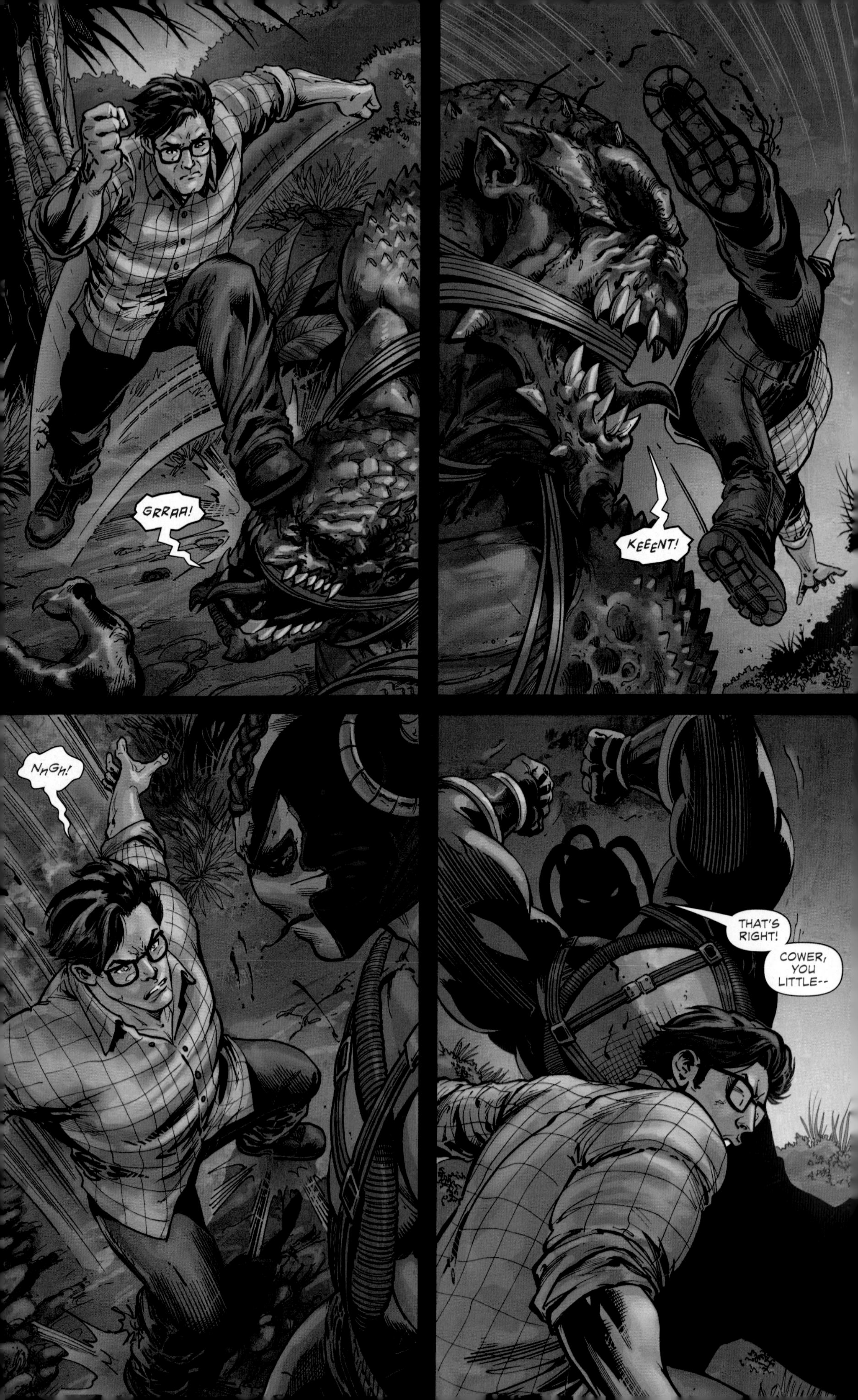
GRRAA!
KEEENT!
NnGh!
THAT'S RIGHT!
COWER, YOU LITTLE--

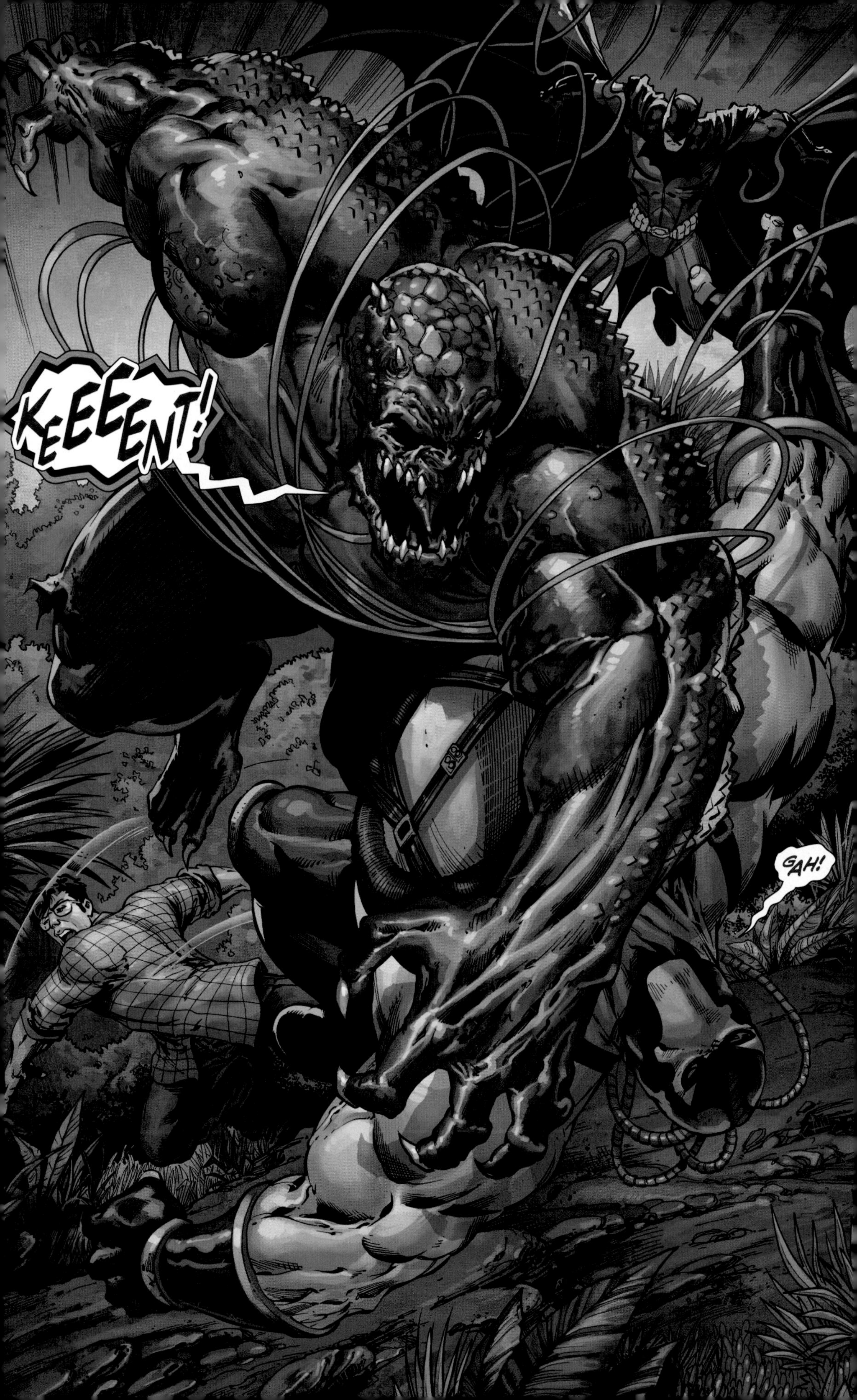
KEEEENT!
GAH!

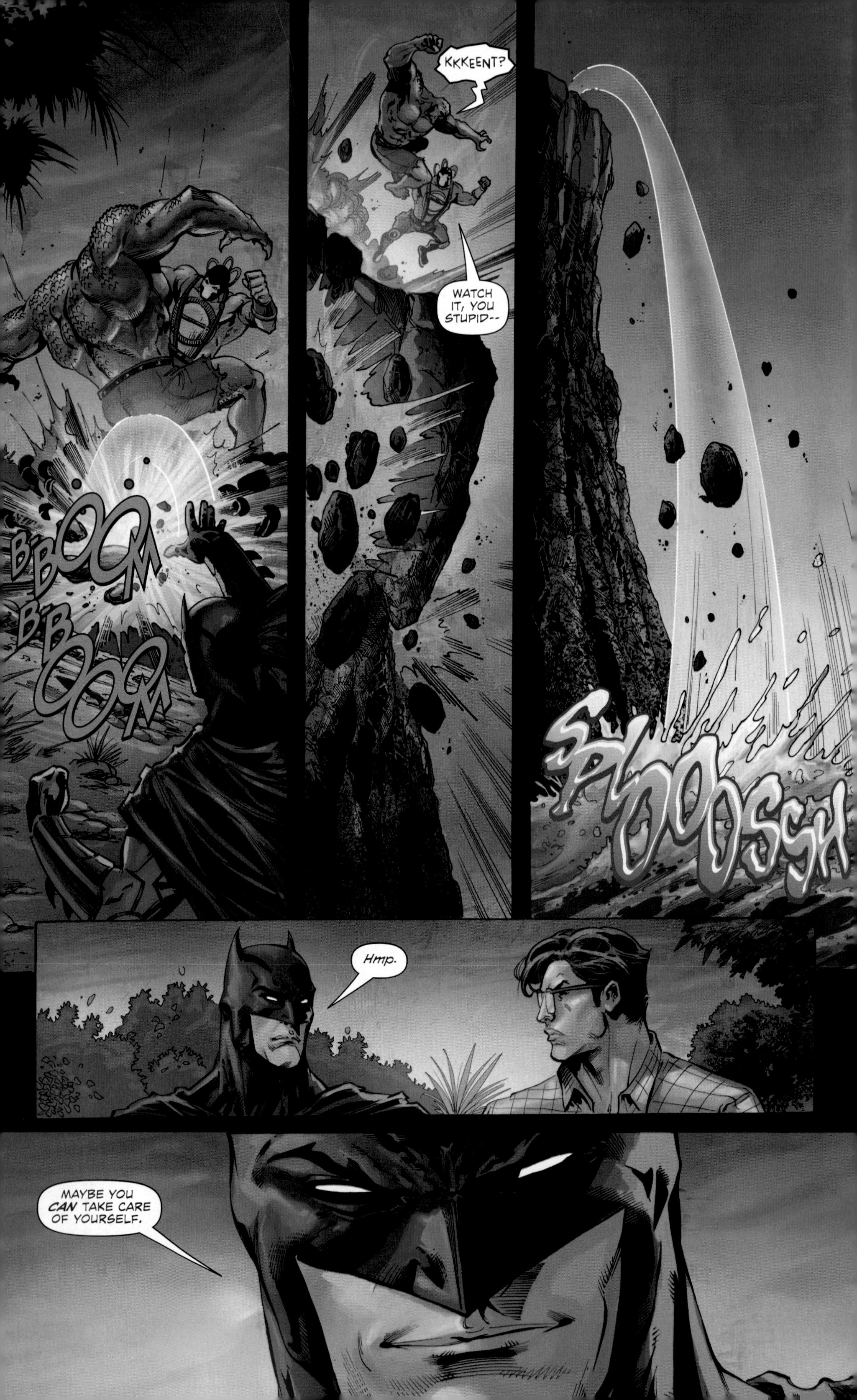
BBOOOM
BBOOOM
KKKEENT?
WATCH IT, YOU STUPID--
SPLOOOSSH
Hmp.
MAYBE YOU *CAN* TAKE CARE OF YOURSELF.

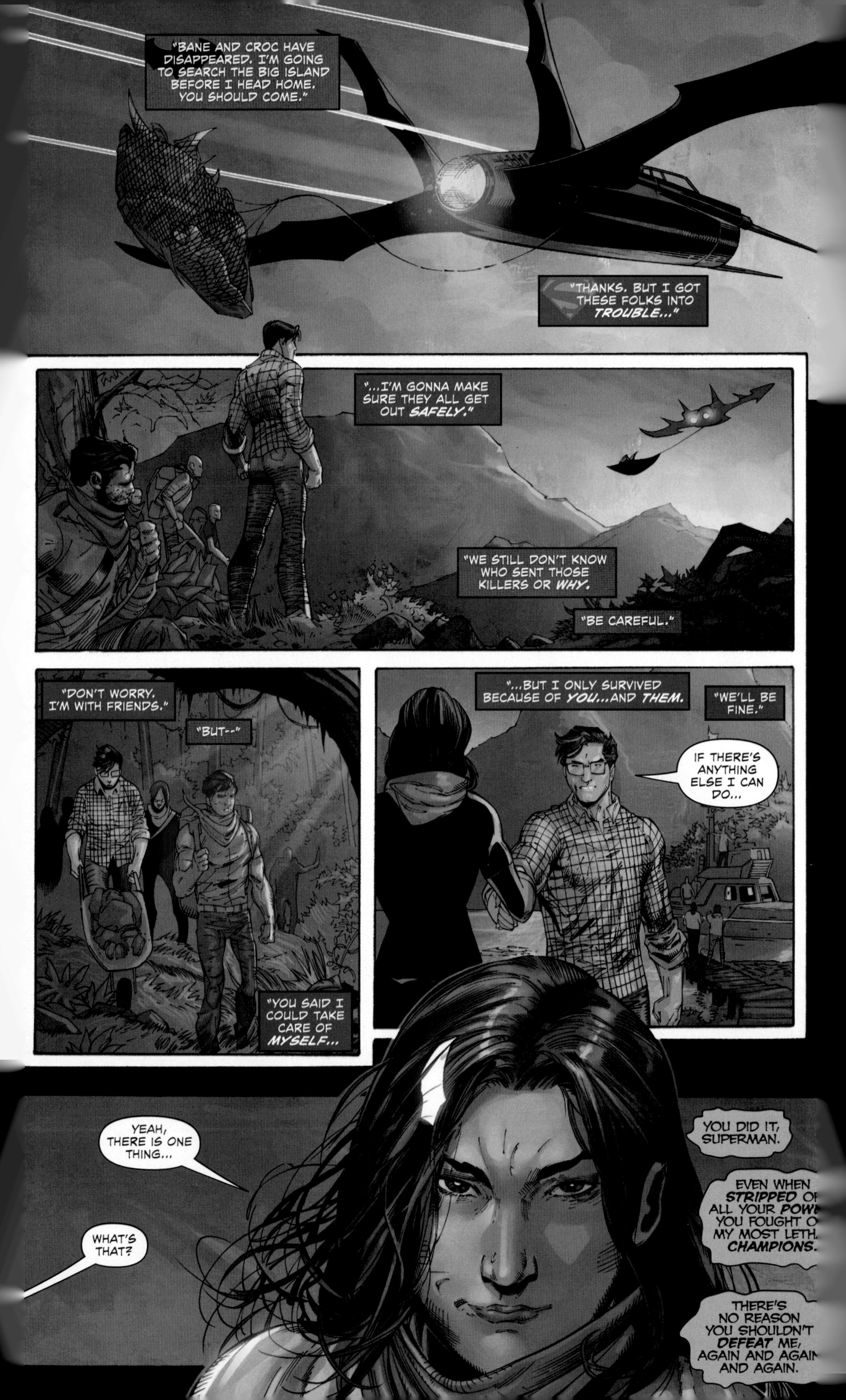
"BANE AND CROC HAVE DISAPPEARED. I'M GOING TO SEARCH THE BIG ISLAND BEFORE I HEAD HOME. YOU SHOULD COME."
"THANKS. BUT I GOT THESE FOLKS INTO TROUBLE..."
"...I'M GONNA MAKE SURE THEY ALL GET OUT SAFELY."
"WE STILL DON'T KNOW WHO SENT THOSE KILLERS OR WHY.
"BE CAREFUL."
"DON'T WORRY. I'M WITH FRIENDS."
"BUT--"
"YOU SAID I COULD TAKE CARE OF MYSELF...
"...BUT I ONLY SURVIVED BECAUSE OF YOU...AND THEM.
"WE'LL BE FINE."
IF THERE'S ANYTHING ELSE I CAN DO...
YEAH, THERE IS ONE THING...
WHAT'S THAT?
YOU DID IT, SUPERMAN.
THERE'S NO REASON YOU SHOULDN'T DEFEAT ME, AGAIN AND AGAIN AND AGAIN.

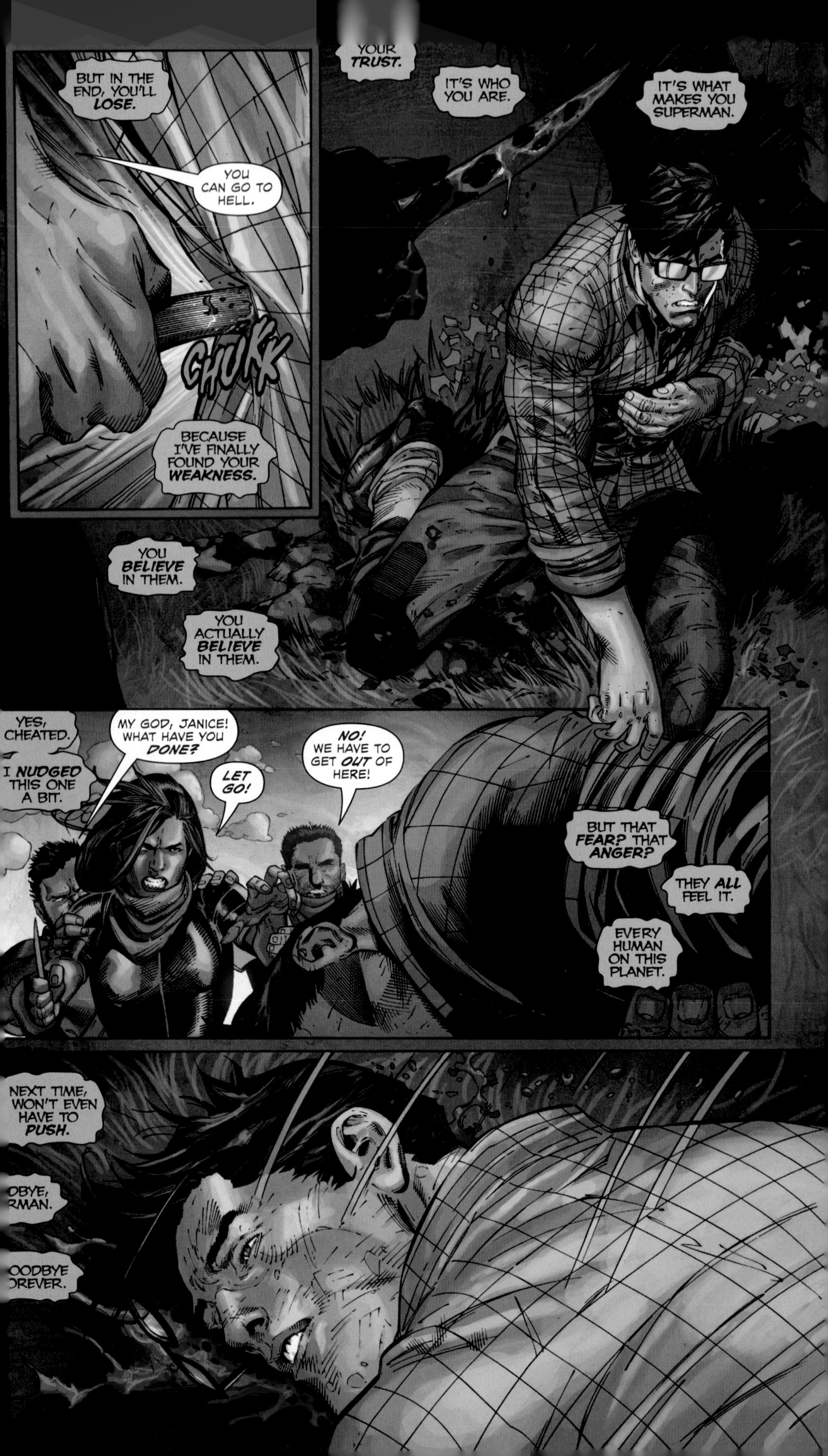
YOUR TRUST.
BUT IN THE END, YOU'LL LOSE.
YOU CAN GO TO HELL.
CHUKK
BECAUSE I'VE FINALLY FOUND YOUR WEAKNESS.
IT'S WHO YOU ARE.
IT'S WHAT MAKES YOU SUPERMAN.
YOU BELIEVE IN THEM.
YOU ACTUALLY BELIEVE IN THEM.
YES, CHEATED.
I NUDGED THIS ONE A BIT.
MY GOD, JANICE! WHAT HAVE YOU DONE?
LET GO!
NO! WE HAVE TO GET OUT OF HERE!
BUT THAT FEAR? THAT ANGER?
THEY ALL FEEL IT.
EVERY HUMAN ON THIS PLANET.
NEXT TIME, WON'T EVEN HAVE TO PUSH.
ODBYE, RMAN.
OODBYE OREVER.

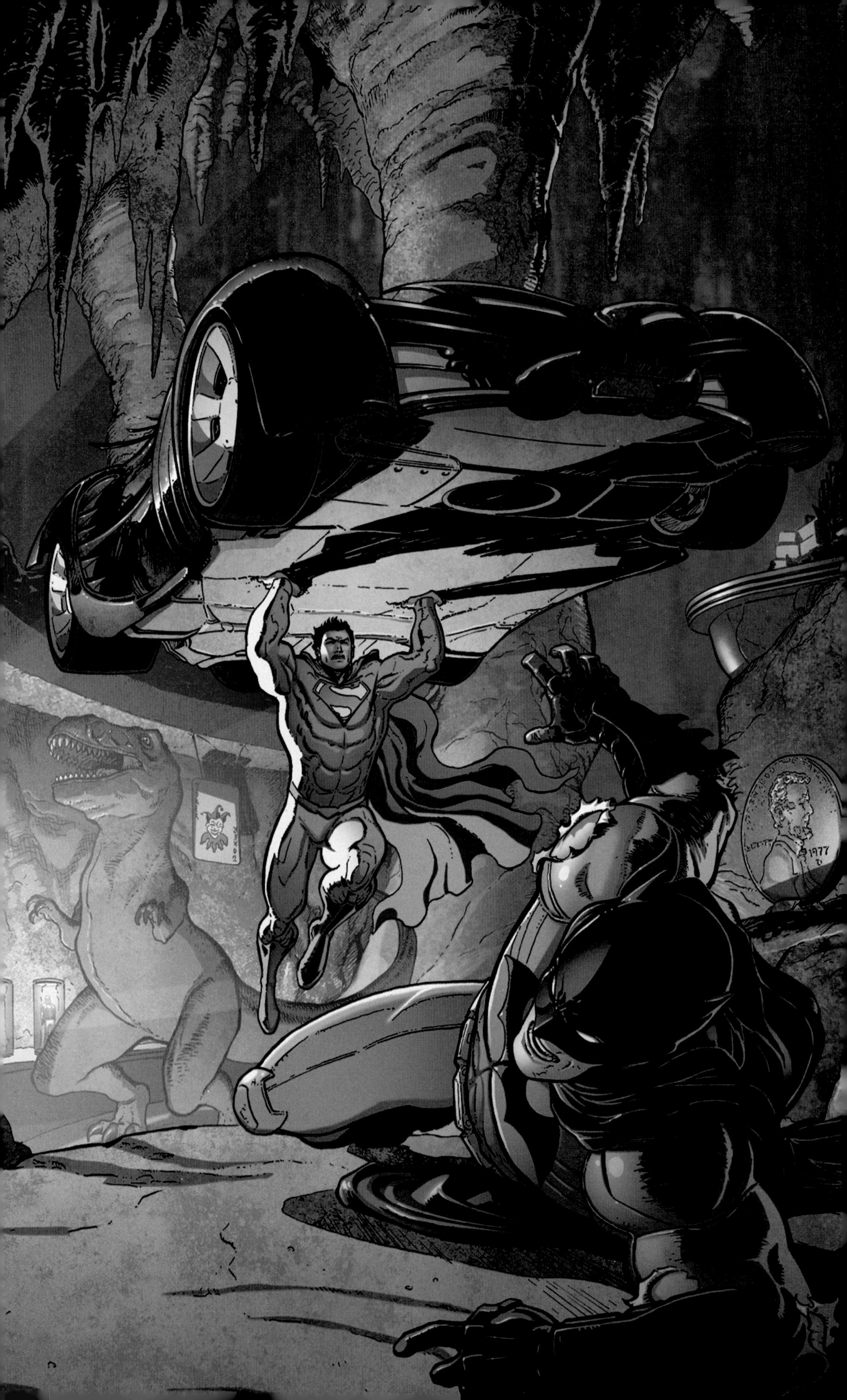
1977

UNDONE

GREG PAK writer **CLIFF RICHARDS, JACK HERBERT, VICENTE CIFUENTES** artists **HI-FI** colorist **ROB LEIGH** letterer
cover by **AARON KUDER** with **WIL QUINTANA**

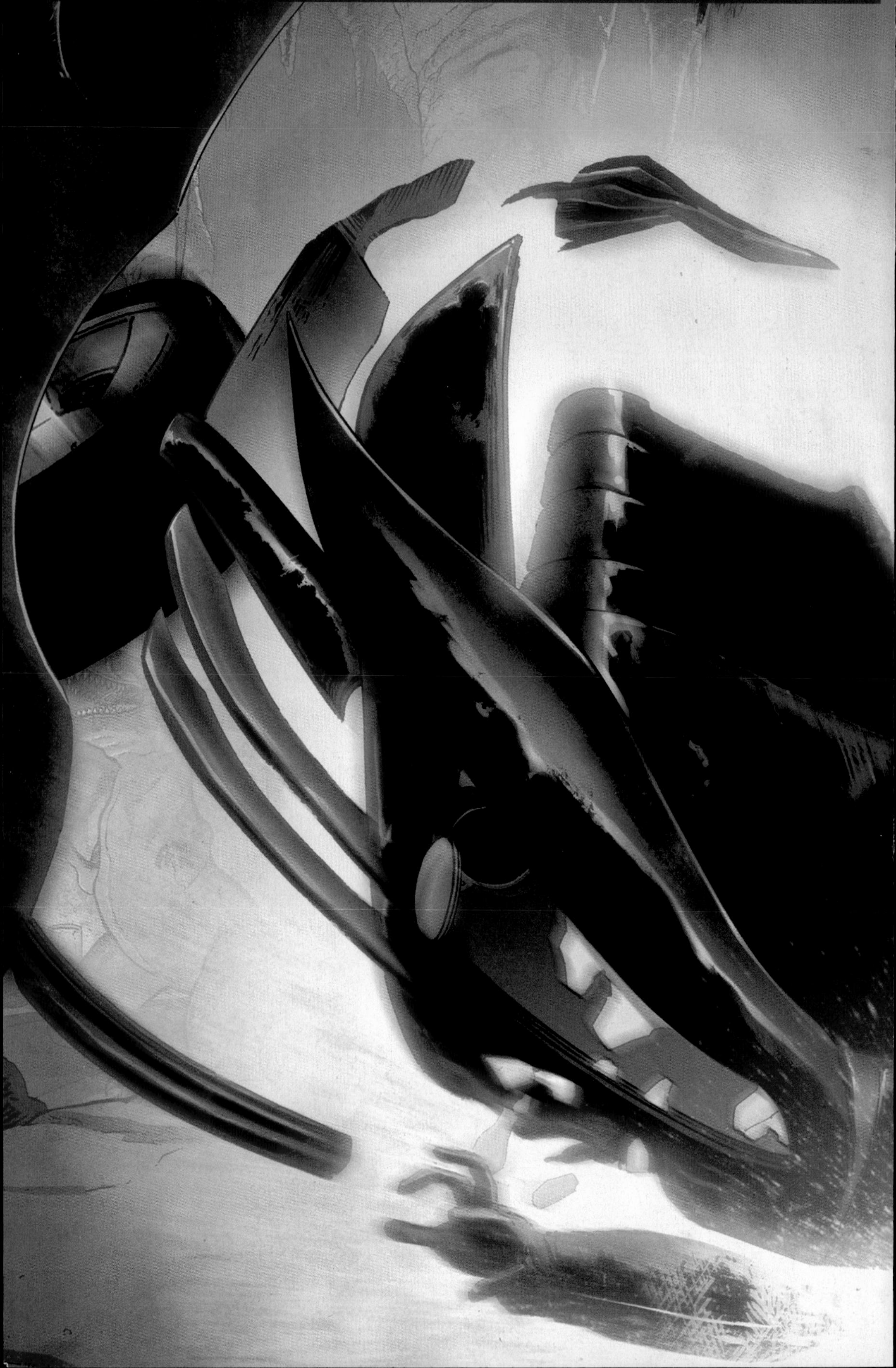

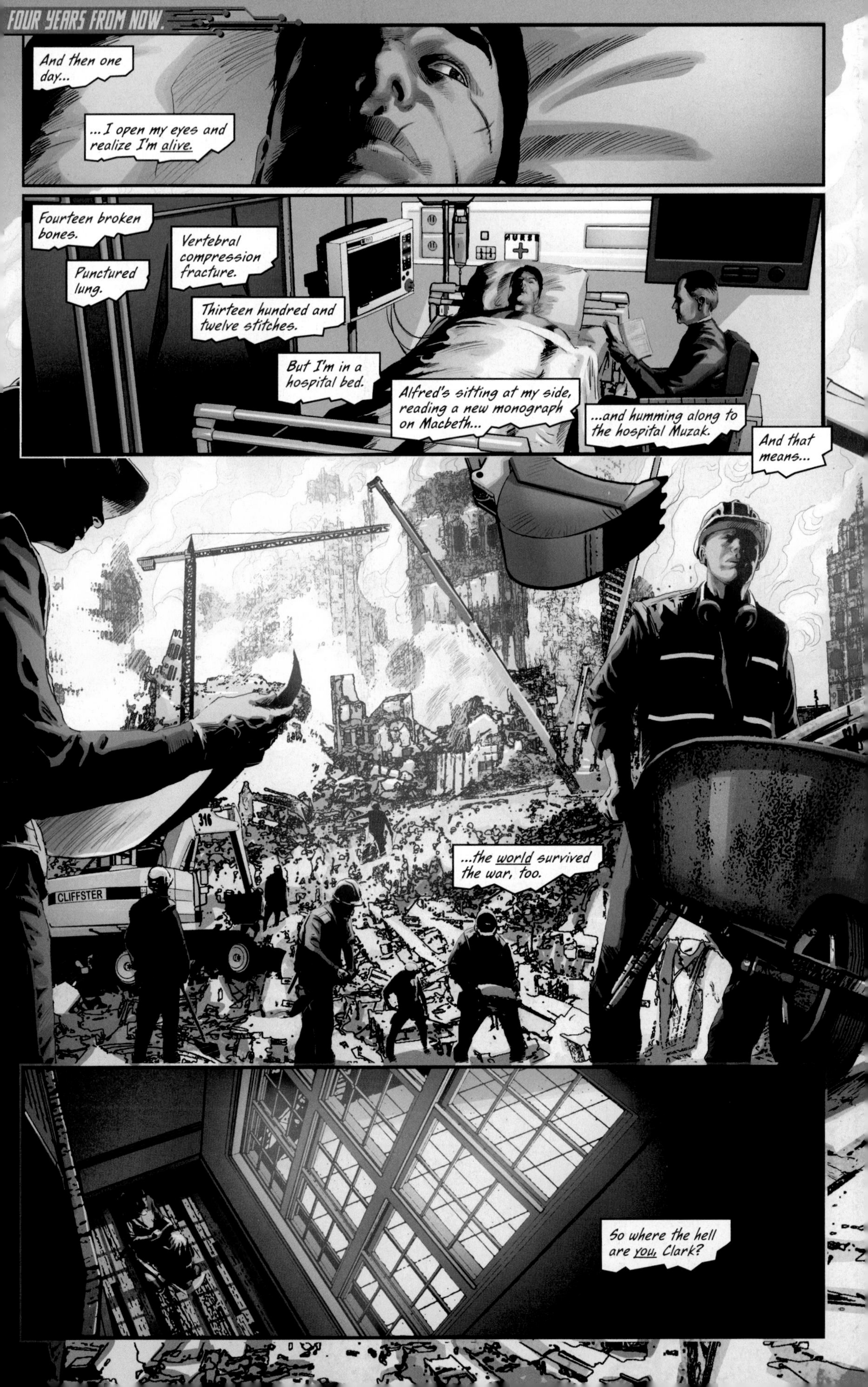
FOUR YEARS FROM NOW.
And then one day...
...I open my eyes and realize I'm alive.
Fourteen broken bones.
Punctured lung.
Vertebral compression fracture.
Thirteen hundred and twelve stitches.
But I'm in a hospital bed.
Alfred's sitting at my side, reading a new monograph on Macbeth...
...and humming along to the hospital Muzak.
And that means...
...the world survived the war, too.
CLIFFSTER
316
So where the hell are you, Clark?

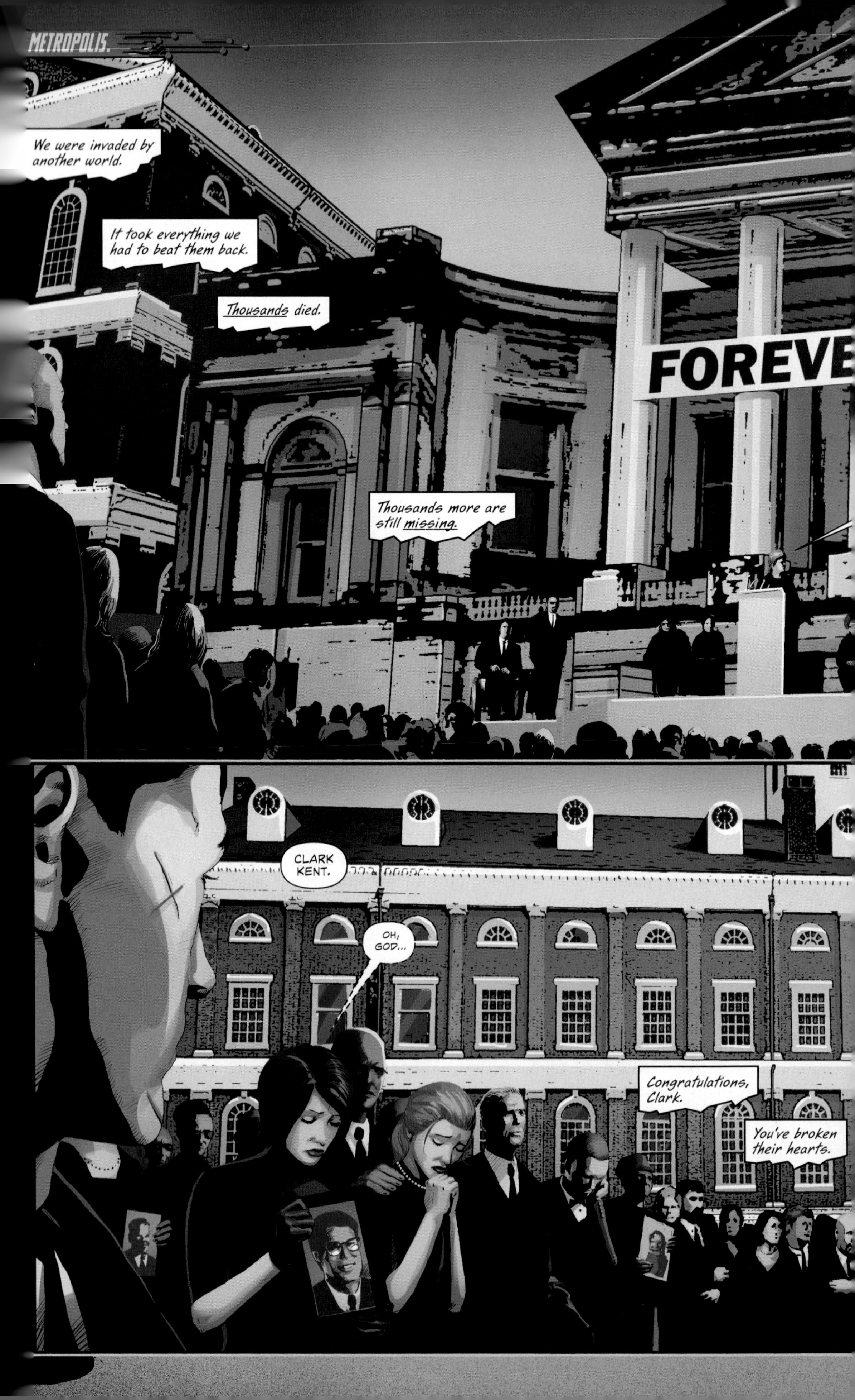
METROPOLIS.
We were invaded by another world.
It took everything we had to beat them back.
Thousands died.
FOREVE
Thousands more are still missing.
CLARK KENT.
OH, GOD...
Congratulations, Clark.
You've broken their hearts.

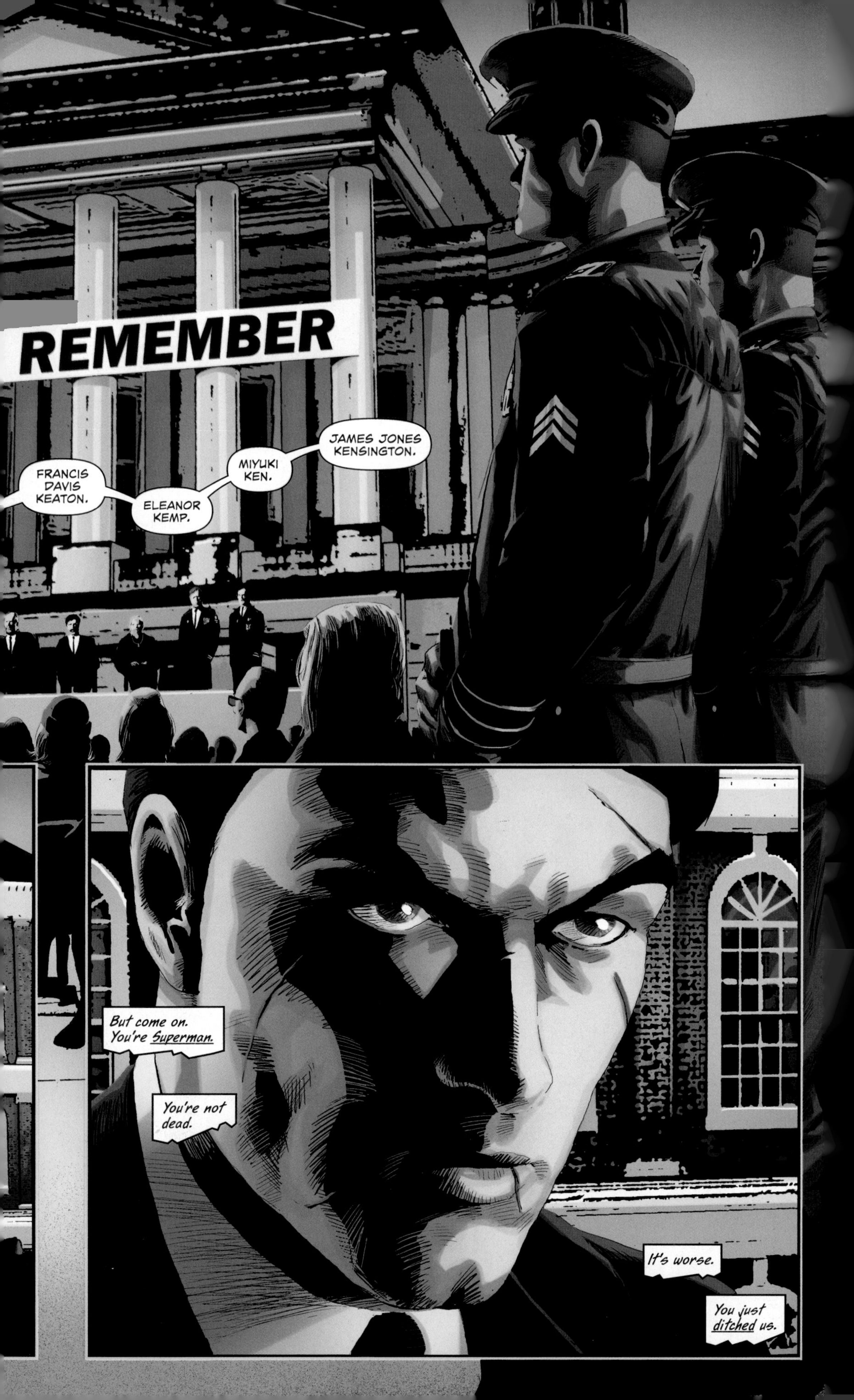
REMEMBER
FRANCIS DAVIS KEATON.
ELEANOR KEMP.
MIYUKI KEN.
JAMES JONES KENSINGTON.
But come on. You're Superman.
You're not dead.
It's worse.
You just ditched us.

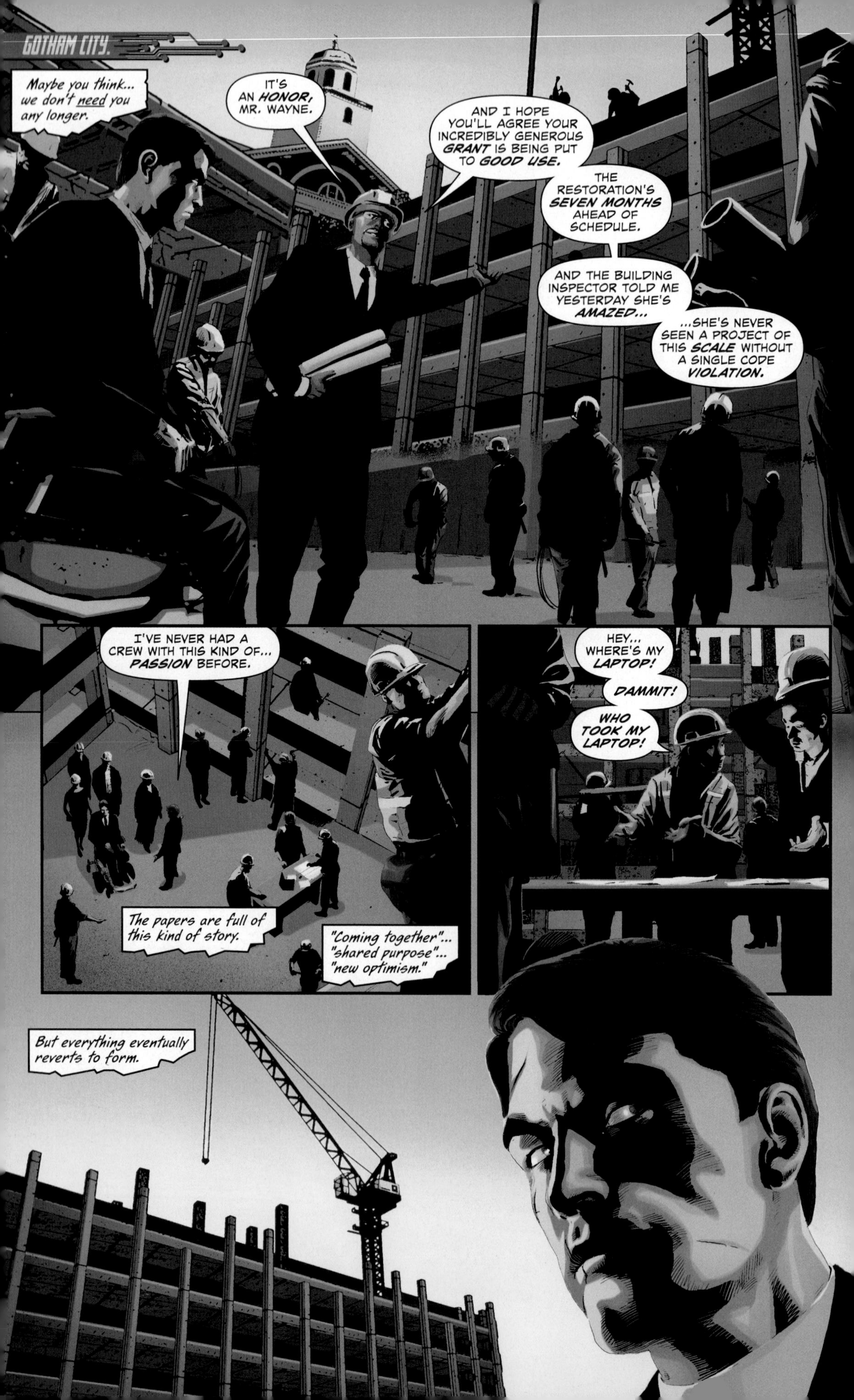
GOTHAM CITY.
Maybe you think... we don't need you any longer.
IT'S AN HONOR, MR. WAYNE.
AND I HOPE YOU'LL AGREE YOUR INCREDIBLY GENEROUS GRANT IS BEING PUT TO GOOD USE.
THE RESTORATION'S SEVEN MONTHS AHEAD OF SCHEDULE.
AND THE BUILDING INSPECTOR TOLD ME YESTERDAY SHE'S AMAZED...
...SHE'S NEVER SEEN A PROJECT OF THIS SCALE WITHOUT A SINGLE CODE VIOLATION.
I'VE NEVER HAD A CREW WITH THIS KIND OF... PASSION BEFORE.
The papers are full of this kind of story.
"Coming together"... "shared purpose"... "new optimism."
HEY... WHERE'S MY LAPTOP!
DAMMIT!
WHO TOOK MY LAPTOP!
But everything eventually reverts to form.

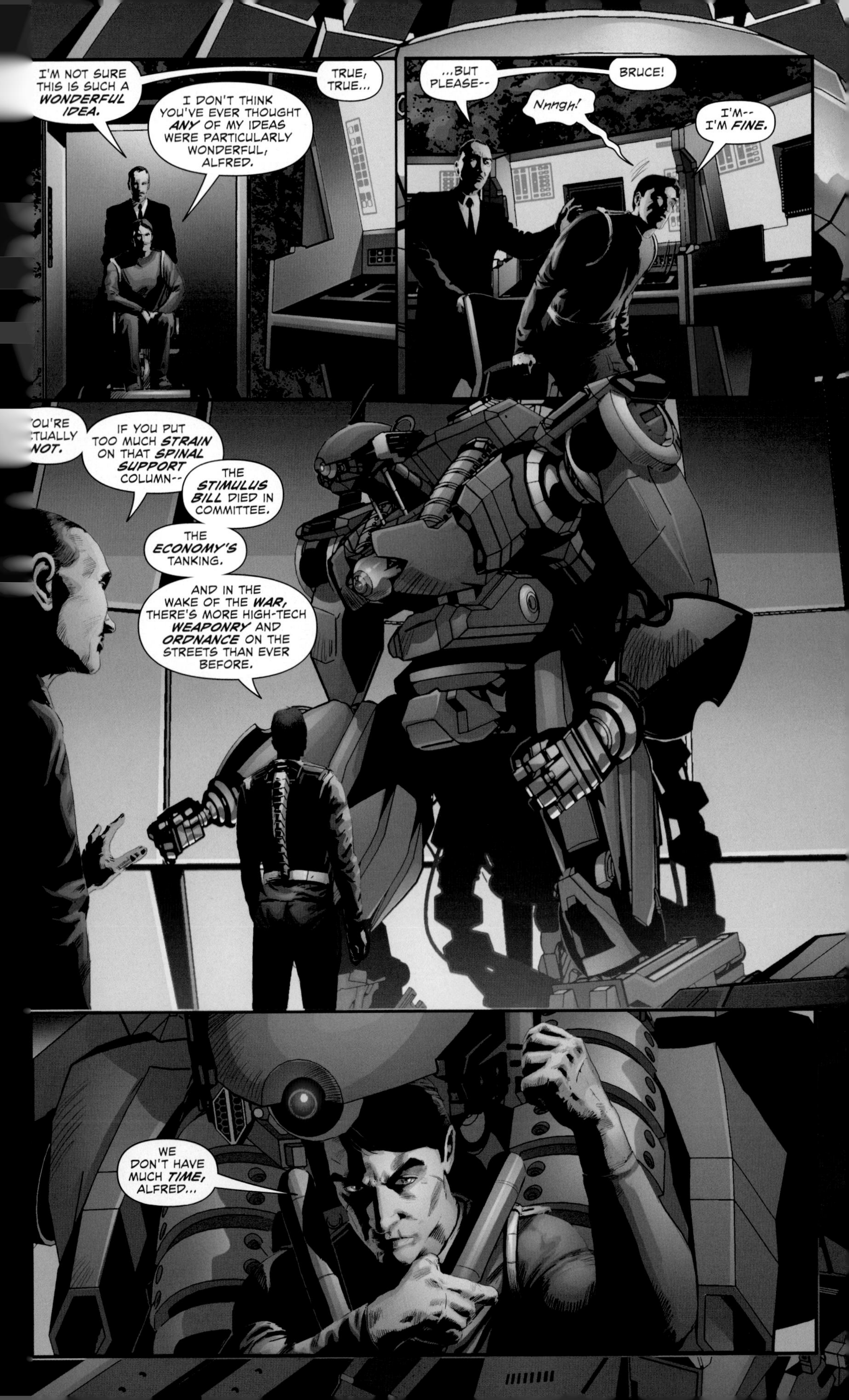
I'M NOT SURE THIS IS SUCH A *WONDERFUL IDEA.*
I DON'T THINK YOU'VE EVER THOUGHT *ANY* OF MY IDEAS WERE PARTICULARLY WONDERFUL, ALFRED.
TRUE, TRUE...
...BUT PLEASE--
BRUCE!
Nnngh!
I'M-- I'M *FINE.*
OU'RE CTUALLY *NOT.*
IF YOU PUT TOO MUCH *STRAIN* ON THAT *SPINAL SUPPORT* COLUMN--
THE *STIMULUS BILL* DIED IN COMMITTEE.
THE *ECONOMY'S* TANKING.
AND IN THE WAKE OF THE *WAR,* THERE'S MORE HIGH-TECH *WEAPONRY* AND *ORDNANCE* ON THE STREETS THAN EVER BEFORE.
WE DON'T HAVE MUCH *TIME,* ALFRED...

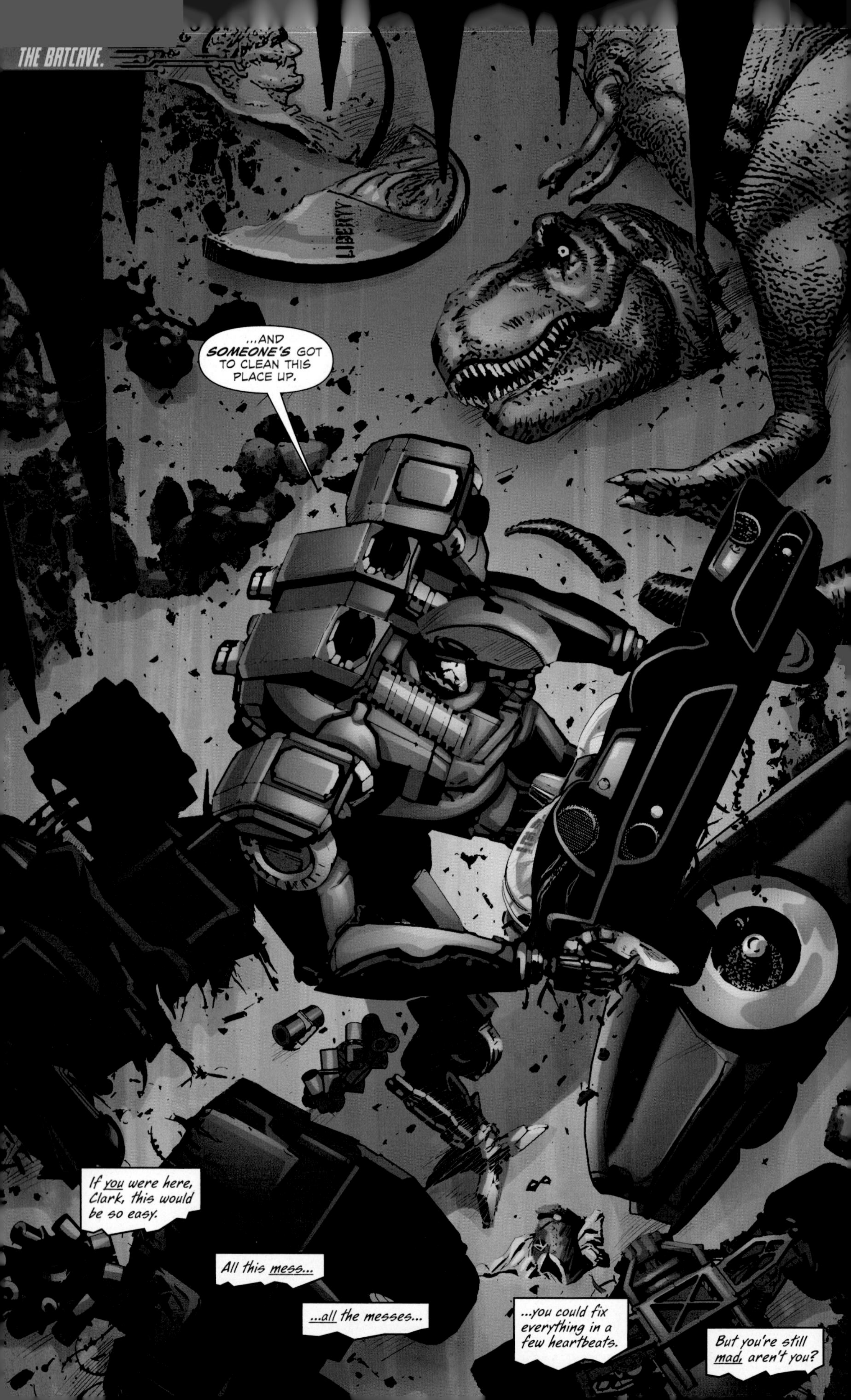
THE BATCAVE.
LIBERTY
...AND SOMEONE'S GOT TO CLEAN THIS PLACE UP.
If you were here, Clark, this would be so easy.
All this mess...
...all the messes...
...you could fix everything in a few heartbeats.
But you're still mad, aren't you?

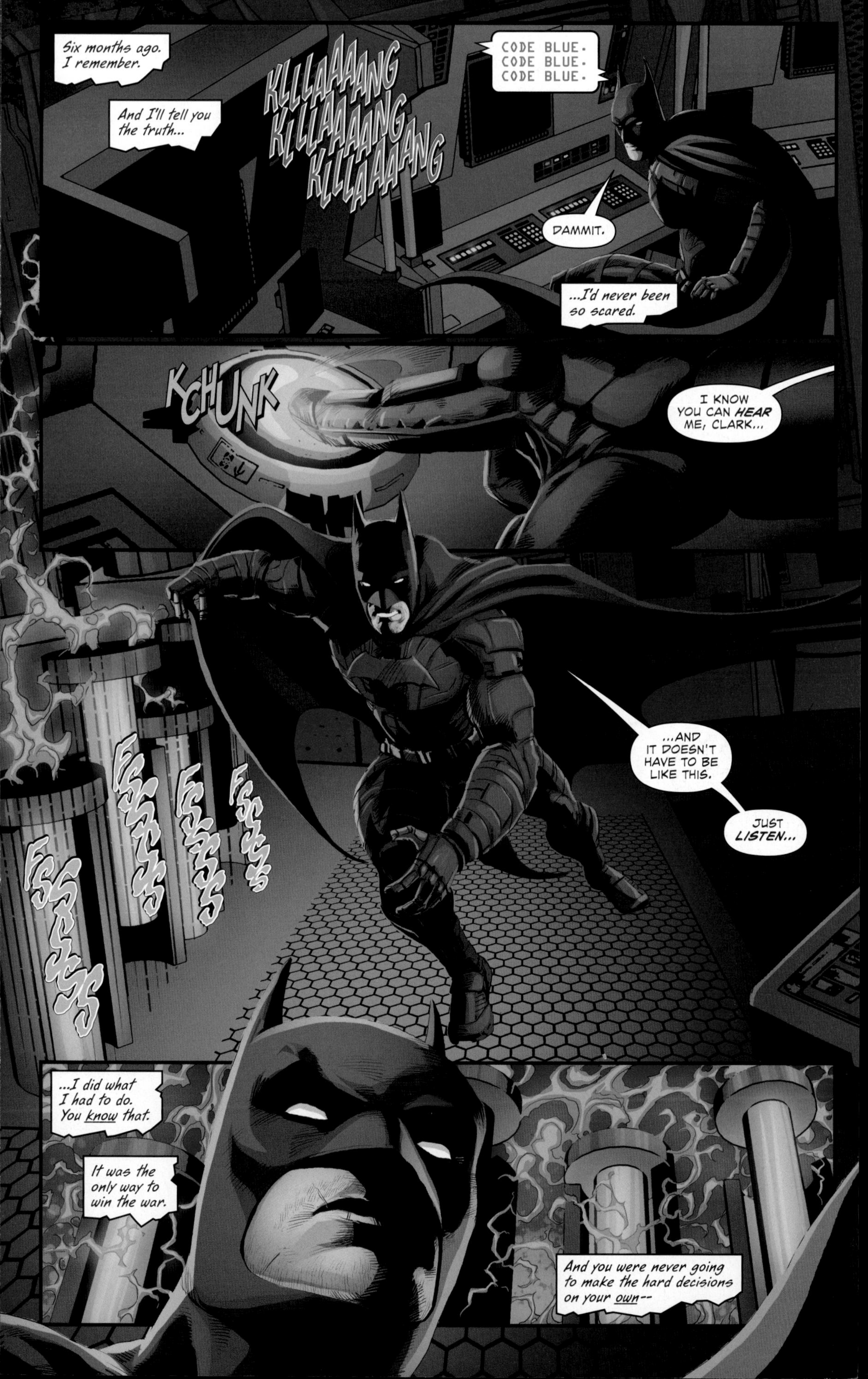
Six months ago. I remember.
And I'll tell you the truth...
KLLLAAAANG KLLLAAAANG KLLLAAAANG
CODE BLUE. CODE BLUE. CODE BLUE.
DAMMIT.
...I'd never been so scared.
KCHUNK
I KNOW YOU CAN HEAR ME, CLARK...
...AND IT DOESN'T HAVE TO BE LIKE THIS.
JUST LISTEN...
FSSSSS FSSSSS FSSSSS FSSSSS
...I did what I had to do. You know that.
It was the only way to win the war.
And you were never going to make the hard decisions on your own--

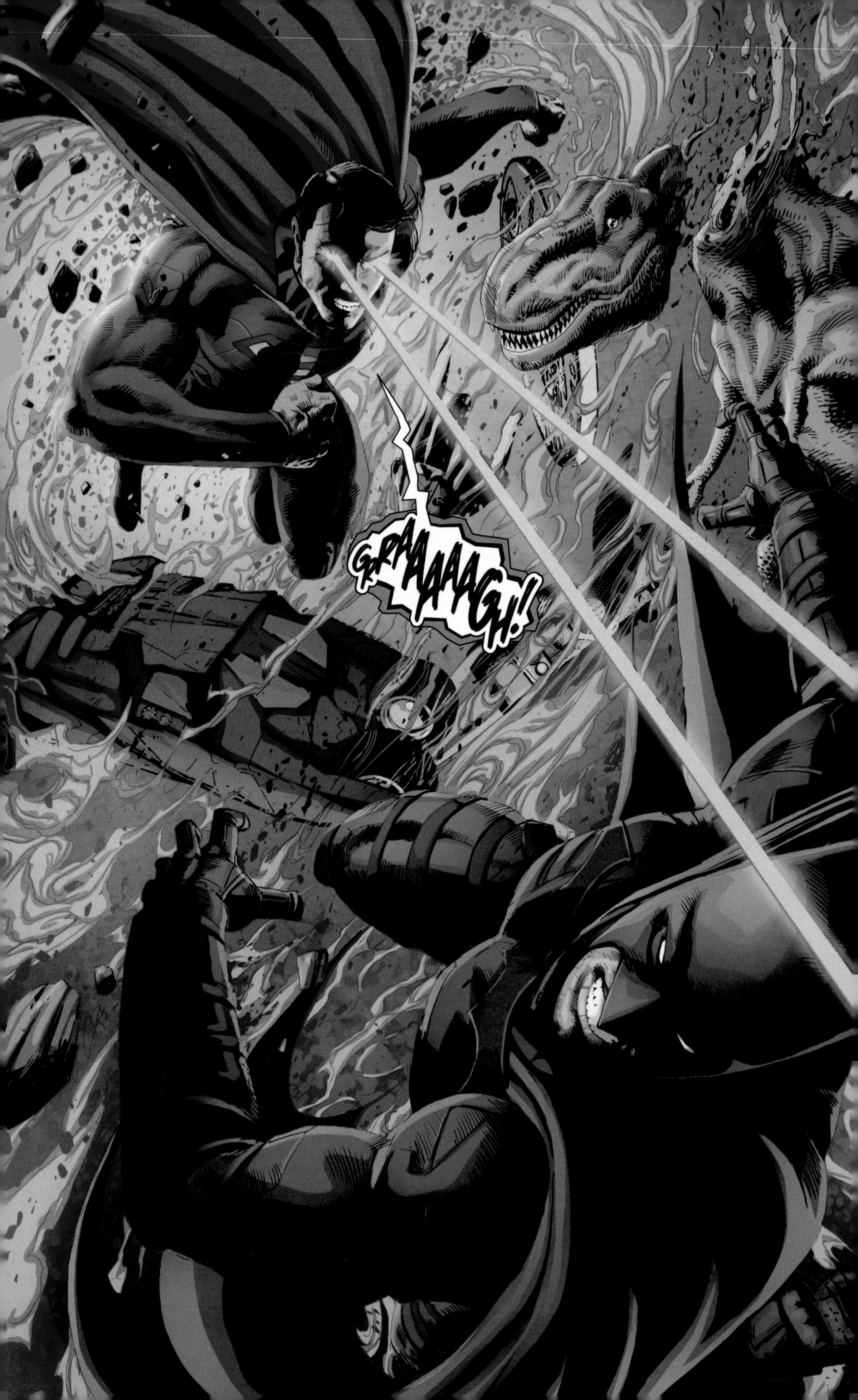
GRRAAAAAAAGH!

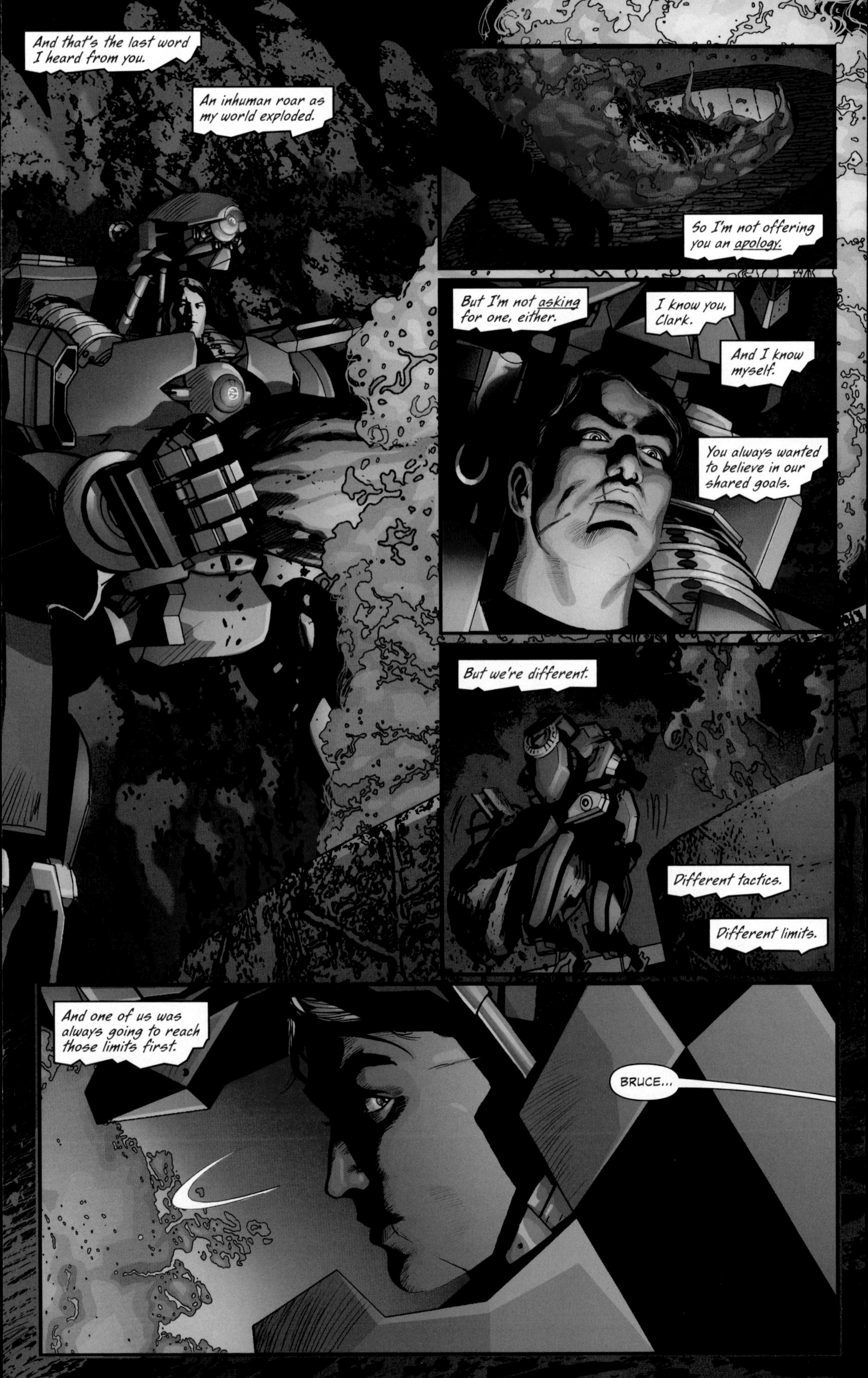
And that's the last word I heard from you.
An inhuman roar as my world exploded.
So I'm not offering you an apology.
But I'm not asking for one, either.
I know you, Clark.
And I know myself.
You always wanted to believe in our shared goals.
But we're different.
Different tactics.
Different limits.
And one of us was always going to reach those limits first.
BRUCE...

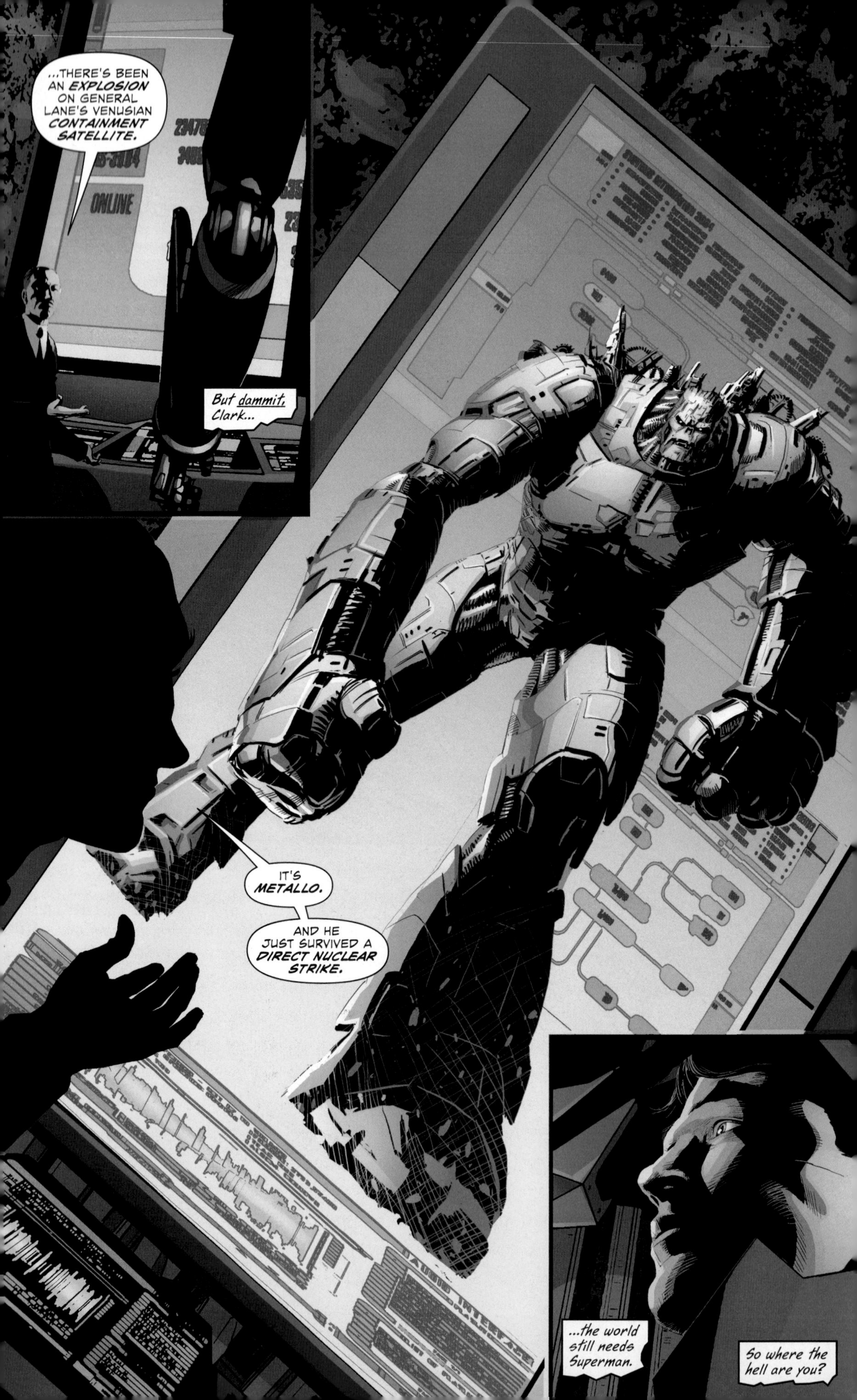

...THERE'S BEEN AN EXPLOSION ON GENERAL LANE'S VENUSIAN CONTAINMENT SATELLITE.
But dammit, Clark...
IT'S METALLO.
AND HE JUST SURVIVED A DIRECT NUCLEAR STRIKE.
...the world still needs Superman.
So where the hell are you?

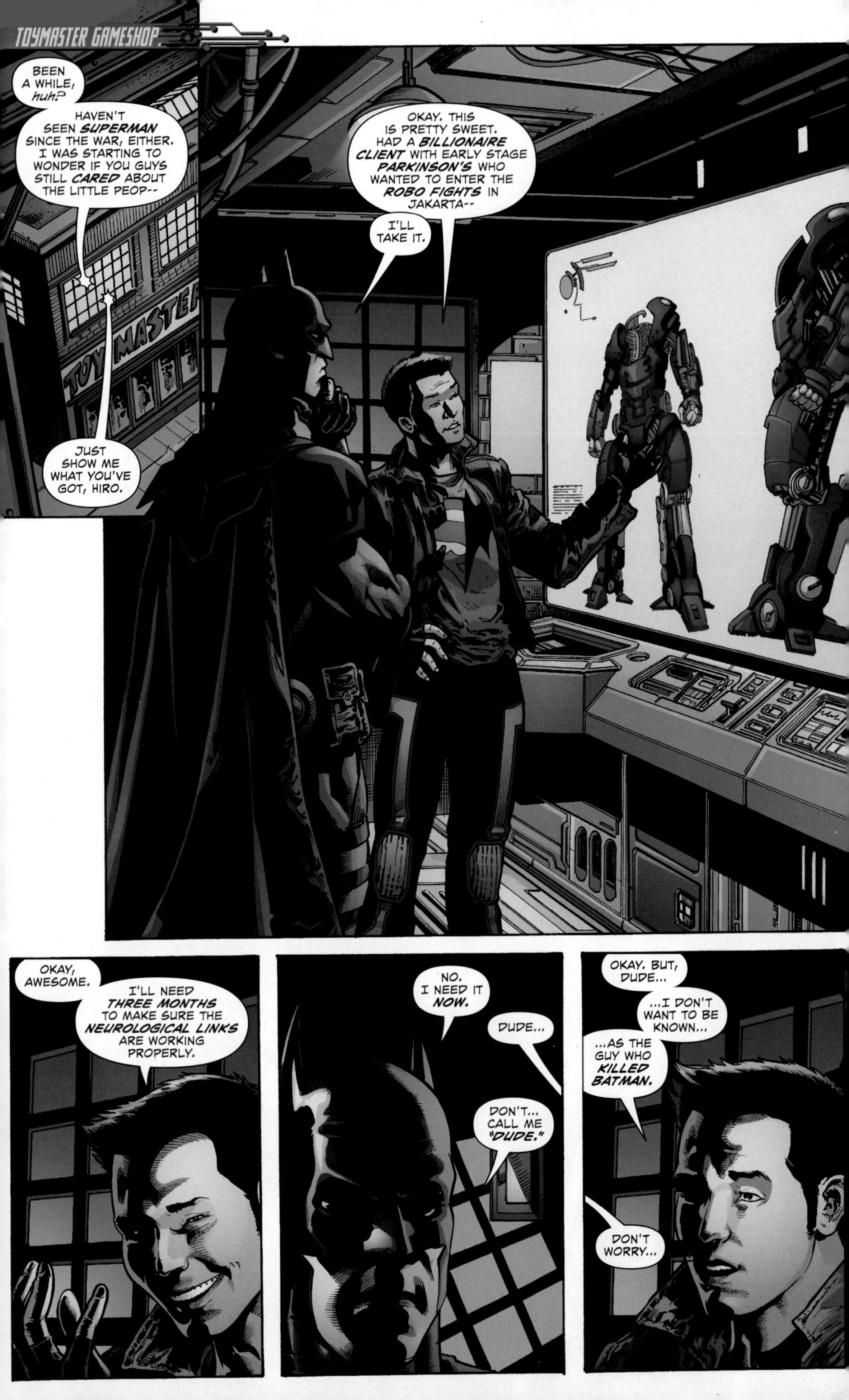
TOYMASTER GAMESHOP.
BEEN A WHILE, huh?
HAVEN'T SEEN SUPERMAN SINCE THE WAR, EITHER. I WAS STARTING TO WONDER IF YOU GUYS STILL CARED ABOUT THE LITTLE PEOP--
JUST SHOW ME WHAT YOU'VE GOT, HIRO.
OKAY. THIS IS PRETTY SWEET. HAD A BILLIONAIRE CLIENT WITH EARLY STAGE PARKINSON'S WHO WANTED TO ENTER THE ROBO FIGHTS IN JAKARTA--
I'LL TAKE IT.
OKAY, AWESOME.
I'LL NEED THREE MONTHS TO MAKE SURE THE NEUROLOGICAL LINKS ARE WORKING PROPERLY.
NO. I NEED IT NOW.
DUDE...
DON'T... CALL ME "DUDE."
OKAY. BUT, DUDE...
...I DON'T WANT TO BE KNOWN...
...AS THE GUY WHO KILLED BATMAN.
DON'T WORRY...

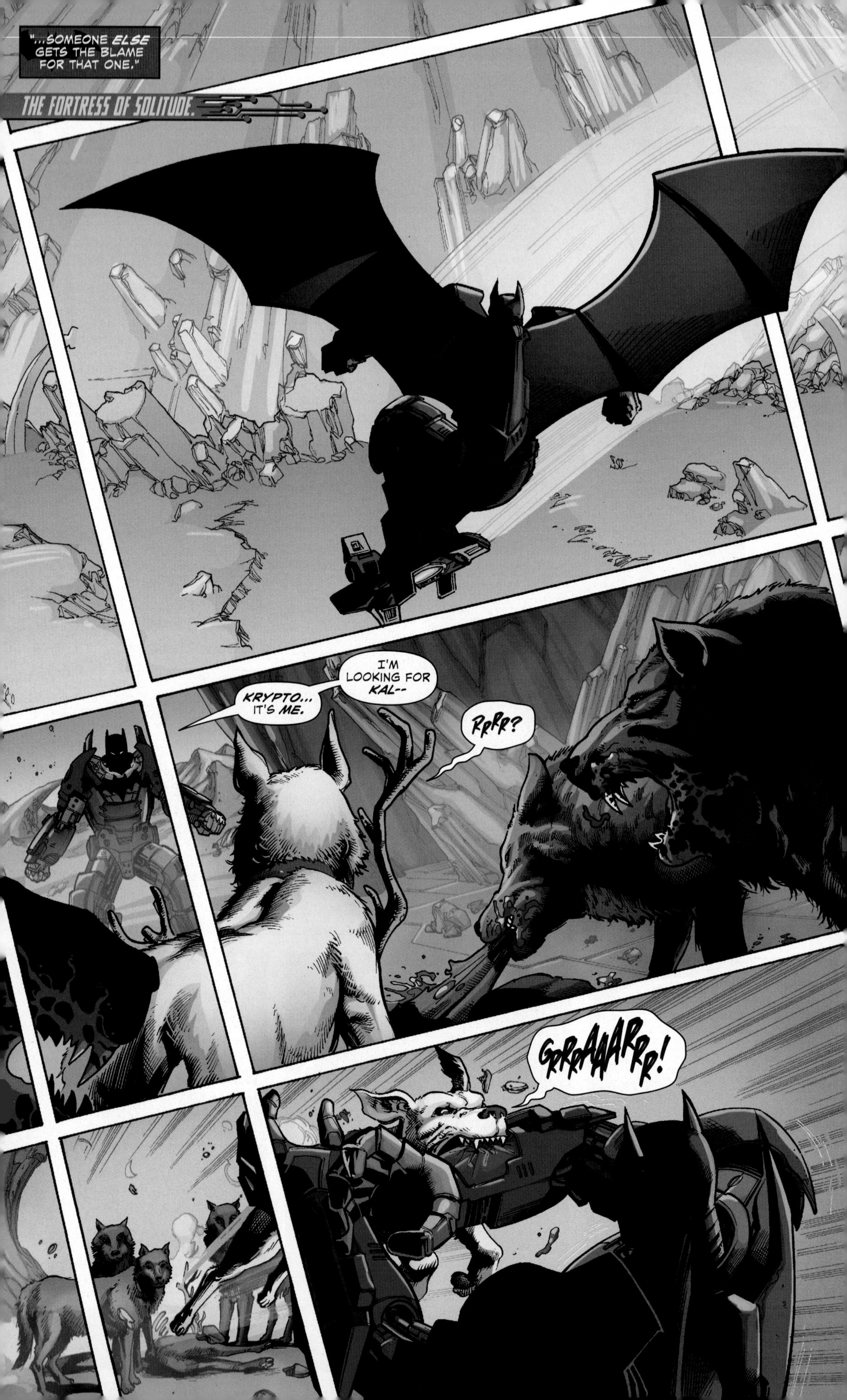
"...SOMEONE ELSE GETS THE BLAME FOR THAT ONE."
THE FORTRESS OF SOLITUDE.
KRYPTO... IT'S ME.
I'M LOOKING FOR KAL--
RRRR?
GRRRAAARRR!

NO, KRYPTO!

KRAAKOOOM

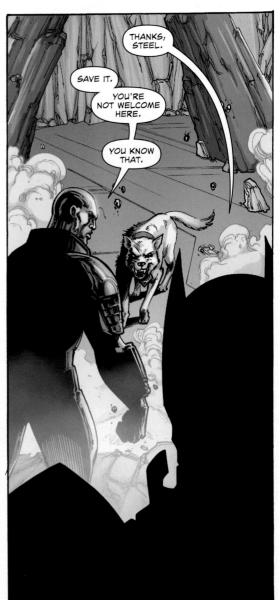

THANKS, STEEL.

SAVE IT. YOU'RE NOT WELCOME HERE.

YOU KNOW THAT.

SOMETHING'S COME UP.

SUPERMAN NEEDS TO KNOW.

IS THIS ABOUT METALLO? I'M HEADING OFF-PLANET TONIGHT WITH CYBORG FOR A SEARCH-AND-DESTROY.

BUT LET'S IMAGINE, JUST FOR THE SAKE OF ARGUMENT, THAT SUPERMAN'S STILL ALIVE.

WHY WOULD HE EVER TRUST ANYTHING YOU HAD TO SAY?

YOU ALREADY USED HIM UP, BATMAN.

YOU'RE ON YOUR OWN, NOW.

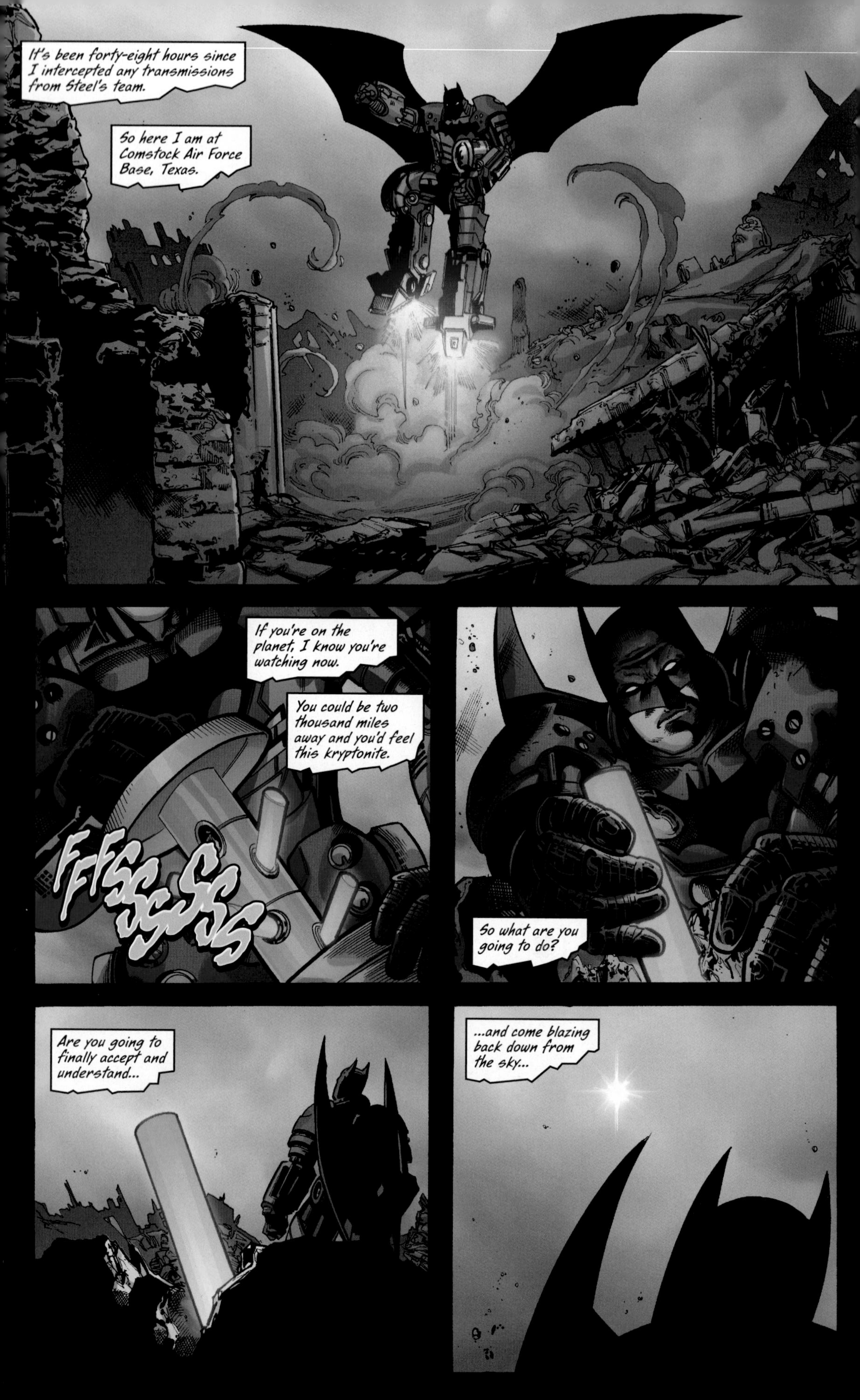
It's been forty-eight hours since I intercepted any transmissions from Steel's team.
So here I am at Comstock Air Force Base, Texas.
If you're on the planet, I know you're watching now.
You could be two thousand miles away and you'd feel this kryptonite.
FFSSSSSS
So what are you going to do?
Are you going to finally accept and understand...
...and come blazing back down from the sky...

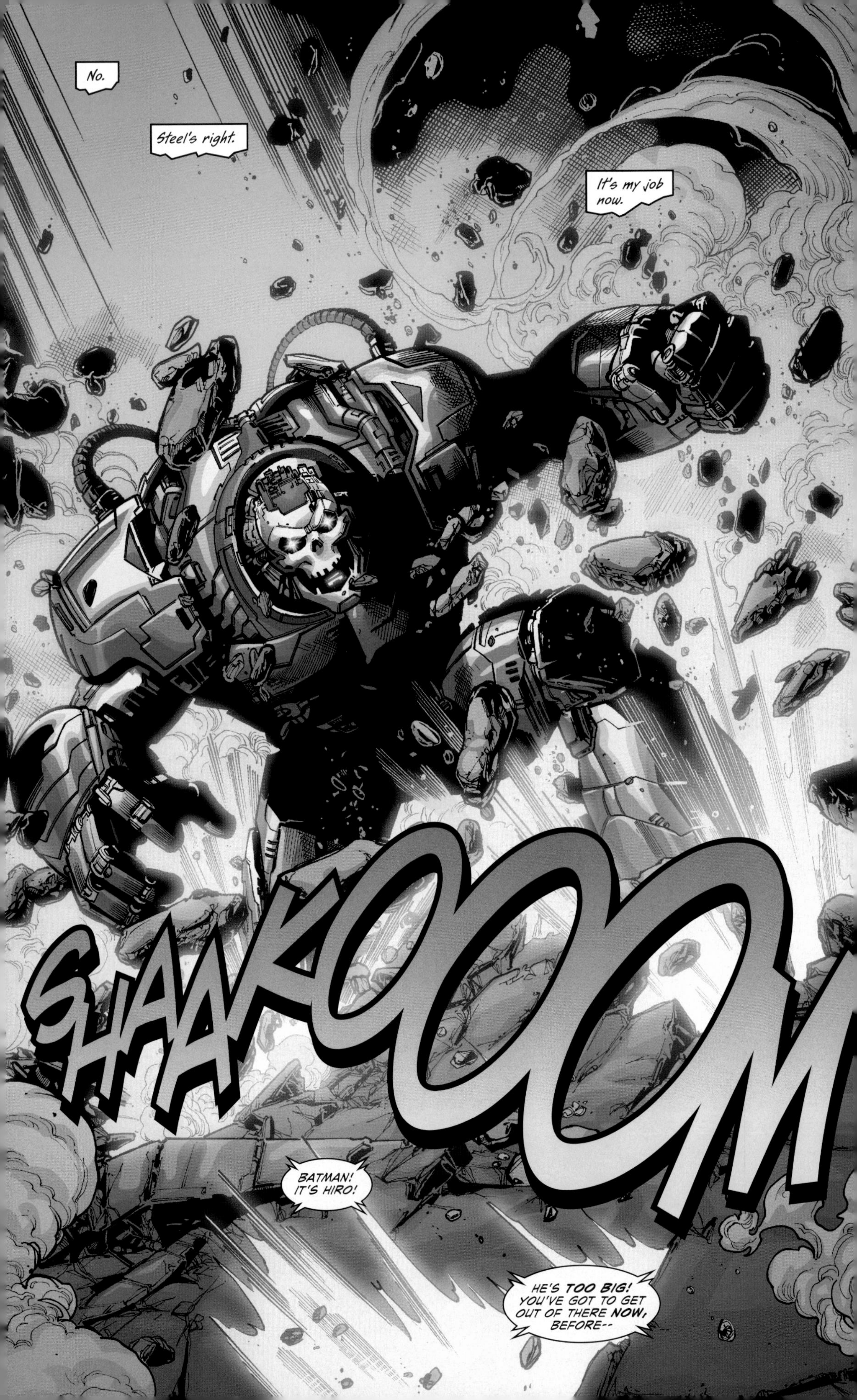
No.
Steel's right.
It's my job now.
SHAKOOOM
BATMAN! IT'S HIRO!
HE'S TOO BIG! YOU'VE GOT TO GET OUT OF THERE NOW, BEFORE--

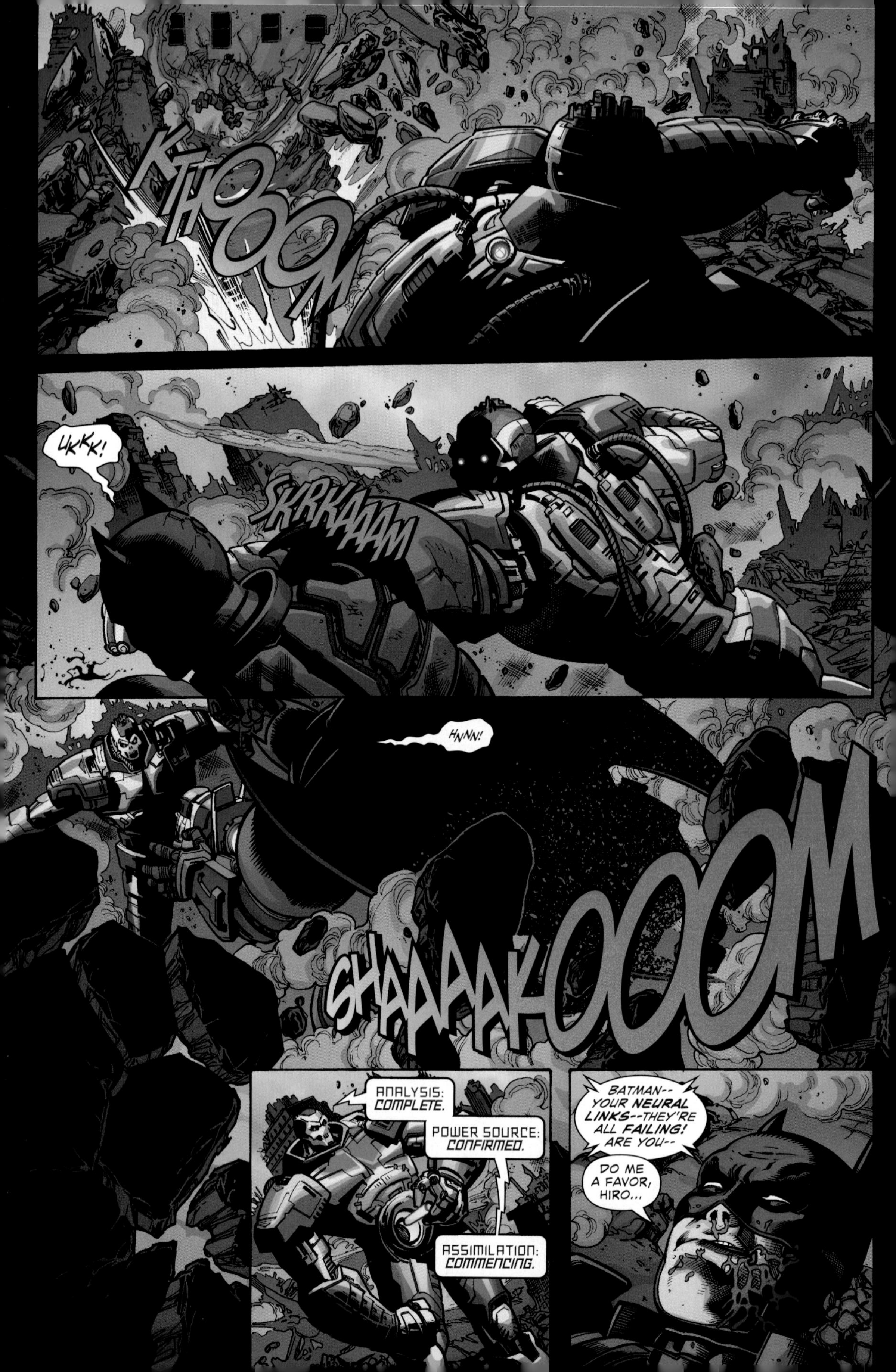
K-THOOOM
UKKK!
SKRKAAAM
HNNN!
SHAAAAKOOOM
ANALYSIS: COMPLETE.
POWER SOURCE: CONFIRMED.
ASSIMILATION: COMMENCING.
BATMAN-- YOUR NEURAL LINKS--THEY'RE ALL FAILING! ARE YOU--
DO ME A FAVOR, HIRO...

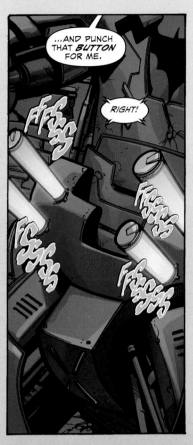

...AND PUNCH THAT *BUTTON* FOR ME.

RIGHT!

FFSSSS FFSSSS FFSSSS

KRYPTONITE LEVELS: *INCREASING!*

SYSTEM-- *OVERLOAD!*

SYSTEM-- *OVERLOAD!*

SYSTEM--

KTHOOM

HA HA!

THAT'S IT, BATMAN!

JUST LIKE WE PLANNED IT!

HEY, WE MAKE A PRETTY GOOD TEAM, *huh?*

BATMAN?

BATMAN!

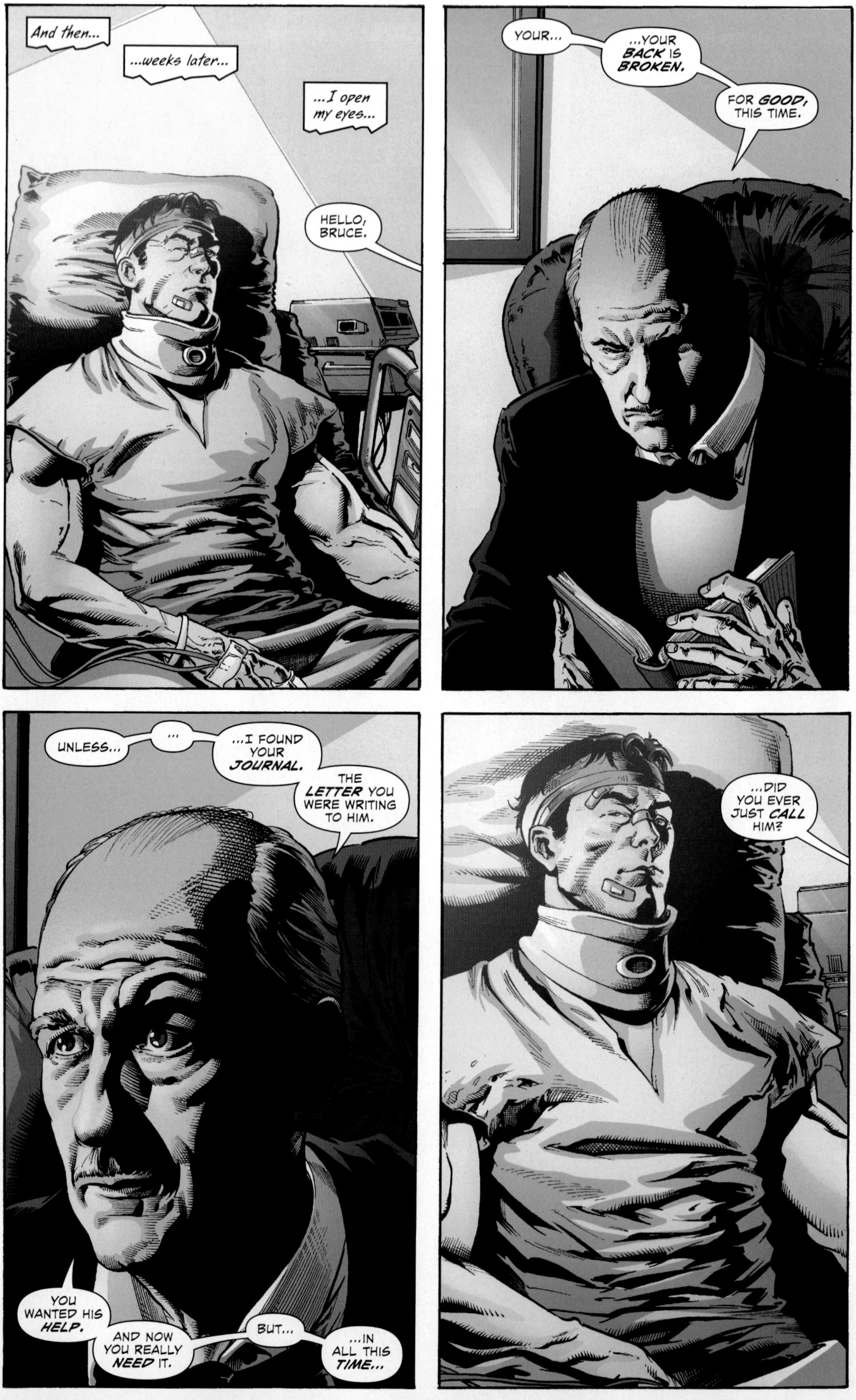
And then...
...weeks later...
...I open my eyes...
HELLO, BRUCE.
YOUR...
...YOUR BACK IS BROKEN.
FOR GOOD, THIS TIME.
UNLESS...
...
...I FOUND YOUR JOURNAL.
THE LETTER YOU WERE WRITING TO HIM.
YOU WANTED HIS HELP.
AND NOW YOU REALLY NEED IT.
BUT...
...IN ALL THIS TIME...
...DID YOU EVER JUST CALL HIM?

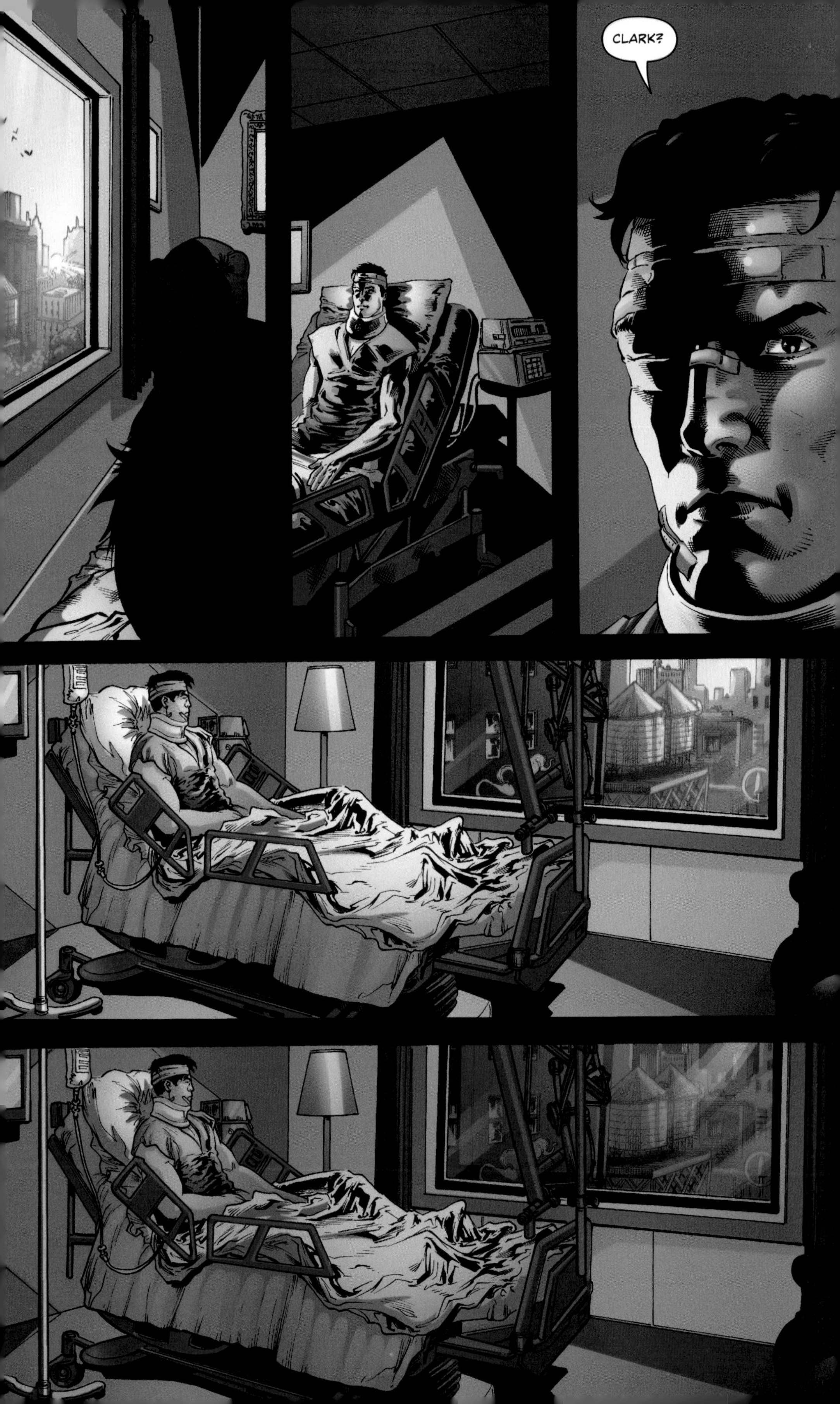
CLARK?

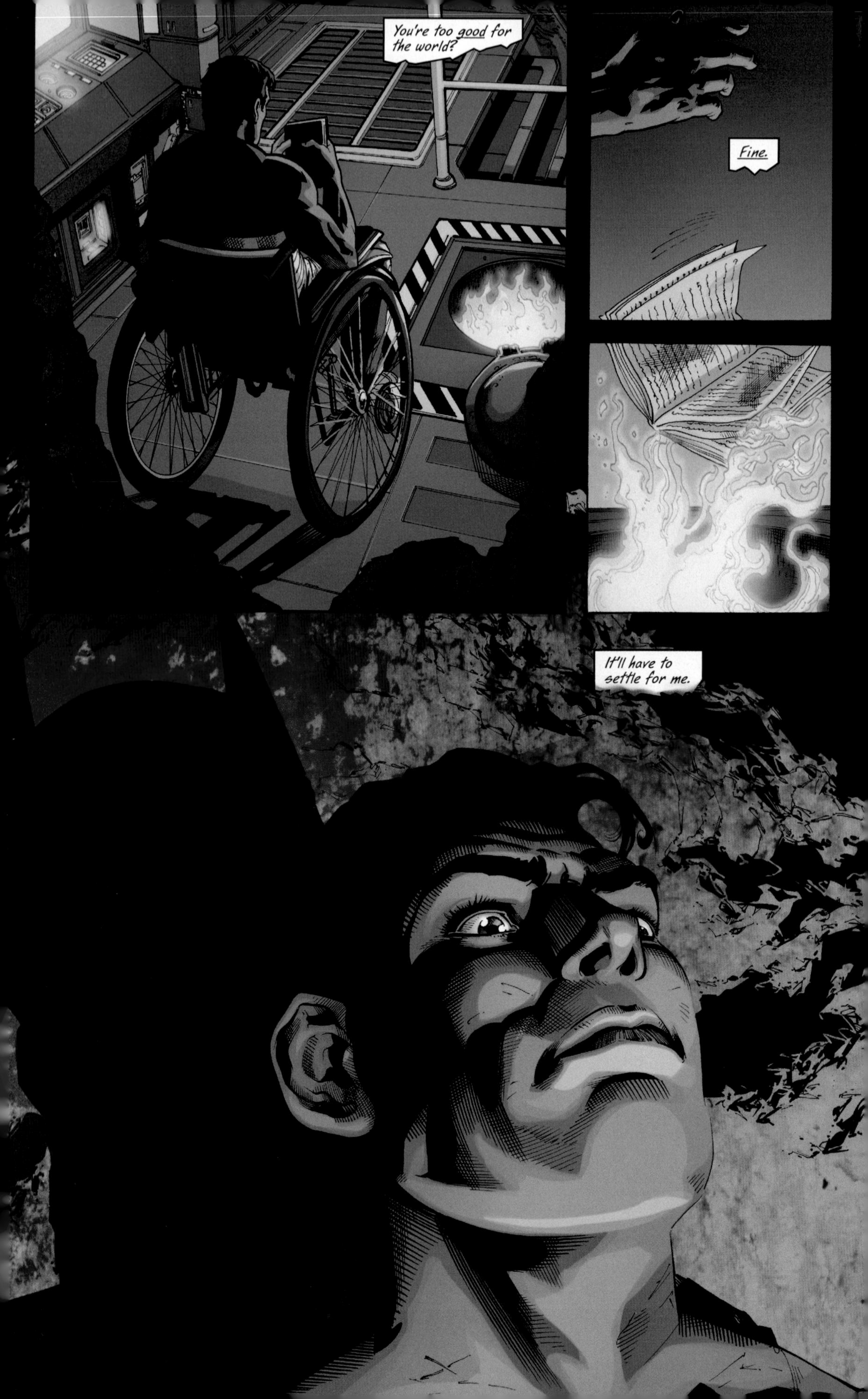
You're too good for the world?
Fine.
It'll have to settle for me.

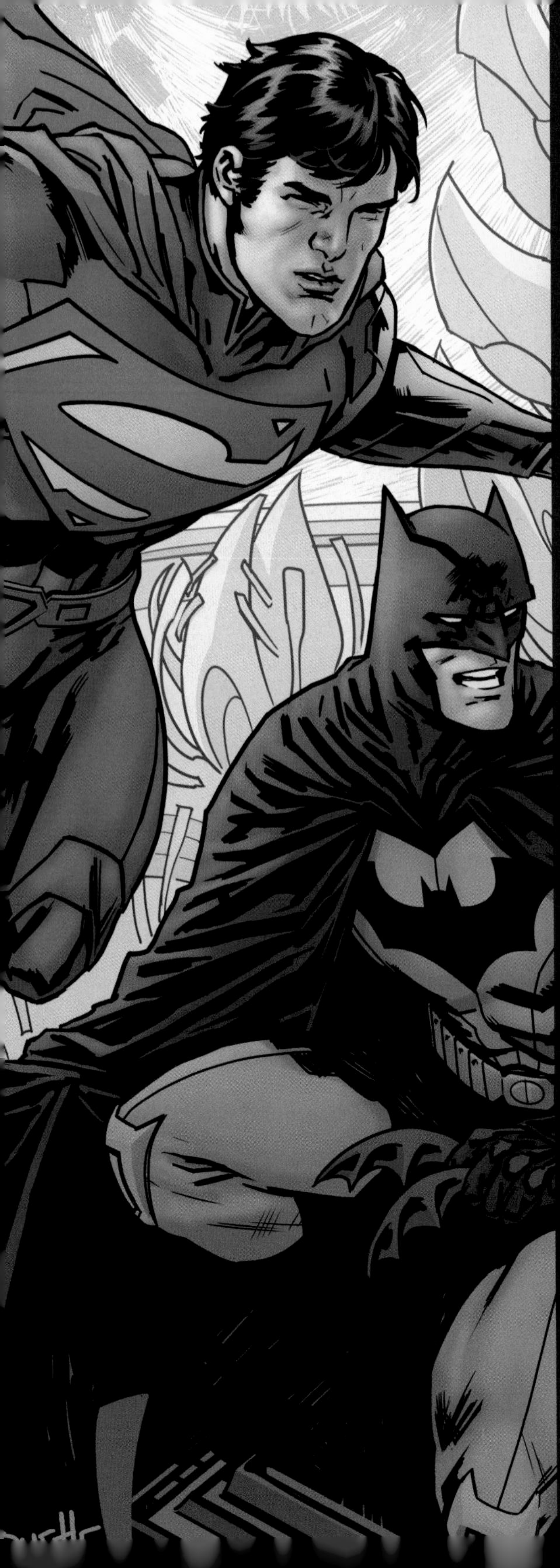

VARIANT COVER GALLERY

BATMAN/SUPERMAN #16
LEGO VARIANT COVER

BATMAN/SUPERMAN #16
VARIANT BY KEVIN WADA

BATMAN/SUPERMAN #17
VARIANT COVER BY DARWYN COOKE

BATMAN/SUPERMAN #17
VARIANT COVER BY LEANDRO FERNÁNDEZ AND ANDREW DALHOUSE

BATMAN/SUPERMAN #18
VARIANT COVER BY JUANJO AND TOMEU MOREY

BATMAN/SUPERMAN #18
FLASH 75TH ANNIVERSARY COVER BY JIM LEE, SCOTT WILLIAMS AND ALEX SINCLAIR

BATMAN/SUPERMAN #19
VARIANT COVER BY JOE QUINONES

BATMAN/SUPERMAN #19
HARLEY QUINN VARIANT COVER BY J.G. JONES AND ALEX SINCLAIR

BATMAN/SUPERMAN #20
VARIANT COVER BY YANICK PAQUETTE AND NATHAN FAIRBAIRN

BATMAN/SUPERMAN #20
MOVIE VARIANT COVER BY TONY HARRIS

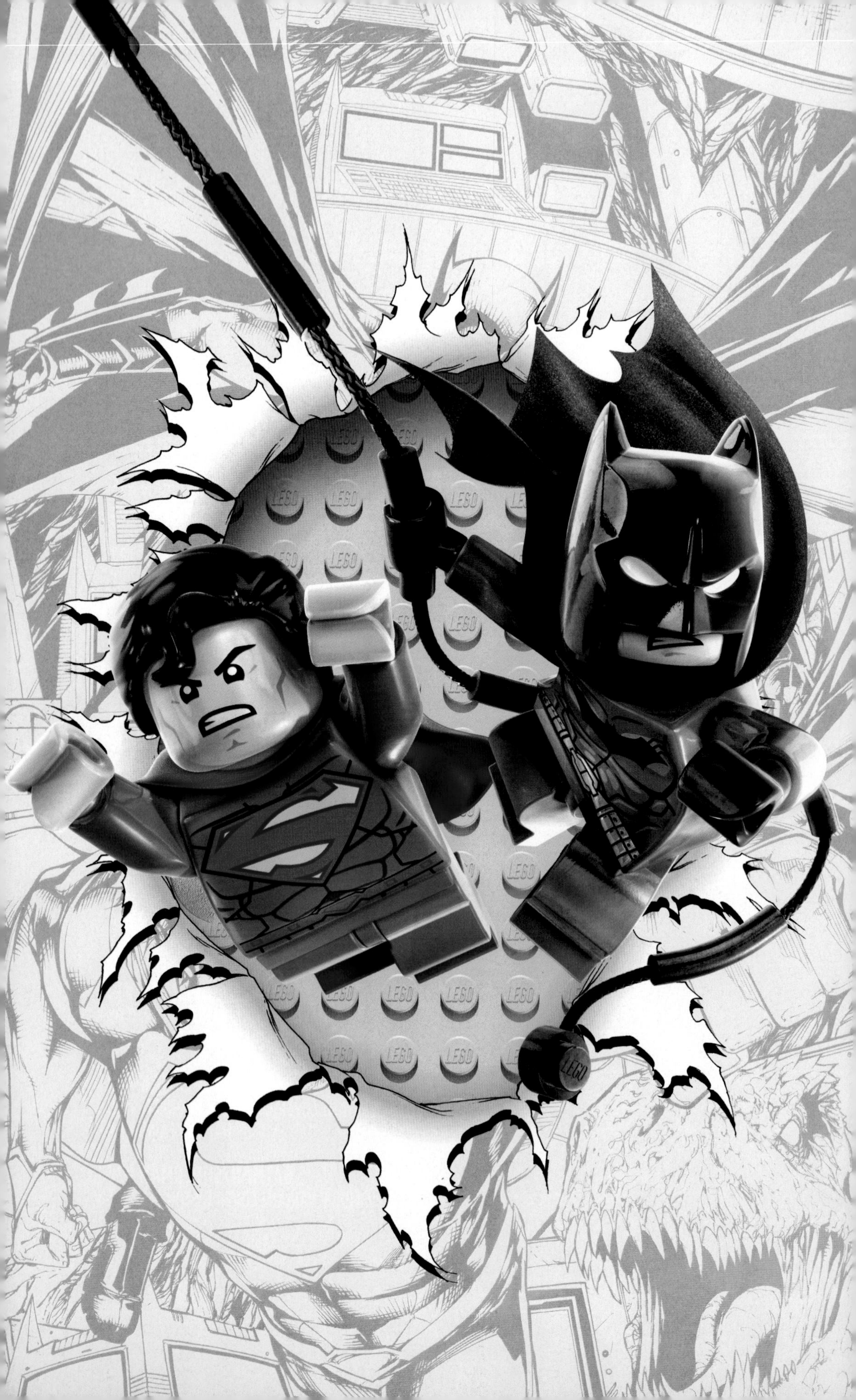

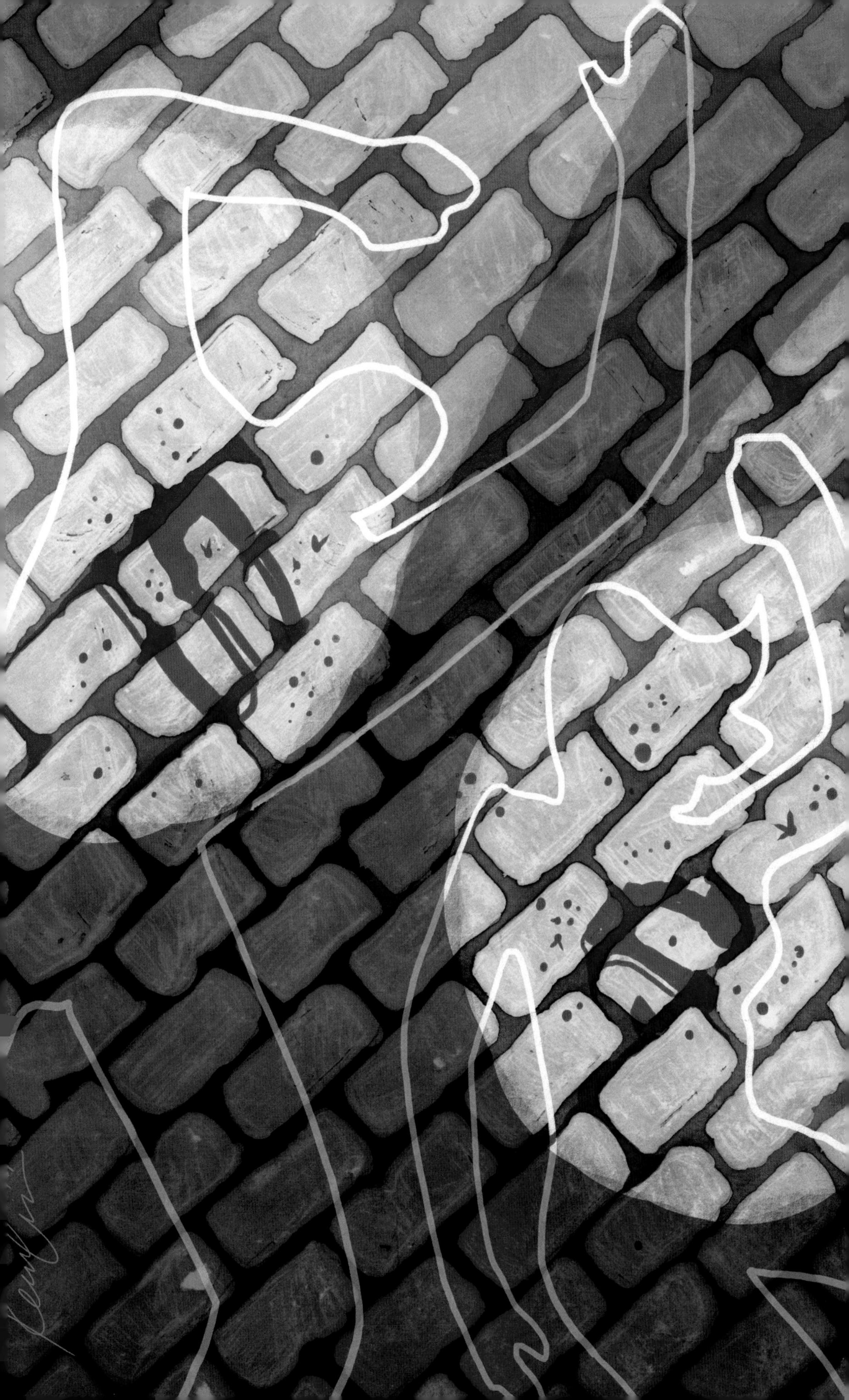

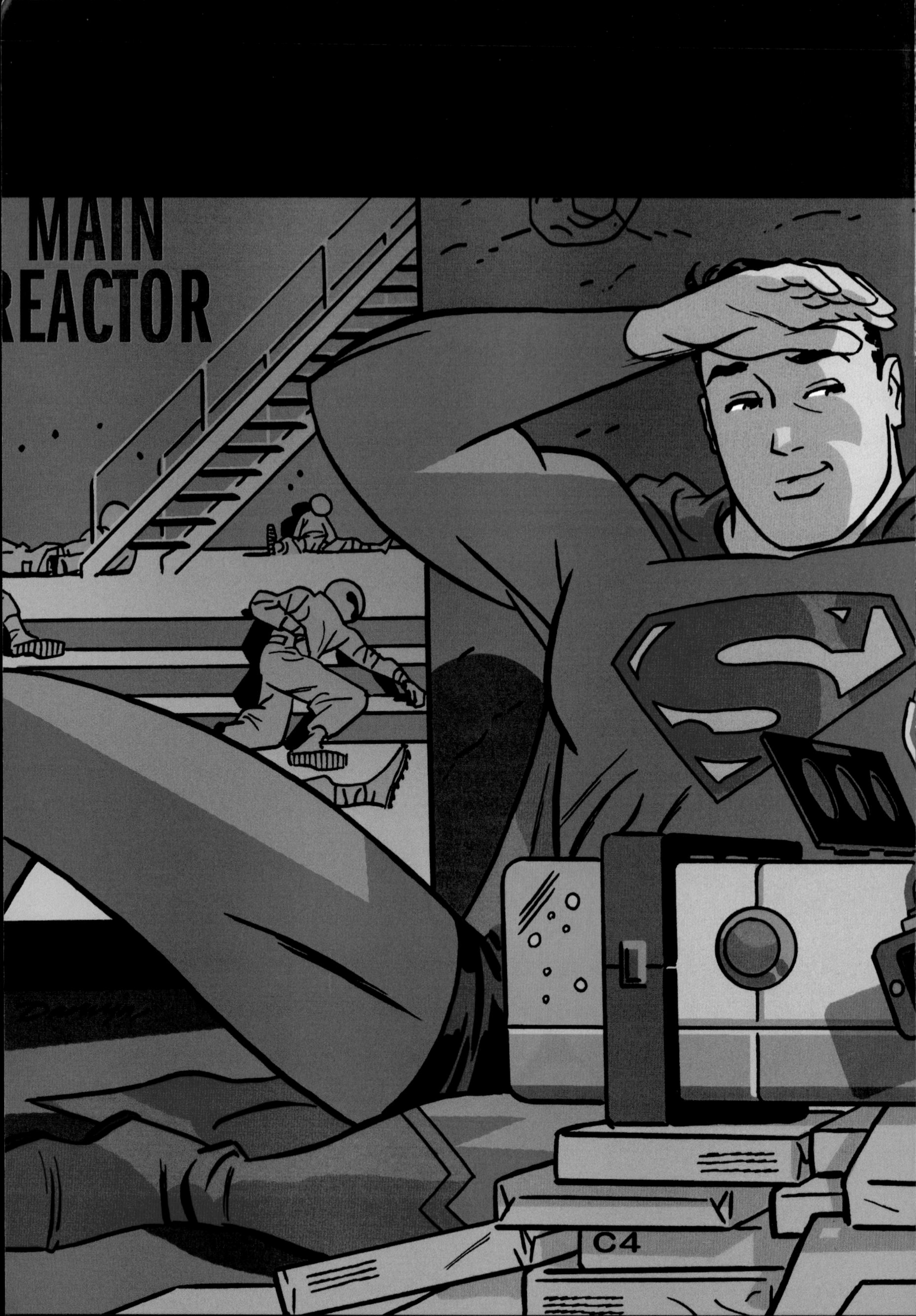
MAIN
REACTOR
C4

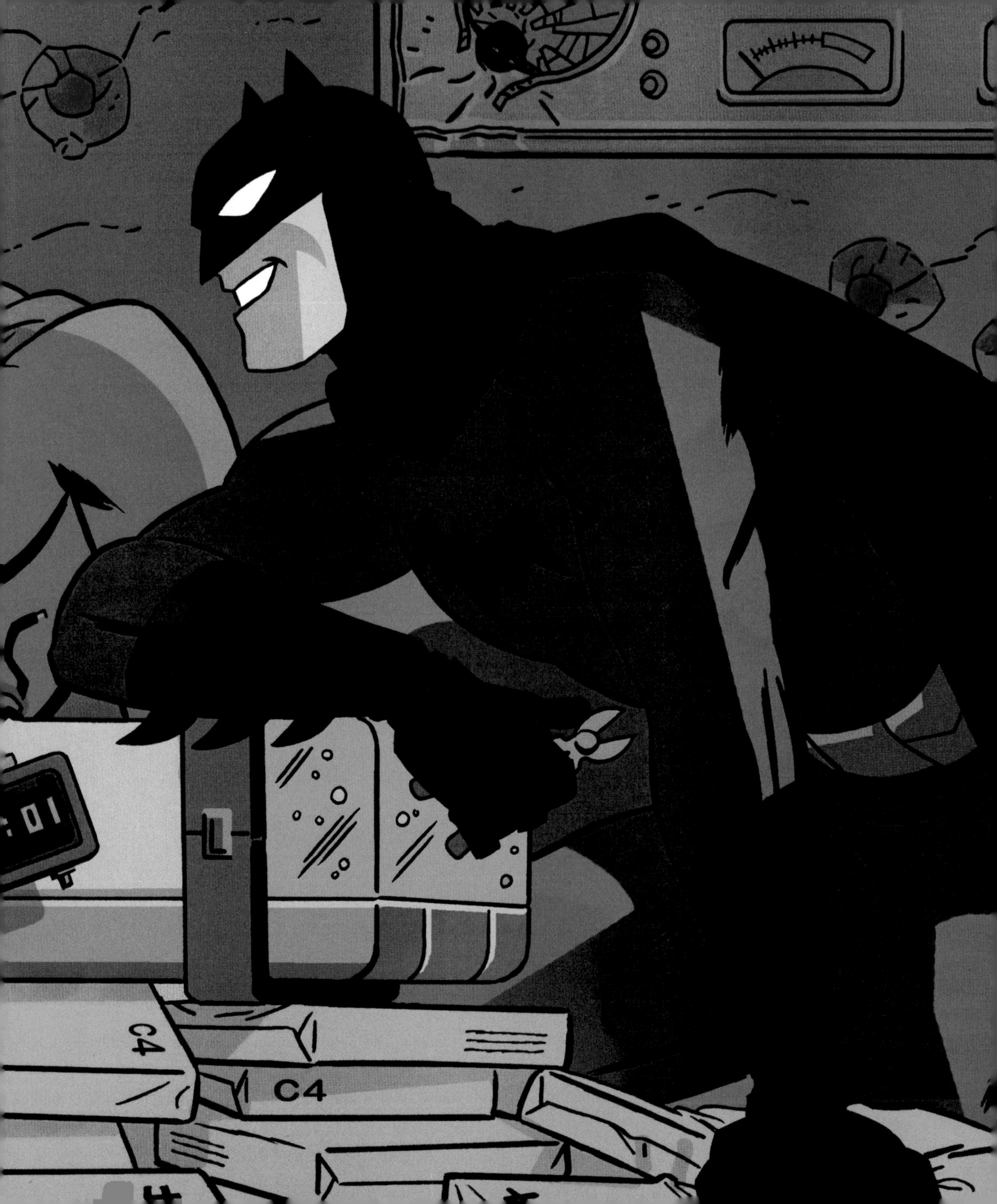
C4
C4

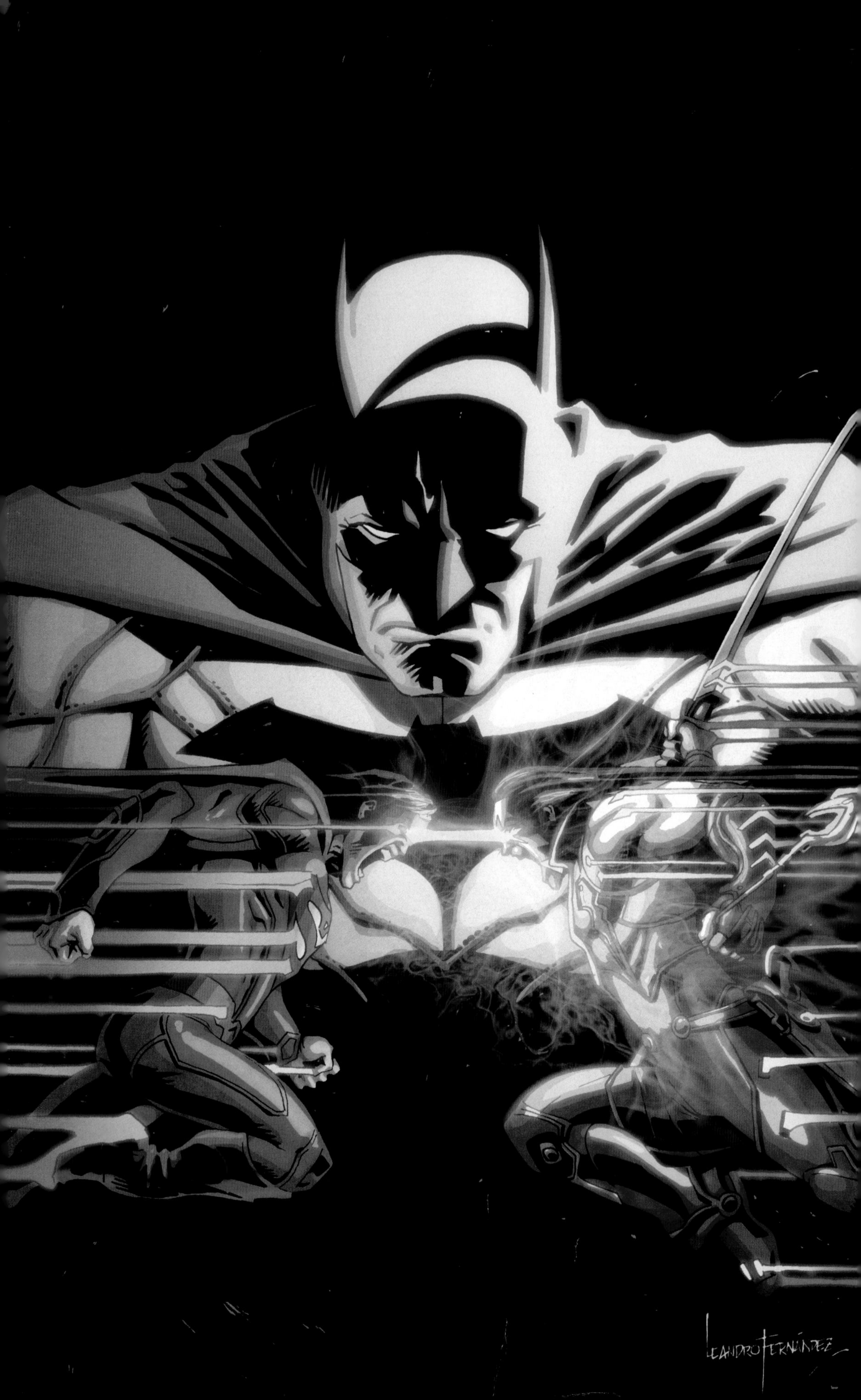
LEANDRO FERNÁNDEZ

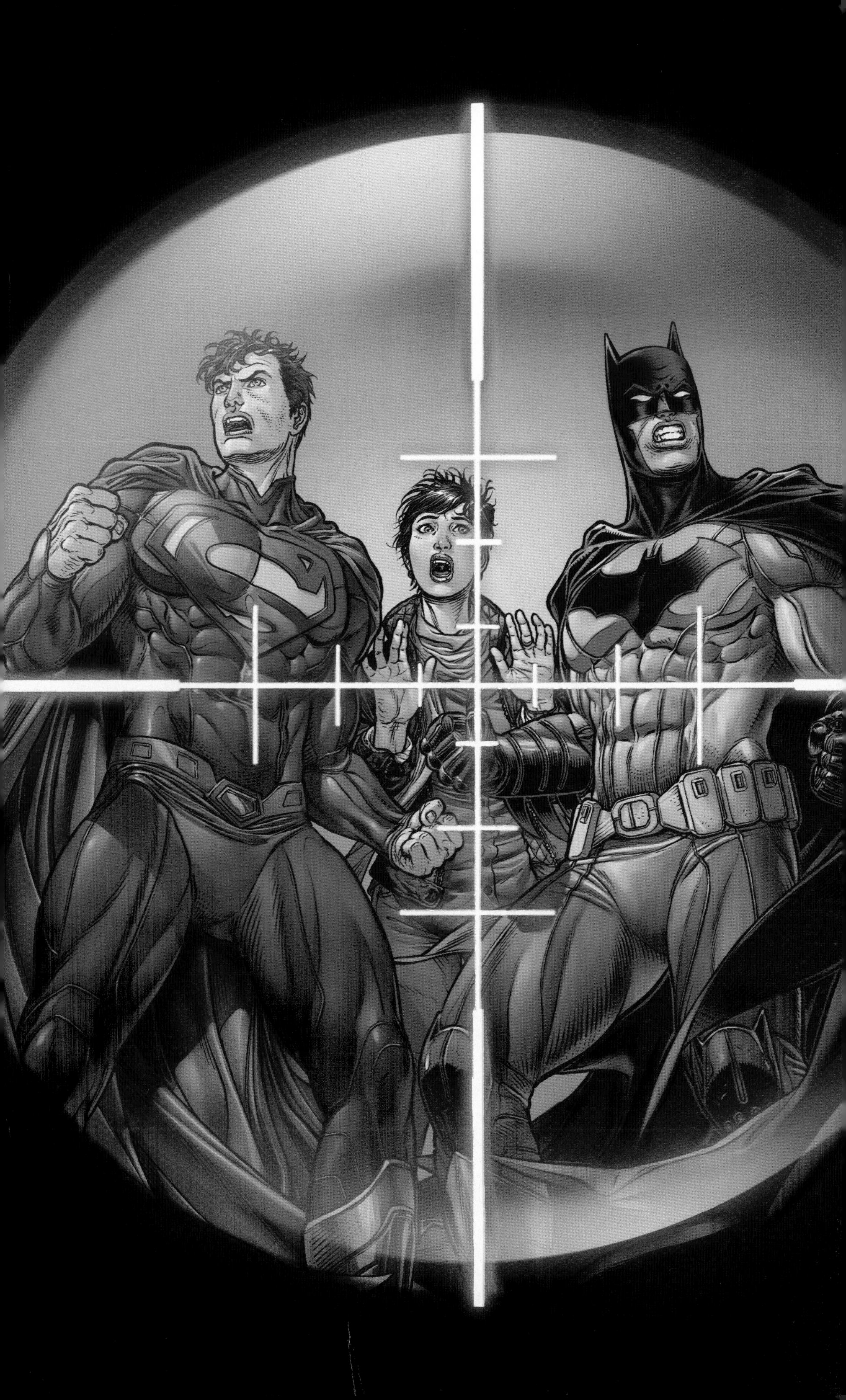

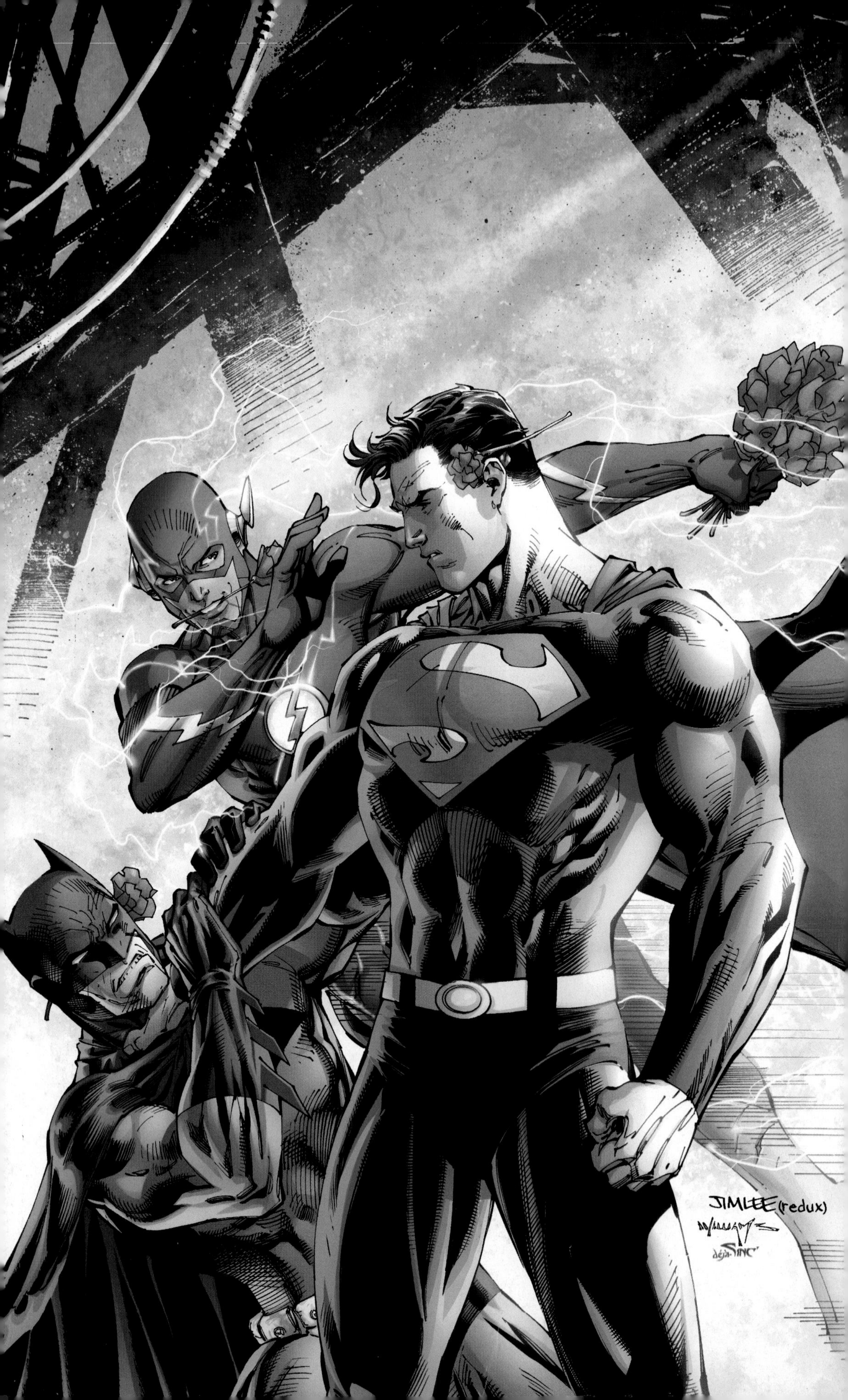
JIMLEE(redux)

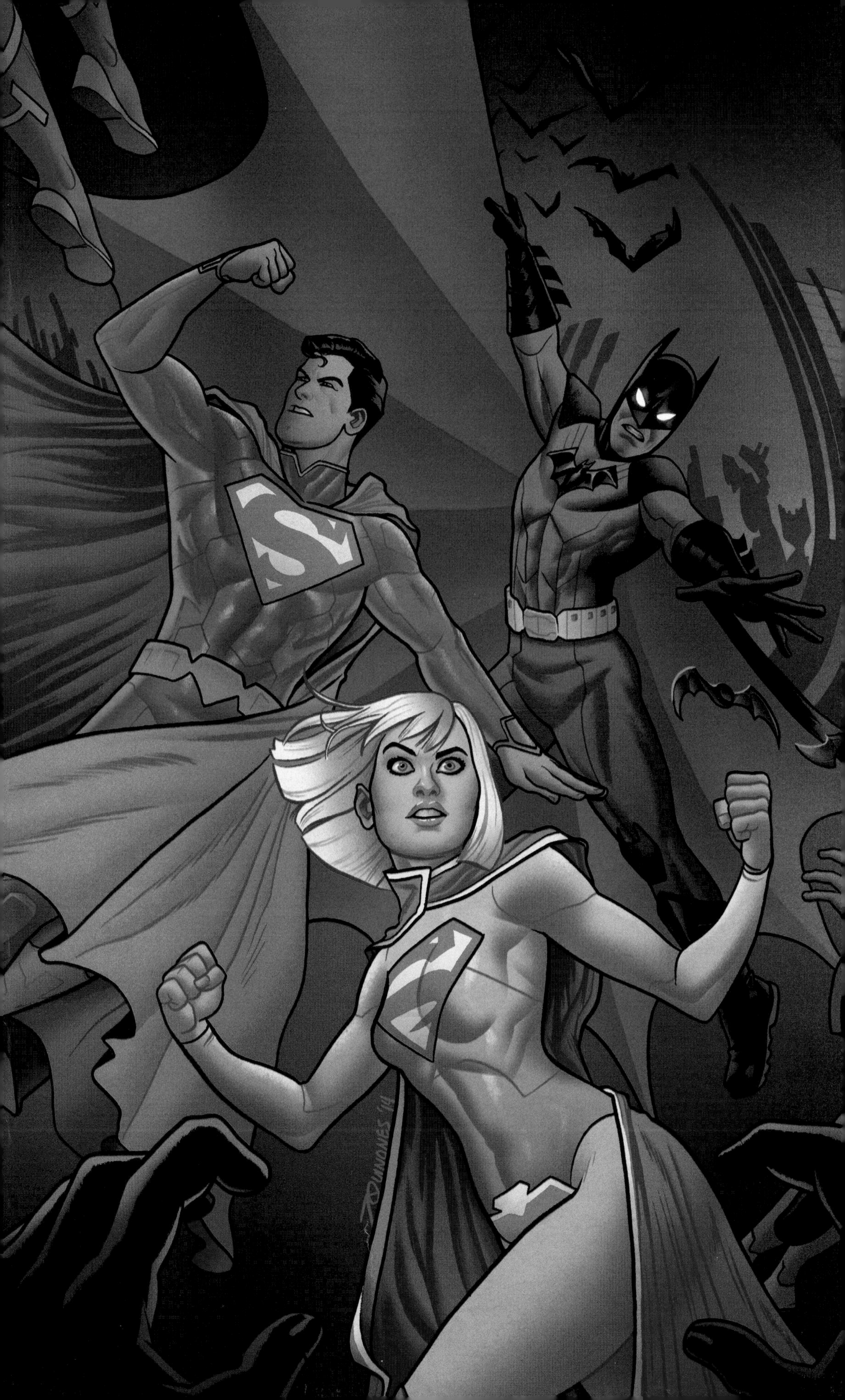

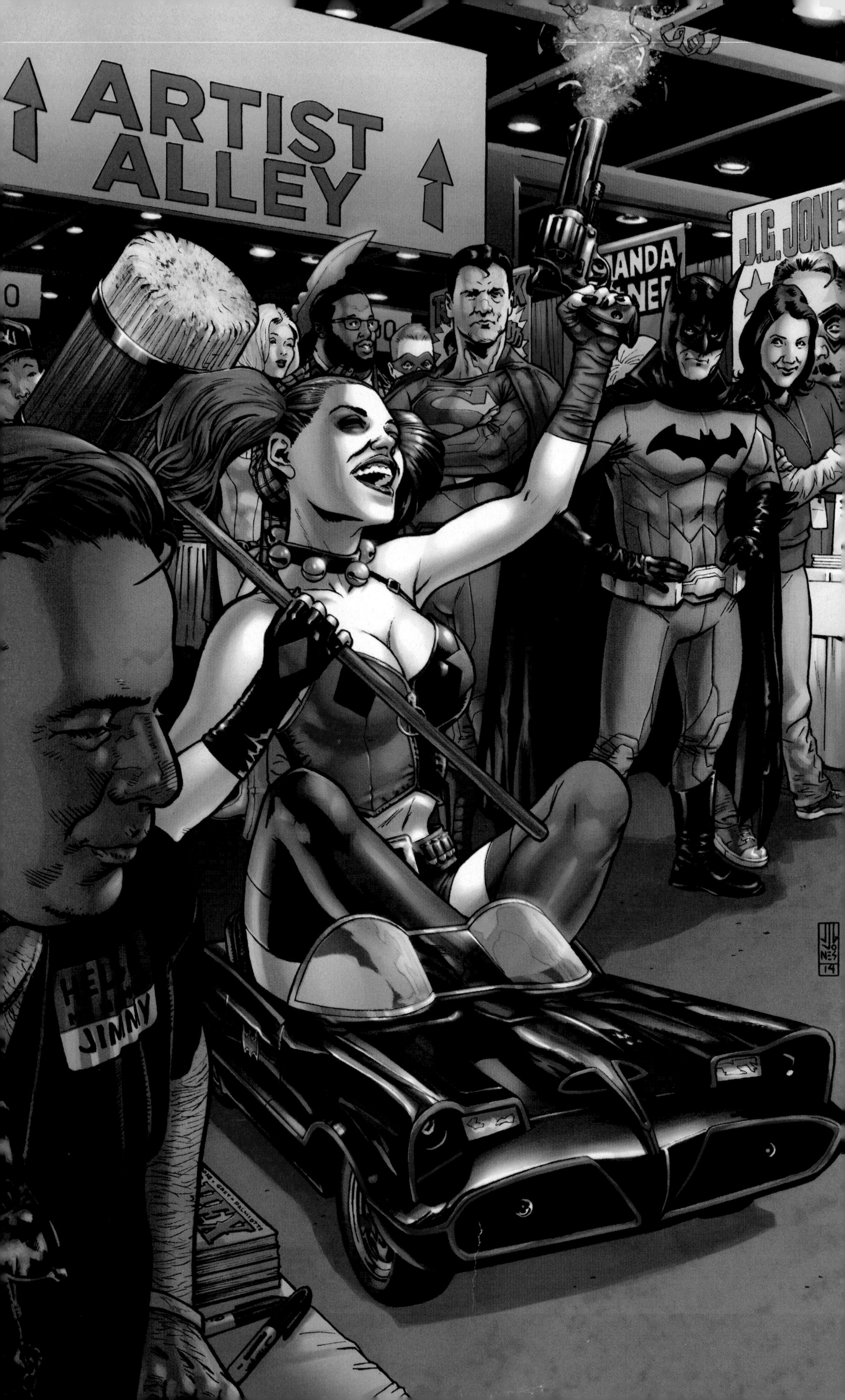
ARTIST
ALLEY
J.G. JONE
JIMMY

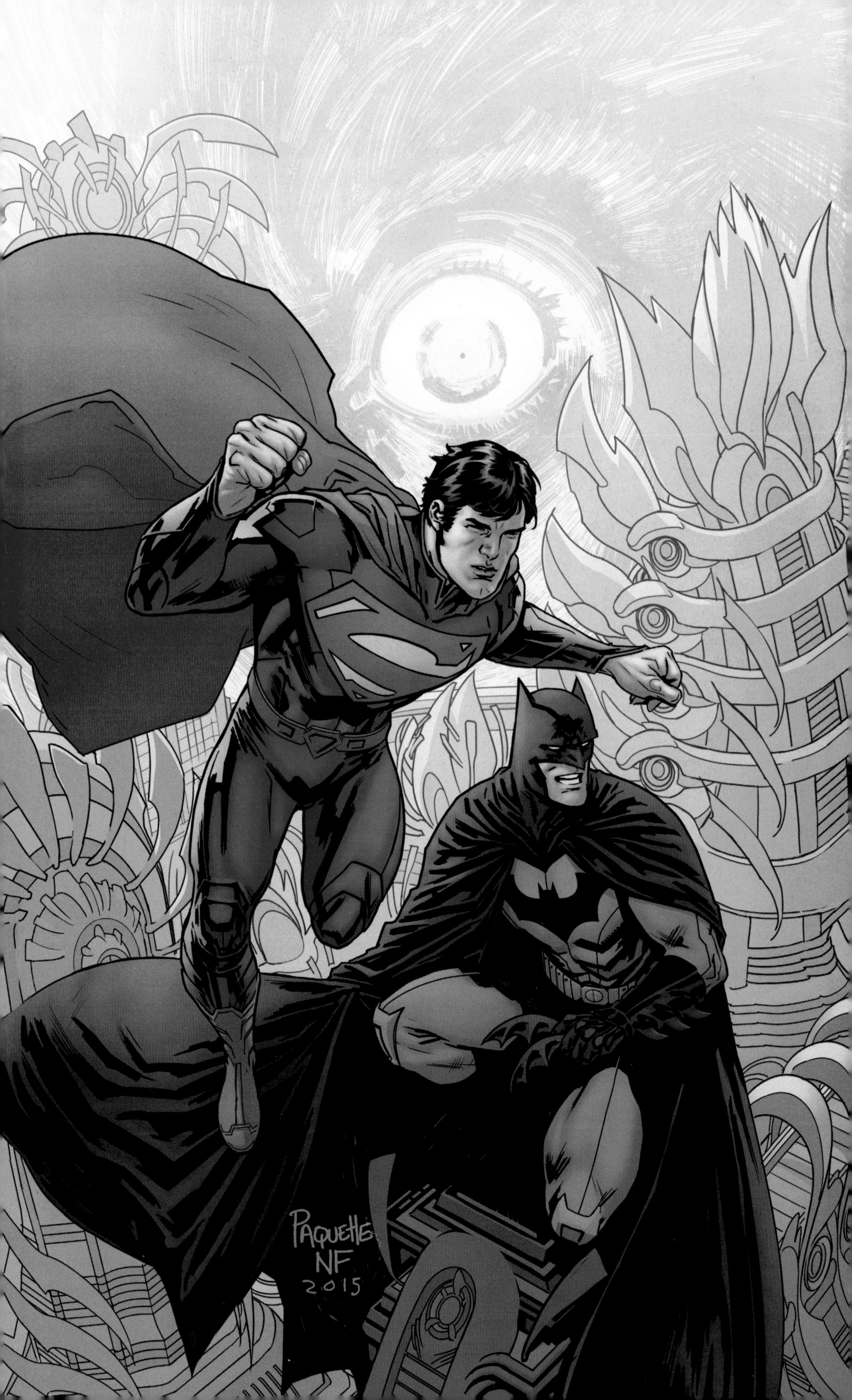
PAQUETTE
NF
2015

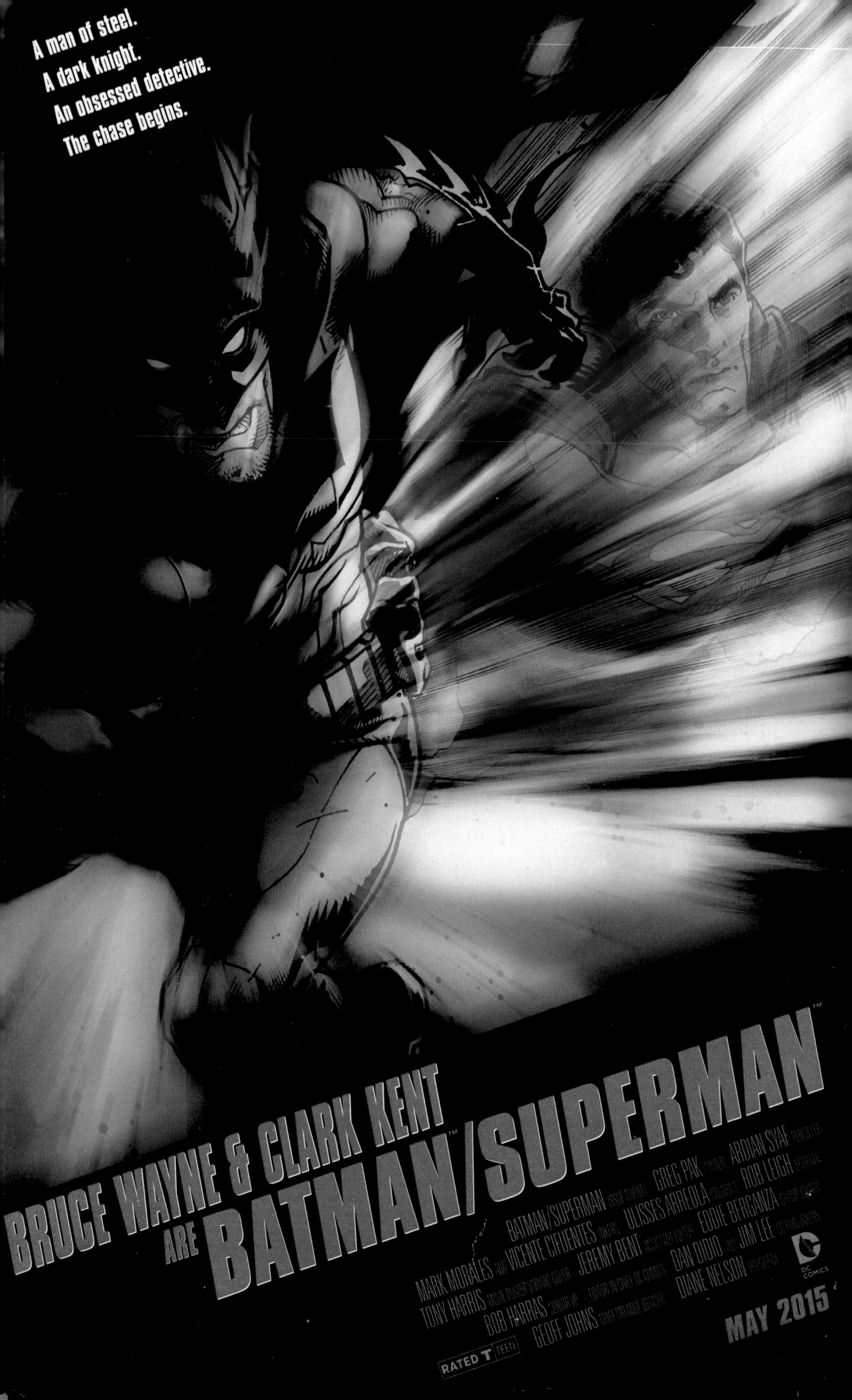
A man of steel.
A dark knight.
An obsessed detective.
The chase begins.
BRUCE WAYNE & CLARK KENT
ARE
BATMAN™/SUPERMAN™
BATMAN/SUPERMAN ISSUE TWENTY GREG PAK WRITER ARDIAN SYAF PENCILLER
MARK MORALES AND VICENTE CIFUENTES INKERS ULISSES ARREOLA COLORIST ROB LEIGH LETTERER
TONY HARRIS MOVIE POSTER VARIANT COVER JEREMY BENT ASSISTANT EDITOR EDDIE BERGANZA GROUP EDITOR
BOB HARRAS SENIOR VP — EDITOR IN CHIEF DC COMICS DAN DIDIO AND JIM LEE CO-PUBLISHERS
GEOFF JOHNS CHIEF CREATIVE OFFICER DIANE NELSON PRESIDENT
DC COMICS
MAY 2015
RATED T TEEN